# English Poetry, 1660-1800

# AMERICAN LITERATURE, ENGLISH LITERATURE, AND WORLD LITERATURES IN ENGLISH: AN INFORMATION GUIDE SERIES

Series Editor: Theodore Grieder, Curator, Division of Special Collections, Fales Library, New York University

Associate Editor: Duane DeVries, Associate Professor, Polytechnic Institute of New York, Brooklyn

*Other books on English literature in this series:*

ENGLISH DRAMA, 1660-1800—*Edited by Frederick M. Link*

ENGLISH DRAMA AND THEATRE, 1800-1900—*Edited by L. W. Conolly and J. P. Wearing*

ENGLISH DRAMA, 1900-1950—*Edited by E.H. Mikhail*

MODERN DRAMA IN AMERICA AND ENGLAND, 1950-1970—*Edited by Richard H. Harris*

ENGLISH FICTION, 1660-1800—*Edited by Jerry C. Beasley*

ENGLISH FICTION, 1900-1950 (volume 1)—*Edited by Thomas Jackson Rice*

ENGLISH FICTION, 1900-1950 (volume 2)—*Edited by Thomas Jackson Rice*

CONTEMPORARY FICTION IN AMERICA AND ENGLAND, 1950-1970—*Edited by Alfred F. Rosa and Paul A. Echholz*

OLD AND MIDDLE ENGLISH POETRY TO 1500—*Edited by Walter H. Beale*

ENGLISH ROMANTIC POETRY, 1800-1835—*Edited by Donald H. Reiman*

ENGLISH POETRY, 1900-1950—*Edited by Emily Ann Anderson*

CONTEMPORARY POETRY IN AMERICA AND ENGLAND, 1950-1975—*Edited by Martin E. Gingerich*

ENGLISH PROSE, PROSE FICTION, AND CRITICISM TO 1660—*Edited by S.K. Heninger, Jr.*

ENGLISH PROSE AND CRITICISM IN THE NINETEENTH CENTURY—*Edited by Harris W. Wilson and Diane Long Hoeveler*

ENGLISH PROSE AND CRITICISM, 1900-1950—*Edited by Christopher C. Brown and William B. Thesing*

AUTHOR NEWSLETTERS AND JOURNALS—*Edited by Margaret C. Patterson*

*in preparation

---

The above series is part of the

## GALE INFORMATION GUIDE LIBRARY

The Library consists of a number of separate series of guides covering major areas in the social sciences, humanities, and current affairs.

General Editor: Paul Wasserman, Professor and former Dean, School of Library and Information Services, University of Maryland

Managing Editor: Denise Allard Adzigian, Gale Research Company

# English Poetry, 1660-1800

## A GUIDE TO INFORMATION SOURCES

*Volume 40 in the American Literature, English
Literature, and World Literatures in English
Information Guide Series*

## Donald C. Mell, Jr.

*Associate Professor
Department of English
University of Delaware
Newark*

***Gale Research Company***
*Book Tower, Detroit, Michigan 48226*

**Library of Congress Cataloging in Publication Data**

Mell, Donald Charles.
   English poetry, 1660-1800.

   (American literature, English literature, and world
literatures in English information guide series ; v. 40)
   Includes index.
   1. English poetry—18th century—Bibliography.
2. English poetry—Early modern, 1500-1700—Bibliography.
I. Title.  II. Series:  Gale information guide library.
American literature, English literature, and world
literatures in English ; v. 40.
Z2014.P7M44   1982   [PR551]   016.821    73-16974
ISBN 0-8103-1230-1

To my father
Donald C. Mell

# VITA

Donald C. Mell, Jr., teaches in the department of English at the University
of Delaware. He received his B.A. and M.A. degrees from Yale University
and Ph.D. from the University of Pennsylvania. Mell is the author of A
POETICS OF AUGUSTAN ELEGY: STUDIES OF POEMS BY DRYDEN, POPE,
PRIOR, GRAY, AND JOHNSON (Rodopi, 1974) and he co-edited CONTEM-
PORARY STUDIES OF SWIFT'S POETRY (University of Delaware Press, 1982).
He has also written a number of articles dealing with forms of satiric mimesis
in eighteenth-century poetry and with the Augustan poet's use of the past.
He is co-editor of a new scholarly edition of the poems of Jonathan Swift to
be published by the University of Delaware Press in 1986.

# CONTENTS

# Contents

# ACKNOWLEDGMENTS

Many people within academia and on the outside have generously contributed their time and support to this project, and I would like to thank them personally.

Provost Leon Campbell, Dean Helen Gouldner, and Zack Bowen, chair of the English department at the University of Delaware, have approved a number of grants under the auspices of the General University Research Funds that made preparation of this book possible. In addition, the entire staff of the Morris Library at Delaware was an invaluable asset. I would thank in particular Marilyn Olson, whose flexible interpretation of library procedures helped facilitate my initial research, and Katharine Wood, who introduced me to the electronic wonders of the OCLC computerized retrieval system and thus reduced substantially the time spent in identifying and locating many items. Heyward Brock, David Erdman, James E. May, Charles Robinson, Elaine Safer, and James Winn shared with me their considerable knowledge of matters bibliographical and I am especially grateful to them for their help. Bill McBride, Elizabeth Mell, Derek vanBever, Carolyn Woj, Mary Beth Zimmerman, and Frank Crotzer did much of the legwork during the preparation of the manuscript, searching through bibliographies and card catalogs, making out entry cards, and assembling materials for my use, and I thank them all for their efforts. I was also fortunate having as colleagues and friends two expert bibliographers of long and wide experience: Jerry Beasley and Leo Lemay good naturedly answered my questions and provided much good advice on methodology and procedures. Theodore Grieder, series editor of American Literature, English Literature, and World Literatures in English, saved me from many blunders through his thoughtful editing of the manuscript. Rita Beasley typed the manuscript from handwritten note cards, and I appreciate her thorough and professional workmanship. I also wish to thank Denise Allard Adzigian for her careful copyediting of the manuscript and for guiding the book through press.

# INTRODUCTION

This Gale information guide is intended for readers ranging from undergraduate students beginning a study of eighteenth-century poetry to graduate students, professional critics, and experts in the field. With this audience in mind, I have followed Alexander Pope's rationale for his poem AN ESSAY ON MAN and, to adapt slightly his phraseology, have steered betwixt critical extremes seemingly opposite, passing over the specialized and arcane in presenting a balanced yet interesting, and an imperfect yet useful, combination of bibliographical, biographical, textual, historical, and critical approaches to English poetry, 1660 to 1800.

Like Pope's thematic intentions, addressed to readers of the ESSAY, my own efforts here should be considered something of a "general map" of the critical landscape, marking out some of the contours, indicating important landmarks, and generally providing guidance through the various responses to the poetry of the age. In so doing, I have concentrated on the criticism of the last fifty years or so, in which serious and important reassessments of the period, especially of the poetry, have occurred; and also a time when romantic theories of art and Victorian moral assumptions, which have tacitly shaped attitudes toward the eighteenth century, have been challenged, rejected, even sometimes reendorsed, always however with a critical terminology and from a perspective thoroughly modern. Although my more or less systematic survey focuses on twentieth-century materials through the year 1979 (and many articles or books that have come to my attention since that date), I also include descriptions of important editions and critiques from both the eighteenth and nineteenth centuries.

In making selections, I have kept in mind three distinct, but not mutually exclusive, qualities that seem always to characterize the best criticism of this or any other period of literary history. First, I have chosen those studies that by general agreement are of historical importance and have influenced the thinking of subsequent commentators; second, I also include those studies of intrinsic merit as imaginative criticism; third, I cite studies that suggest areas for future exploration. In the last group the theses tendered are, more often than not, tentative in nature, and make no pretense to definitiveness, but still have value in opening doors to new possibilities.

# Introduction

## SELECTION OF POETS

The poets selected for treatment fall into five basic groups. First are figures who, in one way or another, significantly contributed to, refined, and extended such popular genres or modes of expression of the period as satire (in all forms); the pastoral, georgic, and reflective-descriptive rural poem; the ode, sonnet, ballad, and hymn; and the sublime and exotic poem. A second group includes poets who somehow reflect the "official" or dominant tastes and spirit of the age, but whose representative activities, if nothing else, set off by comparison the greater writers who transcend the limits of time and history into universal status. A third group consists of those poets whose considerable poetic achievement has been overshadowed by their equally brilliant performances in other forms of writing or genres. The fourth category contains poets of the period in whose work can be located a change of sensibilities, the clear shifting of aesthetic norms, and a fundamental reevaluation of attitudes toward the nature and function of art characterizing the change from classic to romantic. The final classification involves those writers whose unique poetic sensibilities, though perhaps something of an anomaly in the age, hold a certain fascination for the modern reader. Among these thirty-one choices are poets designated as major in the NEW CAMBRIDGE BIBLIOGRAPHY OF ENGLISH LITERATURE (1971), but also many lesser talents who are deserving of a place in one or more of these categories. In an age known for its abundance of scribblers and poetasters (often targets of the best satire), these particular poets, whether major or minor, seem in my judgment the most interesting and worthy of comment.

## ARRANGEMENT

Part 1 of this book is divided into four sections consisting of a bibliography of general reference materials; basic reference works pertaining specifically to the period of 1660 to 1800; background resources; and a list of literary studies devoted to the poetry. The second section (B), which enumerates specialized reference materials, consists of a list of literary histories, guidelines, and collections of poetry and criticism; bibliographies and checklists of secondary studies; scholarly journals and reprint series mainly concerned with the Restoration and eighteenth century; and selected modern collections of essays and festschriften. The third section (C) deals with background resources that provide a wider cultural context in which to view the poetry. Historical, political, social, and economic studies are cited, as well as books and articles on the intellectual history, the philosophical milieu, science, and religion. Studies dealing with the fine arts of the period and studies touching on aesthetics and literary theory conclude this section. The fourth section (D) focuses on the themes, genres, forms and structures, and the diction and prosodic matters relating to the poetry of the period. All items in part 1 are numbered consecutively and arranged alphabetically by author's name, editor's name, or by title, if appropriate.

Part 2 deals exclusively with the thirty-one individual poets. All of these poets are treated under six separate sections when possible, making it easier to locate particular areas of interest. The first section lists important and/or standard editions, collected works, poetical works, and specialized facsimiles or editions of individual poems of note. The determination of the full textual history of a poem and the specialized and complicated nature of such textual research are inappropriate subjects for this present volume, and I have not attempted a full accounting of the numerous eighteenth-century editions, printings, and revisions, or of the appearances of poems in miscellanies or other publications unless they are of particular note. I cite important nineteenth-century editions, especially if no modern scholarly edition exists and the edition is still our best source of the poetry; but I make no attempt to cover all reprints, revisions, and textual alterations except when crucial to understanding problems of canon. The second section lists standard or important editions of the correspondence and also incomplete collections of letters when they provide essential knowledge about the author, as well as diaries and journals. Section 3 contains bibliographies that exist as such and, especially in the case of minor writers, partial bibliographies that appear as appendixes to critical studies, important textual research, and concordances if available. Section 4 lists collections of articles, essays, and festschriften mainly devoted to an individual poet. The fifth section describes books or essays with a clear biographical focus and studies concerned with the life and personal relationships of the poet in question. The final (and longest) section cites noteworthy critical studies of the author. Primary materials of scholarship, such as editions and correspondence, are arranged chronologically to reflect their cumulative nature and dependence on previous scholarly efforts. Citation of editions is chronological, beginning with complete works, including prose, drama, and poetry; complete poems; important selected editions; and individual poems in that order. All other entries are arranged in alphabetical order by author's name, editor's name, or by title if necessary. Because of the large number of entries for Dryden and Pope in section 5, I have further categorized by major poems or groups of poems. This procedure will help facilitate use of what might otherwise seem an unwieldy list.

## CITATION OF EDITIONS

My usual practice is to cite the original place, publisher, and date of a study, so as to reflect as accurately as possible its critical orientation, historical setting, and place in the history of literary criticism. For books that have been substantially revised, I cite the revision and explain in the annotation the extent of changes. If a book is a facsimile reprint, I indicate that information in the citation. For books commonly used in reprint editions, I cite the original date of publication immediately before the reprint date. If a study has been published the same year by two or more presses in different countries, I normally choose the imprint most accessible to the American student or the one that, because of press reputation, best indicates what the reader should expect. I mention only the first city and/or editorial offices for books published by presses with two or more sales outlets.

## ANNOTATIONS

The annotations in the volume are of two basic types: the first type is mainly factual and informative and is used to describe editions, correspondence, bibliographies, concordances, and the like; the second type represents as fully and faithfully as possible the central ideas or arguments as well as the scope and significance of an entry in question, and applies to studies in literary criticism. This second type of annotation, like the first, is mainly descriptive in character; but if the work cited is noteworthy for one reason or another, and if it addresses a critical controversy or interpretive crux of importance to the understanding of the poet or age, I often evaluate the author's handling of the issue and provide relevant cross-references. In the interest of saving space, I have employed a modified form of syntactical ellipsis when doing so does not distort the sense or lead to awkwardness.

## CROSS-REFERENCING

To avoid the clutter resulting from excessive cross-referencing, my policy is to restrict multiple listings for entries in which a comparison of two or more poets or poems constitutes the main focus of the discussion. If a book or article touches on a number of writers during the course of a survey, or if authors are compared or used to illustrate a particular thesis, the annotation itself makes this fact clear.

Essays that originally appeared as journal articles and have subsequently become integral parts of longer, more comprehensive studies, or that appear as chapters of a book-length study, are normally cited in their original journal version. The same holds for essays originating as part of collections or festschriften. In the event that the book-length study is also cited, I have not always indicated this fact through cross-listing, despite occasional overlap. Individual essays in a collection or festschrift are cross-referenced with the titles of collections.

## COVERAGE

I do not include items of the "notes and queries" variety, doctoral dissertations, master's theses, book reviews, or works written in a foreign language but not translated into English; nor have I covered paperback editions, anthologies, casebooks, and other materials designed primarily for the classroom. I regret these omissions, and would remind the reader that short notes often address important matters relating to textual editing, variant readings, and specific borrowings and allusions among poets, and also point out that excellent studies of the poetry and poets of the period have appeared in French, German, and Japanese journals and books. Introductions to such paperback editions and anthologies as the Longman Annotated English Poets Series, Modern Library College Editions, Norton Critical Editions, Rinehart and Riverside Series, and many others often provide valuable critical assessment.

# JOURNAL ABBREVIATIONS

Acronyms conform to the MLA INTERNATIONAL BIBLIOGRAPHY master list of periodicals. Journals cited infrequently are named in full. The acronyms in this list are used consistently throughout the bibliography, except when the journal itself is listed as an entry.

| | |
|---|---|
| AL | AMERICAN LITERATURE: A JOURNAL OF LITERARY HISTORY, CRITICISM, AND BIBLIOGRAPHY |
| ArielE | ARIEL: A REVIEW OF INTERNATIONAL ENGLISH LITERATURE |
| BB | BULLETIN OF BIBLIOGRAPHY |
| BJA | BRITISH JOURNAL OF AESTHETICS |
| BlakeS | BLAKE STUDIES |
| BSUF | BALL STATE UNIVERSITY FORUM |
| BUJ | BOSTON UNIVERSITY JOURNAL |
| BuR | BUCKNELL REVIEW: A SCHOLARLY JOURNAL OF LETTERS, ARTS AND SCIENCE |
| BUSE | BOSTON UNIVERSITY STUDIES IN ENGLISH |
| CE | COLLEGE ENGLISH |
| CentR | CENTENNIAL REVIEW (East Lansing, Mich.) |
| CL | COMPARATIVE LITERATURE (Eugene, Oreg.) |
| ClioI | CLIO: AN INTERDISCIPLINARY JOURNAL OF LITERATURE, HISTORY, AND THE PHILOSOPHY OF HISTORY |
| CLS | COMPARATIVE LITERATURE STUDIES |
| CP | CONCERNING POETRY (Bellingham, Wash.) |
| CQ | CAMBRIDGE QUARTERLY |
| CRITICISM | CRITICISM: A QUARTERLY FOR LITERATURE AND THE ARTS (Detroit, Mich.) |

# Journal Abbreviations

| | |
|---|---|
| DR | DALHOUSIE REVIEW |
| DUJ | DURHAM UNIVERSITY JOURNAL |
| EA | ETUDES ANGLAISES: GRAND-BRETAGNE, ETATS-UNIS |
| EAL | EARLY AMERICAN LITERATURE |
| ECent | EIGHTEENTH CENTURY: THEORY AND INTERPRETATION |
| ECLife | EIGHTEENTH-CENTURY LIFE |
| ECS | EIGHTEENTH-CENTURY STUDIES (Davis, Calif.) |
| EIC | ESSAYS IN CRITICISM: A QUARTERLY JOURNAL OF LITERARY CRITICISM (Oxford, Engl.) |
| Éire | ÉIRE-IRELAND: A JOURNAL OF IRISH STUDIES (St. Paul, Minn.) |
| ELH | [Formerly JOURNAL OF ENGLISH LITERARY HISTORY] |
| ELN | ENGLISH LANGUAGE NOTES (Boulder, Colo.) |
| EM | ENGLISH MISCELLANY: A SYMPOSIUM OF HISTORY, LITERATURE AND THE ARTS |
| EnlE | ENLIGHTENMENT ESSAYS (Chicago, Ill.) |
| ES | ENGLISH STUDIES: A JOURNAL OF ENGLISH LANGUAGE AND LITERATURE |
| HLB | HARVARD LIBRARY BULLETIN |
| HLQ | HUNTINGTON LIBRARY QUARTERLY: A JOURNAL FOR THE HISTORY AND INTERPRETATION OF ENGLISH AND AMERICAN CIVILIZATION |
| HudR | HUDSON REVIEW |
| JAAC | JOURNAL OF AESTHETICS AND ART CRITICISM |
| JBS | JOURNAL OF BRITISH STUDIES |
| JEGP | JOURNAL OF ENGLISH AND GERMANIC PHILOLOGY |
| JHI | JOURNAL OF THE HISTORY OF IDEAS |
| JNT | JOURNAL OF NARRATIVE TECHNIQUE |
| JWCI | JOURNAL OF THE WARBURG AND COURTAULD INSTITUTES |
| KR | KENYON REVIEW |
| KSJ | KEATS-SHELLEY JOURNAL: KEATS, SHELLEY, BYRON, HUNT, AND THEIR CIRCLES |
| L&P | LITERATURE AND PSYCHOLOGY (Teaneck, N.J.) |
| Library | LIBRARY: A QUARTERLY JOURNAL OF BIBLIOGRAPHY |
| MiltonS | MILTON STUDIES |
| MLN | [Formerly MODERN LANGUAGE NOTES] |

| | |
|---|---|
| MLQ | MODERN LANGUAGE QUARTERLY |
| MLR | MODERN LANGUAGE REVIEW |
| MLS | MODERN LANGUAGE STUDIES |
| MP | MODERN PHILOLOGY: A JOURNAL DEVOTED TO RE-SEARCH IN MEDIEVAL AND MODERN LITERATURE |
| Neophil | NEOPHILOLOGUS (Groningen, Netherlands) |
| NLH | NEW LITERARY HISTORY: A JOURNAL OF THEORY AND INTERPRETATION |
| NRam | NEW RAMBLER: JOURNAL OF THE JOHNSON SOCIETY OF LONDON |
| PBA | PROCEEDINGS OF THE BRITISH ACADEMY |
| PBSA | PAPERS OF THE BIBLIOGRAPHICAL SOCIETY OF AMERICA |
| PLL | PAPERS ON LANGUAGE AND LITERATURE: A JOURNAL FOR SCHOLARS AND CRITICS OF LANGUAGE AND LITERA-TURE |
| PMLA | PUBLICATIONS OF THE MODERN LANGUAGE ASSOCIATION OF AMERICA |
| PQ | PHILOLOGICAL QUARTERLY (Iowa City, Iowa) |
| REL | REVIEW OF ENGLISH LITERATURE |
| RES | REVIEW OF ENGLISH STUDIES: A QUARTERLY JOURNAL OF ENGLISH LITERATURE AND THE ENGLISH LANGUAGE |
| RLC | REVUE DE LITTÉRATURE COMPARÉE |
| RLV | REVUE DES LANGUES VIVANTES |
| RMS | RENAISSANCE & MODERN STUDIES |
| SAQ | SOUTH ATLANTIC QUARTERLY |
| SB | STUDIES IN BIBLIOGRAPHY: PAPERS OF THE BIBLIOGRAPH-ICAL SOCIETY OF THE UNIVERSITY OF VIRGINIA |
| SBHT | STUDIES IN BURKE AND HIS TIME |
| SCN | SEVENTEENTH-CENTURY NEWS |
| SCRIBLERIAN | SCRIBLERIAN: A NEWSLETTER DEVOTED TO POPE, SWIFT, AND THEIR CIRCLE |
| SEL | STUDIES IN ENGLISH LITERATURE, 1500-1900 |
| SHR | SOUTHERN HUMANITIES REVIEW |
| SIR | STUDIES IN ROMANTICISM (Boston, Mass.) |
| SLitI | STUDIES IN THE LITERARY IMAGINATION (Atlanta, Ga.) |
| SNL | SATIRE NEWSLETTER |
| SP | STUDIES IN PHILOLOGY |

# Journal Abbreviations

| | |
|---|---|
| SR | SEWANEE REVIEW |
| SSL | STUDIES IN SCOTTISH LITERATURE (Columbia, S.C.) |
| SVEC | STUDIES ON VOLTAIRE AND THE EIGHTEENTH CENTURY |
| TSL | TENNESSEE STUDIES IN LITERATURE |
| TSLL | TEXAS STUDIES IN LITERATURE AND LANGUAGE: A JOURNAL OF THE HUMANITIES |
| UKCR | UNIVERSITY OF KANSAS CITY REVIEW |
| UTQ | UNIVERSITY OF TORONTO QUARTERLY |
| YES | YEARBOOK OF ENGLISH STUDIES |
| YR | YALE REVIEW: A NATIONAL QUARTERLY |

Part 1

GENERAL BIBLIOGRAPHY

# Part 1

# GENERAL BIBLIOGRAPHY

## A. GENERAL REFERENCE MATERIALS

1    ABSTRACTS OF ENGLISH STUDIES. Urbana, Ill.: National Council
of Teachers of English, 1958-- . Ten issues per year.

   Provides abstracts of scholarly articles; since 1972 also covers
   monographs.

2    Altick, Richard D., and Andrew Wright. SELECTIVE BIBLIOGRAPHY
FOR THE STUDY OF ENGLISH AND AMERICAN LITERATURE. 6th ed.
New York: Macmillan, 1979.

   Lists general resource materials, library catalogs, encyclopedias,
   and other valuable references.

3    ARTS AND HUMANITIES CITATION INDEX. Philadelphia: Institute
for Scientific Information, 1977-- . Annual, with interim issues bi-
annually.

   An elaborately cross-referenced bibliography based on 950
   core journals and 125 books in the arts and humanities.
   Indicates footnote citations and frequency of author referral.
   The weekly supplement, CURRENT CONTENTS, provides subject matter index, significant word or phrase listings, table
   of contents, and topic headings.

4    Bateson, F.W., and Harrison T. Meserole, eds. A GUIDE TO ENGLISH
AND AMERICAN LITERATURE. 3rd ed. London: Longman, 1976.

   Valuable aid to research in the format of bibliographical and
   historical essays. Introduces categories and periods with
   thoughtful commentary.

5    BRITISH MUSEUM GENERAL CATALOGUE OF PRINTED BOOKS. London:
Trustees of the British Museum, 1959.

Holdings through 1955 recorded in volumes published between 1955–66. Supplements periodically issued.

6    DICTIONARY OF NATIONAL BIOGRAPHY. 21 vols. London: Oxford Univ. Press, 1917–71.

Information source about obscure figures, as well as data concerning the major authors of the period. Brief bibliographies accompany entries.

7    DISSERTATION ABSTRACTS INTERNATIONAL. Ann Arbor, Mich.: University Microfilms, 1938–– . Monthly.

Abstracts of most doctoral theses. A 1970 index covers the years 1938 to 1969.

8    Downs, Robert B. AMERICAN LIBRARY RESOURCES: A BIBLIOGRAPHI-CAL GUIDE. Chicago: American Library Association, 1951.

Describes holdings in American libraries. Supplements appeared in two volumes, 1962–72, for years 1950–61 and 1960–70.

9    _____ . BRITISH LIBRARY RESOURCES: A BIBLIOGRAPHICAL GUIDE. Chicago: American Library Association, 1973.

Useful information about holdings in British libraries. Companion to American volume, cited above.

10    Harvey, Paul, ed. THE OXFORD COMPANION TO ENGLISH LITERA-TURE. Rev. Dorothy Eagle. 4th ed. Oxford: Clarendon Press, 1967.

Indispensable short guide to English authors, furnishing biographical and bibliographical sketches. Includes comment on literary history, trends, and movements.

11    MLA ABSTRACTS OF ARTICLES IN SCHOLARLY JOURNALS. New York: Modern Language Association, 1972–77. Annual.

Begins with the year 1970 in conjunction with the MLA INTERNATIONAL BIBLIOGRAPHY. Ceased publication in 1976 for year 1975.

12    NATIONAL UNION CATALOG: PRE-1956 IMPRINTS (NUC). Chicago: American Library Association, 1968–– .

Supplements include the NUC 1956–67; also five-year, annual, and monthly supplements appear periodically. A valuable resource for locating bibliographical information and the libraries in which books are held.

13    OCLC. Columbus, Ohio, 1967-- . Formerly Ohio College Library
      Center.

      Computer retrieval system. Data base includes seven million
      volumes found in over two thousand member libraries.

14    RLG/RLIN. Stanford, Calif.: Research Library Group, 1974-- .

      Computer retrieval system. Member libraries are among the
      major research institutions. A smaller data base than OCLC
      (cited above), but more highly refined.

## B. ENGLISH LITERATURE, 1660-1800: REFERENCE MATERIALS

## 1. Histories, Guidebooks, Collections of Poetry, and Criticism

15    Addison, Joseph, and Richard Steele. THE SPECTATOR. Ed. Donald F.
      Bond. 5 vols. Oxford: Oxford Univ. Press, 1965.

      The standard edition of these valuable essays published six
      times weekly between 1711-12 on a variety of social, politi-
      cal, and literary topics. The numbers on the ballad, wit,
      PARADISE LOST, and the creative imagination are central
      essays in the field of aesthetics and literary criticism.

16    Arnold, Matthew. "Essays in Criticism, Second Series" and "The Study
      of Poetry." In THE COMPLETE WORKS OF MATTHEW ARNOLD. Ed.
      R.H. Super. Vol. 9, pp. 161-204. Ann Arbor: Univ. of Michigan
      Press, 1973.

      Still provocative essays from the Victorian viewpoint on poets
      from the period 1660 to 1800.

17    Butt, John. THE MID-EIGHTEENTH CENTURY. Ed. and completed by
      Geoffrey Carnall. Vol. 8 of the OXFORD HISTORY OF ENGLISH
      LITERATURE. Oxford: Clarendon Press, 1979. Tables, Bibliog.

      An account of Johnson; the poetry of 1740 to 1789, drama,
      history, travel writing, memoirs, essays, dialogs, speeches;
      Richardson, Fielding, Smollett, Sterne; and minor fiction.

18    THE CAMBRIDGE HISTORY OF ENGLISH LITERATURE (CHEL). Ed.
      A.W. Ward and Alfred R. Waller. Vols. 8, 9, 10. New York: G.P.
      Putnam, 1912-13.

      Organized similarly to an encyclopedia format with a different
      commentator for each genre or poet or topic. Dated, but
      still of value.

19    Chapman, Robert W.  "Dodsley's Collection of Poems by Several Hands."
      PROCEEDINGS AND PAPERS OF THE OXFORD BIBLIOGRAPHICAL
      SOCIETY, 3 (1933), 269-316.  Collations, Lists, Indexes.

      Compilation and descriptive bibliography of these volumes
      that provide a valuable index to the tastes of the age and
      to which the age owed its knowledge of such poets as Gray,
      Collins, and Johnson.  See no. 26.

20    Chappell, W., and T.W. Ebsworth, eds.  ROXBURGHE BALLADS.  9
      vols.  Hertford, Engl.:  S. Austin, 1871-99.

      Useful collection of popular ballads written during the
      seventeenth and eighteenth centuries.

21    A COMPLETE EDITION OF THE POETS OF GREAT BRITAIN.  Ed.
      Robert Anderson.  13 vols.  London:  T. and A. Arch, 1792-95.

      Standard source for the minor poetry.

22    Courtney, William P.  DODSLEY'S COLLECTION OF POETRY:  ITS
      CONTENTS AND CONTRIBUTIONS:  A CHAPTER IN THE HISTORY OF
      ENGLISH LITERATURE IN THE EIGHTEENTH CENTURY.  1910; rpt.
      New York:  Burt Franklin, 1968.

      Valuable commentary on this famous collection, describing
      contributors, presenting bibliographical details, and dis-
      cussing its reception into the nineteenth century.  See no.
      26.

23    Day, Cyrus L.  "PILLS TO PURGE MELANCHOLY."  RES, 8 (1932),
      177-84.

      Thorough account of the contents and bibliography of this
      collection first published in 1698 and completed in 1720,
      stressing its importance as a source for tunes in Gay's
      BEGGAR'S OPERA and its popularity in the eighteenth-
      century's developing interest in popular culture and anti-
      quarianism.

24    Dennis, John.  THE CRITICAL WORKS.  Ed. Edward Niles Hooker.
      2 vols.  Baltimore:  Johns Hopkins Press, 1939-43.

      Indispensable introduction to a critic whose discussions of
      "the sublime" gave theoretical underpinnings to the emerging
      sensibility of so-called preromanticism.

25    Dobrée, Bonamy.  ENGLISH LITERATURE IN THE EARLY EIGHTEENTH
      CENTURY, 1700-40.  Vol. 7 of the OXFORD HISTORY OF ENGLISH
      LITERATURE.  Oxford:  Clarendon Press, 1959.  Tables.

> Includes comprehensive bibliographical coverage of genre, intellectual history, criticism, and individual authors both major and minor.

26  Dodsley, Robert. COLLECTION OF POEMS BY SEVERAL HANDS. 3 vols. 1748. 4 vols. 1749. 6 vols. 1758. 4 vols. 1775. London: R. and J. Dodsley.

> An important miscellany that printed poems of both major and minor figures. See no. 29.

27  Durfey, Thomas, ed. WIT AND MIRTH: OR PILLS TO PURGE MEL-ANCHOLY. 6 vols. Introd. Cyrus L. Day. Facsim. reproduction of 1876 rpt. of orig. 1719-20 ed. New York: Folklore Library Publishers, 1959.

> Marks the end of an era of intellectual contempt for popular literature and song and the faint beginning of the antiquarian movement of the mid-century.

28  Dyson, Henry V.D., and John Butt, eds. AUGUSTANS AND ROMAN-TICS, 1689-1830. New York: Dover, 1940. Bibliog.

> Deals with backgrounds as a context for a discussion of the literature of the period. Sections on philosophy and economic influences. Includes major and minor poets.

29  Eddy, Donald D. "Dodsley's COLLECTION OF POEMS BY SEVERAL HANDS (Six Volumes) 1758; Index of Authors." PBSA, 60 (1966), 9-30.

> Views the edition of 1758 as "definitive," and indexes the contents and contributions, many of which differ from those in the 1748, 1749, and 1755 editions. See no. 26.

30  Elledge, Scott, ed. EIGHTEENTH CENTURY CRITICAL ESSAYS. 2 vols. Ithaca, N.Y.: Cornell Univ. Press, 1961.

> Invaluable collection of significant essays in criticism and aesthetics.

31  Gosse, Edmund. A HISTORY OF EIGHTEENTH CENTURY LITERATURE, 1660-1780. London: Macmillan, 1889.

> Impressionistic and personalized account of the period, covering major and minor figures and epitomizing Victorian tastes and biases.

32  LATER ENGLISH BROADSIDE BALLADS. Ed. John Holloway and Joan Black. Lincoln: Univ. of Nebraska Press, 1975.

Reprinted from the Madden Collection of broadsides now at the Cambridge University Library, with an introduction to their "large and intricate subjects."

32A    Lonsdale, Roger, ed. DRYDEN TO JOHNSON. Vol. 4: THE HISTORY OF LITERATURE IN THE ENGLISH LANGUAGE. London: Barrie and Jenkins, 1971.

Essays devoted to the major figures, main literary developments, and significant genres of the period, combining information with "individuality of response to the literature itself."

33    McKillop, Alan D. ENGLISH LITERATURE FROM DRYDEN TO BURNS. New York: Appleton-Century-Croft, 1948. Bibliogs.

A student guide to the literature and culture from 1660 to 1780, treating major and minor figures and the important genres.

34    Magill, Frank N., ed. ENGLISH LITERATURE, MIDDLE AGES TO 1800. Pasadena, Calif.: Salem, 1980. Bibliog.

Designed for "augmenting classroom work," but contains biographical and critical materials and up-to-date bibliography with essay-reviews concerning the poet's reputation.

35    MINOR BRITISH POETRY, 1680-1800. Ed. J. Ernest Barlough. Metuchen, N.J.: Scarecrow Press, 1973.

Unannotated collection of the minor verse, valuable in bringing together under a single cover poems difficult to locate elsewhere.

36    MINOR POETS OF THE EIGHTEENTH CENTURY. Ed. Hugh l'Anson Fausset. London: J.M. Dent, 1930.

Selections of minor poetry of the period.

37    Moore, Cecil A. BACKGROUNDS OF ENGLISH LITERATURE, 1700-1760. Minneapolis: Univ. of Minnesota Press, 1953.

Mostly reprinted essays especially of value to the study of popular literature and minor poets of the period. Treats Parnell, Akenside, Thomson and the Wartons, among others.

38    Nichols, John. LITERARY ANECDOTES OF THE EIGHTEENTH CENTURY. 9 vols. London: Nichols and Bentley, 1812-16.

Source of information and biographical data about the age.

39    THE PELICAN GUIDE TO ENGLISH LITERATURE. Ed. Boris Ford. Vol.
      4: FROM DRYDEN TO JOHNSON. 1957. Rev. ed. Baltimore:
      Penguin Books, 1968.

      A good introduction by experts to the various types of litera-
      ture of the period and to some of the critical issues raised
      by the aesthetic assumptions of the age. Treats major poets
      and contains essays on the minor figures, especially the re-
      flective and descriptive poets. Reprints T.S. Eliot's intro-
      duction to the Halewood Books edition (1930) of Johnson's
      LONDON and THE VANITY OF HUMAN WISHES, which
      discusses the "decadent" minor verse of the period.

40    Percival, Milton, ed. POLITICAL BALLADS ILLUSTRATING THE AD-
      MINISTRATION OF SIR ROBERT WALPOLE. Oxford: Clarendon Press,
      1916.

      Considers ballads from the point of view of history, literature,
      and music, and shows them as a minor but still important
      means of political satire. Prints ballads issued from 1725 to
      1742.

41    POEMS ON AFFAIRS OF STATE: AUGUSTAN SATIRICAL VERSE, 1660-
      1714. Ed. George de F. Lord et al. 7 vols. New Haven, Conn.:
      Yale Univ. Press, 1963-75. Footnotes.

      An enormously successful effort to collect over three thousand
      verse satires on contemporary court issues and personalities
      during the fifty-four years between the Restoration and the
      death of Queen Anne when satire on public affairs was an
      important genre. Full textual apparatus and helpful foot-
      notes identifying names, historical circumstances and events,
      literary allusions, and previous critical commentary.

42    THE POETICAL CALENDAR. Ed. Francis Fawkes and William Woty.
      London: D. Leech, 1763.

      An appendix to Dodsley's COLLECTION published in twelve
      monthly installments. See no. 26.

43    Renwick, William L. ENGLISH LITERATURE 1785-1815. Vol. 9 of
      the OXFORD HISTORY OF ENGLISH LITERATURE. Oxford: Clarendon
      Press, 1963. Tables, Bibliogs.

      Emphasizes writers whose characteristic work was published
      in this twenty-five year period and who responded in some
      fashion to the impact of the French Revolution.

44    Rollins, Hyder E., ed. THE PEPYS BALLADS. 8 vols. Cambridge,
      Mass.: Harvard Univ. Press, 1929-32.

## General Bibliography

A collection of popular ballads of the day often relating to political and social concerns as well as to the general human predicament.

44A Rothstein, Eric. RESTORATION AND EIGHTEENTH-CENTURY POETRY 1660-1780. Vol. 3 of the ROUTLEDGE HISTORY OF ENGLISH POETRY. London: Routledge and Kegan Paul, 1981.

Identifies the distinctive character of the poetry and discusses the dominant genres and styles of three periods: the late seventeenth century that emphasizes power; the early eighteenth century characterized by interaction; the final period that stresses sympathy and human feeling. Chronological appendix briefly comments on many individual poems, both major and minor, not covered in the main argument.

45 Rymer, Thomas. THE CRITICAL WORKS. Ed. Curt A. Zimansky. New Haven, Conn.: Yale Univ. Press, 1956.

Excellent edition, including an informative introduction to an often-misunderstood critic.

46 Saintsbury, George. A SHORT HISTORY OF ENGLISH LITERATURE. New York: Macmillan, 1929.

Still a fine, well-written introduction to English literature, but obviously dated.

47 Schilling, Bernard N., ed. ESSENTIAL ARTICLES FOR THE STUDY OF ENGLISH AUGUSTAN BACKGROUNDS. Hamden, Conn.: Archon Books, 1961.

Brings together previously published articles of importance "which time has sanctioned" on such topics as prose style, couplet rhetoric, satire as genre, and philosophical and intellectual backgrounds.

48 Sherburn, George. "The Restoration and Eighteenth Century (1660-1789)." In A LITERARY HISTORY OF ENGLAND. Ed. A.C. Baugh. 2nd ed., rev. New York: Appleton-Century-Crofts, 1967.

Remains an excellent introduction to the critics and literary trends of the period. Especially strong on the minor figures. Includes bibliographical supplements and index in the revised edition. This work is volume 3 of the 1967 edition.

49 Spingarn, Joel E., ed. CRITICAL ESSAYS OF THE SEVENTEENTH CENTURY. 3 vols. Oxford: Clarendon Press, 1908-09.

Still the best anthology of Restoration and late seventeenth-century criticism.

50 Sutherland, James. ENGLISH LITERATURE OF THE LATE SEVENTEENTH CENTURY. Vol. 6 of the OXFORD HISTORY OF ENGLISH LITERATURE. Oxford: Oxford Univ. Press, 1969. Tables, Bibliog.

10

Covers backgrounds, the drama, poetry, essays, letters, journals, biography, history, travel literature, religious writing, philosophy, politics, economics, science, and literary criticism from 1660 to 1700.

51   TONSON'S MISCELLANY, 1684-1709. 6 vols. 5th ed. London: J. Tonson, 1727.

A famous collection initiated by Dryden and continued by Tonson, his publisher. Rivals Dodsley's in the later eighteenth century for importance.

52   Wellek, René. A HISTORY OF MODERN CRITICISM 1750-1950. Vol. 1: THE LATER EIGHTEENTH CENTURY. New Haven, Conn.: Yale Univ. Press, 1955.

Excellent summary of the theoretical basis of neoclassicism and discussion of the "romantic" aesthetic propounded especially by minor English and Scottish aestheticians of the middle and late eighteenth century. Controversial section on Samuel Johnson's theory of art relevant to his poetic sensibility.

53   Wimsatt, William K., and Cleanth Brooks. LITERARY CRITICISM: A SHORT HISTORY. New York: Knopf, 1957.

Historical account of literary ideas from the "new critical" or evaluative perspective, providing valuable commentary on the neoclassical aesthetic in all its complexities and richness. Particularly good on Dryden, Addison, and Johnson.

54   THE WORKS OF THE ENGLISH POETS. Ed. Alexander Chalmers. 21 vols. London: J. Johnson, 1810.

Well-known source for minor figures.

## 2. Bibliographies and Checklists

55   ANNUAL BIBLIOGRAPHY OF ENGLISH LANGUAGE AND LITERATURE. Cambridge, Engl.: Modern Humanities Research Association, 1921-- .

Comprehensive guide, noting dissertations, reviews, anthologies.

56   Bond, Donald F. THE AGE OF DRYDEN. Goldentree Bibliographies in Language and Literature. Spring Grove, Ill.: AHM Publishing, 1970.

Selective and unannotated listings of editions and secondary readings in pamphlet format.

57   _____. THE EIGHTEENTH CENTURY. Goldentree Bibliographies in Language and Literature. Spring Grove, Ill.: AHM Publishing, 1975.

Selective and unannotated listings of editions and secondary readings in pamphlet format.

58   Case, Arthur E. A BIBLIOGRAPHY OF ENGLISH POETIC MISCELLANIES,
     1525-1750. Oxford: Oxford Univ. Press, 1935.

     Based on holdings at the British Museum, Bodleian, Yale, and
     Harvard libraries. Descriptive and analytical in nature.

59   Cordasco, Francesco. EIGHTEENTH CENTURY BIBLIOGRAPHIES. Metuchen,
     N.J.: Scarecrow Press, 1970.

     Includes a handlist of critical studies on Young.

60   _____. A REGISTER OF 18TH CENTURY BIBLIOGRAPHIES AND REFERENCES:
     A CHRONOLOGICAL QUARTER-CENTURY SURVEY. Detroit: Gale Research
     Co., 1968.

     List of bibliographies and bibliographical aids, 1926-48, and some
     1949 notices.

61   Crum, Margaret. FIRST-LINE INDEX OF ENGLISH POETRY, 1500-1800, IN
     MANUSCRIPTS OF THE BODLEIAN LIBRARY, OXFORD. 2 vols. Oxford:
     Clarendon Press, 1969.

     Aims at making accessible the poetical holdings in a form similar
     to the "Manuscript Index of First and Last Lines" in the Department
     of Manuscripts of the British Library.

62   Day, Cyrus L., and Eleanor B. Murrie. ENGLISH SONG-BOOKS 1651-1702:
     A BIBLIOGRAPHY WITH A FIRST-LINE INDEX OF SONGS. London: Bibli-
     ographical Society of Oxford, 1937.

     Lists, describes, and indexes all the secular songbooks published in
     England and Scotland between 1651 and 1702, and also miscellaneous
     works containing the words and music of two or more songs.

63   Dyson, A.E., ed. ENGLISH POETRY: SELECT BIBLIOGRAPHICAL GUIDES.
     London: Oxford Univ. Press, 1971.

     Lists major texts, biographies, correspondence, bibliographies,
     and background materials on Dryden (James Kinsley), Pope (Geof-
     frey Tillotson) and Blake (David V. Erdman), as well as providing
     a critical overview of the changing opinions about these poets
     throughout the years.

64   ENGLISH BIBLIOGRAPHICAL SOURCES. London: Gregg, 1964-66.

     An eighteenth-century "publishers' weekly" noting books, sermons,
     pamphlets, and basis for the proposed EIGHTEENTH-CENTURY
     SHORT-TITLE CATALOGUE. Reprints extant trade catalogs of
     new books in the GENTLEMAN'S, LONDON, and BRITISH maga-
     zines to 1766, and identifies authors.

65     Foxon, David F. ENGLISH VERSE 1701-1750: A CATALOGUE OF SEPARATELY PRINTED POEMS WITH NOTES ON CONTEMPORARY COLLECTED EDITIONS. 2 vols. Cambridge: Cambridge Univ. Press, 1975.

> Invaluable research tool. A monumental piece of scholarship.

66     _____. LIBERTINE LITERATURE IN ENGLAND, 1660-1745. New Hyde, N.Y.: University Books, 1965.

> Comprehensive checklist.

67     Lund, Roger D. RESTORATION AND EARLY EIGHTEENTH-CENTURY ENGLISH LITERATURE, 1660-1740: A SELECTED BIBLIOGRAPHY OF RESOURCE MATERIALS. New York: Modern Language Association, 1980.

> Valuable (but selective) listing of library materials, such as current periodicals, bibliographies, and concordances for the study of the literature of the period. Of special significance are the inclusion of minor figures, checklists of translations, considerations of publishing and bookselling, and background references.

68     MLA INTERNATIONAL BIBLIOGRAPHY OF BOOKS AND ARTICLES ON THE MODERN LANGUAGES AND LITERATURES. New York: Modern Language Association of America, 1970-- . Annual.

> From 1922 to 1969 the bibliography was the June issue of PMLA. Comprehensive coverage of books, collections, festschriften, and articles. Published in separate volumes.

69     Moore, Cecil A. ENGLISH POETRY OF THE EIGHTEENTH CENTURY. New York: Holt, 1935. Bibliog., indexes.

> Lists sources for critical and biographical studies through 1934.

70     NEW CAMBRIDGE BIBLIOGRAPHY OF ENGLISH LITERATURE (NCBEL). Ed. George Watson. Vol. 2: 1660-1800. Cambridge: Cambridge Univ. Press, 1971.

> Standard bibliographical source. Lists collections, editions, miscellanies, individual printings, as well as major critical works. A revision of F.W. Bateson's CAMBRIDGE BIBLIOG-RAPHY OF ENGLISH LITERATURE (1941).

71     Osborne, Mary T. ADVICE-TO-A-PAINTER POEMS 1635-1856: AN ANNOTATED FINDING LIST. Austin: Univ. of Texas Press, 1949.

> Collects and examines "one of the smaller genres" in English literary history, indicating some of the important characteristics of this coherent group of poems.

72    Tobin, James E. EIGHTEENTH CENTURY ENGLISH LITERATURE AND
ITS CULTURAL BACKGROUND: A BIBLIOGRAPHY. New York: Ford-
ham Univ. Press, 1939.

>Divided into sections on cultural matters and literature, in-
cluding literary criticism, genre, foreign literatures, and
individual authors. Designed to serve the professional
scholar and the undergraduate or graduate student searching for a thesis topic.

73    Williams, Iolo A. SEVEN XVIIITH CENTURY BIBLIOGRAPHIES. London:
Dulau, 1924.

>Dated and incomplete bibliography of figures in the period.

74    Wing, Donald. SHORT-TITLE CATALOGUE, 1641-1700. 3 vols. New
York: Index Society, 1945-51; Vol. 1, 2nd ed., rev. and enl. New
York: Index Committee of MLA, 1972.

>Attempts a listing of every English publication, except
periodicals, within the terminal dates. An eighteenth-
century continuation is in progress. Remains a high point
in bibliographical scholarship.

75    YEAR'S WORK IN ENGLISH STUDIES. London: English Association,
1921-- . Annual.

>Provides short summaries of important articles and books in
review essay format, beginning in 1919.

## 3. Learned Journals and Reprint Series

76    AUGUSTAN REPRINT SOCIETY (ARS), 1946-- . Biannual.

>Offers facsimile reproductions of important manuscripts and
texts in the William Andrews Clark Library collection, University of California at Los Angeles. Introductions provide
a context for the featured work.

77    EIGHTEENTH CENTURY: A CURRENT BIBLIOGRAPHY (ECCB), 1971-
76. Annual.

>An expanded version of "English Literature, 1660-1800: A
Current Bibliography," which appeared annually in PQ from
1926 to 1970. These bibliographies through 1970 have been
concurrently reprinted and indexed under the title ENGLISH
LITERATURE, 1660-1800: A BIBLIOGRAPHY OF MODERN
STUDIES. See no. 82.

78  EIGHTEENTH CENTURY: A CURRENT BIBLIOGRAPHY (ECCB), 1976-- . Annual.

>   A continuation of no. 77. Published for the American Society for Eighteenth-Century Studies (ASECS) by AMS Press as a separate volume. The best annotated guide to the period. Short reviews are by well-known critics.

79  EIGHTEENTH CENTURY: A JOURNAL OF THEORY AND INTERPRETATION (ECent), 1979-- . 3 times per year. Formerly STUDIES IN BURKE AND HIS TIME (SBHT), 1959-78.

>   Specializes in essays "concerned with the application of twentieth-century theory and methodology to the eighteenth century." Chronologically enlarged to include 1660-1800. Volumes 1-8 were published as BURKE NEWSLETTER.

80  EIGHTEENTH-CENTURY LIFE (ECLife), 1974-- . Quarterly. Publication of East Central ASECS.

>   Articles on all aspects of the period, usually short.

81  EIGHTEENTH-CENTURY STUDIES (ECS), 1967-- . Quarterly.

>   The journal of ASECS, emphasizing essays of interdisciplinary nature and of general interest to scholars of the period.

82  ENGLISH LITERATURE 1660-1800: A BIBLIOGRAPHY OF MODERN STUDIES, 1926-70. 6 vols. Princeton, N.J.: Princeton Univ. Press, 1970.

>   Invaluable collection of bibliographies of this period. Later volumes indexed more fully than those covering the early years. Excellent research tool for student of the period interested in trends and changing critical tastes. See no 77.

83  ENLIGHTENMENT ESSAYS (EnlE), 1970-- . Quarterly.

>   Devoted to all aspects of American, British, and Continental history, literature, and culture.

84  JOHNSONIAN NEWS LETTER, 1940-- . Quarterly.

>   Includes notes and reviews of the literature of the later eighteenth century, but also lists articles for the earlier years and often prints reviews of major scholarly productions relevant to the period as a whole. Delightfully written and a joy to consult.

85    PHILOLOGICAL QUARTERLY (PQ), 1976-79.

One issue a year is devoted to review articles on English
literature from 1660 to 1800, among them "Studies in
Restoration Literature" and "Studies in Augustan Literature,"
written by experts. Has been discontinued.

86    RESTORATION: STUDIES IN ENGLISH LITERARY CULTURE, 1660-1700
(Restoration), 1977-- . Biannual.

Includes short articles, notes, short reviews, professional
news, announcements of conferences, and queries. An excellent guide to recent scholarship.

87    SATIRE NEWSLETTER (SN), 1963-73.

Articles devoted to the nature and function of satire,
ancient and modern. Also includes original satire.

88    SCRIBLERIAN, 1968-- . Biannual.

Since 1979, includes reviews and commentary on the early
novelists, theologians, and philosophers. Brief reviews of
foreign and domestic articles on major and minor poets as
well as of material pertaining to history, religion, and
philosophy; longer reviews of important books and a section
devoted to brief comments on other works; prints information on scholarly activities pertaining to the Scriblerians.
The best single review journal of the early period and a must
for any student of the age.

89    SEVENTEENTH-CENTURY NEWS (SCN), 1941-- . Biannual.

Includes short articles, abstracts, and book reviews of
studies of Restoration figures.

90    STUDIES IN EIGHTEENTH-CENTURY CULTURE: PROCEEDINGS OF
THE AMERICAN SOCIETY FOR EIGHTEENTH-CENTURY STUDIES (SECC),
1971-- . Annual.

Prints selected papers from ASECS national and regional
meetings. Highly interdisciplinary.

91    STUDIES IN ENGLISH LITERATURE, 1500-1900 (SEL), 1961-- .
Quarterly.

Summer issue publishes articles dealing with the period
1660-1800 and also a valuable review essay, "Recent
Studies in the Restoration and Eighteenth Century."

92    STUDIES ON VOLTAIRE AND THE EIGHTEENTH CENTURY (SVEC),
1955-- . 12 times per year.

Publication of the Voltaire Foundation. Ranges from full-length monographs to shorter essays covering material pertinent to British and American subjects.

## 4. Selected Modern Collections and Festschriften

93    Anderson, Howard, and John S. Shea, eds. STUDIES IN CRITICISM AND AESTHETICS, 1660-1800: ESSAYS IN HONOR OF SAMUEL HOLT MONK. Minneapolis: Univ. of Minnesota Press, 1967.

Valuable essays pertaining to eighteenth-century poetry, prose, criticism, and aesthetic principles.

94    Bond, William H., ed. EIGHTEENTH-CENTURY STUDIES IN HONOR OF DONALD F. HYDE. New York: Grolier Club, 1970.

Beautifully printed commemorative volume honoring a scholar-philanthropist who nourished and supported literary studies devoted to Johnson and his circle.

95    Boys, Richard C., ed. STUDIES IN THE LITERATURE OF THE AUGUSTAN AGE: ESSAYS COLLECTED IN HONOR OF ARTHUR ELLICOTT CASE. New York: Gordian Press, 1966.

Articles written from 1917 to 1951 representing "much of the best scholarship" of that thirty-five year period.

96    Brady, Frank, John Palmer, and Martin Price, eds. LITERARY THEORY AND STRUCTURE: ESSAYS IN HONOR OF WILLIAM K. WIMSATT. New Haven, Conn.: Yale Univ. Press, 1973.

Essays address the special literary qualities of the age and critical issues raised by eighteenth-century poetry and poets.

97    Brissenden, R.F., ed. STUDIES IN THE EIGHTEENTH CENTURY, I: PAPERS PRESENTED AT THE DAVID NICHOL SMITH MEMORIAL SEMINAR, CANBERRA, 1966. Toronto: Univ. of Toronto Press, 1968.

Essays, some of which deal with poets and poetry of the period.

98    _____. STUDIES IN THE EIGHTEENTH CENTURY, II: PAPERS PRESENTED AT THE SECOND DAVID NICHOL SMITH MEMORIAL SEMINAR, CANBERRA, 1970. Toronto: Univ. of Toronto Press, 1973.

Essays on a wide range of eighteenth-century cultural and literary topics.

99    Brissenden, R.F., and T.C. Eade, eds. STUDIES IN THE EIGHTEENTH CENTURY, III: PAPERS PRESENTED AT THE THIRD DAVID NICHOL SMITH MEMORIAL SEMINAR, CANBERRA, 1973. Toronto: Univ of Toronto Press, 1976.

Essays on all aspects of eighteenth-century British and Continental literature and culture.

100  Bronson, Bertrand Harris. FACETS OF THE ENLIGHTENMENT: STUDIES IN ENGLISH LITERATURE AND ITS CONTEXTS. Berkeley: Univ. of California Press, 1968.

Reprinted essays, many of which are devoted to eighteenth-century poets and poetry.

101  Brower, Reuben. MIRROR ON MIRROR: TRANSLATION, IMITATION, PARODY. Cambridge, Mass.: Harvard Univ. Press, 1974.

Previously published (or read) essays intended to show that translation, imitation, and parody are forms of poetic creation and, therefore, literary art.

102  Butt, John. POPE, DICKENS, AND OTHERS: ESSAYS AND ADDRESSES. Edinburgh: Edinburgh Univ. Press, 1969.

Diverse essays.

103  Camden, Carroll, ed. RESTORATION AND EIGHTEENTH-CENTURY LITERATURE: ESSAYS IN HONOR OF ALAN DUGALD McKILLOP. Chicago: Univ. of Chicago Press, 1963.

Valuable essays.

104  Champion, Larry S., ed. QUICK SPRINGS OF SENSE: STUDIES IN THE EIGHTEENTH CENTURY. Athens: Univ. of Georgia Press, 1974.

Although stressing the fiction of the period, contains several original essays on the poetry.

105  Clifford, James L., ed. EIGHTEENTH-CENTURY ENGLISH LITERATURE: MODERN ESSAYS IN CRITICISM. New York: Oxford Univ. Press, 1959.

Previously printed essays of note covering all aspects of the period.

106  _____. MAN VERSUS SOCIETY IN EIGHTEENTH-CENTURY BRITAIN: SIX POINTS OF VIEW. Cambridge: Cambridge Univ. Press, 1968.

Excellent essays on a variety of academic disciplines addressing the topic of individual opportunities for self-realization in the period.

107  Clifford, James L., and Louis A. Landa, eds. POPE AND HIS CONTEMPORARIES: ESSAYS PRESENTED TO GEORGE SHERBURN. New York: Oxford Univ. Press, 1949.

Valuable essays devoted to the age of Pope.

108     Ehrenpreis, Irvin.  LITERARY MEANING AND AUGUSTAN VALUES.
        Charlottesville:  Univ. Press of Virginia, 1974.

        Previously published articles exploring a number of widespread
        critical assumptions about "the relation of style to meaning
        and of literary value to both." Of major importance.


108A    Harth, Phillip, ed.  NEW APPROACHES TO EIGHTEENTH-CENTURY
        LITERATURE.  New York: Columbia Univ. Press, 1974.

        Essays characterizing new directions in the study of literature,
        1660-1800, as well as seeking better answers to old questions.


109     Hilles, Frederick W., ed.  THE AGE OF JOHNSON: ESSAYS PRESENTED
        TO CHAUNCEY BREWSTER TINKER.  New Haven, Conn.: Yale Univ.
        Press, 1949.

        Festschrift of essays by Yale students of Tinker on, among other
        topics, the poets and poetry of the eighteenth century.


110     Hilles, Frederick W., and Harold Bloom, eds.  FROM SENSIBILITY TO
        ROMANTICISM: ESSAYS PRESENTED TO FREDERICK A. POTTLE.  New
        York: Oxford Univ. Press, 1965.

        Essays on the problems associated with the "shift of sensibility"
        that occurred between the Augustan period and romanticism.


111     Hilson, J.C., Monica M.B. Jones, and John R. Watson, eds.
        AUGUSTAN WORLDS: ESSAYS IN HONOR OF A.R. HUMPHREYS.
        Leicester, Engl.: Leicester Univ. Press, 1978.

        A festschrift contributing to the debate on the meaning of
        Augustan and Augustanism as these concepts are manifest in
        individual authors and designate an intellectual and cultural
        milieu.


112     Hughes, Peter, and David Williams, eds.  THE VARIED PATTERN:
        STUDIES IN THE EIGHTEENTH CENTURY.  Toronto: A.M. Hakkert,
        1971.

        Essays related to the art, aesthetics, literary criticism, and
        general intellectual background of the period.


113     Jensen, H. James, and Malvin R. Zirker, Jr., eds.  THE SATIRIST'S
        ART.  Bloomington: Indiana Univ. Press, 1972.

        The editors contribute a valuable introduction and afterword,
        both of which summarize arguments presented in the essays
        while addressing such general topics as satire and its rela-
        tionship to panegyric, use of personae, satire's rhetorical
        function, and the question of its corrective or reforming
        intention.

114    JOHNSON, BOSWELL AND THEIR CIRCLE: ESSAYS PRESENTED TO LAWRENCE FITZROY POWELL IN HONOUR OF HIS EIGHTY-FOURTH BIRTHDAY. Oxford: Clarendon Press, 1965.

       Collection of essays "in which new material is published or fresh interpretation advanced."

115    Jones, Richard Foster, ed. THE SEVENTEENTH CENTURY: STUDIES IN THE HISTORY OF ENGLISH THOUGHT AND LITERATURE FROM BACON TO POPE. Stanford, Calif.: Stanford Univ. Press, 1951.

       Excellent representation of the achievement of the "history of ideas" approach to seventeenth-century literature and intellectual thought.

116    Keast, William R. SEVENTEENTH-CENTURY ENGLISH POETRY: MODERN ESSAYS IN CRITICISM. Rev. ed. London: Oxford Univ. Press, 1971.

       Retains seventeen essays originally published in 1962 and adds new selections published since that date. Covers most of the earlier period to 1660, but provides materials important for the understanding of Restoration poetry.

117    Ker, William P. ON MODERN LITERATURE: LECTURES AND ADDRESSES. Ed. Terence Spencer and James Sutherland. Oxford: Clarendon Press, 1955.

       Hitherto unpublished essays on Butler, Dryden, Pope, Gray, Goldsmith, Crabbe, Blake, Cowper, and others.

118    Love, Harold. RESTORATION LITERATURE: CRITICAL APPROACHES. London: Methuen, 1972.

       Essays reflecting "the strongest assertion in post-medieval times of what might be called the Mediterranean component in British culture."

119    Martz, Louis L., and Aubrey Williams, eds. THE AUTHOR IN HIS WORK: ESSAYS ON A PROBLEM IN CRITICISM. Intro. by Patricia Meyer Spacks. New Haven, Conn.: Yale Univ. Press, 1978.

       Although only five essays deal specifically with poetry written between 1660 and 1800, the collection addresses issues raised by the persona approach to eighteenth-century literature as practiced by Maynard Mack, to whom this volume is dedicated.

120    Miller, Henry Knight, Eric Rothstein, and G.S. Rousseau, eds. THE
       AUGUSTAN MILIEU: ESSAYS PRESENTED TO LOUIS LANDA. Oxford:
       Clarendon Press, 1970.

       Eclectic collection of scholarly essays reflecting the range
       of Landa's own work.


121    Patterson, Daniel W., and Albrecht B. Strauss, eds. ESSAYS IN
       ENGLISH LITERATURE OF THE CLASSICAL PERIOD. SP, Extra Series,
       no. 4 (1967): entire issue.

       Ten essays by students, colleagues, and friends of Dougald
       MacMillan.


122    Paulson, Ronald, ed. SATIRE: MODERN ESSAYS IN CRITICISM.
       Englewood Cliffs, N.J.: Prentice-Hall, 1971.

       Good essays dealing with the origins, theory, and practice
       of satire. Reprints many classic studies.


123    Rogers, Pat, ed. THE EIGHTEENTH CENTURY. New York: Holmes
       and Meier, 1978.

       Expert discussions of eighteenth-century culture in its various
       aspects with chapters and bibliography on literature and
       society (P. Rogers), politics (W.A. Speck), religion and
       ideas (J.V. Price), science (G.S. Rousseau), and the visual
       arts (P. Willis).


124    Sutherland, James, and F.P. Wilson, eds. ESSAYS ON THE EIGHTEENTH
       CENTURY PRESENTED TO DAVID NICHOL SMITH IN HONOR OF HIS
       SEVENTIETH BIRTHDAY. Oxford: Clarendon Press, 1945.

       Essays celebrating a great eighteenth-century scholar.


125    Swedenberg, H.T., Jr., ed. ENGLAND IN THE RESTORATION AND
       EARLY EIGHTEENTH CENTURY: ESSAYS ON CULTURE AND SOCIETY.
       Berkeley and Los Angeles: Univ. of California Press, 1972.

       William Andrews Clark lectures at the University of California
       at Los Angeles.


126    Tillotson, Geoffrey. AUGUSTAN STUDIES. London: Athlone Press,
       1961.

       Original and previously published essays.


127    Wasserman, Earl R., ed. ASPECTS OF THE EIGHTEENTH CENTURY.
       Baltimore: Johns Hopkins Press, 1965.

       Essays addressing "the complex and many-faceted nature of
       the eighteenth century."

128 Watt, Ian, ed. THE AUGUSTAN AGE: APPROACHES TO ITS
LITERATURE, LIFE, AND THOUGHT. New York: Fawcett, 1968.

A good introduction to the period, reprinting previously
published essays, and rightfully warning in the introduction
about too-easy identification of the literary and cultural
situation with that of Augustan Rome. Section on the poetry.

129 Wellek, René, and Alvaro Ribeiro, eds. EVIDENCE IN LITERARY
SCHOLARSHIP: ESSAYS IN MEMORY OF JAMES MARSHALL OSBORN.
Oxford: Clarendon Press, 1979.

Festschrift devoted to a well-known eighteenth-century
scholar and antiquarian with many contributions addressed
to topics of the period 1660 to 1800.

130 Williams, Kathleen, ed. BACKGROUNDS TO EIGHTEENTH-CENTURY
LITERATURE. Scranton, Pa.: Chandler, 1971. Bibliog.

Reprints many significant essays dealing with all aspects of
the period, and provides a helpful chronology of cultural
and historical events.

131 Wimsatt, William K. THE VERBAL ICON: STUDIES IN THE MEANING
OF POETRY. Knoxville: Univ. of Kentucky Press, 1954.

Previously published essays, some revised for this collection.

132 Winters, Ivor. FORMS OF DISCOVERY: CRITICAL AND HISTORICAL
ESSAYS ON FORMS OF THE SHORT POEM IN ENGLISH. Denver:
Alan Swallow, 1967.

Contains two important essays on eighteenth-century poetry.

## C. ENGLISH LITERATURE, 1660-1800: BACKGROUND RESOURCES

## 1. Historical, Political, Social, and Economic Studies

133 Ashton, John. SOCIAL LIFE IN THE REIGN OF QUEEN ANNE TAKEN
FROM ORIGINAL SOURCES. London: Chatto and Windus, 1919.

Describes dress, food, leisure, clubs, sports, music, and
other aspects of life in the early part of the century through
the help of original sources such as the periodical essay,
newspapers, and diaries.

134 Ashton, Thomas S. AN ECONOMIC HISTORY OF ENGLAND: THE
EIGHTEENTH CENTURY. London: Methuen, 1955.

Ashton describes the economic and social life of England during the period--not as a professional economist, but as layman asking questions relevant to the general human application of economics.

135　Atherton, Herbert M. POLITICAL PRINTS IN THE AGE OF HOGARTH: A STUDY OF IDEOGRAPHIC REPRESENTATION OF POLITICS. Oxford: Clarendon Press, 1974. Illus.

Treatment of satiric prints from around 1727 to 1763, showing how this golden age of English graphic satire owes much to the common stock of ideas, themes, and myths presented in opposition pamphlets and to the political rhetoric in the early and middle decades of the century.

136　Aubrey, John. BRIEF LIVES. Ed. Andrew Clark. 2 vols. Oxford: Clarendon Press, 1898.

Good source for biographical information about Butler and other Restoration authors.

137　Beasley, Jerry C. "Portraits of a Monster: Robert Walpole and Early Prose Fiction." ECS, 14 (1981), 406-31.

Although primarily concerned with fiction, a lucid account of Walpole's almost mythological status as an enemy of the arts and culture and as representative of a new political and economic system that threatened the older social and moral order, and therefore a prime satiric target of such opposition poets as Swift, Pope, and Gay.

138　Beljame, Alexander. MEN OF LETTERS AND THE ENGLISH PUBLIC IN THE EIGHTEENTH CENTURY: 1660-1744, DRYDEN, ADDISON, POPE. Ed. B. Dobrée. Trans. E.O. Lorimer. London: Kegan Paul, Trench, Trubner, 1948.

Standard study of changing status of the writer vis a vis society in the period, with special emphasis on matters such as patronage and the relation of writers to politics and the court.

139　Biddle, Sheila. BOLINGBROKE AND HARLEY. New York: Knopf, 1974.

An account of the personal and political quarrels between two powerful and talented public statesmen in the early eighteenth century, the one, Bolingbroke, a Tory ideologist, viewing politics in terms of party loyalty and commitment and the other, Harley, a moderate and nominal Tory, committed to a scheme of nonparty government emphasizing the independence and autonomy of the monarchy.

140   Boswell, James. THE YALE EDITIONS OF THE PRIVATE PAPERS OF
      JAMES BOSWELL. Ed. F.A. Pottle et al. 15 vols. New York:
      McGraw-Hill, 1950-- .

      Contains invaluable information, comment, and a uniquely
      personalized perception of the life and times of the mid
      and late eighteenth century.


141   Brewer, John. PARTY IDEOLOGY AND POPULAR POLITICS AT THE
      ACCESSION OF GEORGE III. Cambridge: Cambridge Univ. Press,
      1976.

      A study of parliamentary politics and the political and social
      life outside of government, designed to provide understanding
      of the presuppositions underlying eighteenth-century politics
      and of the process of political transformation occurring
      throughout the century aided and abetted by George III's
      policies and the arguments over ideology carried on by the
      political elite of the time.


142   Brewer, Stella M. DESIGN FOR A GENTLEMEN: THE EDUCATION
      OF PHILIP STANHOPE. London: Chapman and Hall, 1963.

      An account of Lord Chesterfield's son, the recipient of his
      famous correspondence, whose education and life epitomized
      the making of a gentleman of culture during the eighteenth
      century.


143   Bronson, Bertrand H. "Printing as an Index of Taste." In his FACETS
      OF THE ENLIGHTENMENT: STUDIES IN ENGLISH LITERATURE AND
      ITS CONTEXTS. Berkeley and Los Angeles: Univ. of California Press,
      1968, pp. 326-65.

      Explores the importance of type design, printing, and the
      physical appearance of a book as a sociological and artistic
      index to taste in the period. See no. 100.


144   Cannon, John. PARLIAMENTARY REFORM, 1640-1832. Cambridge:
      Cambridge Univ. Press, 1973.

      Focuses on parliamentary change and reform movements from
      the early army debates of 1647 to the controversies surround-
      ing the Wilkes era, emphasizing continuities and similarities
      in the attitudes concerning change and the fundamentally
      conservative nature of the eighteenth-century political
      settlement.


145   Carswell, John. THE SOUTH SEA BUBBLE. Stanford, Calif.: Stanford
      Univ. Press, 1960.

      Views the economic upheaval of the South Sea Year during

1720, when stock from the South Sea Company was inflated from 128 to 1,000, as the culmination of one commercial revolution and the beginning of the Industrial Revolution. Includes biographical sketches of the court of directors.

146    Christian, Ian R.  MYTH AND REALITY IN LATE-EIGHTEENTH-CENTURY BRITISH POLITICS AND OTHER PAPERS.  Berkeley:  Univ. of California Press, 1970.

Essays directed to particular themes in the history of England: the central direction of government under limited monarchy; the inner workings of the political system and public administration; and movements for constitutional reform prior to the impact of the French Revolution.

147    Clarendon, Edward Hyde, First Earl of.  HISTORY OF THE REBELLION AND CIVIL WARS IN ENGLAND.  Ed. W.D. Macray.  6 vols.  Oxford:  Clarendon Press, 1888.

Standard edition of this important narrative of a period in English history that strongly influenced the politics, religion, and literature of the Restoration and early eighteenth century.

148    Clark, Sir George.  THE LATER STUARTS, 1660-1714.  2nd ed.  Oxford:  Clarendon Press, 1955.

A history of England under the later Stuarts, discussing religious disputes, the limits of royal power, and the consolidation of England under a constitutional monarchy despite two wars against the Dutch, two against the French, the Nine Years War (under William III, 1689-97), and the War of the Spanish Succession (1702-13).

149    Collins, Arthur Simons.  AUTHORSHIP IN THE DAYS OF JOHNSON: A STUDY OF THE RELATION BETWEEN AUTHOR, PATRON, PUBLISHER, AND PUBLIC, 1726-1780.  London:  R. Holden, 1927.

An account of the profession of letters in the eighteenth century with special attention to the diminishment of patronage from Pope's time and the growing public support of authors by about 1760.

150    Davis, Herbert.  STELLA:  A GENTLEWOMAN OF THE EIGHTEENTH CENTURY.  New York:  Macmillan, 1942.

Basing his thesis on his vast knowledge of and insights into the Swift-Stella relationship, Davis discusses Stella as representative of a new, middle-class gentlewoman, replacing the older, aristocratic court lady depicted in Renaissance literature.

151    Dickinson, H.T. BOLINGBROKE. London: Constable, 1970.

A biography of an historically important but highly controversial politician-statesman-philosopher, intimately involved
in the ideological battles of his day between landed and
monied interests, in the opposition to Walpole and the Whig
oligarchy, in the rise of Deism and challenge to orthodox
Christianity, and in the philosophical arguments underlying
Enlightenment thought.

152    _____ . LIBERTY AND PROPERTY: POLITICAL IDEOLOGY IN
EIGHTEENTH-CENTURY BRITAIN. New York: Holmes and Meier,
1977.

Challenges Namier's belief that understanding of a political
institution or a society occurs only through analysis of its
components and argues that the ideas and arguments constituting
political ideology affect political and social orders, and that
what men thought and said about civil government influenced
what they actually did.

153    Dickson, Peter George Muir. THE FINANCIAL REVOLUTION IN
ENGLAND: A STUDY IN THE DEVELOPMENT OF PUBLIC CREDIT,
1688-1756. London: Macmillan, 1967.

A detailed study of foreign investment and the system of
government borrowing and national debt of which it was a
part from the end of the seventeenth century through the
South Sea Bubble, the Walpole administration, and the years
immediately following his fall in 1742.

154    Dodington, George Bubb. THE POLITICAL DIARY OF GEORGE BUBB
DODINGTON. Eds. John Carswell and Lewis Arnold Dralle. Oxford:
Clarendon Press, 1965.

A record of the political and literary activities of an important eighteenth-century figure who befriended Fielding,
Young, and Thomson, among others, and whose DIARY was
viewed as documentation of political corruption and as proof
of the need for reform.

155    Evelyn, John. THE DIARY OF JOHN EVELYN. Ed. E.S. de Beer.
6 vols. Oxford: Clarendon Press, 1955.

Many firsthand accounts of historical events and important
figures of the period 1640 to 1706.

156    Foord, Archibald. HIS MAJESTY'S OPPOSITION, 1714-1830. Oxford:
Clarendon Press, 1964.

Tends to minimize Whig-Tory ideological differences and to

stress division along the lines of court-country, arguing that
the hostility to Walpole was a negative unifying force but
that agreement on positive aims and policies was less clear.

157    George, M. Dorothy. ENGLAND IN JOHNSON'S DAY. New York:
Harcourt Brace, 1928.

Selections from a wide variety of poets, novelists, and
essayists commenting on the life, letters, and cultural
phenomena of the period 1709 to 1784. Introduction somewhat dated and oversimplified.

158    _____. ENGLAND IN TRANSITION: LIFE AND WORK IN THE
EIGHTEENTH CENTURY. Middlesex, Engl.: Penguin Books, 1931.

Studies the social conditions of the eighteenth century,
especially the lot of the poor and government response to
poverty, the emerging force of humanitarianism, the revolution in agriculture, the Industrial Revolution, and child labor.

159    _____. ENGLISH POLITICAL CARICATURE: A STUDY OF OPINION
AND PROPAGANDA. 2 vols. Oxford: Clarendon Press, 1959.

Fascinating discussion of pictorial propaganda in England,
with sections ranging from loyalist and monarchist examples
of the 1660s to representations of the Fox-Pitt crisis in 1784.

160    _____. ENGLISH SOCIAL LIFE IN THE EIGHTEENTH CENTURY:
ILLUSTRATED FROM CONTEMPORARY SOURCES. London: Sheldon
Press, 1923.

Prints extracts from relevant documents pertaining to the
social life of England in an age of transition. Treats
wages, standards of living, the plight of the poor, housing,
agriculture, and economics.

161    _____. LONDON LIFE IN THE EIGHTEENTH CENTURY. London:
Kegan Paul, Trench, Trubner, 1925.

Good account of working conditions and the life of the
poor in London, showing that the upheaval associated with
the Industrial Revolution had less effect on the social and
economic fabric of the city than in the newer, less stable,
and often badly administered parishes.

162    Haley, Kenneth H.D. THE FIRST EARL OF SHAFTESBURY. Oxford:
Clarendon Press, 1968.

A full-length biography of Dryden's "false Achitophel,"
who influenced many important issues in the seventeenth

century and remains a man of "considerable personal and
psychological attraction" to the historian.

163   Halsband, Robert. THE LIFE OF LADY MARY WORTLEY MONTAGU.
Oxford: Clarendon Press, 1956.

A biographical account of a learned lady writer, diplomat,
popularizer of smallpox inoculation, patron of the arts, and
satiric target of Alexander Pope.

164   _____. LORD HERVEY: EIGHTEENTH-CENTURY COURTIER. New
York: Oxford Univ. Press, 1974.

A life of a colorful, enigmatic, and complex member of
George II's court, intimately connected with its members,
its political life and Sir Robert Walpole. Hervey was the
model for Sporus, Pope's famous satiric portrait in the "Epistle
to Dr. Arbuthnot."

165   Hammond, John Lawrence, and Barbara Hammond. THE RISE OF
MODERN INDUSTRY. London: Methuen, 1947.

An attempt to place the Industrial Revolution in an historical
context and to discuss its significance and the causes that
determined the age and the society in which it originated.

166   Hanson, Laurence W. CONTEMPORARY PRINTED SOURCES FOR
ENGLISH AND IRISH ECONOMIC HISTORY, 1701-1750. Cambridge:
Cambridge Univ. Press, 1963.

Includes materials relating to economic affairs published
during the period, excluding public acts, estate acts, and
bills, but noting pleadings before Parliament and other
matters relating to legislation.

167   _____. GOVERNMENT AND THE PRESS 1665-1763. Oxford: Clarendon Press, 1936.

A study of the relationship between government and the newspaper press as pertains to politics from the expiration of the
Licensing Act of 1662 to the publication of NORTH BRITON
NO. 45, and the legal consequences following the prosecution
of Wilkes.

168   Hart, Jeffrey. VISCOUNT BOLINGBROKE: TORY HUMANIST. London:
Routledge and Kegan Paul, 1965.

Tory humanists, like Bolingbroke, took their classical system
of values seriously and realized the threats to these values
from commerce, individualism, urbanized society, and moral
relativism.

169    Hill, Christopher. REFORMATION TO INDUSTRIAL REVOLUTION, 1530-1780. Vol. 1: THE MAKING OF MODERN ENGLISH SOCIETY. New York: Pantheon, 1967.

Discusses those special features of English history which are different from that of other European countries during this period, explaining how successful political revolutions led to greater commercial influence over government.

170    Holmes, Geoffrey. BRITISH POLITICS IN THE AGE OF ANNE. London: Macmillan, 1967.

A comprehensive study using the basic conflict of attitudes, policy, and principle embodied in the names Whig and Tory as a vehicle to a deeper understanding of this special era of English political life.

171    Holmes, Geoffrey, and William Arthur Speck, eds. THE DIVIDED SOCIETY: PARTIES AND POLITICS IN ENGLAND, 1694-1716. New York: St. Martin's Press, 1967.

A useful reproduction of excerpts relating to struggle for mastery between Whigs and Tories that dominates the English political scene during the period of the Septennial Bill, promoted by the Whigs to prolong their tenure of office for a duration of seven years.

172    Hook, Judith. THE BAROQUE AGE IN ENGLAND. London: Thames and Hudson, 1976.

A cultural history of the English baroque sensibility and the age and society which sustained and fostered it, concluding that the English artists were not adapting or copying a continental fashion, but producing original contributions to European culture, often "great monuments, great paintings and music, and some of the greatest works of English literature."

173    Humphreys, Arthur R. THE AUGUSTAN WORLD: LIFE AND LETTERS IN EIGHTEENTH-CENTURY ENGLAND. London: Methuen, 1954.

Argues from the conviction that the society in which literature is produced shapes the themes and methods of presentation and, therefore, examines the social, economic, political, religious, moral, and aesthetic influences on the literature of the period. Treats major and minor figures.

174    Jones, James R. THE FIRST WHIGS: THE POLITICS OF THE EXCLUSION CRISIS. London: Oxford Univ. Press, 1961.

Discusses the various competing political groups during Charles II's reign.

175    Kenyon, John P. THE POPISH PLOT. London: Heinemann, 1972.

Discusses the political complexities of this central event in
Dryden's literary career.

176    _____. REVOLUTION PRINCIPLES: THE POLITICS OF PARTY, 1689-
1720. Cambridge: Cambridge Univ. Press, 1977.

Reexamines alleged "Lockean" influence on Whig political
and constitutional themes, finding instead that "experience
and history were in fact to be the keynotes of the Whigs'
political philosophy after the Revolution" and that their
main political problem was not so much to establish an abstract constitutional theory as to "offset entrenched theories
of Toryism."

177    Kramnick, Isaac. BOLINGBROKE AND HIS CIRCLE. Cambridge,
Mass.: Harvard Univ. Press, 1968.

Discusses the "style of thought" and habit of mind Bolingbroke shared with his literary supporters Swift, Gay, and
Pope based on aristocratic attitudes toward politics and
society and beliefs in traditional humanism they saw threatened by corruptions of the Walpole government, the emergence of a new monied class, and the projecting spirit of
entrepreneurism.

178    Lecky, William Edward Hartpole. A HISTORY OF ENGLAND IN THE
EIGHTEENTH CENTURY. 3 vols. London: Longmans, Green, 1892.

Comprehensive history of the social, political, religious,
and economic aspects of England, stressing the "permanent
forces" and "enduring features" of the period.

179    Lynch, Kathleen M. JACOB TONSON, KIT-CAT PUBLISHER. Knoxville: Univ. of Tennessee Press, 1971.

Biographical review of the heritage and educational background of Tonson's "many-faceted career," as well as a discussion of his connection with Dryden, the Kit-Cat group,
and his rise to fame through such authors as Addison, Steele,
Congreve, and Prior and through publication of the classics
and of Spenser and Milton.

180    Macaulay, George B. THE HISTORY OF ENGLAND FROM THE
ACCESSION OF JAMES THE SECOND. Ed. Charles Harding Firth.
6 vols. London: Macmillan, 1913.

Chapter 3 of volume 1, "State of England in 1685," remains
a lively "Whig interpretation" of the period and is still
relevant.

181    Marshall, Dorothy. ENGLISH PEOPLE IN THE EIGHTEENTH CENTURY. London: Longmans, Green, 1956.

Analyzes the social structure of England just before and just after the first impact of "mechanical invention" as background for an understanding of the resulting transformation of England into an industrial nation.

182    _____. THE ENGLISH POOR IN THE EIGHTEENTH CENTURY: A STUDY OF SOCIAL AND ADMINISTRATIVE HISTORY. London: George Routledge and Sons, 1926.

An account of ways the Poor Laws affected the laboring poor in the late seventeenth and eighteenth centuries and of contemporary attitudes toward the fact of poverty.

183    Mathias, Peter. THE FIRST INDUSTRIAL NATION: AN ECONOMIC HISTORY OF ENGLAND, 1700-1914. London: Methuen, 1969.

Comprehensive survey of a variety of factors leading to the industrialization of England during the eighteenth century, taking into account social, philosophic, and religious aspects as well as the more familiar matters of poverty, climate, geography, and other directly related influences.

184    Mingay, G.E. ENGLISH LANDED SOCIETY IN THE EIGHTEENTH CENTURY. London: Routledge and Kegan Paul, 1963.

An important study from estate records of land ownership as the foundation of eighteenth-century social, economic, and political life.

185    Namier, Sir Lewis B. ENGLAND IN THE AGE OF THE AMERICAN REVOLUTION. London: Macmillan, 1930.

Applies the "Namierian" approach made famous in his earlier study of George III's accession to the later years of his reign.

186    _____. THE STRUCTURE OF POLITICS AT THE ACCESSION OF GEORGE III. 2 vols. London: Macmillan, 1929.

Highly influential interpretation of the national political system, arguing that the real groupings were based on familial and electoral interests, not party ideology. Analyzes genealogical as well as political relationships in various localities.

187    Ogg, David. ENGLAND IN THE REIGN OF CHARLES II. 2 vols. Oxford: Clarendon Press, 1934.

Standard narrative history of the period dealing with social,

economic, and political conditions and the wars, French
influence, and constitutional crises of 1681 and various
Stuart reactions to them.

188 _____. ENGLAND IN THE REIGNS OF JAMES II AND WILLIAM
III. Oxford: Clarendon Press, 1955.

A sequel to his history of Charles II's reign, mingling narrative
and descriptive and analytical approaches to this seventeen-
year emergence of England as a major European power.

189 Owen, John B. THE EIGHTEENTH CENTURY, 1714-1815. London:
Thomas Nelson, 1974.

A "self-confessed member of the so-called 'Namier School,'"
attempts a synthesis of his mentor's findings about the structure of English politics in the period as a corrective to the
Whig interpretation and misrepresentations by other Namierian
dogmatists.

190 Pepys, Samuel. THE DIARY OF SAMUEL PEPYS. Ed. Robert Latham
and William Matthews. 11 vols. projected. Berkeley and Los Angeles:
Univ. of California Press, 1970-- .

Famous source of firsthand accounts of the life and times of
Charles II's court, especially on such matters as the Dutch
war, the fire of London, the plague, and the theaters of
the age.

191 Percy, Thomas. THE PERCY LETTERS. Ed. David Nichol Smith,
Cleanth Brooks, A.F. Falconer et al. Vols. 1-5. Baton Rouge:
Louisiana State Univ. Press, 1944-57. Vols. 6-7. New Haven, Conn.:
Yale Univ. Press, 1961, 1977.

Volume 3 (the Percy-Warton correspondence) and volume 7
(the Percy-Shenstone correspondence) are especially valuable
resources for information pertaining to the ballad revival in
particular and antiquarianism in general.

192 _____. RELIQUES OF ANCIENT ENGLISH POETRY. Ed. Henry B.
Wheatley. 3 vols. 1886; rpt. New York: Dover, 1966.

Famous collection of ballads representative of the antiquarian
interest of the period.

193 Pinkus, Philip. GRUB STREET STRIPPED BARE. Hamden, Conn.: Archon,
1968.

Deals with the "historical substance" of the Grub Street
hacks through their own writings and by viewing them in

their historical setting. Treats publishers, authors, and political pamphleteers.

194     Plant, Marjorie. THE ENGLISH BOOK TRADE: AN ECONOMIC HISTORY OF THE MAKING AND SALE OF BOOKS. New York: R.R. Bowker, 1939.

An economic history of book selling, including institutional structure, supply and demand factors, business practices used and discarded, and the social dimensions of the industry.

195     Plumb, J.H. ENGLAND IN THE EIGHTEENTH CENTURY. Baltimore: Penguin Books, 1950.

The best single account of the history, politics, economic trends, and religious and social changes characterizing the period.

196     _____. THE FIRST FOUR GEORGES. London: Batsford, 1956.

Lively and sympathetic description of the Hanoverian royal family.

197     _____. THE GROWTH OF POLITICAL STABILITY IN ENGLAND, 1675–1725. London: Macmillan, 1967.

Gives more weight to the importance of the role of Whig-Tory divisions and political differences than his earlier studies, but maintains that such oppositions are but one of a complex mixture of local and familial rivalries characterizing the politics of the period.

198     _____. ROBERT WALPOLE: THE KING'S MINISTER. London: Cresset, 1970.

Discusses Walpole's main concern with domestic matters and his influence over Parliament, but also indicates the close connections between foreign affairs and domestic politics that shaped his foreign policy, bringing his criticism but establishing his significance as a European statesman. See no. 199.

199     _____. SIR ROBERT WALPOLE: THE MAKING OF A STATESMAN. London: Cresset, 1956.

Standard life of the most controversial political figure (for Augustan satirists) of the period, correcting nineteenth-century distortions of his contributions to the development of constitutional government and objectively analyzing his abilities and achievements as well as his imperfections and failures. See no. 198.

200    Pocock, John Greville Agard.  THE MACHIAVELLIAN MOMENT:
       FLORENTINE POLITICAL THOUGHT AND THE ATLANTIC REPUBLICAN
       TRADITION.  Princeton, N.J.:  Princeton Univ. Press, 1975.

         Part 3 shows that the English and American political tradi-
         tions reflected republican and Machiavellian as well as
         Lockean and Burkean constitutionalist concepts and values.


201    Realey, Charles B.  THE EARLY OPPOSITION TO SIR ROBERT WAL-
       POLE, 1720-1727.  Lawrence:  Univ. of Kansas Press, 1931.

         A detailed study of the parliamentary opposition to Walpole
         between 1721 and 1727, illustrating the challenging character
         of the original opposition and its subsequent intensification
         up to his fall in 1742.


202    Richardson, A.E.  GEORGIAN ENGLAND:  A SURVEY OF SOCIAL
       LIFE, TRADE, INDUSTRIES AND ART FROM 1700-1820.  New York:
       Charles Scribner's Sons, 1931.  Illus.

         Using contemporary sources, traces the salient features and
         characteristics of this period, focusing on less familiar sub-
         jects such as the activities of daily life and the materials
         producing the art, industry, and architecture of the eighteenth
         century.


203    Rogers, Pat.  GRUB STREET:  STUDIES IN A SUBCULTURE.  London:
       Methuen, 1972.

         Valuable study of the social implications of "duncehood,"
         as well as testimony to the fact that Augustan satire was
         built on historical particulars and contemporary life.


204    Sedgwick, Romney, ed.  LORD HERVEY'S MEMOIRS.  London: William
       Kimber, 1952.

         An intimate account of the first ten years of George II's
         reign from the viewpoint of his most famous courtier and
         favorite of Queen Caroline.


205    Speck, William Arthur.  STABILITY AND STRIFE:  ENGLAND, 1714-
       1760.  Cambridge, Mass.:  Harvard Univ. Press, 1977.

         Outlines the constitutional, social, economic, and religious
         context of Westminster politics, of cabinet parliamentary
         debates, and of ministerial charges in order to explain the
         transition of British politics from party divisions in Queen
         Anne's reign to a stable oligarchy in George II's final years.


206    _____.  TORY AND WHIG:  THE STRUGGLE IN THE CONSTITUENCIES,
       1701-1715.  London:  Macmillan, 1970.

Despite the weakening of the Tories as a national political force and the simultaneous disintegration of the Whigs into factionalism during the reign of Queen Anne, these rival parties were cohesive institutions of shared political and religious policy.

207   Steegman, John. THE RULE OF TASTE FROM GEORGE I AND GEORGE IV. London: Macmillan, 1936.

Using the word taste to mean both individual discernment, criticism, and perception, as well as generally agreed upon aesthetic standards, explores the changing tastes among the elite class in the arts of architecture, gardening, and painting from the 1730s to around 1832.

208   Straka, Gerald M., ed. THE REVOLUTION OF 1688 AND THE BIRTH OF THE ENGLISH NATION. 2nd ed. Lexington, Mass.: D.C. Heath, 1973.

Excerpts from both contemporary political and philosophical tracts and from the views of modern historians.

209   Summerson, John. GEORGIAN LONDON. Baltimore: Penguin Books, 1963. Illus.

A useful outline of the architectural history of London during the period.

210   Trevelyan, George M. ENGLAND UNDER QUEEN ANNE. 3 vols. London: Longmans, Green, 1931-34.

Essential historical account of the English social, political, and economic circumstances of 1701 to 1714, with biographical portraits of the major figures involved.

211   _____. THE ENGLISH REVOLUTION, 1688-1689. New York: Henry Holt, 1939.

Interprets the true glory and merit of this bloodless revolution as the prudence and wisdom that prevailed throughout the inflammatory circumstances of the Seven Bishops namely, Sancroft, Archbishop of Canterbury, and six others who petitioned that the clergy be excused from reading James II's DECLARATION OF INDULGENCE, and sees the circumstances as a legacy for future generations of political change without violence.

212   _____. ILLUSTRATED ENGLISH SOCIAL HISTORY. Vol. 2: THE AGE OF SHAKESPEARE AND THE STUART PERIOD. Vol. 3: THE EIGHTEENTH CENTURY. London: Longmans, Green, 1951.

Explores all aspects of English life in the period: public
and private, economic, social, and artistic.

213   Turberville, Arthur S. ENGLISH MEN AND MANNERS IN THE
EIGHTEENTH CENTURY. Oxford: Clarendon Press, 1926.

Comprehensive account from a biographical point of view,
describing outstanding groups of statesmen, politicians, and
other representatives of the "Classical or Augustan Age."

214   _____, ed. JOHNSON'S ENGLAND: AN ACCOUNT OF THE LIFE
AND MANNERS OF HIS AGE. 2 vols. Oxford: Clarendon Press,
1933.

Descriptive account of life, institutions, luxuries, entertain-
ment, the theater, medicine, and other aspects of the
eighteenth century. Shrewd choice of commentators and
essayists.

215   Walcott, Robert, Jr. ENGLISH POLITICS IN THE EARLY EIGHTEENTH
CENTURY. Cambridge, Mass.: Harvard Univ. Press, 1956.

Applies the Namier methodology to the last parliament of
William III and Queen Anne's first three, analyzing the
many-faceted relationships involving one thousand members
of Commons.

216   Walpole, Horace. THE YALE EDITION OF HORACE WALPOLE'S
CORRESPONDENCE. Ed. W.H. Lewis et al. 42 vols. New Haven,
Conn.: Yale Univ. Press, 1937-80.

Standard edition.

217   Whiteley, John Harold. WESLEY'S ENGLAND: A SURVEY OF EIGH-
TEENTH CENTURY SOCIAL AND CULTURAL CONDITIONS. London:
Epworth Press, 1938.

General cultural history of the age, especially of those
aspects that either influenced or were influenced by John
Wesley and Methodism.

218   Williams, Basil. THE WHIG SUPREMACY 1714-1760. Oxford: Clarendon Press, 1939.

Comprehensive and detailed study of the life, times, history,
arts, and literature, positing a "rare unity" of political
interests and national stability between an earlier and later
period of turmoil and doubt.

219    Williams, E. Neville.  LIFE IN GEORGIAN ENGLAND.  London:
       B.T. Batsford, 1962.

       A brief but fully illustrated account of English life in the
       period, stressing the particular character of the English
       people, demographic phenomena, the social class system,
       and general cultural life.

220    Wilson, Charles.  ENGLAND'S APPRENTICESHIP, 1603–1763.  New
       York:  St. Martin's Press, 1965.

       Sets out the main conclusions of economic historians about
       England's past, taking into account the social context and
       the impact of politics.

221    Wood, Anthony à.  ATHENAE OXONIENSES.  Ed. Philip Bliss.  5 vols.
       London:  F.G. and J. Rivington, 1813–20.

       Biographical information on numerous Restoration authors.

## 2. Philosophy, Science, and Religion

222    Becker, Carl L.  THE HEAVENLY CITY OF THE EIGHTEENTH-CENTURY
       PHILOSOPHERS.  New Haven, Conn.:  Yale Univ. Press, 1932.

       Famous but controversial thesis that the philosophers remade
       Augustine's city into their own secular heavenly city, em-
       phasizing the affinities of the age of Voltaire with the
       Middle Ages and its differences from modern society.  See
       no. 254.

223    Bennett, Gareth V.  THE TORY CRISIS IN CHURCH AND STATE, 1688–
       1730:  THE CAREER OF FRANCIS ATTERBURY, BISHOP OF ROCHESTER.
       Oxford:  Clarendon Press, 1975.

       Focuses on this immensely important Anglican divine, cham-
       pion of the High Church cause after the revolution of 1688,
       as a central religio-political figure in the midst of the
       shattering of the church–state alliance and the resultant
       bitterness and agitation that caught up the great literary
       figures of the day.

224    Boulton, James T.  THE LANGUAGE OF POLITICS IN THE AGE OF
       WILKES AND BURKE.  London:  Routledge and Kegan Paul, 1963.

       Valuable as background to political literature during Wilkes's
       election, 1769–71, and the controversies surrounding Burke's
       REFLECTIONS 1790–93.

225     Bush, Douglas. SCIENCE AND ENGLISH POETRY: A HISTORICAL SKETCH, 1590-1950. New York: Oxford Univ. Press, 1950.

        Chapter 2 discusses the impact of the new science, of the materialism of Hobbes, and of Renaissance naturalism on late seventeenth-century thought. Chapter 3 presents the emergence of the three important eighteenth-century concepts of Newtonianism, rationalism, and sentimentalism. Brief but lucid presentation.

226     Butt, John. "Science and Man in Eighteenth-Century Poetry." In POPE, DICKENS, AND OTHERS: ESSAYS AND ADDRESSES. Edinburgh: Edinburgh Univ. Press, 1969, pp. 91-110.

        The eighteenth century inherited three related problems from the seventeenth-century advances in science: how to assimilate these new discoveries, how to reconcile science with traditional beliefs and values, and how to strike a balance between science and human studies. Treats Pope and Thomson. See no. 102.

227     Cassirer, Ernst. THE PHILOSOPHY OF THE ENLIGHTENMENT. Trans. Fritz C.A. Koelln and James P. Pettegrove. Princeton, N.J.: Princeton Univ. Press, 1951.

        Deservedly classic study viewing the philosophy of the age as a unity by noting its development, its intellectual energy, and "the enthusiasm with which it attacks all its various problems."

228     Clark, George Norman. SCIENCE AND SOCIAL WELFARE IN THE AGE OF NEWTON. Oxford: Clarendon Press, 1937.

        Focuses on the years 1660 to 1700 as a period of changing relationships between science and economic life that brought about modern institutionalizing and socializing of scientific technology.

229     Cragg, Gerald R. THE CHURCH AND THE AGE OF REASON, 1648-1789. New York: Atheneum, 1960.

        Discusses the variety of challenges to Christian orthodoxy and institutional dynasty and authority in the period, indicating the important figures and movements giving rise to modern Christianity and the intertwining of the ecclesiastical and political that often made change and reform risky.

230     _____. FROM PURITANISM TO THE AGE OF REASON: A STUDY OF CHANGES IN RELIGIOUS THOUGHT WITHIN THE CHURCH OF ENGLAND, 1660 TO 1700. Cambridge: Cambridge Univ. Press, 1966.

A study restricted to the developments in religious thought and philosophy after the extremes of Puritanism and the emergence of toleration based on reason.

231    Crane, R.S.  "Anglican Apologetics and the Idea of Progress, 1699-1745."  MP, 31 (1934), 273-306.

An account of the "significant contributions" made to the formulation and influence of "progressivist ways of thinking" in England by writers whose motivation was not enthusiam for the advancement of science or the freeing of the mind from prejudices, but rather the defense of revealed religion against its detractors.

232    Davies, Horton. WORSHIP AND THEOLOGY IN ENGLAND FROM WATTS AND WESLEY TO MAURICE, 1690-1850. Princeton, N.J.: Princeton Univ. Press, 1961.

A comprehensive account of the salient features of Anglican and nonconformist traditions in worship and architecture throughout the period, discussing the inroads made by Deism in Trinitarian orthodoxy and the subsequent yielding of "rationalistic moralism" to evangelicalism and the religion of sentiment in the middle of the century.

233    Dickinson, H.T.  "Henry St. John:  A Reappraisal of the Young Boling-broke."  JBS  7 (1968), 33-55.

Bolingbroke's early years explain his inconsistent character, thought, purpose, intellect, but make more interesting his literary talent and political life.

234    Fairchild, Hoaxie Neale.  RELIGIOUS TRENDS IN ENGLISH POETRY. 6 vols.  New York:  Columbia Univ. Press, 1939-68.

Volume 1, 1700-1740, "Protestantism and the Cult of Senti-ment," and volume 2, 1740-1780, "Religious Sentimentalism in the Age of Johnson," study the religious element in poetry of the period from an historical viewpoint, defining the term broadly enough to include ideas or concepts--even those scientific or philosophic in import--with any religious implica-tions.

235    Gay, Peter.  THE ENLIGHTENMENT:  AN INTERPRETATION.  2 vols. New York:  Knopf, 1966, 1969.

Although emphasizing continental thought and culture, a comprehensive analysis of the critical dialectic between pagan and Christian inheritances in the establishment of enlightenment philosophy.

236    Green, Stanley. SHAFTESBURY'S PHILOSOPHY OF RELIGION AND
       ETHICS: A STUDY OF ENTHUSIASM. Athens: Ohio Univ. Press,
       1967.

       A full-length study of one of the "philosophic greats" of
       the Enlightenment, whose "moral sense" school of ethics,
       optimistic metaphysics, attacks on the God of retribution,
       and contributions to the Deistic movement made him an
       important figure in the transition from Cambridge Platonism
       to the ethical intuitionism and liberal theology characterizing
       the early and middle eighteenth century.


237    Harris, Ronald W. REASON AND NATURE IN THE EIGHTEENTH
       CENTURY. New York: Barnes and Noble, 1969.

       Examines the assumption that the eighteenth century witnessed
       a disintegration of the great Renaissance humanistic tradition
       as a result of the new science, the growth of individualism,
       and the empirical philosophies of Hobbes, Locke, and Hume;
       but asserts that in literature the tradition was "outwardly
       strong" while forces of change subverted the structure of
       thought from within.


238    Howell, Wilbur J. EIGHTEENTH-CENTURY BRITISH LOGIC AND
       RHETORIC. Princeton, N.J.: Princeton Univ. Press, 1971.

       Treats the major eighteenth-century writings on logic and
       rhetoric, placing them in chronological order to relate them
       to the preceding and following centuries, concluding that
       the changes that took place in the theories are the result
       of the impact of the new science.


239    Humphreys, Arthur R. "Literature and Religion in Eighteenth-Century
       England." JOURNAL OF ECCLESIASTICAL HISTORY, 3 (1952), 159-90.

       An authoritative analysis of the effects of religion on
       eighteenth-century writers and their public.


240    Kuhn, Reinhard. THE DEMON OF NOONTIDE: ENNUI IN WESTERN
       LITERATURE. Princeton, N.J.: Princeton Univ. Press, 1976.

       A learned study of the idea of boredom or ennui, a crucial
       feature in the formation of Western man, presenting material
       especially relevant to the study of poets of the middle and
       late part of the century.


241    Lovejoy, Arthur O. ESSAYS ON THE HISTORY OF IDEAS. Baltimore:
       Johns Hopkins Press, 1948.

       Discussions of the intellectual background of the eighteenth

century. Five essays on the concept of nature as an aesthetic
norm and on relationships between Deism and classicism.

242 _____. THE GREAT CHAIN OF BEING: A STUDY OF THE HISTORY
OF AN IDEA. Cambridge, Mass.: Harvard Univ. Press, 1936.

Discusses the history and implications of this metaphysical
construct on Renaissance and seventeenth-century writers,
and its contribution to the understanding of man's place in
the universe and idea of nature and to the concept of pleni-
tude in the eighteenth century. A highly influential book
and idea, often applied to the literature in a heavy-handed
way.

243 _____. REFLECTIONS ON HUMAN NATURE. Baltimore: Johns
Hopkins Press, 1961.

A brilliant set of lectures by the dean of the history of
ideas approach to literature, accounting for a number of
conceptions held about human motivation and their implications for man's cultural, political, and economic life.

244 Manuel, Frank E. THE EIGHTEENTH CENTURY CONFRONTS THE
GODS. Cambridge, Mass.: Harvard Univ. Press, 1959.

A discussion of themes involving the nature of the gods,
pointing out a discernible sequence or shift from one type
of theory to another during the course of the century, 1680-
1780.

245 Mazzeo, Joseph Anthony, ed. REASON AND THE IMAGINATION:
STUDIES IN THE HISTORY OF IDEAS, 1600-1800. New York:
Columbia Univ. Press, 1962.

Collection of distinguished scholars and students, contributing
distinguished essays in honor of their mentor Marjorie Hope
Nicolson in "the very idiom" of her expertise.

246 Mossner, Ernest C. BISHOP BUTLER AND THE AGE OF REASON: A
STUDY IN THE HISTORY OF THOUGHT. New York: Macmillan, 1936.

Studies Joseph Butler's ANALOGY OF RELIGION (1736)
as an index to the intellectual developments of the period,
particularly in respect to the new science, natural philosophy
and Deism, the decline of rational religion, Hume's skepticism, and Wesley's evangelicalism.

247 Nicolson, Marjorie Hope. NEWTON DEMANDS THE MUSE: NEWTON'S
"OPTICKS" AND THE EIGHTEENTH CENTURY POETS. Princeton, N.J.:
Princeton Univ. Press, 1946.

Argues that Newton's OPTICKS (1704), not his PRINCIPIA (1687), had the greatest impact on the literary imagination, especially between 1727 and 1757, the date of Burke's ENQUIRY.

248        . PEPY'S DIARY AND THE NEW SCIENCE. Charlottesville: Univ. Press of Virginia, 1965.

Helpful in identifying many of the actual scientists and virtuosi on which Samuel Butler based his satires against the new science.

249        . SCIENCE AND THE IMAGINATION. Ithaca, N.Y.: Great Seal Books, 1956.

Previously published essays addressing the connections between science and literature, many touching on poets from 1660 to 1800.

250    Ober, William B. BOSWELL'S CLAP AND OTHER ESSAYS: MEDICAL ANALYSES OF LITERARY MEN'S AFFLICTIONS. Carbondale: Southern Illinois Univ. Press, 1979.

Believes that relevant medical information about writers throws light on certain aspects of their life and writing and helps resolve literary problems. Discusses Collins, Cowper, Smart, and Rochester.

251    Patrides, C.A., and Raymond B. Waddington, eds. THE AGE OF MILTON: BACKGROUNDS TO SEVENTEENTH-CENTURY LITERATURE. Manchester, Engl.: Manchester Univ. Press, 1980. Bibliog., chronology.

Though not directly related to Restoration poetry, this volume nonetheless provides a rich context for a fuller comprehension of the poetry and prose of the middle years, especially the scientific, political, educational, and aesthetic background.

252    Purver, M. THE ROYAL SOCIETY: CONCEPT AND CREATION. Cambridge: MIT Press, 1967.

Good account of the founding of the Royal Society in 1660, the impact of the new philosophy, and the new scientific attitude it espoused, focusing especially on the emergence of the "true Baconian philosophy."

253    Raven, Charles F. NATURAL RELIGION AND CHRISTIAN THEOLOGY. Cambridge: Cambridge Univ. Press, 1953.

Good introduction to the important controversy involving the challenge of natural religion to the supernaturalism of tradi-

tional orthodoxy, explaining how the attempt to reconcile
the dualism between the orders of nature and of grace ran
afoul of deeply ingrained Roman Catholic and Protestant
theological assumptions.

254    Rockwood, Raymond O., ed. CARL BECKER'S HEAVENLY CITY RE-
VISITED. Ithaca, N.Y.: Cornell Univ. Press, 1958.

A symposium designed to provide critiques of Becker's version
of intellectual history by a number of distinguished eighteenth-
century intellectual historians. See no. 222.

255    Roston, Murray. PROPHET AND POET: THE BIBLE AND THE GROWTH
OF ROMANTICISM. Evanston, Ill.: Northwestern Univ. Press, 1965.

Argues that the rediscovery of biblical poetry in the eighteenth
century created a "gateway" to a new literary world by providing an "august literary model" under whose aegis the mid-
century poets could break away from the restraints of neoclassicism.

256    Sprat, Thomas. THE HISTORY OF THE ROYAL SOCIETY. Ed. Jackson
I. Cope and Harold Whitmore Jones. St. Louis: Washington Univ.
Studies, 1958.

Makes Sprat's text available and usable by printing a facsimile of the 1667 text, annotating and explaining this
valuable document in the intellectual and literary history
of the later seventeenth century.

257    Stephen, Leslie. HISTORY OF ENGLISH THOUGHT IN THE EIGH-
TEENTH CENTURY. 2 vols. New York: G.P. Putnam, 1876.

Famous monumental study of the period, emphasizing the
personalities, but controversial in its treatment of Deism and
the religious history of the period.

258    Sykes, Reverend Norman. CHURCH AND STATE IN ENGLAND IN THE
EIGHTEENTH CENTURY. Hamden, Conn.: Archon Books, 1962.

Detailed study of the important matter of church appointments,
preferment, and the general relationships between religious
institutions and politics.

259    Willey, Basil. THE EIGHTEENTH CENTURY BACKGROUND: STUDIES
ON THE IDEA OF NATURE IN THE THOUGHT OF THE PERIOD. London:
Chatto and Windus, 1940.

Treats the changing concepts of the protean term "nature,"
discussing its meaning in the categories of natural religion,

Deism, and physicotheology as well as in literature and
philosophy up through Wordsworth.

260        . THE SEVENTEENTH CENTURY BACKGROUND: STUDIES IN
THE THOUGHT OF THE AGE IN RELATION TO POETRY AND RELIGION.
London:  Chatto and Windus, 1933.

Classic study of the effects of contemporary thought and
"climates of opinion" on poetry and religion of the age,
especially in respect to the traditional "ideas of Truth and
Fiction" challenged by Locke's new epistemology.

## 3.  Fine Arts

261     Archer, John.  "Character in English Architectural Design."  ECS,  12
(1979),  339-71.

Deals with the development of the concept of character in
landscape and architectural design and its relationship to
eighteenth-century aesthetic theory and practice.

262     Clark, Kenneth.  THE GOTHIC REVIVAL:  AN ESSAY ON THE HISTORY
OF TASTE.  Rev. ed.  New York:  Scribners, 1950.

Although Gothic architecture never disappeared in England,
its revival in Horace Walpole's fiction and villa and in the
mid-century poets resulted from eighteenth-century scholarly
interest in the language, literature, and antiquities of
medieval Europe.

263     Hunt, John Dixon, and Peter Willis, eds.  THE GENIUS OF THE PLACE:
THE ENGLISH LANDSCAPE GARDEN 1620-1820.  New York:  Harper
and Row, 1975.  Illus.

An anthology, combining the expertise of an art historian
and a literary scholar and offering a glimpse of the vast
literature on England's great contribution to Europe.  Excerpts are taken from contemporary sources.

264     Hussey, Christopher.  ENGLISH COUNTRY HOUSES, 1715-1840.  3
vols.  London:  Country Life, 1955.

Comprehensive narrative of the development of English domestic architecture as manifest in the large country estates,
some privately owned and others part of the National Trust.
Lists architects, builders, and specifications.

265        .  ENGLISH GARDENS AND LANDSCAPES, 1700-1750.  London:
Country Life, 1967.

Illustrates the chief existing gardens and garden architecture on the grounds of country houses and relates them to the revolution in the conceptualization and execution of gardens originating in England.

266 _____. THE PICTURESQUE: STUDIES IN A POINT OF VIEW. London: Putnam, 1927.

A pioneering book about visual romanticism and still useful historical introduction to and appreciation of the visual values as reflected in literature, architecture, art, and gardening at the turn of the century.

267 Irwin, David. ENGLISH NEOCLASSICAL ART: STUDIES IN INSPIRATION AND TASTE. Greenwich, Conn.: New York Graphic Society, 1966.

Intended as a preliminary discussion of "the influence of the 'antique' taste" on poetry and sculpture from the 1760s to the 1820s.

268 Jones, Barbara. FOLLIES AND GROTTOES. London: Constable, 1953. Illus.

Fascinating study of the curious psychological impulse to create architectural follies—idiosyncratic, incongruous, amateurish, self-indulgent, and tasteless structures.

269 Lee, Rensselaer. UT PICTURA POESIS: THE HUMANISTIC THEORY OF PAINTING. New York: W.W. Norton, 1967.

A classic treatment of the fundamental assumption "that good painting, like good poetry, is the ideal imitation of human action" with the thesis that painters and poets strive to express general, not local, truths through subject matter drawn from what was universally known and found to be interesting in such sources as Scripture and classical antiquity.

270 Malins, Edward. ENGLISH LANDSCAPING AND LITERATURE, 1660-1840. London: Oxford Univ. Press, 1966.

Political and social ideals of "reasoned freedom" and the Aristotelian concept of "moderate" improvement of nature by art executed "direct influence" on theories about and the formation of English landscapes early in the eighteenth century, as did Longinus' distinctions between sublimity and beauty in the later years.

271 Manwaring, Elizabeth W. ITALIAN LANDSCAPE IN EIGHTEENTH CENTURY ENGLAND: A STUDY CHIEFLY OF THE INFLUENCE OF

CLAUDE LORRAIN AND SALVATORE ROSA ON ENGLISH TASTE, 1700-1800. London: Frank Cass, 1925.

Classic study of the impact on the English poetic conscious-ness of a conception of landscape derived from the practices of two contrasting painters, and a discussion of the influence of English conceptions of Italian landscape beauty on the literature of the period.

272     Myers, Robert M. HANDEL, DRYDEN, AND MILTON. London: Barnes and Barnes, 1956.

A valuable treatment of Handel's links with such dominant literary figures of the period as Dryden and Milton, empha-sizing the ways he utilized their texts and how the critics continually associated Handel with the literary greats; also provides complete and authentic texts of two compositions based on the works of these two poets.

273     Paulson, Ronald. EMBLEM AND EXPRESSION: MEANING IN ENGLISH ART OF THE EIGHTEENTH CENTURY. London: Thames and Hudson, 1975.

Discusses the changing mode of painting and visual repre-sentation during the 1750s manifest in the work of Hogarth and later painters from "meaning based primarily on explicit readable structures to meaning based primarily on spatial or formal structures."

274     _____. HOGARTH: HIS LIFE, ART, AND TIMES. 2 vols. New Haven, Conn.: Yale Univ. Press, 1971.

Shows how Hogarth's background, milieu, life, and aesthetic principles "contributed to produce and define his unique kind of art" and considers his "comic history paintings" central to his career. Interesting interpretations of the illustrations for Butler's HUDIBRAS (1663-78). A monumental study.

275     _____. HOGARTH'S GRAPHIC WORKS. 2 vols. New Haven, Conn.: Yale Univ. Press, 1965. Illus.

Complete collection of prints reproduced from originals with excellent notes and discussion of circumstances surrounding the production. Introduction treats biographical, critical, and bibliographical aspects.

276     Reynolds, Sir Joshua. DISCOURSES ON ART. Ed. Robert R. Wark. New Haven, Conn.: Yale Univ. Press, 1975.

An excellent edition providing an accurate text, collations listing changes, plates illustrating problems discussed, and explanatory comments. An introductory essay discusses the setting and historical circumstances in which the discourses were written and the audience intended.

277    Richardson, Jonathan.  AN ESSAY ON THE THEORY OF PAINTING. London: W. Bowyer, 1715.

Succeeded Kneller as England's most famous portrait painter, and his treatise on painting as a liberal art was an early eighteenth-century statement of the important sister arts concept.

278    Simpson, Claude M.  THE BRITISH BROADSIDE BALLAD AND ITS MUSIC. New Brunswick, N.J.: Rutgers Univ. Press, 1966.

Valuable study of broadside ballad tunes, which prints melodies, briefly explains political or historical significance, and lists the numerous settings and authors.

279    Tinker, Chauncey Brewster.  PAINTER AND POET: STUDIES IN THE LITERARY RELATIONS OF ENGLISH PAINTING. Cambridge, Mass.: Harvard Univ. Press, 1939.

Explores the proposition that the work of painters clearly reflects the literary movements and aesthetic concerns of the age.

280    Willis, Peter.  CHARLES BRIDGEMAN AND THE ENGLISH LANDSCAPE GARDEN. London: A. Zwemmer, 1977.

Creator of Stowe in Buckinghamshire, the most celebrated landscape of his day, Bridgeman was royal gardener to George II, a collaborator with Vanbrugh, a friend and confidant of famous writers of the day, and the most important figure in the transition from geometrical gardens in the early 1700s to a freer, natural landscape.

281    Wittkower, Rudolph.  ARCHITECTURAL PRINCIPLES IN THE AGE OF HUMANISM. 3rd ed. London: Tirauti, 1962.

Important study of the philosophy and intellectual context underlying architectural modes of proportion, symmetry, and balance of the Palladian movement in the early eighteenth century.

282    _____.  PALLADIO AND ENGLISH PALLADIANISM. London: Thames and Hudson, 1974.

Thirteen previously published essays on all aspects of the Palladian revival in England, some dealing with the particulars of design and others devoted to the cultural and artistic implications of the movement.

283    Woodbridge, Kenneth. LANDSCAPE AND ANTIQUITY: ASPECTS OF ENGLISH CULTURE AT STOURHEAD 1718 TO 1838. Oxford: Clarendon Press, 1970.

An account of various influences to be seen at Stourhead, showing the variety of classical strains that are realized in its design and setting, as well as the cultural context in which it developed.

## 4. Aesthetics and Literary Theory

285    Abrams, Meyer H. THE MIRROR AND THE LAMP: ROMANTIC THEORY AND THE CRITICAL TRADITION. New York: Oxford Univ. Press, 1953.

A classic study of romantic literary theory against the background of eighteenth-century aesthetics which conclusively shows how much romanticism is developed from, as well as a "deliberate reaction" to, eighteenth-century aesthetics.

286    Allen, B. Sprague. TIDES IN ENGLISH TASTE, 1619-1800: A BACKGROUND FOR THE STUDY OF LITERATURE. 2 vols. Cambridge, Mass.: Harvard Univ. Press, 1937.

Studies the intellectual and emotional forces molding art as well as literature and sees them as part of a larger whole, imparting a common and characteristic quality to such widely differing manifestations of beauty as poetry, textiles, ceramics, landscape gardening, and architecture.

287    Allison, Alexander Ward. TOWARD AN AUGUSTAN POETIC: EDMUND WALLER'S "REFORM" OF ENGLISH POETRY. Lexington: Univ. of Kentucky Press, 1962.

Examined in the context of Restoration and eighteenth-century poetry, Waller's subject matter, manner, and metrical practices can be viewed as an early model for the couplet rhetoric of Pope and others.

288    Appleton, William W. THE CYCLE OF CATHAY: THE CHINESE VOGUE IN ENGLAND DURING THE SEVENTEENTH AND EIGHTEENTH CENTURIES. New York: Columbia Univ. Press, 1951.

Treats the English interest in China, beginning at 1600 with the founding of the East India Company and ending around 1800, focusing on the myths and legends fabricated in the vogue of chinoiserie and the general flowering of interest in things Chinese.

289    Bate, Walter Jackson.  FROM CLASSIC TO ROMANTIC:  PREMISES
       OF TASTE IN EIGHTEENTH-CENTURY ENGLAND.  New York:
       Harper, 1946.

            Respected discussion of the shifting conceptions of taste and
            aesthetic judgments in the eighteenth century under the
            general rubric of classicism and romanticism.

290    Bond, Donald F.  "'Distrust' of Imagination in English Neo-Classicism."
       PQ, 14 (1935), 54-69.

            An early corrective of the stereotype concerning poetic
            theory and expression as "rationalistic," demonstrating that
            rationalism applied only to the prose and that in no place
            is it argued that poetry should be devoid of the imagination
            or fancy.  See no. 47.

291    Bredvold, Louis I.  "The Tendency Toward Platonism in Neo-Classical
       Esthetics."  ELH, 1 (1934), 91-119.

            A comprehensive discussion of affinities between ideas of
            form and beauty in the eighteenth century and the aesthetic
            and metaphysical traditions of Platonism and Neo-Platonism.
            Early defense of the so-called "artificial" and formal quali-
            ties of the neoclassical age.

292    Brett, R.L.  THE THIRD EARL OF SHAFTESBURY:  A STUDY IN EIGH-
       TEENTH-CENTURY LITERARY THEORY.  London:  Hutchinson's University
       Library, 1951.

            Concentrates on Shaftesbury's aesthetic and literary theories
            and their influence on not only eighteenth-century criticism
            but also on the poets and poetry of the period.

293    Congleton, James E.  THEORIES OF PASTORAL POETRY IN ENGLAND,
       1684-1798.  Gainesville:  Univ. of Florida Press, 1952.

            A comprehensive account of theories of pastoral poetry ad-
            vanced in England from Creech's translation of Rapin's
            treatise (1684) through Blair's essay in 1783, identifying
            their classical and continental sources.

294    Crane, Ronald S., ed.  CRITICS AND CRITICISM:  ANCIENT AND
       MODERN.  Chicago:  Univ. of Chicago Press, 1952.

            Important essays by members of the so-called formalist or
            Chicago School espousing critical theories directly bearing
            on the aesthetic implications and interpretation of the poetry
            of the period.

295 _____. THE IDEA OF THE HUMANITIES AND OTHER ESSAYS CRITICAL AND HISTORICAL. 2 vols. Chicago: Univ. of Chicago Press, 1967.

Impressive writings on literary history, criticism, and the history of ideas, establishing the "intellectual foundations" of the humanistic perspective.

296 _____. "On Writing the History of English Criticism, 1650-1800." UTQ, 22 (1953), 376-91.

Important essay setting forth the criteria for establishing "the internal character of any critical discourse."

296A Engell, James. THE CREATIVE IMAGINATION: ENGLIGHTENMENT TO ROMANTICISM. Cambridge, Mass.: Harvard Univ. Press, 1981.

A comprehensive and learned treatment of philosophical and aesthetic formulations from 1650 to 1820, mentioning hundreds of figures and concluding that Romanticism was the great achievement of the Enlightenment, not a reaction to it, and that the instrument of this achievement was the imagination.

297 Foerster, Donald M. HOMER IN ENGLISH CRITICISM: THE HISTORICAL APPROACH IN THE EIGHTEENTH CENTURY. New Haven, Conn.: Yale Univ. Press, 1947.

Investigates the increasingly historical approach to Homer during the eighteenth century and the dependence on the ILIAD and ODYSSEY as sources for information about early literature and society.

298 Gilpin, William. THREE ESSAYS ON PICTURESQUE BEAUTY: ON PICTURESQUE TRAVEL; ON SKETCHING LANDSCAPE: TO WHICH IS ADDED A POEM; ON LANDSCAPE PAINTING. London: R. Blamire, 1794.

The seminal essay on the "picturesque," defining this quality as the kind of beauty that looks well in a picture, meaning the landscape art admired in his age--the controlled depiction of idealized nature.

299 Greene, Donald. "Augustinianism and Empiricism: A Note on Eighteenth-Century English Intellectual History." ECS, 1 (1967), 33-68.

An important corrective to easy labelling of the Restoration and early eighteenth century as the age of reason, the neo-classical age, or the enlightenment in favor of two assumptions and beliefs shared by all in the period: the fallen and imperfect nature of man and the experience of the senses as the true source of man's knowledge.

300 _____. "What Indeed Was Neo-Classicism?" JBS, 10 (1970), 69-79.

A reply to attempts defining the term neoclassicism in a vacuum without a full "awareness of historical continuity."

301  Hagstrum, Jean H. THE SISTER ARTS: THE TRADITION OF LITERARY PIC-
     TORIALISM AND ENGLISH POETRY FROM DRYDEN TO GRAY. Chicago:
     Univ. of Chicago Press, 1958.

     Combines a valuable survey of the tradition of literary pictorialism
     and ut pictura poesis with an in-depth treatment of Dryden, Pope,
     Thomson, Collins, and Gray by application of the method of lit-
     erary history and analysis to the pictorial imagery often charac-
     terizing their work.

302  Hipple, Walter J. THE BEAUTIFUL, THE SUBLIME, AND THE PICTURESQUE
     IN EIGHTEENTH-CENTURY BRITISH AESTHETIC THEORY. Carbondale:
     Southern Illinois Univ. Press, 1957.

     Comprehensive survey of major contributors to the field of eigh-
     teenth-century aesthetics from Addison to Dugald Stewart, view-
     ing ideas of beauty, sublime, picturesque, and taste as shaped by
     the writer's metaphysical beliefs, psychological make-up, and
     method of argumentation.

303  Hunt, John Dixon. THE FIGURE IN THE LANDSCAPE: POETRY, PAINTING,
     AND GARDENING DURING THE EIGHTEENTH CENTURY. Baltimore:
     Johns Hopkins Press, 1976.

     Excellent study of "the human consequences" of garden design,
     exploring how the landscape garden "promoted and answered imag-
     inative experience" and "how poetry emerged from the alliance
     among what Horace Walpole called the 'three new Graces.'"

304  Jackson, Wallace. THE PROBABLE AND THE MARVELOUS: BLAKE, WORDS-
     WORTH, AND THE EIGHTEENTH-CENTURY CRITICAL TRADITION. Athens:
     Univ. of Georgia Press, 1978.

     Proposes "yet another approach" to the mid and later eighteenth-
     century poetic and critical traditions, stressing the "radical in-
     terest in the poetic marvelous" and the exploration of passions
     that "reveal the magnitude of the human spirit." An interesting
     alternative to the preromantic, post-Augustan, or age of sensibil-
     ity explanations of the period 1750 to 1800.

305  Jensen, H. James. THE MUSES' CONCORD: LITERATURE, MUSIC, AND
     THE VISUAL ARTS IN THE BAROQUE AGE. Bloomington: Indiana Univ.
     Press, 1978.

     An ambitious and exhaustively argued account of the philosophic
     and psychological underpinnings and the associated rhetorical
     practices charcterizing the rationalistic and imaginative qualities
     of baroque art.

306  Johnson, James William. THE FORMATION OF ENGLISH NEO-CLASSICAL
     THOUGHT. Princeton, N.J.: Princeton Univ. Press, 1967.

Attempts to expand previous understandings of both historical and philosophic influences on the literature of 1660 to 1800 by studying English Hellenism, Roman republicanism, patriotic literature, Byzantine culture, and Dutch humanism.

307 _____. "What Was Neo-Classicism?" JBS, 9 (1969), 49-70.

Cautioning against overreaction to Victorian prejudices about the period 1660 to 1800, counters recent refusals to generalize about the period by proposing a "loosely connected pattern of attitudes and assumptions" about God, man, and nature revealed through a number of recurring literary forms and conventions.

308 Korshin, Paul J. "The Evolution of Neoclassic Poetics." ECS, 2 (1968), 102-37.

Explores the changing attitudes toward "the idea of poetry" in Cleveland, Denham, and Waller to explain the emergence of the new poetic called "neoclassical poetry."

309 _____. FROM CONCORD TO DISSENT: MAJOR THEMES IN ENGLISH POETIC THEORY 1640-1700. Menston, Yorkshire, Engl.: Scolar Press, 1973.

By examination of the poetry itself, describes the changing features of seventeenth-century poetics as a movement from metaphysical roughness and complexity to the rational public poetry of the Restoration transformed into a "poetics of dissent" when the underlying political and moral traditions are threatened by historical change and revolutionary aesthetics. Treats Dryden and Oldham.

310 Lewis, C.S. "Addison." In ESSAYS ON THE EIGHTEENTH CENTURY PRESENTED TO DAVID NICHOL SMITH IN HONOUR OF HIS SEVENTIETH BIRTHDAY. Ed. James Sutherland and F.P. Wilson. Oxford: Clarendon Press, 1945, pp. 1-14.

Touches on Addison's defense of "Chevy Chase" and the ballad in general as indicative of new directions in eighteenth-century aesthetic theory. See no. 124.

311 Lipking, Lawrence. "A History of the Future." In NEW APPROACHES TO EIGHTEENTH-CENTURY LITERATURE. Ed. Phillip Harth. New York: Columbia Univ. Press, 1974, pp. 157-76.

A wide-ranging and speculative essay recommending that future inquiries into the period accept it on its own terms at the same time that modern concerns and techniques of analysis are brought to bear on a rich and diverse literature. See no. 108A.

312 _____. THE ORDERING OF THE ARTS IN EIGHTEENTH-CENTURY
ENGLAND. Princeton, N.J.: Princeton Univ. Press, 1970.

A comprehensive study of the relationship between the sister
arts of music, painting, and literature as revealed in the
massive treatises by Walpole, Reynolds, Hawkins, Charles
Burney, and Johnson that span the middle to late eighteenth
century.

313 Lovejoy, Arthur O. "On the Discrimination of Romanticisms." PMLA
39 (1924), 229-53.

Determines, at their most fundamental level, "three 'Romanticisms,'" sharing few common elements and characterized by
significant differences insofar as their ethical and aesthetic
principles are concerned. Especially valuable introduction
to the critical issues raised by the mid-century and later
poets.

314 MacLean, Kenneth. JOHN LOCKE AND THE ENGLISH LITERATURE
OF THE EIGHTEENTH CENTURY. New Haven, Conn.: Yale Univ.
Press, 1936.

An early study of the influence of the ESSAY CONCERN-
ING HUMAN UNDERSTANDING (1690), on theories of the
mind, perception, ideas, and knowledge and on Addison, Pope,
Thomson, Sterne, and Johnson.

315 Maclean, Norman. "From Action to Image: Theories of the Lyric in
the Eighteenth Century." In CRITICS AND CRITICISM: ANCIENT
AND MODERN. Ed. Ronald S. Crane. Chicago: Univ. of Chicago
Press, 1952, pp. 408-60.

An important and lengthy discussion of the shifting critical
opinions of the lyric as essentially ethical and shaped by
classical poetry and theory, to a more modern view of it
as expressing the poet's inner spirit and private self. See
no. 294.

316 Marks, Emerson R. THE POETICS OF REASON: ENGLISH NEOCLASSI-
CAL CRITICISM. New York: Random House, 1968.

A lucidly written account of the criticism from both historical and evaluative perspectives. The best introduction to a
complex subject.

317 Marsh, Robert. FOUR DIALECTICAL THEORIES OF POETRY: AN AS-
PECT OF ENGLISH NEOCLASSICAL CRITICISM. Chicago: Univ. of
Chicago Press, 1965.

Examines four independent theories of poetry and speculates

on the "formative causes," the nature of the theoretical problems addressed, and the means employed to solve them in order to discover a unifying factor in neoclassical criticism.

318    Monk, Samuel Holt. THE SUBLIME: A STUDY OF CRITICAL THEORIES IN EIGHTEENTH-CENTURY ENGLAND. Ann Arbor: Univ. of Michigan Press, 1960.

When originally published (1935), a pioneering study of the aesthetics of the sublime, showing not only its impact after the 1750s but also its presence in the criticism and poetic theories of the earlier years.

319    Peckham, Morse. "Toward a Theory of Romanticism." PMLA, 66 (1951), 5-23.

A far-reaching, suggestive, often brilliant theory of historical romanticism viewed as a participation in a dynamic organicism involving the rejection of a static mechanistic metaphysic (eighteenth century) and acceptance of a constantly evolving order whose values are change, imperfection, growth, creativity, and diversity.

320    Røstvig, Maren-Sofie. THE HAPPY MAN: STUDIES IN THE METAMORPHOSES OF A CLASSICAL IDEAL. 2 vols. Vol. 1: 1600-1700. Oslo: Akademisk forlag, 1954; vol 2: 1700-1760. Oslo: Oslo Univ. Press, 1958.

Volume 2 is the standard survey of Virgil's influence on eighteenth-century nature poetry, especially the shaping given it by the beatus ille and O fortunatos nimium themes of his Georgics.

321    Swedenberg, H.T. THE THEORY OF EPIC IN ENGLAND, 1650-1800. Berkeley: Univ. of California Press, 1944.

A thorough treatment of the backgrounds and themes informing the English theory of epic; cites classical and Italian treatises, English theorists from 1650 to 1800, and the main characteristics used as criteria for analysis, such as fable, action, moral, the probable and marvelous, machines, characters, and language.

322    Tuveson, Ernest Lee. THE IMAGINATION AS A MEANS OF GRACE: LOCKE AND THE AESTHETICS OF ROMANTICISM. Berkeley: Univ. of California Press, 1960.

A discussion of the changing conceptions of art and of the artist in the eighteenth century in terms of the emerging

romantic aesthetic of the creative imagination as surrogate
for religious grace.

323   Wellek, René. DISCRIMINATIONS: FURTHER CONCEPTS OF CRITI-
CISM. New Haven, Conn.: Yale Univ. Press, 1970.

Collection of essays on literary theory as well as on intellectual and literary history often addressing issues raised by such
terms as classicism and romanticism.

324   Wimsatt, William K. "The Affective Fallacy." In THE VERBAL ICON:
STUDIES IN THE MEANING OF POETRY. Knoxville: Univ. of
Kentucky Press, 1954, pp. 21-39.

Warns against the confusion between a work of art and its
"results," that is between "what it is, and what it does."
An important essay and the subject of much recent controversy.
See no. 131.

325   _____ . "The Concrete Universal." In THE VERBAL ICON: STUDIES
IN THE MEANING OF POETRY. Knoxville: Univ. of Kentucky
Press, 1954, pp. 69-83.

Argues for the existence of a core meaning, a general idea
or "concrete universal," in every work of art despite the
changing particulars of language, critical terminology, and
interpretation. See no. 131.

326   Wimsatt, William K., and Monroe L. Beardsley. "The Intentional
Fallacy." In THE VERBAL ICON: STUDIES IN THE MEANING OF
POETRY. Knoxville: Univ. of Kentucky Press, 1954, pp. 3-18.

Provocative and much disputed essay arguing that "the design or intention of the author is neither available nor de-
sirable as a standard for judging the success of a work of
literary art." Raises important critical issues. See no. 131.

## D. ENGLISH POETRY, 1660-1800: LITERARY STUDIES

## 1. Theme

328   Atkins, G. Douglas. "The Ancients, the Moderns, and Gnosticism."
SVEC, 151 (1976), 149-66.

A discussion of Gnosticism as an historical phenomenon of
early Christianity and its relationship to the Augustan conflict between the ancients and the moderns, focusing on
Dryden, Swift, and Pope as figures "directly confronting
tendencies, aims, and desires that may best be viewed as
Gnostic."

329     Bate, Walter Jackson. THE BURDEN OF THE PAST AND THE ENGLISH
        POET. New York: Norton, 1970.

        A highly influential and much referred to study of the eigh-
        teenth century as peculiarly the pivotal period when the
        legacy of the past became an oppressive burden and conse-
        quently forced the poet into literary self-consciousness as
        he contemplated the difficulties of achieving anything new.

330     Bateson, F.W. ENGLISH POETRY: A CRITICAL INTRODUCTION.
        London: Longmans, Green, 1950.

        Contains chapters on Swift's "Description of the Morning"
        (1709) and Gray's ELEGY (1751) that stress the economic,
        historical, and political backgrounds of the poems.

331     Battestin, Martin C. THE PROVIDENCE OF WIT: ASPECTS OF FORM
        IN AUGUSTAN LITERATURE AND THE ARTS. Oxford: Clarendon Press,
        1974.

        An important but disputed thesis that both the literature and
        art produced in the eighteenth century attest (directly or
        implicitly) to the age's faith in the attributes of order, pro-
        portion, and balance reflecting "the ontological assumptions
        of the Christian humanist tradition." An especially thorough
        and painstaking treatment of minor poetry and its theological,
        scientific, and philosophical expressions of design in nature
        paralleling the theme of order in the major productions.

332     Blom, T.E. "Eighteenth-Century Reflexive Process Poetry." ECS,
        10 (1976), 52-72.

        Such "reflexive-process poets" as Cowper, Goldsmith, Lloyd,
        and Gray "depict themselves as aliens whose existence in a
        world of confusing and contradictory values motivates a fond,
        backward glance to a never-to-be recovered yesteryear of
        simplicity, order, health, and prosperity," and share the
        conviction that only through the employment of "transitions,
        to dramatize the irreconcilable nature of polarized issues"
        can the poet mediate between the opposites of his revolu-
        tionary age.

333     Bogel, Fredric V. "Structure and Substantiality in Late Eighteenth-
        Century Literature." SBHT, 15 (1973-74), 143-54.

        The two intersecting dimensions of human experience under-
        lying Northrop Frye's terms "product" and "process" give impetus
        to the greatest writers of the late eighteenth century where
        the insistence on design, on the a priori, and on being is
        complemented by a similar insistence on temporality, empiri-
        cal discovery, and on becoming. Treats Smart, Collins, and
        Gray.

334    Boys, Richard C.  SIR RICHARD BLACKMORE AND THE WITS.  Ann
       Arbor:  Univ. of Michigan Press, 1949.

       A full discussion of the background and circumstances of the
       literary quarrel surrounding Blackmore's poetic efforts and
       the satiric attacks on his tastes, literary abilities, and status
       as city poet.  Prints the texts of the poetry in question,
       both pro and con Blackmore.


335    Bronson, Bertrand H.  "The Pre-Romantic or Post-Augustan Mode."  ELH,
       20 (1953), 15-28.

       This particular era of poetry is "too close to the triumphs
       of Dryden and Pope to be able to forget them . . . but it
       is also discontented, restless, uncommitted, unwilling to stay,
       yet undetermined to go."  See no. 100.


336    _____.  "When Was Neoclassicism?"  In STUDIES IN CRITICISM AND
       AESTHETICS, 1660-1800:  ESSAYS IN HONOR OF SAMUEL HOLT
       MONK.  Ed. Howard Anderson and John S. Shea.  Minneapolis:  Univ.
       of Minnesota Press, 1967, pp. 13-35.

       A provocative treatment of the presence of neoclassicism in
       the literary age of 1660 to 1800, viewing it "as in fact a
       period when the spirit of Classicism steadily refined its values,
       grew increasingly assured in its declaration of them, and
       never knew better their true and vital meaning and importance
       than when on the verge of losing them."  See nos. 93,
       100, 130.


337    Budick, Sanford.  "The Demythological Mode in Augustan Verse."  ELH,
       37 (1970), 389-414.

       A learned and challenging discussion, drawing on modern
       theology and Scripture, about processes of demythologizing
       and proclaiming and destruction of old authority and creation
       of a new order as "cultural revision at the deepest level of
       communal consciousness."


338    _____.  POETRY OF CIVILIZATION:  MYTHOPOEIC DISPLACEMENT
       IN THE VERSE OF MILTON, DRYDEN, POPE, AND JOHNSON.  New
       Haven, Conn.:  Yale Univ. Press, 1974.

       Beginning with Plato's dialectical procedures, studies the
       history of mythmaking in the public poetry of Horace and
       Juvenal, the addition of the biblical paradigm in Milton,
       and ends with chapters where the process of mythic dis-
       placement, antimythic reversion, and resurrected antece-
       dent is fully traced.

339    Burgum, Edwin G.   "The Neo-Classical Period in English Literature:
       A Psychological Definition."   SR, 52 (1944), 247-65.

       A sociopsychological investigation of contrasting neoclassical
       concepts in France and England around 1700, noting that in
       England social relationships and the presence of Milton chal-
       lenged complacent aristocratic aesthetic values that "became
       hypnotized by the image of its own insignificance in the work
       of Pope."


340    Butt, John.  THE AUGUSTAN AGE.  London:  Hutchinson's University
       Library, 1950.

       Concentrates on the major poets (and Johnson) and con-
       siders their achievement against the background of the
       age.


341    _____.  "Pope and the Opposition to Walpole's Government."  In
       POPE, DICKENS, AND OTHERS:  ESSAYS AND ADDRESSES.  Edin-
       burgh:  Edinburgh Univ. Press, 1969, pp. 111-26.

       Discusses Pope's excursion into politics during 1733 to 1740
       and describes his political poetry of that period as voicing
       generally held moral objections to Walpole's regime and as
       successfully arousing the public conscience.  See no. 102.


342    Byrd, Max.  LONDON TRANSFORMED:  IMAGES OF THE CITY IN
       THE EIGHTEENTH CENTURY.  New Haven, Conn.:  Yale Univ. Press,
       1978.

       Traces the recurrent images that mock the humanist imagina-
       tion's attempt to control and understand the diverse and form-
       less energies constituting a depersonalized and modernized
       London.  Discusses Pope, Swift, Gay, and Blake.


343    _____.  VISITS TO BEDLAM:  MADNESS AND LITERATURE IN THE
       EIGHTEENTH CENTURY.  Columbia:  Univ. of South Carolina Press,
       1974.

       A study of the universal ambiguity of madness and irrational-
       ity--as both a curse and blessing--in the eighteenth century,
       drawing on the imaginative literature of the Augustan period
       in analyzing the complex response to madness.


344    Carnochan, W.B.  "Augustan Satire and the Gates of Dreams:  A
       Utopian Essay."  STUDIES IN THE LITERARY IMAGINATION, 5, ii (1972),
       1-18.

       Interesting discussion of the scholarly controversy sparked by
       Virgil's reference (AENEID, 6.  893-99) to the gates of
       dreams, of Pope's use of this "summary image" of the Augustan

satirists' descent into the underworld of folly, and of implications for the meaning of Augustan satire as "a continuous
struggle between the realms of dream and waking."

345    Carver, Larry. "The Restoration Poets and Their Father King." HLQ,
       40 (1977), 333-351.

       A study of the idea of king as father of his country (pater
       patriae) as a major image in the Restoration poetry of praise
       of 1660 to 1690, indicating satirical treatment of the topic
       by anticourt poets and its eventual loss of symbolic meaning
       and significance.

346    Davie, Donald. THE LATE AUGUSTANS. London: Heinemann, 1965.

       Argues that English poets of the later eighteenth century,
       for whom the country and natural world were so compelling
       and pervasive a subject, "saw what was happening to rural
       England without understanding why it was happening."

347    DePorte, Michael V. NIGHTMARES AND HOBBYHORSES: SWIFT,
       STERNE, AND AUGUSTAN IDEAS OF MADNESS. San Marino, Calif.:
       Huntington Library, 1974.

       An illuminating study of theories of insanity in the eighteenth
       century, from both a medical and psychological perspective,
       and their function in the works of Swift and Sterne.

348    Dobrée, Bonamy. "The Theme of Patriotism in the Poetry of the Early
       Eighteenth Century." PBA, 85 (1949), 49-65.

       Isolates the universal and permanent emotion of patriotism
       as manifested in widely differing ways during the first half
       of the century, citing such major and minor figures as
       Thomson, Tickell, Watt, Philips, Dyer, Prior, Young, and
       Pope.

349    Doughty, Oswald. ENGLISH LYRIC IN THE AGE OF REASON.
       London: D. O'Conner, 1922.

       Argues that the intellectual climate of the age of reason
       suppressed emotion and human feeling and consequently
       stifled the lyric impulse, only for it to reappear in the
       ballad revival, medievalism, and literature of sensibility.
       Treats major and minor figures. Dated but encyclopedic
       in coverage.

350    _____. "The English Malady of the Eighteenth Century." RES, 2
       (1926), 257-69.

59

Both Englishmen and foreigners alike felt that "England lay under the curse of 'Spleen,'" a morbid streak in the temper of the eighteenth century. Good survey of major and minor poems addressing the topic.

351     Edwards, Thomas R. IMAGINATION AND POWER: A STUDY OF POETRY ON PUBLIC THEMES. New York: Oxford Univ. Press, 1971.

Fascinating study of ways poets have imagined the public world, showing that this engagement tells us more about the individual poet and the nature of poetry than about the politics of the actual historical occasion and, thus, humanizes the poet, producing an imaginative awareness of man's condition, the state of society, and the role of the poet that implicitly criticizes his own rhetorical distortions of feeling. Treats Butler, Dryden, Pope, Gray, and Blake.

352     Ehrenpreis, Irvin. "Explicitness in Augustan Literature." In his LITERARY MEANING AND AUGUSTAN VALUES. Charlottesville: Univ. Press of Virginia, 1974, pp. 1-48.

Argues that the characteristic mode of English poetry of 1660 to 1760 is explicit and direct rendering of doctrine or meaning--rather than the implicit strategies of allusion, allegory, or irony. An important attack on literary and moral biases and distortions during the past forty years of Augustan literary criticism. See no. 108.

353     _____. "Personae." In RESTORATION AND EIGHTEENTH-CENTURY LITERATURE: ESSAYS IN HONOR OF ALAN DUGALD McKILLOP. Ed. Carroll Camden. Chicago: Univ. of Chicago Press, 1963, pp. 25-37.

Attacks such critical concepts as mask, persona, and the terms referring to a dramatic or fictional speaker in recent discussions of Swift and Pope as falsely implying that "sentiments expressed in a literary work are not to be attributed to the author himself." An important challenge to rhetorical theories of criticism. See nos. 103 and 108.

354     _____. "Poverty and Poetry: Representations of the Poor in Augustan Literature." In THE MODERNITY OF THE EIGHTEENTH CENTURY. Ed. Louis Milic. Cleveland: Press of Case Western Reserve Univ., 1971, pp. 3-35.

Contends that the Augustans, as well as Thomson, Fielding, Sterne, and Goldsmith, gave a distorted picture of the poor, stereotyping them as loyal, industrious workers or welfare chiselers, and that only Johnson wrote of the poor as a suffering humanity.

355   Emery, Clark.  "The Poet and the Plough."  AGRICULTURAL HISTORY,
      16 (1942), 9-15.

      The "extended didactic poem," dealing with agriculture and
      the achievements of science, was designed not only to popu-
      larize agrarian life in England, but also to provide a rhymed
      textbook of instructions on such a technological subject as
      the raising of sheep.  Makes passing reference to Dyer,
      Smart, and Cowper.

356   England, A.B.  BYRON'S DON JUAN AND EIGHTEENTH-CENTURY
      LITERATURE:  A STUDY OF SOME RHETORICAL CONTINUITIES AND
      DISCONTINUITIES.  Lewisburg, Pa.:  Bucknell Univ. Press, 1975.

      Points out the closer relationship of DON JUAN to the
      "burlesque style" of Butler and Swift than to the "dominant
      Augustan tradition" of Pope, whose rhetorical structures re-
      flect a "vision of an ordered universe."  Valuable compari-
      sons of Pope and Swift (as poet).

357   Erskine-Hill, Howard.  "Augustans on Augustanism:  England, 1655-
      1759."  RENAISSANCE AND MODERN STUDIES, 11 (1967), 55-83.

      Examines important passages in which the Augustans use the
      word Augustan on the theory that the terms in which an age
      sees and describes itself can tell us as much or more about
      its character than the terminologies of later critics.

358   Fabricant, Carole.  "Binding and Dressing Nature's Loose Tresses: The
      Ideology of Augustan Landscape Design."  STUDIES IN EIGHTEENTH-
      CENTURY CULTURE, 8 (1979), 109-35.

      Perceptive study of connections between women and land-
      scape as revealed in the images and language of poetry,
      painting, and landscape architecture, expressing the society's
      deepest contradictions:  "the era's rage for order in a world
      perceived--whether rightly or wrongly--to be on the verge
      of chaos, filled with threatening irrational forces needing
      to be fenced out (or, alternately, 'tamed' and incorporated
      within)."

359   Feder, Lillian.  MADNESS IN LITERATURE.  Princeton, N.J.: Prince-
      ton Univ. Press, 1980.

      Far-reaching discussion of madness as a theme in myth and in
      literature, identifying its presence in personal responses to
      political, social, and cultural pressures.  Touches on Cowper,
      Smart, Winchilsea, and Swift.

360   Fitzgerald, Margaret M.  FIRST FOLLOW NATURE:  PRIMITIVISM IN
      ENGLISH POETRY, 1725-1750.  New York: King's Crown Press, 1947.

Whether looking back to a lost golden age (chronological
primitivism) or attempting to renew lost innocence (cultural
primitivism), the eighteenth-century writer expresses a common desire for a natural mode of existence. Treats both
major and minor figures.

361    Frye, Northrop. "Towards Defining an Age of Sensibility." ELH, 23
       (1956), 144-52.

       An important essay rejecting the term pre-romantic to define
       mid-century poetry and offering sensibility as a more accurate
       description of the transitional stage between literature as
       product (Augustan) and literature as process (Romantic). See
       nos. 107 and 130.

362    Fussell, Paul. THE RHETORICAL WORLD OF AUGUSTAN HUMANISM:
       ETHICS AND IMAGERY FROM SWIFT TO BURKE. Oxford: Clarendon
       Press, 1965.

       An excellent account of the fundamental unity of the humanist
       ethical tradition nourished by classical literature and history
       and of the image-systems and rhetorical strategies through
       which this tradition is articulated by Swift and Pope in the
       beginning of the period and by Reynolds, Johnson, and Burke
       in the later eighteenth century.

363    Goad, Caroline. HORACE IN THE ENGLISH LITERATURE OF THE
       EIGHTEENTH CENTURY. New Haven, Conn.: Yale Univ. Press, 1918.

       Comprehensive study of the use made of Horace by poets,
       novelists, and dramatists of the period. Valuable in that it
       attempts to account for all allusions and quotations and to
       note the editions used and the conscious or inadvertent
       changes of the original wording.

364    Golden, Morris. "The Imagining Self in the Eighteenth Century." ECS,
       3 (1969), 4-27.

       By particular reference to Pope, Thomson, and Smart, an
       attempt to counteract the excesses of rhetorical criticism by
       repersonalizing the poetry of the period through consideration
       of private visions and idiosyncrasies of the authors.

365    Goldgar, Bertrand A. "Satires on Man and 'the Dignity of Human
       Nature.'" PMLA, 80 (1965), 535-41.

       Important discussion of attacks during the early eighteenth
       century on satires against mankind, showing that they were
       thought to be affronts to human dignity (perversions of the

true function of satire) motivated by antisocial impulses--all
reactions stemming from the new optimistic appraisal of human
nature and the popular literature of sensibility.

366        . WALPOLE AND THE WITS: THE RELATION OF POLITICS
TO LITERATURE, 1722-1742. Lincoln: Univ. of Nebraska Press, 1976.

A valuable study of the interrelations between politicians
and men of letters in the Walpole period, addressing such
questions as the nature of the literary opposition, the extent of its common ideology, personal and private motivations,
and the status of literary art itself in an increasingly materialistic and commercialized world.

367   Goldstein, Laurence. RUINS AND EMPIRE: THE EVOLUTION OF A
THEME IN AUGUSTAN AND ROMANTIC LITERATURE. Pittsburgh:
Univ. of Pittsburgh Press, 1977.

Describes the literary tradition of ruins, especially as it
operates in the role of antagonist in the drama of human
salvation: "a means of mortifying in the public those
worldly desires which caused the great empires . . . to
decline and fall." Chapters on Dyer and Goldsmith, as
well as on the graveyard literature.

368   Greene, Donald. THE AGE OF EXUBERANCE: BACKGROUNDS TO
EIGHTEENTH-CENTURY ENGLISH LITERATURE. New York: Random
House, 1970.

An informed discussion of the historical, philosophical, and
aesthetic backgrounds of the literature while demonstrating
the exuberant, various, inventive, imaginative, and always
passionate nature of the art and literature of the period.
Particularly valuable as a corrective to stereotypes (largely
derived from Victorian biases) concerning the roles played
by reason, the classics, religion, and rules in this complex
age.

369        . "The Study of Eighteenth-Century Literature: Past, Present,
and Future." In NEW APPROACHES TO EIGHTEENTH-CENTURY
LITERATURE. Ed. Phillip Harth. New York: Columbia Univ. Press,
1974, pp. 1-32.

A lament, often witty and always trenchant, over the Victorian prejudices regarding the eighteenth century as well
as the demonstrated ignorance of some modern critics of the
period, coupled with a plea for deeper interdisciplinary
understanding and for recognition of the relevance of the
masterpieces of Swift, Pope, and Johnson. See no. 108A.

370    Guilhamet, Leon. THE SINCERE IDEAL: STUDIES ON SINCERITY IN
       EIGHTEENTH-CENTURY ENGLISH LITERATURE. Montreal: McGill-
       Queen's Univ. Press, 1974.

       Notes the impulse toward personal sincerity in English poetry
       beginning around 1750, and studies the search by various
       poets of the period for this ideal in their patterns of imagery,
       ideological positions, and poetic voice. Treats major and
       minor figures.

371    Hardin, Richard F., ed. SURVIVALS OF PASTORAL. Humanistic
       Studies, no. 52. Lawrence: Univ. of Kansas Publications, 1979.

       Some essays devoted to the pastoral mode in eighteenth-
       century poetry.

372    Havens, Raymond D. "Assumed Personality, Insanity, and Poetry."
       RES, NS 4 (1953), 26-37.

       A seminal essay shifting the critical problem raised by the
       forgeries of Chatterton and Macpherson from the question
       of whether those authors wrote such poems to why they were
       able to do so, as well as addressing the matter of insanity
       in Collins, Smart, Cowper, and Blake, concluding that
       fictional identities and mental disease constituted two im-
       portant ways of loosening the restraints of neoclassical
       decorum and freeing creative genius.

373    _____. THE INFLUENCE OF MILTON ON ENGLISH POETRY.
       Cambridge, Mass.: Harvard Univ. Press, 1922.

       Famous study of Milton's impact on English poetry, but
       also a critical evaluation of the particular poets and poems
       he influenced, paying special attention to the principal
       types of unrhymed verse, to the awakening of the lyric,
       and to the tradition of the sonnet. Covers poetry from
       1660 to 1837.

374    _____. "Simplicity, A Changing Concept." JHI, 14 (1953), 3-32.

       Comprehensive study, in the history of ideas tradition, of
       the search for simplicity as an ideal in a variety of human
       and artistic areas, despite the often conflicting definitions
       attached to the term.

375    Hollander, John. THE UNTUNING OF THE SKY: IDEAS OF MUSIC
       IN ENGLISH POETRY 1500-1700. Princeton, N.J.: Princeton Univ.
       Press, 1961.

       Contains excellent insights into Dryden's achievement in
       versifying musical doctrine through his skillful adaptation of

"the celebration of singing to singing of that celebration" and fusion of poetic and musical theory.

376   Hopkins, Kenneth. THE POETS LAUREATE. New York: Library Publishers, 1955.

General inquiry into the biography and the personalities of these official poets who were often the targets of much unmerciful satire in the age. Prints selections from these often notorious poetasters.

377   Johnson, William Bruce. "The Idealization of the Familiar and the Poetics of the English Enlightenment." EnIE, 6, i (1975), 19-26.

The genesis of Thomson's SEASONS and Goldsmith's DESERTED VILLAGE affords a broad view of the eighteenth-century reconciliation of idealizing, generalizing, and universalizing impulses with contemporary interest in sensational psychology, empiricism, and the familiar.

378   Johnston, Arthur. "Poetry and Criticism after 1740." In THE HISTORY OF LITERATURE IN THE ENGLISH LANGUAGE. Vol. 4. Ed. Roger Lonsdale. London: Barrie and Jenkins, 1971, pp. 357-98.

A survey of poetry and criticism as a rediscovery of Spenser, Milton, classical and biblical poetry, and folk and ballad art through acts of the poetic imagination nurtured by a sense of alienation from human society. See no. 32A.

379   Jones, Richard Foster. "The Background of the Attack on Science in the Age of Pope." In POPE AND HIS CONTEMPORARIES: ESSAYS PRESENTED TO GEORGE SHERBURN. Ed. James L. Clifford and Louis A. Landa. New York: Oxford Univ. Press, 1949, pp. 96-113.

A classic study of the opposition to experimental science in the late seventeenth-century and its influence on the anti-scientific satire of the Augustans. See no. 107.

380   Jones, William Powell. "The Idea of the Limitations of Science from Prior to Blake." SEL, 1 (1961), 97-114.

From Prior through Cowper to Blake, the limitations of science as adequate explanation for the ultimate workings of nature was a pervasive theme of literature; but whereas Pope chided man's scientific presumptions for measuring stars and tides, Blake attacked science with "belligerent hostility," believing that it destroyed the imagination and stifled the creative spirit of poetry.

381   _____. THE RHETORIC OF SCIENCE: A STUDY OF SCIENTIFIC

IDEAS AND IMAGERY IN EIGHTEENTH-CENTURY ENGLISH POETRY. Berkeley: Univ. of California Press, 1966.

"The first attempt to describe and assess the whole story of scientific ideas and imagery," accounting for Newton's influence as well as that of the microscope, astronomy, and the new science of natural history, medicine, minerals, and shells. Especially strong on Thomson.

382    Knox, Norman. THE WORD "IRONY" AND ITS CONTEXT, 1500-1755. Durham, N.C.: Duke Univ. Press, 1961.

A classic study of the history of the word irony from the early sixteenth through the middle of the eighteenth century, describing the actual presence of irony in the writings of authors to show range and variety of meanings.

383    Krieger, Murray. THE CLASSIC VISION: THE RETREAT FROM EXTREMITY IN MODERN LITERATURE. Baltimore: Johns Hopkins Press, 1971.

Treats, among other topics and poems, Pope's "Eloisa to Abelard," (1717) "The Rape of the Lock," (1714) and Johnson's THE VANITY OF HUMAN WISHES (1749) and his elegy "On the Death of Dr. Robert Levet" (1782) as exemplifying the final effort of the classic disposition to affirm structures of order against the incursion of "the god seen in men's hearts."

384    Kropf, Carl R. "Unity and the Study of Eighteenth-Century Literature." ECent, 21 (1980), 25-40.

Objects to recent attempts to impose postromantic organic theories of order and unity on the literature and argues for a different inquiry into the critical assumptions eighteenth-century audiences brought to language.

385    Leavis, F.R. REVALUATION: TRADITION AND DEVELOPMENT IN ENGLISH POETRY. London: Chatto and Windus, 1949.

Connects Pope's poetry with the wit traditions of both Donne and Jonson and views Samuel Johnson's poetry as reviving this traditional morality of craft and artistic discipline later in the century. The refinement of sensibility by poets of the mid-century, however, represents a deviation from the central moral and aesthetic norms of the age. A provocative, if somewhat dated, viewpoint.

386    McKillop, Alan D. "Local Attachment and Cosmopolitanism--The

Eighteenth-Century Pattern." In FROM SENSIBILITY TO ROMANTI-
CISM: ESSAYS PRESENTED TO FREDERICK A. POTTLE. Ed. Frederick
W. Hilles and Harold Bloom. New York: Oxford Univ. Press, 1965,
pp. 191-218.

> A careful tracing of the interplay between poetic emphasis
> on local scenery, circumstances, beliefs, and sentiments
> and themes and motifs derived from traditional and general-
> ized philosophic concerns. Treats Gray, Akenside, Gold-
> smith, Thomson, and Hill. See no. 110.

387    Manlove, Colin N.  LITERATURE AND REALITY, 1600-1800.  London:
Macmillan, 1978.

> Discusses inclusiveness, the amount and extent of reality
> that absolutist writers of the period admitted into their art
> at a time when the definition of reality was becoming
> problematical, various, and relative. Treats Dryden, Pope,
> Thomson, Gray, Johnson, Goldsmith, Crabbe, and Cowper.

388    Maresca, Thomas E.  "Language and Body in Augustan Poetic."  ELH,
37 (1970), 374-388.

> Beginning with Dryden's MACFLECKNOE and ending with
> Pope's DUNCIAD, Maresca discusses the "network of ideas"
> (mainly Neo-Platonic and Christian) informing such satiric
> oppositions as language and body, word and thing in Augus-
> tan literature.

389    Miles, Josephine.  ERAS AND MODES IN ENGLISH POETRY.  Berkeley:
Univ. of California Press, 1964.

> Characterizes as "the prevailing eighteenth-century poem"
> that patriotic celebration of commercialism rooted in the
> classical heroic mode but shaped into a native English
> "panoramic and panegyrical verse, emotional, pictorial,
> noble, universal, and tonal, rising to the height of heaven
> and of feeling in the style traditionally known as grand or
> sublime."

390    Miner, Earl.  "From Narrative to 'Description' and 'Sense' in Eighteenth-
Century Poetry."  SEL, 9 (1969), 471-87.

> Describes the change from the narrative verse of the Restora-
> tion to the poetry of description, conversation, persuasion,
> and feeling or sentiment as indicative of the loss of faith
> in the meaningfulness of heroic or courtly modes of action
> and views Pope as the one eighteenth-century poet who
> keeps in balance these different poetic tendencies.

391  _____. THE RESTORATION MODE FROM MILTON TO DRYDEN. Princeton, N.J.: Princeton Univ. Press, 1974.

Steers between exclusively critical or historical approaches to the later seventeenth century and examines the marked shift from lyrical conceptions of experience to narrative conceptions and the changing attitudes toward human experience implicit in such a change. Excellent treatment of Dryden and Butler.

392  Moore, Cecil A. "The Return to Nature in English Poetry of the Eighteenth Century." SP, 14 (1917), 243-291.

Treating mostly minor figures, argues that the poets in the age of Pope did not uniformly despise or neglect physical nature and that the return to nature movement began early in the period and developed gradually throughout. See no. 37.

393  _____. "Shaftesbury and Ethical Poets in England." PMLA, 31 (1916), 264-325.

Early recognition of the importance of Shaftesbury's CHARACTERISTICS (1711) to the theological and ethical dimensions of eighteenth-century verse, especially his theory of benevolence, idea of sensibility, and humanitarian thesis. See no. 37.

394  Morris, David B. THE RELIGIOUS SUBLIME: CHRISTIAN POETRY AND CRITICAL TRADITION IN 18TH-CENTURY ENGLAND. Lexington: Univ. Press of Kentucky, 1972.

Excellent analysis of the idea of the sublime as a force liberating the eighteenth-century imagination "from all that was little, petty, natural, regular, and safe" and as a dominant literary quality that "spans the chasm separating Pope's 'Messiah' from Blake's prophetic books."

395  Nevo, Ruth. THE DIAL OF VIRTUE: A STUDY OF POEMS ON AFFAIRS OF STATE IN THE SEVENTEENTH CENTURY. Princeton, N.J.: Princeton Univ. Press, 1963.

Studies the seventeenth-century political poems (excluding broadsides) as both "history between the lines" and as an index to stylistic problems peculiar to this type of verse, and concludes that the antithetical quality of couplet rhetoric reflects the dialectical opposition of political and religious forces at the same time that it indicates the century's desire for order and unity.

396     Nicolson, Marjorie Hope.  MOUNTAIN GLOOM AND MOUNTAIN
        GLORY.  Ithaca, N.Y.: Cornell Univ. Press, 1959.

        Deals with scientific and philosophic backgrounds of the new
        eighteenth-century aesthetic of the great and sublime and
        the accompanying changes in the idea of nature and in the
        responses to mountain scenery.

397     Parkin, Rebecca Price.  "The Journey Down the Great Scale Reflected
        in Two Neoclassical Elegies."  EnlE, 1, iii/iv (1970), 197-204.

        An interesting attempt to trace the one hundred-year journey
        of literary history and sensibility in the eighteenth century
        from elitist classicism to "human concern for the common
        man" through analysis of two elegies:  Dryden's "To Oldham"
        (1684) and Johnson's "On Levet" (1783).

398     Paulson, Ronald.  "What is Modern in Eighteenth-Century Literature."
        STUDIES IN EIGHTEENTH-CENTURY CULTURE, 1 (1971), 75-86.

        Sees a kinship between modern concerns and eighteenth-
        century literature in their mutual preoccupations with self-
        reflexiveness, with disconnectedness, and with the "use of
        metaphor to reveal rather than overcome difference."  A
        contribution to a symposium on "The Modernity of the Eigh-
        teenth Century."

399     Peake, Charles.  "Poetry 1700-1740."  In THE HISTORY OF LITERA-
        TURE IN THE ENGLISH LANGUAGE.  Vol. 4.  Ed. Roger Lonsdale.
        London: Barrie and Jenkins, 1971, pp. 164-89.

        Treats major and minor poets, popular genres, and a variety
        of poetic modes against the background of an age marked by
        strong forces making for both stability and conformity as well
        as change and experiment.  See no. 32A.

400     Price, Martin.  "The Sublime Poem: Pictures and Powers."  YR, 58
        (1969), 194-213.

        An excellent discussion of the many meanings and uses of
        the term and idea of the sublime in the eighteenth century,
        describing the phenomenon as "an experience of transcendence,
        a surpressing of conventions or reasonable limits, an attempt
        to come to terms with the unimaginable.  The moment of the
        sublime was a transport of spirit, and at such a moment the
        visible object was eclipsed or dissolved."

401     _____ .  TO THE PALACE OF WISDOM: STUDIES IN ORDER AND
        ENERGY FROM DRYDEN TO BLAKE.  Garden City, N.Y.: Doubleday,
        1964.

A comprehensive study of major and minor figures in terms of
a dialectic between ideas of order, restraint, and moderation
and those producing stress, excess, and freedom under the
rubric of Pascal's categories of flesh, mind, and charity,
emphasizing the manifestation of these conflicts in the popular poetic forms of the early, middle, and late periods.

402    Rawson, Claude J.  "Order and Misrule:  Eighteenth-Century Literature
       in the 1970's."  ELH, 42 (1975), 471–505.

       A brilliant critique of recent trends in the study of eighteenth-
       century literature, singling out:  (1) the tendency of the his-
       tory of ideas approach to reductivism and oversimplification
       that ignores the role of ambiguity or the play of irony; (2)
       nostalgia for plain literal meaning at the expense of allusive
       subtleties and complexity of attitudes; and (3) eagerness to
       elevate misrule and the interest of the period in ideas of
       madness and irrationality into a new orthodoxy of moral
       value.  See nos. 108, 331, 343, and 347.

403    Reed, Amy Louise.  THE BACKGROUND OF GRAY'S ELEGY:  A STUDY
       IN THE TASTE FOR MELANCHOLY POETRY 1700–1751.  New York:
       Columbia Univ. Press, 1924.

       A justly famous study of the pervasiveness and popularity of
       poems of romantic melancholy during the seventeenth and
       eighteenth centuries, whatever their influence on nineteenth-
       century Romanticism.

404    Renwick, William L.  "Notes on Some Lesser Poets of the Eighteenth
       Century."  In ESSAYS ON THE EIGHTEENTH CENTURY PRESENTED TO
       DAVID NICHOL SMITH IN HONOUR OF HIS SEVENTIETH BIRTHDAY.
       Ed. James Sutherland and F.P. Wilson.  Oxford:  Clarendon Press, 1945,
       pp. 130–46.

       A defense of minor eighteenth-century poetry which rational-
       izes its stock-in-trade poetic devices and conventions and
       which views it as mature and cultivated verse communicating
       the values of "humility, moderation, and common sense."
       See no. 124.

405    Rivers, Isabel.  THE POETRY OF CONSERVATISM 1600–1745:  A STUDY
       OF POETS AND PUBLIC AFFAIRS FROM JONSON TO POPE.  Cam-
       bridge, Engl.:  Rivers Press, 1973.

       Good survey of the relationship of poetry to the public world
       of government and politics, exploring the tensions that exist
       between the mythologies of conservatism, involving a divinely-
       ordained universe, a hierarchical view of society, and the
       realities of moral disorder and social and political fragmentation.

406    Rogers, Pat. THE AUGUSTAN VISION. New York: Barnes and Noble, 1974.

    Stresses the unmodernity of the age by examining the social, political, moral, and religious backgrounds informing the literary forms and tastes of the age.

407    Saintsbury, George. THE PEACE OF THE AUGUSTANS. London: G. Bell, 1916.

    A famous, although usually discredited, account that often replaces nineteenth-century distortions of the age with an equally distorted thesis about the literature "as a place of rest and refreshment."

408    Sampson, H. Grant. THE ANGLICAN TRADITION IN EIGHTEENTH-CENTURY VERSE. The Hague: Mouton, 1971.

    Points out that Anglican religious poetry flourished during the eighteenth century, especially among minor talents, and that the range of interests was wide, extending from moral sentiment, mysticism, and meditation to theological dispute.

409    Sams, Henry W. "Anti-Stoicism in Seventeenth- and Early Eighteenth-Century England." SP, 41 (1944), 65-78.

    Attacks on Stoicism and the Stoics were so various and widespread as to be nearly universal among English writers of the period, reflecting their basic faith in liberty of conscience, freedom of enterprise, and the dignity of human passion.

410    Shuster, George N. THE ENGLISH ODE FROM MILTON TO KEATS. New York: Columbia Univ. Press, 1940.

    Well-known historical survey of the English ode, concentrating on such matters as its formal characteristics, relationship to musical expression, and effects on the prosody of lyric verse. Chapters on Dryden and the Restoration, on the Augustans, and on Collins, Gray, and the revitalized imagination.

411    Sickels, Eleanor M. THE GLOOMY EGOTIST: MOODS AND THEMES OF MELANCHOLY FROM GRAY TO KEATS. New York: Columbia Univ. Press, 1932.

    Especially good on graveyard poetry and poets, literature of ruins, and poems involving melancholia, especially those found in Dodsley's COLLECTION OF POEMS BY SEVERAL HANDS, (1748-58).

412    Sitter, John E. "Theodicy at Midcentury: Young, Akenside, and Hume."
       ECS, 12 (1978), 90-106.

       By application of a combination of Locke's and Hume's
       epistemologies and ontologies, shows striking similarities
       between Young's NIGHT THOUGHTS (1742-45) and Aken-
       side's THE PLEASURES OF IMAGINATION (1744). The
       egocentric, private, internalized consciousness informing
       this imagined reality represents an "attempt to order the
       world according to new procedures," in contrast to the
       empirical, externalized, objective visual theodicy of Pope's
       ESSAY ON MAN (1733-34). An important study.

413    Solomon, Stanley J. "Conflicting Sensibility in Death Poetry: 1740
       to the Romantic Age." EnlE, 2, ii (1971), 67-81.

       The genre of death poetry was largely unsuccessful in the
       eighteenth century because of conflicting poetic sensibilities
       associated with humanistic rationalism and deism and with
       traditional Christian hope and consolation.

414    Spacks, Patricia Meyer. THE INSISTENCE OF HORROR: ASPECTS OF
       THE SUPERNATURAL IN EIGHTEENTH-CENTURY POETRY. Cambridge,
       Mass.: Harvard Univ. Press, 1962.

       An early study of supernaturalism in the so-called age of
       reason, showing that although the criticism of the age only
       reluctantly justified use of supernatural materials, the prac-
       ticing poets considered the irrational an important aspect of
       the human consciousness.

415    _____. THE POETRY OF VISION: FIVE EIGHTEENTH-CENTURY
       POETS. Cambridge, Mass.: Harvard Univ. Press, 1967.

       Studies the function of visual imagery in Thomson, Collins,
       Gray, Smart, and Cowper (poets of sensibility) in the frame-
       work of contemporary critical theory and poetic convention.
       An important contribution to the modern understanding of
       the function of the visual component of poetry in the period.

416    Spencer, Jeffry B. HEROIC NATURE: IDEAL LANDSCAPE IN ENGLISH
       POETRY FROM MARVELL TO THOMSON. Evanston, Ill.: Northwestern
       Univ. Press, 1973.

       A comprehensive study of the thematic and pictorial features
       of poetic landscapes, accounting for their complex com-
       bination of allegory, myth, and symbol, together with politi-
       cal, religious, social, and aesthetic preoccupations.

417    Staver, Frederick. "'Sublime' as Applied to Nature." MLN, 70 (1955),
       484-87.

The term sublime referred to a memorable or heightened literary passage, and was not applied to sensational appearances
in nature until around 1742.

418    Stern, Bernard Herbert.  THE RISE OF ROMANTIC HELLENISM IN
ENGLISH LITERATURE, 1732-1786.  Menasha, Wis.:  George Banta,
1940.

A comprehensive account of the resurgence of classicism
(especially of the Greek variety) during the middle and
late eighteenth century in a new, sentimentalized, and
romantic form.  Treats Thomson, Akenside, Joseph Warton,
Collins, and Dodsley's COLLECTION OF POEMS BY
SEVERAL HANDS (1748-58).

419    Stevick, Philip.  "Miniaturization in Eighteenth-Century English Literature."  UTQ, 38 (1968), 159-73.

"The reduction of scale in the eighteenth century is a tactic
so rich and various that its purpose and effect in no two
works . . . are quite alike," and it is a trope so central
to the eighteenth-century imagination that it rivals the more
familiar terms nature and wit.  Treats Prior and Pope.

420    Sutherland, James.  ENGLISH SATIRE.  Cambridge:  Cambridge Univ.
Press, 1958.

Discusses the origins of satire in the forms of lampoon and
the invective, its basic functions, and the ways it differs
from comedy, citing as examples many eighteenth-century
poems.

421    _____.  "The Impact of Charles II on Restoration Literature."  In
RESTORATION AND EIGHTEENTH-CENTURY LITERATURE:  ESSAYS
IN HONOR OF ALAN DUGALD McKILLOP.  Ed. Carroll Camden.
Chicago:  Univ. of Chicago Press, 1963, pp. 251-63.

Although not gifted as a writer himself, Charles II, through
close association with major and minor authors, influenced
the literature of his country more than any other English
ruler except Elizabeth I.  See no. 103.

422    _____.  A PREFACE TO EIGHTEENTH-CENTURY POETRY.  Oxford:
Clarendon Press, 1948.

A traditional study replete with routine generalizations
about such concepts as rationality, generality, the elitist
audience, refinement, decorum, and the importance of
genre in the eighteenth century.

423    Sutherland, William Owen Sheppard, Jr. THE ART OF THE SATIRIST:
       ESSAYS ON THE SATIRE OF AUGUSTAN ENGLAND. Austin: Univ.
       of Texas Press, 1965.

       Analyzes the principles and assumptions distinctive to the
       unity of satire, and discusses Pope's RAPE OF THE LOCK
       (1714) and DR. ARBUTHNOT (1735), Butler's HUDIBRAS
       (1663-78), and Dryden's ABSALOM AND ACHITOPHEL
       (1681), among other works, as historically oriented or
       occasional satire also "symbolizing something of a wide
       or universal significance."


424    Tave, Stuart. THE AMIABLE HUMORIST. Chicago: Univ. of Chicago
       Press, 1960.

       Traces the history of the idea of humor in the eighteenth
       and early nineteenth centuries by relating it to certain
       aesthetic principles and attitudes toward man and nature
       to show that during the period a new form of amiable humor
       emerged in which objects of comic ridicule were not fools
       or knaves, but rather models of good nature, and that the
       resulting satire was more tolerant than bitter. An important
       study.


425    Thackeray, William Makepeace. THE ENGLISH HUMOURISTS OF THE
       EIGHTEENTH CENTURY. London: Grey Walls Press, 1949.

       The most notorious of Victorian denunciations of the Augustan
       satiric mode, labelling Swift as amoral, raging, and obscene
       and Pope as a ruthless little tyrant attacking the poetasters
       of Grub Street, but curiously accurate in sensing aggression
       and other complex psychological factors motivating satire.


426    Thorpe, Peter. EIGHTEENTH CENTURY ENGLISH POETRY. Chicago:
       Nelson-Hall, 1975. Bibliog.

       For the student reader, treats the poetry by genre and pro-
       vides a chapter on backgrounds of the verse.


427    _____. "Harold Bloom's Revisionary Ratios and the Augustan Satirists."
       SHR, 13 (1979), 181-96.

       Turns Bloom's theory about the anxiety of influence in re-
       cent poetry on its head by arguing (employing Bloom's own
       vocabulary) that the eighteenth-century satirists actively
       sought the appearance of the influence of their classical
       predecessors "and wore it like a badge" as a mark of poetic
       excellence.


428    _____. "Some Fallacies in the Study of Augustan Poetry." CRITICISM,
       9 (1967), 326-36.

Although Augustan studies have produced first-rate scholarly results, the purely critical side of the endeavor has been hampered by three persistent orientations: the organic fallacy, ambivalence fallacy, and metaphysical fallacy, and not until good minds overcome these biased and unfruitful approaches and begin a detached and objective assessment of Augustan poetry on its own merit will criticism "get at the truth" behind this verse.

429     Tickell, Richard Eustace. THOMAS TICKELL AND THE EIGHTEENTH CENTURY POETS (1685-1740). CONTAINING NUMEROUS LETTERS AND POEMS HITHERTO UNPUBLISHED. London: Constable, 1931.

Valuable collection of letters, poems, and other items connected with Tickell's literary friends, providing insights into their personalities.

430     Tillotson, Geoffrey. "Matthew Arnold and Eighteenth-Century Poetry." In ESSAYS ON THE EIGHTEENTH CENTURY PRESENTED TO DAVID NICHOL SMITH IN HONOUR OF HIS SEVENTIETH BIRTHDAY. Ed. James Sutherland and F.P. Wilson. Oxford: Clarendon Press, 1945, pp. 252-73.

Unlike his clear understanding of Victorian culture, Arnold's views of the historical and literary past in general and of Pope and the eighteenth century in particular are flawed by incomplete knowledge, narrow perspectives, and quotations out of context. See no. 124.

431     Tillyard, E.M.W. POETRY DIRECT AND OBLIQUE. London: Chatto and Windus, 1934.

An early challenge to the Arnoldian thesis about prose poetry in the age and to Eliot's concept of a seventeenth-century dissociation of sensibility, as well as a thoughtful appreciation of the poetic and passionate qualities informing Dryden's rhetoric of argumentation.

432     Trickett, Rachel. THE HONEST MUSE: A STUDY IN AUGUSTAN VERSE. Oxford: Clarendon Press, 1967.

Demonstrates the interplay between real and ideal in the characteristic Restoration genres of panegyric, elegy, and satire, and traces the developing sense of a fundamental realism, of seeing things as they are, in the poetry of Dryden, Pope, and Johnson even at "its most political and formal."

433     Vieth, David M. "Divided Consciousness: The Trauma and Triumph of Restoration Culture." TSL, 22 (1977), 46-62.

Argues that in response to the changing cultural dynamics of the period, literature shaped itself in four different, but not mutually exclusive, ways, reflecting providentialism and a many-sided awareness through an irony employing open-ended forms or generating negative, reversible meaning.

434    Viner, Jacob. "Satire and Economics in the Augustan Age of Satire." In THE AUGUSTAN MILIEU: ESSAYS PRESENTED TO LOUIS LANDA. Ed. Henry Knight Miller, Eric Rothstein, and G.S. Rousseau. Oxford: Clarendon Press, 1970, pp. 77-101.

Points out the "continuous and profound complacency" among the upper classes toward England's economic health reflected in the satire that ridiculed men, morals, and manners, but ignored institutions vitally affecting the great majority of the English population. See no. 120.

435    Wallerstein, Ruth. STUDIES IN SEVENTEENTH-CENTURY POETIC. Madison: Univ. of Wisconsin Press, 1950.

A memorable study in the manner of the history of ideas school, analyzing the funeral elegy, Marvell's poetry, and Dryden's early poems, to determine the extent of Renaissance platonism in the seventeenth-century aesthetic context.

436    Wasserman, Earl R. ELIZABETHAN POETRY IN THE EIGHTEENTH CENTURY. Urbana: Univ. of Illinois Press, 1947.

The neoclassical attitude toward the Elizabethans was more complex than demonstrated by the caricatures provided by apologists or preromantic critics, and despite Elizabethan violations of such critical precepts as correctness and regularity, the neoclassical reader responded to the energy, invention, and furor poeticus of Elizabethan writing.

437    _____. "Nature Moralized: The Divine Analogy in the Eighteenth Century." ELH, 20 (1953), 39-76.

The "myth of an analogically ordered universe" is further weakened in the period by the emergence of a rhetorical tradition, Lockean associationism, and the new science, all forces which replaced the tradition of correspondences and the concept of a unity between idea and language.

438    _____. THE SUBTLER LANGUAGE: CRITICAL READINGS OF NEO-CLASSIC AND ROMANTIC POEMS. Baltimore: Johns Hopkins Press, 1959.

Subtle and sophisticated analyses of Dryden's "Epistle to Charleton" (1662), Denham's "Cooper's Hill" (1642), and

Pope's "Windsor Forest" (1713) as self-sustaining, coherent
verbal constructs and also as lyric expressions of "publicly
acknowledged conceptions of nature and cosmic order."

439   Watkins, W.B.C. PERILOUS BALANCE: THE TRAGIC GENIUS OF
      SWIFT, JOHNSON AND STERNE. Princeton, N.J.: Princeton Univ.
      Press, 1939.

      Mostly biographical interpretation of such factors as physical
      disease, melancholic temperament, and sense of the tragic
      affecting the artistic vision of these three complex writers.

440   Wedgwood, C.V. POETRY AND POLITICS UNDER THE STUARTS.
      Cambridge: Cambridge Univ. Press, 1960.

      A classic study of poetry and power under the Stuarts,
      recognizing the complexity of the political, social, and
      religious issues confronting these monarchs, but remarking
      on the use of poetry as a weapon of attack and vehicle
      of praise in the areas of political, religious, and social
      controversy.

441   Weinbrot, Howard D. AUGUSTUS CAESAR IN "AUGUSTAN" ENGLAND:
      THE DECLINE OF A CLASSICAL NORM. Princeton, N.J.: Princeton
      Univ. Press, 1978.

      A well-researched attack on the use of the term Augustan
      to describe the literary period from 1660 to 1800, citing
      evidence of hostility toward Augustus' political principles
      in light of English Whig ascendency in the 1730s. Includes
      an interesting revisionist interpretation of Pope's "Epistle to
      Augustus" (1737), not as ironic contrast between Horace's
      honest praise with his own ironic version, but as outright
      attack both on Horace and Augustus.

442   Wells, Henry W. "The Seven Against London: A Study in the Satirical
      Tradition of Augustan Poetry." SR, 47 (1939), 514-23.

      Delightful critique of the interrelated strands of Augustan
      satire appropriately cast in original heroic couplets and
      based on poems of Prior, Gay, Pope, Swift, Young, Cowper,
      and Blake.

443   Williams, George G. "The Beginnings of Nature Poetry in the Eigh-
      teenth Century." SP, 27 (1930), 583-608.

      Nature poetry in the eighteenth century differs materially
      from previous seventeenth-century examples, and not until
      this period did the interest in nature become "an elaborate
      cult, a self-conscious worship" that depended on "personified
      Nature for wisdom, spiritual comfort, and holiness."

444    Williams, Raymond.  THE COUNTRY AND THE CITY.  London: Chatto
and Windus, 1973.

Argues that the pastoral ideal of classical literature is a
lyrical evasion of the harsh realities surrounding production
and the economic exploitation of the capitalist Industrial
Revolution.  Interesting Marxist reading.

445    _____.  "'Nature's Threads.'"  ECS, 2 (1968), 45-57.

Brief but suggestive analysis of "transition from reflection
to retrospect" in the eighteenth century through the changing forms of poetic consciousness and a newly emerging
romantic sensibility in which nature is opposed to industry,
poetry to trade, and myths of human isolation and community
are seen against "the real social pressures of time."

446    Williamson, George.  "The Restoration Revolt Against Enthusiasm."
SP, 30 (1933), 571-603.

Views this often-noted revolt as really the culmination of
important philosophical assumptions flowering in the first
half of the seventeenth century variously manifested in
religious and scientific skepticism and in new literary styles,
especially by "the emphasis of 'statement' in Dryden's
poetry" and the Arnoldian "prose virtues" characterizing
neoclassical poetry.

447    Wilson, John Harold.  COURT SATIRES OF THE RESTORATION.
Columbus:  Ohio State Univ. Press, 1976.

Selection of personal satires dealing with court personalities,
literary and theatrical figures, and the various scandals and
outrages that engaged public interest.  Contains (1) headnotes
and annotations explaining historical circumstances and (2)
brief biographies.

448    _____.  THE COURT WITS OF THE RESTORATION:  AN INTRODUC-
TION.  Princeton, N.J.:  Princeton Univ. Press, 1948.

Good discussion of the interrelationships of Buckingham,
Dorset, Etherege, Rochester, Sedley, and Wycherley, the
literary rakes that flourished around Charles II's court,
pointing out similarities in their literary tastes and thinking.

449    Wimsatt, William K.  "The Augustan Mode in English Poetry."  ELH,
20 (1953), 1-14.

A perceptive discussion of Augustan poets who at their most
characteristic were "laughing poets of an heightened un-
reality" who found most amusing a world of "inverted,
chaotic reality" which was redeemed into meaning and order by
their "force of wit."  See nos. 128 and 131.

450 _____. "Imitation as Freedom, 1717-1798." NLH, 1 (1970), 215-36.

>A brilliant discussion of the proposition that poetic freedom, invention, and independence were the result of the enabling restraints of "imitation or free-running parallel" in the following three areas: burlesque of Greek and Roman classics; forgery of the British archaic and primitive past; and serious parody of the native English classics from Chaucer through Pope.

450A Winn, James A. UNSUSPECTED ELOQUENCE: A HISTORY OF THE RELATIONS BETWEEN POETRY AND MUSIC. New Haven, Conn.: Yale Univ. Press, 1981.

>A comprehensive historical account of the relationship between music and poetry by an accomplished flutist, musicologist, and literary critic that synthesizes and generalizes upon diverse materials from the two arts. An ambitious and informative study, especially helpful regarding the idea of imitation in the eighteenth century.

451 Winters, Ivor. "The Sentimental-Romantic Decadence of the 18th and 19th Centuries." In his FORMS OF DISCOVERY: CRITICAL AND HISTORICAL ESSAYS ON THE FORMS OF THE SHORT POEM IN ENGLISH. Denver: Alan Swallow, 1967, pp. 147-88.

>Discussion of representative poems by Dyer, Collins, Gray, Smart, and Crabbe as exhibiting "a rebellion against the authority of the rational mind . . . formulated by two closely related doctrines": Shaftesbury's sentimentalism and Locke's concept of the association of ideas. See no. 132.

## 2. Genre

452 Aubin, Robert A. TOPOGRAPHICAL POETRY IN EIGHTEENTH-CENTURY ENGLAND. New York: Modern Language Association, 1936.

>Focuses on poetry generated by specific localities and nameplaces to map out changing tastes and ideas in this subspecies of descriptive verse. Contains exhaustive bibliography of such poems.

453 Bloom, Edward A., and Lillian D. Bloom. SATIRE'S PERSUASIVE VOICE. Ithaca, N.Y.: Cornell Univ. Press, 1979.

>Despite the protean nature of satire and the controversies surrounding its function, the affirmative impulse is the hallmark of the best satire deriving from the satirist's basic humanitas, his concern for everything human and his underlying faith in man's capacity for moral awareness. Major and minor satirists treated.

454 Bond, Richmond P. ENGLISH BURLESQUE POETRY 1700-1750. Cambridge, Mass.: Harvard Univ. Press, 1932.

>Classic study of the story of the Augustan burlesque tradition, pro-

viding essays on a wide variety of forms and practices and a valuable register of poems written from 1700 to 1750 with commentary,
category of burlesque demonstrated, date, and source. Treats,
among others, Pope, Gray, Philips, Carey, Browne, and Shenstone.

455   Bredvold, Louis I. "The Gloom of the Tory Satirists." In POPE AND HIS
      CONTEMPORARIES: ESSAYS PRESENTED TO GEORGE SHERBURN. Ed. James
      L. Clifford and Louis L. Landa. Oxford: Clarendon Press, 1949, pp. 1-19.

      Famous corrective to charges that the Augustan satirists were
      pathologically pessimistic and excessively negative, claiming for
      satire the exhilarating and tonic effect of toughminded realism.
      See no. 107.

456   _____. "A Note in Defence of Satire." ELH, 7 (1940), 253-64.

      Well-known rationalization of satire, rejecting charges that it is
      personal and vindicative and emphasizing the conviction of right-
      eousness, reasonableness, and moral idealism shared by the satirist
      and his audience.

458   Brown, Marshall. "The Urbane Sublime." ELH, 45 (1978), 236-54.

      Argues perceptively that the satiric and sublime poets wrote on a
      basis of common stylistic suppositions, that there is more unity than
      diversity in early eighteenth-century poetry, and that the dominant
      style--manifest in Gray, Collins, and Young--is the "urbane
      sublime," "a social, urbane, highly cultivated, self-confident,
      temperate and easy kind of humor."

459   Callan, Norman. "Augustan Reflective Poetry." In FROM DRYDEN TO
      JOHNSON. Vol. 4 of PELICAN GUIDE TO ENGLISH LITERATURE. Ed.
      Boris Ford. 1957. Rev. ed. Baltimore: Penguin Books, 1968, pp. 346-71.

      Laments the one-sided view of the eighteenth century that stresses
      the satirical tradition, and shows instead that the preponderance
      of poetry of rural meditation and reflection was influenced (as
      was the satirical one) by the Roman poet Horace. Treats such
      figures as Dyer, Lady Winchilsea, Thomson, Gray, Collins,
      Shenstone, Goldsmith, and Cowper. See no. 39.

460   Carnochan, W.B.  "Satire, Sublimity, and Sentiment: Theory and
      Practice in Post-Augustan Satire." PMLA, 85 (1970), 260-67.

      Post-Augustan satire preferred Juvenal over Horace, but the
      use of Juvenal was selective and emphasized his sublimity,
      pathos, and rational piety, not his obscenity, wit, and
      rhetorical control.

461    Chalker, John. THE ENGLISH GEORGIC: A STUDY IN THE DEVELOP-
       MENT OF A FORM. Baltimore: Johns Hopkins Press, 1969.

       A thorough treatment of the influence of Virgil's GEORGICS
       on eighteenth-century poetry, emphasizing reasons the form
       and theme attracted a variety of adaptations and transforma-
       tions by diverse poets of the period.

462    Deane, Cecil V. ASPECTS OF EIGHTEENTH-CENTURY NATURE
       POETRY. Oxford: B. Blackwell, 1935.

       Methods of composition in landscape poetry are analogous
       to or often identified with the aims of landscape painters,
       but "poetic in substance and execution."

463    Donaldson, Ian. "The Satirists' London." EIC, 23 (1975), 101-22.

       Discusses city life as the setting for satire, showing how the
       recognizable details of urban life lend realism to the mode,
       but that the truth of the satirists' vision relies on distortion,
       suppression, and manipulation of facts.

464    Draper, John W. THE FUNERAL ELEGY AND THE RISE OF ENGLISH
       ROMANTICISM. New York: New York Univ. Press, 1929.

       Treats elegiac poetry starting with the seventeenth-century
       showing its fascination with the physical fact of death and
       the idea of Christian hope as instances of poetic tours de
       force rather than as genuine grief or sociological concern.

465    Elkin, Peter K. THE AUGUSTAN DEFENCE OF SATIRE. Oxford:
       Clarendon Press, 1973.

       Invaluable study of the aims, nature, and function of satire
       held by the chief practitioners of the age, which concludes
       that their defense of its moral value (Swift excepted) on
       corrective and reformative grounds was inadequate. Distinc-
       tions between modern and eighteenth-century satire especially
       helpful.

466    Elliott, Robert C. THE POWER OF SATIRE: MAGIC, RITUAL, ART.
       Princeton, N.J.: Princeton Univ. Press, 1960.

       An important study of the origin of satire in primitive magic
       and incantatory effects, along with a survey of its "towering
       achievements" throughout history. Chapters on Swift and the
       role of satire in society.

467    Farley-Hills, David. THE BENEVOLENCE OF LAUGHTER: COMIC
       POETRY OF THE COMMONWEALTH AND RESTORATION. London:
       Macmillan, 1974.

Describes the much-neglected comic verse of the Restoration as a uniquely serious response to the contradictions and perplexities of the age and to the intellectual confusion and doubt characterizing its thinkers and artists. Chapters on Butler, Dryden, and Rochester.

468    Feingold, Richard. NATURE AND SOCIETY: LATER EIGHTEENTH-CENTURY USES OF THE PASTORAL AND GEORGIC. New Brunswick, N.J.: Rutgers Univ. Press, 1978.

Studies reasons for the artistic failure of Georgic and pastoral fictions as expressive opportunities in the later period, and concludes that these failures are directly related to the ways poets of nature viewed historical change and the new implications of agricultural and industrial expansion.

469    Foster, John Wilson. "The Measure of Paradise: Topography in Eighteenth-Century Poetry." ·ECS, 9 (1975-76), 232-56.

Topographical poetry (a subclass of eighteenth-century landscape poetry) relies not so much on techniques of painting and gardening as on scientific advances in surveying and topography where the eye becomes a physical instrument accounting for the visual, physical, and externalized organization of the verse.

470    _____. "A Redefinition of Topographical Poetry." JEGP, 69 (1970), 394-406.

Defines five structural characteristics of the genre: creation of three-dimensional space, use of space as pattern, use of time-projections, use of extended metaphor, and formation of a controlling moral vision.

471    Hagstrum, Jean H. "Verbal and Visual Caricature in the Age of Dryden, Swift, and Pope." In ENGLAND IN THE RESTORATION AND EARLY EIGHTEENTH CENTURY: ESSAYS ON CULTURE AND SOCIETY. Ed. H.T. Swedenberg, Jr. Berkeley: Univ. of California Press, 1972, pp. 173-95.

Discusses the age's fondness for analogies between painting and poetry and describes satire as involving the art of making formal pictures of two kinds: the emblematic caricature, reducing the subject to contempt by insulting comparisons; and the portrait caricature, maintaining a realistic surface but rendering the original ridiculous by means of a distorting line. See no. 125.

471A    Harth, Phillip. "The New Criticism and Eighteenth-Century Poetry."
        CRITICAL INQUIRY, 7 (1981), 521-37.

        Provides a useful overview of the impact of the New Criti-
        cism and its attendant objective, anti-scientific, impersonal
        theories of art on recent criticism of Augustan poetry, and
        notes challenges mounted in the 1970s to this particular
        "monogeneric" theory of art.

472     Hibbard, George R. "The Country House Poem of the Seventeenth
        Century." JWCI, 19 (1956), 159-74.

        A valuable study of poems in praise of the English country
        house, beginning with Jonson's PENSHURST (1616) and ending
        with a discussion of the moral implications of that tradition
        focused in Pope's satirical attack on Timon's villa, symboliz-
        ing the vision of wealth, nature, and art. See no. 1533.

473     Hopkins, Kenneth. PORTRAITS IN SATIRE. London: Barrie Books,
        1958.

        Includes long and heavily biographical and descriptive essays
        on Churchill and Peter Pindar as exemplary of the decline
        of satire in the Silver Age.

474     Horsely, Lee. "Vox Populi in Political Literature of 1710." HLQ,
        38 (1975), 335-53.

        Interesting discussion of inconsistent attitudes toward the mob
        and the general populace in the political propaganda of the
        times, pointing out that Tories welcomed support of the
        masses while Whigs attacked Tory delusion and that, though
        allegiances changed in this volatile period, the satirists
        uniformly maintained that mob irrationality was a threat to
        civilized values.

475     Jack, Ian. AUGUSTAN SATIRE: INTENTION AND IDIOM IN
        ENGLISH POETRY, 1660-1750. Oxford: Clarendon Press, 1952.

        Close stylistic analysis of representative satires of the
        Augustan age determining both intentions of the poems
        and their generic category. Treated are HUDIBRAS (1663-
        78), MAC FLECKNOE (1678), ABSALOM AND ACHITOPHEL
        (1681), RAPE OF THE LOCK (1714), EPISTLES TO SEVERAL
        PERSONS, Horatian Imitations, DUNCIAD (1742), and
        VANITY OF HUMAN WISHES (1749).

476     Joseloff, Samuel H. "Social Satire and the Pastoral Form: The Town
        Eclogue." EnlE, 3, iii/iv (1972), 192-97.

The conventional pastoral motif contrasting rural and urban life to praise country values is altered in the town eclogue where for satiric purposes urban shepherds embody the corruptions of the city.

477    Kernan, Alvin. THE CANKERED MUSE: SATIRE OF THE ENGLISH RENAISSANCE. New Haven, Conn.: Yale Univ. Press, 1959.

Ostensibly addressing the themes and practices of Elizabethan satire, this book provides invaluable background material for understanding the importance of rhetorical convention, the concept of persona, and the tradition of the satirist satirized in the period of 1660 to 1800.

478    _____. THE PLOT OF SATIRE. New Haven, Conn.: Yale Univ. Press, 1965.

Helpful discussions of Pope's DUNCIAD and Gay's TRIVIA as sophisticated satirical art, the one displaying the energies of duncery that finally are both everything and nothing, the other depicting a city tour reported by a walker who magnifies the details of urban life into epic proportions as the result of a limited perspective which reduces "a complex city with all its human interactions into trivia."

479    Kinsley, William. "'The Malicious World' and the Meaning of Satire." GENRE, 3 (1970), 137-55.

Argues (from the main example of Timon's villa in Pope's EPISTLE TO BURLINGTON) that the audience has an important role in determining satire's meaning and that as a mode of ridicule it reaches outside itself to include a dynamics of extraliterary forces that enrich and sharpen its effects.

480    Kitchin, George. A SURVEY OF BURLESQUE AND PARODY IN ENGLISH. Edinburgh: Oliver and Boyd, 1931.

Chapters 3, 4, and 5 exhaustively survey major and minor parodic poets. Treats Butler, Prior, Swift, Gay, Thomas Warton, Philips, Goldsmith, and Crabbe, among others, and explains the main features of the targets of poems of ridicule.

481    Kropf, Carl R. "Libel and Satire in the Eighteenth Century." ECS, 8 (1974-75), 153-68.

Discusses the influence of libel law on methods of satire in the eighteenth century, and concludes that it did not actually determine the forms of satire but rather did much to encourage the use of innuendo.

482    Kupersmith, William.    "Vice and Folly in Neoclassical Satire."   GENRE, 11 (1978), 45-62.

Despite Dryden's often misleading comparisons of his satiric predecessors Horace and Juvenal, his opinions, as expressed in THE DISCOURSE OF SATIRE (1693), were widely held and accepted in the late seventeenth century and were useful to both Swift and Pope.

483    Ledger, Marshall A.   "The Decline of Verse Satire:   Small Thanks to William Gifford."   EnlE, 5, i (1974), 48-56.

Gifford is an unworthy heir of Pope's Augustan verse satire and a poor model for later Byronic practice because he descended to personal and tasteless invective without artistic merit.

484    Levine, Jay A.   "The Status of the Verse Epistle Before Pope."   SP 59 (1962), 658-84.

Studies the theory and practice of the verse epistle preceding Pope's popularization in his Horatian imitations and ethic epistles, indicating its form and concern with individual, social, and political matters expressed in an intimate style.

485    Leyburn, Ellen D.   SATIRIC ALLEGORY: MIRROR OF MEN.   New Haven, Conn.: Yale Univ. Press, 1956.

Treats allegorical satire as a subgenre, and includes a chapter on ABSALOM AND ACHITOPHEL as biblical narrative and a species of this satirical type.

486    Lockwood, Thomas.   "On the Relationship of Satire and Poetry after Pope."   SEL, 14 (1974), 387-402.

This history of verse satire after Pope "is the history of a genre trying to accommodate itself to the shift in ideas about what makes a poem."   With Dryden and Pope, for example, Juvenal's theme "whatever men do" was adequate, but later this focus became the province of the novel. Thus, the choice was "either to be a poet and not a satirist, or else a satirist and not a poet--but not both."

487    Lord, George de Forest.   HEROIC MOCKERY: VARIATIONS ON EPIC THEMES FROM HOMER TO JOYCE.   Newark: Univ. of Delaware Press, 1977.

Emphasizes the comedy and exuberant playfulness of Pope's RAPE OF THE LOCK and DUNCIAD rather than treating these satires as mock-heroic strategies.

489   Maresca, Thomas E. EPIC TO NOVEL. Columbus: Ohio State Univ. Press, 1974.

Examines the novel's replacement of the epic as the major literary form in English through examination of Renaissance commentaries on Virgil's AENEID and Augustan parodic versions of the epic as an indication of just what readers expected and why from these literary forms. Treats Dryden, Pope, Swift, and Fielding.

490   Mell, Donald C. A POETICS OF AUGUSTAN ELEGY: STUDIES OF POEMS BY DRYDEN, POPE, PRIOR, SWIFT, GRAY, AND JOHNSON. Amsterdam: Rodopi, N.V., 1974.

Defines the Augustan elegiac mode as a tension of conflicting opposites, displaying concepts of order, ideality, and eternity in opposition to disorder, reality, and time, and as exemplifying the Augustan faith in the capacity of art to rescue life and meaning from mortality.

491   Moore, Cecil A. "Whig Panegyric Verse 1700-1760: A Phase of Sentimentalism." PMLA, 41 (1926), 362-401.

Whig poetry constitutes a distinct chapter in eighteenth-century literature, shunning the lampoon, eulogy, and invective characterizing Restoration political verse and advocating party ideals and principles rather than personalities. See no. 37.

492   Munker, Dona F. "The Paultry Burlesque Stile: Seventeenth-Century Poetry and Augustan 'Low Seriousness.'" SCN, 33 (1975), 14-22.

An expansion of Restoration verse satires, the "Augustan low style" is characterized by realistic diction, short stressed lines, a conversational and easy tone, and interest in ordinary experience based on empirical knowledge of the world. Treats Rochester, Swift, and Horace.

493   O'Neill, John H. "Sexuality, Deviance, and Moral Character in the Personal Satire of the Restoration." ECLife, 2, i (1975), 16-19.

Examines the nature and purpose of sexual allegations in the Restoration lampoon, such as masturbation, impotency, satyriasis, and nymphomania, to see what they reveal about the poet's art and the social mores which he and his audience shared. Discusses Rochester.

494   _____. "An Unpublished 'Imperfect Enjoyment' Poem." PLL, 13 (1977), 197-202.

Discusses imperfect enjoyment poems as a subgenre during the Restoration, and credits two anonymous poetasters for providing us with the knowledge of the order of composition of their work and possible influence of one poem on another.

495    Paulson, Ronald. THE FICTIONS OF SATIRE. Baltimore: Johns Hopkins Press, 1967.

Views satire as simultaneously mimetic in form and rhetorical in effect, presenting, exploring, and analyzing human folly and evil as well as convincing the reader of his moral responsibility.

496    Peltz, Catherine Walsh. "The Neo-Classic Lyric, 1660-1725." ELH, 11 (1944), 92-116.

Studies the origin, continuance, and increasing dominance of the neoclassic lyric tradition that had its roots in Renaissance England, was shaped by critical precepts of Aristotle and Horace, nourished by translation and imitations of the classic lyric genres--the irregular ode, elegy, pastoral, and epigram--and reached its highest achievement in the verses of Rochester, Congreve, and Prior.

497    Pinkus, Philip. "The New Satire of Augustan England." UTQ, 38 (1968), 136-58.

"The pretense to human reason is the most persistent irony in Augustan satire. Ultimately, it is the impact of rationalism on the neo-classical period that brought about this irony and in effect helped create the profound sense of incongruity which formed the new satire of the Augustan period."

498    Quaintance, Richard. "French Sources of the Restoration 'Imperfect Enjoyment' Poem." PQ, 42 (1963), 190-99.

An important discussion, particularly of two French versions of the imperfect enjoyment poem that influenced English adaptations, showing the conventional aspects as well as the artful alterations by Etherege, Aphra Behn, and Rochester.

499    Randolph, Mary Claire. "Candour in Eighteenth-Century Satire." RES, 20 (1944), 45-62.

Studies the fortunes in the eighteenth century of the idea of candour and its associations with the satiric vision of reality, showing the "decay of the genus satire" as "faithfully mirrored in the deterioration of this single critical term."

500    Rogers, Pat. "Drayton Modernis'd: An Augustan Version of England's Heroicall Epistles." ES, 53 (1972), 112-23.

The vogue for Ovidian imitations in the early eighteenth century exemplifies the continuing high interest in adaptations, paraphrases, and modernization ranging from the seventeenth on into the nineteenth centuries and involving major and minor authors.

501    Sambrook, A.J. "An Essay on Eighteenth-Century Pastoral, Pope to Wordsworth, Part I." TRIVIUM, 5 (1970), 21-35; "Part II." TRIVIUM, 6 (1971), 103-15.

In the eighteenth-century pastoral, "we may see change in ideas about art and society, the growth of sentimental humanitarianism and of subjectiveness, the influence of cultural naturalism and regionalism, and even the stirrings of radical feeling." Part 2 focuses on Goldsmith's THE DESERTED VILLAGE (1770) as a successful combination of "the contemporary fact of rural oppression" with an "appealing, idealistic yet plausible retrospective peasant Arcadia, to make a myth that could serve a radical cause."

502    Seidel, Michael. SATIRIC INHERITANCE, RABELAIS TO STERNE. Princeton, N.J.: Princeton Univ. Press, 1979.

A dense and difficult study of satire "as a literary system of discontinuities and subversions" of traditions, inheritances, and transferences, both individual and cultural. Sees satire as a deforming mode that deprives its subjects of "progressive hereditas" while thriving on its regressive vitality.

503    Selden, Raman. ENGLISH VERSE SATIRE 1590-1765. London: George Allen and Unwin, 1978.

Surveys theories as well as the practice of verse satire from the Elizabethan to the Augustan period, using as a vocabulary of analysis the traditional distinctions between Horatian and Juvenalian forms.

504    Toliver, Harold. PASTORAL FORMS AND ATTITUDES. Berkeley: Univ. of California Press, 1971.

Explores the Augustan balance of nature and art, noting strains between the celebration of the pastoral ideal of art and nature's entanglements in economic and social realities.

505    Weinbrot, Howard D. THE FORMAL STRAIN: STUDIES IN AUGUSTAN IMITATION AND SATIRE. Chicago: Univ. of Chicago Press, 1969.

Historical inquiry determining both a genealogy and essential features of Augustan imitation and formal verse satire to aid the modern reader in understanding and evaluating the poetic successes or failures of this genre. Chapters on Young, Pope, and Johnson.

506    Wilkinson, Andrew M.  "The Decline of English Verse Satire in the Middle Years of the Eighteenth Century."  RES, NS 3 (1952), 222-33.

The decline of satire was not due to overt opposition, but was rather the result of a revised estimate of human nature, which is the source of what is commonly called sentimentalism.

507    _____.  "The Rise of English Verse Satire in the Eighteenth Century." ES, 34 (1953), 97-108.

Many things contributed to the preeminence of this form of satire from 1660 to 1740--among them the Augustans' conception of truth; devotion to the intellect, moral position, and sense of an ordered universe; and respect for the classics and Boileau and social and political institutions. The satirist both accepted and rejected the pessimism and optimism implied by this intellectual atmosphere.

508    Worcester, David.  THE ART OF SATIRE.  Cambridge, Mass.: Harvard Univ. Press, 1940.

Famous enumeration of the various devices and forms of expression characterizing the satiric mode:  burlesque, irony, invective, tragedy, and comedy.

## 3. Poetic Forms and Structures

509    Boyce, Benjamin.  "Sounding Shells and Little Prattlers in the Mid-Eighteenth-Century English Ode."  ECS, 8 (1975), 245-64.

Focuses on the images of sounding shells and babes or infants, demonstrating how these tropes contribute in the mid-century to the complicated blending of manners, motifs, and moods characterizing these coterie and fashionably ornamental poems. Treats Collins, Joseph Warton, Gray, and Smart.

510    Bronson, Bertrand H.  "Personification Reconsidered."  In NEW LIGHT ON DR. JOHNSON: ESSAYS ON OCCASION OF HIS 250TH BIRTHDAY.  Ed. Frederick W. Hilles.  New Haven, Conn.: Yale Univ. Press, 1959, pp. 189-231.

Thoughtful, far-reaching defense of personification in neo-classical verse generally and in Johnson's particular employment (especially in the Levet elegy), identifying its metaphorical function and establishing its suitability as expression of universal truths about human significance. See no. 1372.

511  Brooks, Harold F. "The 'Imitation' in English Poetry, Especially in Formal Satire before the Age of Pope." RES, 25 (1949), 124-40.

The deliberate use of classical models by formal verse satirists in the Restoration and early eighteenth century is an outgrowth of the Renaissance concept of enriching the modern and vernacular by translating and borrowing from ancient literature.

512  Brower, Reuben A. "Form and Defect of Form in Eighteenth-Century Poetry: A Memorandum." CE, 29 (1968), 535-41.

Using R.P. Blackmur's distinction between underlying or felt literary form and mere technical or mechanical coherence, warns against ignoring obvious artistic deficiencies in Dryden, Prior, Gray, and Thomson.

513  Castle, Terry J. "Lab'ring Bards: Birth Topoi and English Poetics 1660-1820." JEGP, 78 (1979), 193-208.

Traces the childbirth figure as an underlying image signifying the creative process, showing how such imaginative conceptions reveal not only epistemological presuppositions, but also important changes in aesthetic theory.

514  Cohen, Ralph. "The Augustan Mode in English Poetry." ECS, 1 (1967), 3-32.

A key, if difficult, essay among recent attempts to define the mode of Augustan poetry by structural or organizational features--such as spatial concepts inclusive of imagery, metaphor, prosody, and allusion reflecting larger scientific and religious beliefs embracing analogies between men, nature, and God--rather than by means of intellectual history.

515  _____. "On the Interrelations of Eighteenth-Century Literary Forms." In NEW APPROACHES TO EIGHTEENTH-CENTURY LITERATURE. Ed. Phillip Harth. New York: Columbia Univ. Press, 1974, pp. 33-78.

Argues that no literary work in the eighteenth century can be understood and appreciated without recognizing that it is a combination of parts, forms, conventions, and genre

and that such categories in the period were never pure
and rigid, but part of a family of expressive modes. See
no. 108A.

516    Fry, Paul H. THE POET'S CALLING IN THE ENGLISH ODE. New
       Haven, Conn.: Yale Univ. Press, 1980.

       A complex and dense discussion (chapters 3, 4, 5) of the
       public, epideictic qualities of Dryden's odes that are char-
       acterized as personal and dissident as well, displaying the
       disruptions of daemonic forces of nature paradoxically given
       voice in the unnatural and artificial poetic diction of Gray's
       and Collins' nervous odes of the mid-century.

517    Greene, Donald J. "'Logical Structure' in Eighteenth-Century Poetry."
       PQ, 31 (1952), 315-36.

       A witty and brilliant attack on nineteenth- and early
       twentieth-century critical stereotypes involving so-called
       logical or rational structures in the poetry, demonstrating
       that in fact the age was anti-Reason and empirical and
       that the structure of a poem of Pope's surely reveals as
       rich and complex an imaginative organization as any romantic
       poem.

518    Hughes, Peter. "Allusion and Expression in Eighteenth-Century Litera-
       ture." In THE AUTHOR IN HIS WORK: ESSAYS ON A PROBLEM IN
       CRITICISM. Ed. Louis L. Martz and Aubrey Williams. Intro. by
       Patricia Meyer Spacks. New Haven, Conn.: Yale Univ. Press, 1978,
       pp. 297-311.

       Discusses the allusive mode in eighteenth-century literature
       and sees in the technique of expressive repetition (versus
       mimetic reference) a solution to the burden of the past
       through the writers' efforts to make the way back a new
       way forward. Pope's and Dryden's original parodies and
       imitations condemn contemporary dunces while conveying
       respect for their literary forebearers. Difficult but worthy
       essay. See no. 119.

519    McGuinness, Rosamond. ENGLISH COURT ODES: 1660-1820. Oxford:
       Clarendon Press, 1971.

       A study of court odes performed on the birthday of a
       monarch and on the New Year as a social phenomenon of
       contemporary aesthetic values, and as a means for under-
       standing both connections between music and literature and
       the patronage system.

520    Oates, Mary I. "Jonson, Congreve, and Gray: Pindaric Essays in
       Literary History." SEL, 19 (1979), 387-406.

Surveys representative Pindaric odes as documenting the
change from a didactic-mimetic Renaissance aesthetic to
a view of the art as concerned with the image of the poet.

521    Randolph, Mary Claire. "The Structural Design of the Formal Verse
       Satire." PQ, 21 (1942), 368-84.

       A classic study of the dramatic framework of satura as an
       A-B structure, A representing the presentation of some vice,
       folly, or corruption, and B the affirmation of an ideal,
       norm, or positive standard of value. See nos. 47 and 122.

522    Thorpe, Peter. "The Nonstructure of Augustan Verse." PLL, 5 (1969),
       235-51.

       Using representative poems by Denham, Dryden, Rochester,
       Pope, Gray, and Johnson, demonstrates that a lack of
       unity, structure, coherence, and design (in the usual sense
       of these terms) does not detract from the beauty and force
       of the poetic art, asserting that truth in literature involves
       chaos as well as order.

523    Wasserman, Earl R. "The Inherent Values of Eighteenth-Century Personi-
       fication." PMLA, 65 (1950), 435-63.

       Argues that because personification is a device, not a
       product, of art, its aesthetic value lies in its organic
       relationship to the work of art as a whole and that it
       serves the same artistic purpose in the eighteenth century
       as does symbolism for the twentieth century: fusing con-
       crete and abstract, physical and moral.

524    Williamson, George. "The Rhetorical Pattern of Neo-Classical Wit."
       MP, 32 (1935), 55-81.

       A wit of vibrant oppositions gives the neoclassical couplet
       its distinctive form, and though the pattern began with
       Jonson and extended through Dryden, the expressive im-
       pulse here represented was focused in Waller.

525    Wimsatt, William K. "The Structure of Romantic Nature Imagery." In
       THE AGE OF JOHNSON: ESSAYS PRESENTED TO CHAUNCEY BREW-
       STER TINKER. Ed. Frederick W. Hilles. New Haven, Conn.: Yale
       Univ. Press, 1949, pp. 291-303.

       Helpful remarks on neoclassic poetic structure in comparison
       with that of metaphysical and romantic practices. See nos.
       109 and 131.

## 4. Language and Versification

526     Adams, Percy G.   GRACES OF HARMONY.   Athens: Univ. of Georgia
        Press, 1977.

        A detailed analysis of consonant and vowel sounds that
        occur in stressed syllables, based on the assumption that
        poetry is composed for the speaking voice. Treats Dryden,
        Pope, Thomson, and Johnson.

527     Ames, George T.   "The Structure of the Augustan Couplet."   GENRE,
        9 (1976), 37-58.

        Basically a statistical survey of prosodic qualities character-
        izing the heroic couplet in (mostly) Dryden and Pope, con-
        cluding that its internal structure suits aphoristic rather than
        narrative progression, and that as the emphasis shifts from
        a narrative function to a concentration of complex meanings
        within static decasyllabic confines, the rhetorical design
        is "a model . . . of a much larger way of looking at and
        dealing with the world."

528     Arthos, John.   THE LANGUAGE OF NATURAL DESCRIPTION IN
        EIGHTEENTH-CENTURY POETRY.   Ann Arbor: Univ. of Michigan
        Press, 1949.

        Studies the relationship of the "stock diction" of eighteenth-
        century descriptive verse to the language widely used in the
        naturalist and scientific writings of the period, both English
        and continental.

529     Bailliet, Conrad A.   "The History and Rhetoric of the Triplet."   PMLA,
        80 (1965), 528-34.   Table.

        An offspring of the pentameter couplet, this rhetorical
        device had a period of growth, maturity, and demise,
        flourishing in the period of Dryden just before the apex
        of the couplet, after the couplet had become loose and
        open, and before its use violated the decorum and polish
        represented by Pope's practice. Contains a table of
        occurrences.

529A    Brogan, Terry V.F.   ENGLISH VERSIFICATION, 1570-1980: A REFER-
        ENCE GUIDE WITH A GLOBAL APPENDIX.   Baltimore: Johns Hopkins
        Univ. Press, 1981.   Index, bibliog.

        Collects, lists, classifies by subject, summarizes, describes,
        and evaluates all known printed studies on English versifica-
        tion from their origin in the Renaissance, Ascham's THE
        SCHOLEMASTER (1570), through 1980; places English

versification within the larger frame of all versification
systems of the world. Cross-referenced and indexed by
poet and author. Appendix provides a selective bibliography on other languages.

530    Brown, Wallace Cable. THE TRIUMPH OF FORM: A STUDY OF THE
       LATER MASTERS OF THE HEROIC COUPLET. Chapel Hill: Univ. of
       North Carolina Press, 1948.

       An early new critical approach to couplet rhetoric in se-
       lected poems by Gay, Johnson, Churchill, Young, Cowper,
       Goldsmith, and Crabbe, emphasizing each poet's ability to
       adapt subject to form and generally assessing his artistic
       achievement.

531    Chapin, Chester F. PERSONIFICATION IN EIGHTEENTH-CENTURY
       ENGLISH POETRY. New York: Columbia Univ. Press, 1955.

       Against a background of poetic theory and practice, studies
       personified abstraction in the period and distinguishes be-
       tween two types--metaphysical and allegorical--by analyzing
       their purpose and function in the eighteenth century.

532    Davie, Donald. ARTICULATE ENERGY: AN ENQUIRY INTO THE
       SYNTAX OF ENGLISH POETRY. New York: Harcourt Brace, 1955.

       Short but insightful comment on the function of eighteenth-
       century syntax, distinguishing between the Augustan assump-
       tion that syntax carry a weight of poetic meaning and the
       romantic notion of syntactical forms carrying no sense, only
       feeling.

533    _____. THE LANGUAGE OF SCIENCE AND THE LANGUAGE OF
       LITERATURE, 1700-1740. London: Steed and Ward, 1963.

       Argues that science and poetry are not antagonistic and
       that the vocabulary of poetry demonstrates not only inno-
       vative uses of the new language of science, but also the
       impact of scientific meanings on old words.

534    _____. PURITY OF DICTION IN ENGLISH VERSE. London: Chatto
       and Windus, 1952.

       Interesting speculations on language and metaphor, espe-
       cially as illustrated by poets of the mid and late eighteenth
       century, which conclude that uses often censured as merely
       conventional are in fact poetically functional.

535    Empson, William. SEVEN TYPES OF AMBIGUITY. Norfolk, Conn.:
       New Directions, 1949.

Brilliant analysis of verbal ingenuity and complexity of motive in, among other poems, Pope's DUNCIAD, DR. ARBUTHNOT, and MORAL ESSAYS.

536    Fussell, Paul. POETIC METER AND POETIC FORM. New York: Random House, 1965.

Good study of the rhythmical and formal dimensions of poetry, citing many examples from eighteenth-century verse.

537    _____. THEORY OF PROSODY IN EIGHTEENTH-CENTURY ENGLAND. New London: Connecticut College, 1954.

Exhaustive survey of prosodic treatises from 1657 to 1900 and examination of theories of verse structure manifested in the rhythmical structure of the heroic line, poetic contractions, and the beginnings of what became romantic prosody.

538    Groom, Bernard. THE DICTION OF POETRY FROM SPENSER TO BRIDGES. Toronto: Univ. of Toronto Press, 1955.

Historical treatment of the vocabulary of selected poets to determine its contribution to the quality of their work. Sections on Dryden, Pope, Prior, Thomson, Young.

539    Hamilton, Kenneth G. THE TWO HARMONIES: POETRY AND PROSE IN THE SEVENTEENTH CENTURY. Oxford: Clarendon Press, 1963.

Interesting discussion of the changing concepts about the nature and function of language in the period as a result of the emergence of the scientific attitude, the idea of reasoning based on spatial rather than linguistic analogies, the separation of words and thought, and the new emphasis in the eighteenth century on passions or emotions as the true subject of poetry.

540    Humphreys, Arthur R. "A Classical Education and Eighteenth-Century Poetry." SCRUTINY, 8 (1939-40), 193-207.

Seconding Coleridge's contention that writing Latin verses had a pejorative effect on poetic language of the eighteenth century, argues that the classical creed of elegance, correctness, and rhetoric debilitated the energies and linguistic exuberance inherent in poetic creation.

541    Miles, Josephine. "The Primary Language of Poetry in the 1740's and the 1840's." In her THE CONTINUITY OF POETIC LANGUAGE. Berkeley and Los Angeles: Univ. of California Press, 1951, pp. 161-382.

By means of charts and statistics describes the language
used in poetry for these two decades as an index to the
kind of poetry written, its syntactical structure, critical
status, and to some of the qualities the poetry shares with
the prose of the time period.

542    Parker, David.  "Periphrasis in Eighteenth-Century English Verse and
the Function of the Direct Article."  Neophil, 59 (1975), 147-56.

The combined use of periphrasis and the article the generates
an ambiguity that permits a poet writing in English to emu-
late the effects of Latin, and thus blur the distinctions between the particular and the general, an effect welcomed
and one that possibly accounts for the popularity of the
direct article in the age.

543    Piper, William Bowman.  THE HEROIC COUPLET.  Cleveland:  Press
of Case Western Reserve Univ., 1969.

Comprehensive historical account of the closed couplet in
English literature illustrating its function and appropriateness
for public, conversational, and social poetry in poets ranging from Chaucer to Crabbe, but emphasizing its popularity
in the poetry of 1660 to 1800.

544    Thompson, Elbert N.S.  "The Octosyllabic Couplet."  PQ, 18 (1939),
257-68.

Points out that whereas the more familiar and acceptable
heroic couplet derives in part from Latin elegiac meter
and the principles of Italian metrics, the octosyllabic
couplet is essentially the offspring of Old English poetry
and accentual Latin hymns, a "more ancient and respected
lineage."

545    Tillotson, Geoffrey.  "Augustan Poetic Diction I, II, and III."  In his
AUGUSTAN STUDIES.  London:  Athlone Press, 1961, pp. 13-110.

Classic study of the relationship between Augustan poetic
theory and practice, demonstrating the linguistic appropriateness and aesthetic function of a special language for
poetry and levels of diction.  Treats major and minor
figures.  See no. 126.

546    _____.  "The Manner of Proceeding in Certain Eighteenth- and Early
Nineteenth-Century Poems."  In his AUGUSTAN STUDIES.  London:
Athlone Press, 1961, pp. 111-46.

Meticulous discussion of patterns of word order in Pope
(with references to Johnson, Gray, and Wordsworth),

emphasizing the quality of ordinary prose syntax in his couplet configurations and the age's concern for method and design in contrast to early nineteenth-century preference for continuity and sense of movement. See no. 126.

547 _____. "The Methods of Description in Eighteenth- and Nineteenth-Century Poetry." In RESTORATION AND EIGHTEENTH-CENTURY LITERATURE: ESSAYS IN HONOR OF ALAN DUGALD McKILLOP. Ed. Carroll Camden. Chicago: Univ. of Chicago Press, 1963, pp. 235-38.

Comparisons of brief passages from Thomson, Pope, Gray, Wordsworth, and Milton reveal the important contribution of syntax to the overall descriptive effect. See no. 103.

548 Tucker, Susie I. PROTEAN SHAPE: A STUDY IN EIGHTEENTH-CENTURY VOCABULARY AND USAGE. London: Athlone Press, 1967.

Studies usage, pronunciation, and decorum to help the modern reader understand contemporary attitudes toward language in both a theoretical and practical sense.

549 Wasserman, Earl R. "The Return of the Enjambed Couplet." ELH, 7 (1940), 239-52.

Chronicles some of the major events in the return to English poetry after Pope of the run-on couplet championed by Dryden, citing the following reasons for the reappearance: to provide relief from monotony induced by couplet rhetoric; experimentation with Miltonic blank verse and stanzaic poems; romantic and melancholic thematic concerns; and recognition of Dryden's achievement.

550 Youngren, William H. "Generality in Augustan Satire." In IN DEFENSE OF READING: A READER'S APPROACH TO LITERARY CRITICISM. Ed. Reuben A. Brower and Richard Poirier. New York: Dutton, 1962, pp. 206-34.

Examples from Dryden, Pope, and Johnson are analyzed against the backdrop of contemporary philosophical and linguistic theories of abstraction and generalization to show that generality and verbal particularity in individual poems are complementary aspects of a single language characteristic.

Part 2

INDIVIDUAL AUTHORS

# MARK AKENSIDE (1721-70)

## A. MAJOR EDITIONS

551  THE POEMS OF MARK AKENSIDE, M.D.  Ed. Jeremiah Dyson.
London: W. Boyer and J. Nichols, 1772.

Although recognized as incomplete, this edition is the
basis for subsequent modern editions.

552  POETICAL WORKS OF AKENSIDE AND DYER.  Ed. Robert A. Willmott.
London: G. Routledge, 1855.

Draws heavily on Dyce edition (1834).  See no. 553.

553  POETICAL WORKS OF MARK AKENSIDE.  Ed. Alexander Dyce.  Aldine
edition.  Boston: Little, Brown, 1865.

Essentially a reprint of the Aldine Poets edition (1834)
with corrections and improvements through recollation of
the texts.  A short life acts as a preface to this standard
edition.

554  THE PLEASURES OF IMAGINATION: A POEM: IN THREE BOOKS.
London: R. Dodsley, 1754.

Important early edition and basis for later printings.

## B. BIBLIOGRAPHY AND TEXTUAL STUDIES

555  Chapman, Robert W.  "A Note on the First Edition of THE PLEASURES
OF IMAGINATION."  RES, 1 (1925), 346-48.

Reprints of first editions of popular poems often pose serious
editorial questions for the modern scholar, and Akenside's
PLEASURES presents a number of such editorial cruxes.

556    Hart, Jeffrey. "Akenside's Revisions of THE PLEASURES OF IMAGINA-
TION." PMLA, 74 (1959), 67-74.

>Akenside's extensive revisions of THE PLEASURES OF IMAG-
INATION (1744) reveal his involvement in the political
and cultural history of the period, his painstaking care for
poetical niceties, and a general increase in poetic powers.

557    See no. 562.

558    Silber, C. Anderson. "The Evolution of Akenside's THE PLEASURES OF
THE IMAGINATION: The Missing Link Established." PBSA, 65 (1971),
357-63.

>Attempts to establish the "hereditary connection" between
PLEASURES and the later, incomplete version published
by Jeremiah Dyson with an altered title (THE PLEASURES
OF THE IMAGINATION [1770]) by noting minor revisions
and textual variants.

559    See no. 73.

560    Williams, Ralph M. "Two Unpublished Poems by Mark Akenside." MLN,
57 (1942), 626-31.

>Prints for the first time two odes, "not among Akenside's
best productions," but thoroughly characteristic of the poet
at the time they were composed, the one reflecting his
liberal, Whiggish attitudes, the other a defense against
attacks made on Akenside by Alexander Monro and Bishop
Warburton.

## C. BIOGRAPHY

561    Bucke, Charles. ON THE LIFE, WRITINGS, AND GENIUS OF AKEN-
SIDE; WITH SOME ACCOUNT OF HIS FRIENDS. London: J. Cochrane,
1832.

>Lengthy biography by Akenside's admirer, although marred
by irrelevant material, questionable evidence, and biased
evaluations.

562    Houpt, Charles T. MARK AKENSIDE: A BIOGRAPHICAL AND CRITI-
CAL STUDY. 1944; Folcroft, Pa.: Folcroft Press, 1970. Bibliog.

>Good modern look at Akenside organized chronologically,
except in the chapter containing critical analyses of the
odes, where materials are approached topically.

## D. CRITICISM

563   Aldridge, Alfred Owen. "Akenside and Imagination." SP, 42 (1945), 769-92.

Objects to viewing Akenside's theory of the imagination as an anticipation of romantic organicism and contends that it is better seen against the background of "established moral and aesthetic traditions of the eighteenth century."

564   _____. "Akenside and the Hierarchy of Beauty." MLQ, 8 (1947), 65-67.

Akenside's presentation of differing degrees of beauty in THE PLEASURES OF IMAGINATION reflect the sources of his theories of the perception of beauty as a blend of Addison, Hutcheson, and Shaftesbury, the eighteenth-century Platonist who held (with Plato) that the mind immediately recognizes beauty by reference to an idea of perfection existing within oneself.

565   _____. "The Eclecticism of Mark Akenside's THE PLEASURES OF IMAGINATION." JHI, 5 (1944), 292-314.

Describes Akenside as eclectic in his desire to reconcile the "two divergent streams of thought, rationalism and empiricism" and drawing, therefore, from an array of classical and contemporary philosophical sources--including Shaftesbury, Addison, Leibniz, Plato, and Lucretius--in his evocation of both an a priori and empirically understood harmony of all things.

566   Buck, Howard. "Smollett and Akenside." JEGP, 31 (1932), 10-26.

Considers the biographical relationship of the two men and the "infusion of personal satire" in the novel PEREGRINE PICKLE through the caricature of Dr. Akenside under the name of "the Physician."

567   Gosse, Edmund. "Mark Akenside, Poet and Physician." LIVING AGE, 311 (1921), 787-91.

Discursive essay on the affinity of physicians for writing poetry, citing a number of such instances in English literary history.

568   Hartman, Geoffrey H. "Reflections on the Evening Star: Akenside to Coleridge." In NEW PERSPECTIVES ON COLERIDGE AND WORDSWORTH. Ed. Geoffrey H. Hartman. New York: Columbia Univ. Press, 1972, pp. 85-131.

An interesting but often difficult discussion of the creative
process illustrated by different poetic perspectives on and
approaches to the star image from Akenside to Wordsworth,
concluding that the eighteenth-century lyric generally has
structural problems with "development or manner of proceeding" and that in "Ode to the Evening Star" Akenside
has not found a satisfying "developmental pattern" to reflect his romantic theme of the developing consciousness.
Touches also on Macpherson, Blake, and Gray.

569   Kallich, Martin.   "Association of Ideas and Akenside's PLEASURES OF
IMAGINATION."  MLN, 62 (1947), 166-73.

Akenside was one of the first poets to give the psychological theories of associationism popular literary expression,
and PLEASURES demonstrates the importance of the mental
activity known as "association, or connection, of ideas"
to his fundamental concept of the imagination.

570   Mahoney, John L.   "Addison and Akenside: The Impact of Psychological Criticism on Early English Romantic Poetry."   BJA, 6 (1966), 365-
74.

Despite widespread understanding of Locke's sensationalist
psychology in the early eighteenth century, there is no
direct evidence that Akenside actually read the philosopher.
More likely, he familiarized himself with the ideas concerning the role of the imaginative faculty in the epistemological process through Locke's "popularizer," Joseph Addison in the SPECTATOR (issue nos. 409-21).

571   _____.   "Akenside and Shaftesbury: The Influence of Philosophy on
English Romantic Theory."   Discourse, 4 (1961), 241-47.

A brief discussion of changing ideas of man and nature
epitomized by the work of Shaftesbury, a philosopher of
aesthetics and morality whose influence on Akenside's
poetry can be well documented.

572   Marsh, Robert.   "Akenside and Addison: The Problem of Ideational
Debt."   MP, 59 (1961), 36-48.

A comparative examination of such matters as artistic intentions and methods behind Akenside's THE PLEASURES OF
IMAGINATION and Addison's SPECTATOR papers on "The
Pleasures of the Imagination," stressing the differences
between blank verse and philosophical prose and the function of "poetic" expression as it affects the ideas and
doctrines these two authors have in common.

# Mark Akenside

573      Norton, John. "Akenside's THE PLEASURES OF IMAGINATION: An Exercise in Poetics." ECS, 3 (1970), 366-83.

> Not simply a descriptive poem extolling the beauties of the universe, but a serious attempt to confront problems of value and knowledge of general interest to eighteenth-century readers.

574      Potter, George R. "Mark Akenside, Prophet of Evolution." MP, 24 (1926), 55-64.

> An excursion into eighteenth-century science and philosophy, arguing for the exceptional nature of Akenside's evolutionary beliefs.

575      Priestley, F.E.L. "Science and the Poet." DR, 38 (1958), 141-53.

> Argues that the relationship between science and poetry has not always been "amicable" and that when Akenside explains the processes of refraction and internal reflection which produce the rainbow (in THE PLEASURES OF IMAGI-NATION), the poetry never rises above mere technical description to deal with the human implications of the phenomenon.

576      Smith, Lyle E. "Akenside's 'A British Philippic': New Evidence." PBSA, 68 (1974), 418-77.

> Traces the complex bibliographical history of this poem that not only aroused "a nation to war but also indirectly contributed to the eventual downfall of Walpole's ministry."

577      ten Hoor, G.J. "Akenside's THE PLEASURES OF IMAGINATION in Germany." JEGP, 38 (1939), 96-106.

> German critics of the eighteenth century considered Aken-side's famous poem as a perfect example of the Lehrgedicht, a poem that presents a complete system of truths as its principal subject matter and provides support and proof for its arguments--all embellished with the chorus of poetry.

# WILLIAM BLAKE (1757-1827)

The amount of published material on Blake, especially since the bicentenary in 1957, is staggering and the content often intellectually formidable. There are, for example, two learned journals devoted exclusively to Blake criticism and scholarship. Moreover, to be counted among Blake scholars are some of the most important, but often challenging, literary critics and editors. In a selective bibliography such as this, it is possible to give only a brief indication of the amount, range, and depth of Blake scholarship. My hope is that the selections here will provide the reader with a balanced introduction to the two main trends in the criticism--those studies emphasizing mythological-archetypal-symbolic approaches and those oriented toward historical-political perspectives on Blake's art.

The inclusion of Blake in this guide has the virtue of pragmatism, chronology, and the authority of the NEW CAMBRIDGE BIBLIOGRAPHY OF ENGLISH LITERATURE (1971), but nevertheless creates a number of problems. To be sure, he lived the greater part of his life in the eighteenth century, developed his characteristic style of writing and formed his attitudes in the context of the latter part of the century. He shared with such earlier poets as Gray, Collins, Smart, and Cowper an affinity for the prophetic mode of poetry and visionary experience, and with Chatterton and Macpherson a penchant for mythmaking. As several commentators convincingly show, Blake knew and understood fully the characteristics of neoclassicism and philosophical tenets of the Enlightenment he so thoroughly and radically rejected. Yet, despite his clear connections with the eighteenth century, critics often find Blake more congenial to the conceptualizations and aesthetic principles of romantic poetry and the nineteenth century generally, than to the dominant neoclassical sensibility of the eighteenth century. Thus the background resources and literary studies cited in part 1 need to be supplemented by similar studies oriented toward romanticism and detailed in the extensive section devoted to Blake bibliography. The student would be well advised to consult this section for a far wider context in which to view Blake.

The other major difficulty facing any literary bibliographer, certainly one working within spatial limitations, is to do justice to Blake's work as a professional engraver and printer. Blake's illustrations of his own works, which he called

illuminated printing, and his illustrations of others' works for commercial purposes are worthy of consideration as texts.  Blake continually warned against
the unnatural separation of the two mediums of his artistic expression, poetry
and painting, and the visual element looms large in his imaginative vision and
mythological system, as recent studies indicate.  Unfortunately, this extra
dimension of Blake's art is often unfamiliar to the literary scholar.

It is not possible here to list the immense number of facsimiles and illuminated
books depicting Blake's composite art, but excellent reproductions exist that
are notably true to the original color and line detail.  Many are issued by
the Trianon Press for the Blake Trust.  Also, a number of public and private
institutions and museums, in both England and the United States, own special
collections of Blakeana and make slides, transparencies, posters, and postcards
suitable for classroom use.

## A.  MAJOR EDITIONS

578    THE WORKS OF WILLIAM BLAKE, POETIC, SYMBOLIC, AND CRITI-
       CAL.  Ed. Edwin John Ellis and William Butler Yeats.  3 vols.  London:
       Bernard Quaritch, 1893.

       > A famous and pioneering critical edition, but often a pro-
       > duct of the editors' own mythopoeic needs rather than an
       > accurate representation of Blake; the editing or rearranging
       > of materials often reinforces their mythic fabrications.

579    THE POETICAL WORKS OF WILLIAM BLAKE: A NEW AND VERBATIM
       TEXT FROM THE MANUSCRIPT ENGRAVED AND LETTERPRESS ORIGI-
       NALS.  Ed. John Sampson.  Oxford:  Clarendon Press, 1905.

       > An influential early twentieth-century edition and basis
       > for more recent texts.

580    THE COMPLETE WRITINGS OF WILLIAM BLAKE, WITH VARIANT
       READINGS.  Ed. Geoffrey Keynes.  London:  Oxford Univ. Press, 1966.

       > Edited text supplying and regularizing Blake's idiosyncratic
       > punctuation.  Variant readings and deletions in both poetry
       > and prose bracketed with main text.  The fruit of many
       > revisions and corrections since 1925.  Still considered by
       > some as a standard text.

581    THE POETRY AND PROSE OF WILLIAM BLAKE.  Ed. David V. Erdman.
       Commentary by Harold Bloom.  Garden City, N.Y.:  Doubleday, 1965.

       > Schematic arrangement of poems with deletions and variants
       > in notes.  Blake's minimal and idiosyncratic punctuation
       > and his use of capitalization and accidents are retained.
       > Standard modern edition.

582 THE POEMS OF WILLIAM BLAKE. Ed. William H. Stevenson. Text by David V. Erdman. London: Longman, 1971.

Based on the Erdman text but with modernized spelling, capitalization, and punctuation. Contains only the poetry; also rearranges sheets of THE FOUR ZOAS; adopts plate order of two earliest copies for text of MILTON.

583 WILLIAM BLAKE'S WRITINGS. Ed. Gerald E. Bentley, Jr. 2 vols. Oxford: Clarendon Press, 1978. Notes.

Volume 1 presents engraved and etched writings; volume 2, a transcription into conventional typography and manuscript. The purpose of the edition "is to present Blake's writing in a form as close to the originals as type will permit."

584 BLAKE'S POETRY AND DESIGNS. Norton Critical Series. Ed. Mary Lynn Johnson and John E. Grant. New York: W.W. Norton, 1979. Illus.

Contains authoritative texts, related prose, selected criticism, and thirty-two color and eighty monochrome reproductions of whole pages or details from Blake's illuminated books.

585 Binyon, Laurence. ENGRAVED DESIGNS OF WILLIAM BLAKE. New York: Scribner, 1926. Illus.

Important early publication of Blake's engravings.

586 Erdman, David V. THE ILLUMINATED BLAKE. Garden City, N.Y.: Doubleday-Anchor, 1974. Illus.

Black and white reproductions of all of Blake's illuminated works with plate-by-plate commentary.

587 THE NOTEBOOK OF WILLIAM BLAKE: A PHOTOGRAPHIC AND TYPOGRAPHIC FACSIMILE. Ed. David V. Erdman. Oxford: Clarendon Press, 1973. Illus.

Typographical facsimile of each page juxtaposed with photographic reproductions, making use of improved photography and printing methods. Effectively arranged presentation of this Rossetti Manuscript first published in facsimile by Geoffrey Keynes in 1935.

588 THE NOTEBOOK OF WILLIAM BLAKE: A PHOTOGRAPHIC AND TYPOGRAPHIC FACSIMILE. Ed. David V. Erdman. Rev. ed. New York: Readex Books, 1977. Illus.

Takes into account objections by some scholars and critics
to certain identifications and interpretations in the earlier
version of 1973. See no. 587.

589   THE PICKERING MANUSCRIPT OF WILLIAM BLAKE. Intro. Charles
      Ryskamp. New York: Pierpont Morgan Library, 1972.

      Facsimile reproduction of the manuscript.

590   WILLIAM BLAKE, TIRIEL, FACSIMILE AND TRANSCRIPT OF THE MANU-
      SCRIPT REPRODUCTION OF THE DRAWINGS, AND A COMMENTARY
      ON THE POEM. Ed. Gerald E. Bentley, Jr. Oxford: Clarendon
      Press, 1967.

      Introduction discusses the history and significance of both
      the drawings and the manuscript.

591   WILLIAM BLAKE'S DESIGNS FOR EDWARD YOUNG'S NIGHT THOUGHTS:
      A COMPLETE EDITION. Ed. David V. Erdman, John E. Grant, Edward
      J. Rose, and Michael J. Tolley. 2 vols. Oxford: Clarendon Press,
      1979. Illus.

      Sumptuous edition of the 537 watercolor drawings and forty-
      three engravings that constitute Blake's most ambitious pic-
      torial work--the page-for-page illustrations of all nine
      nights of Young's NIGHT THOUGHTS (1742-45) described
      as "an illuminated serial fresco of irony, comedy, and
      prophecy."

## B. CORRESPONDENCE

592   THE LETTERS OF WILLIAM BLAKE WITH RELATED DOCUMENTS. Ed.
      Geoffrey Keynes. 3rd ed., rev. and enl. Oxford: Clarendon Press,
      1980.

      Standard edition. Includes letters to Blake, plates, figures,
      and register of documents.

## C. BIBLIOGRAPHY, TEXTUAL STUDIES, AND CONCORDANCES

593   Bentley, Gerald E., Jr. BLAKE BOOKS: ANNOTATED CATALOGUES
      OF WILLIAM BLAKE'S WRITINGS IN ILLUMINATED PRINTING, IN
      CONVENTIONAL TYPOGRAPHY AND IN MANUSCRIPT . . . REPRO-
      DUCTIONS OF HIS DESIGNS, BOOKS WITH HIS ENGRAVINGS,
      CATALOGUES, BOOKS HE OWNED, AND SCHOLARLY AND CRITI-
      CAL WORKS ABOUT HIM. Oxford: Clarendon Press, 1977.

      Revised and expanded edition of the work begun by Bentley

and Nurmi in 1964 (below) with principal changes and improvements as follows:  lucidly rewritten section on Blake's writings and commercial engravings; inclusion of Japanese items; periodical notices corrected and revised for accuracy of fact and comment; a list of books owned by Blake; a comprehensive review of the scholarship and criticism, including a breakdown of articles published in BLAKE NEWSLETTER and BLAKE STUDIES through 1973. An excellent essay examining Blake's reputation and interpreters introduces this exceedingly detailed and comprehensive example of Blakean scholarship.  Monumental work. See no. 594.

594    Bentley, Gerald E., Jr., and Martin Nurmi, eds.  A BLAKE BIBLIOGRAPHY.  Minneapolis:  Univ. of Minnesota Press, 1964.

A comprehensive coverage (at the time) of Blake's works and secondary materials devoted to his art, including reviews.  Exhaustively cross-referenced.  See no. 593.

595    Erdman, David V.  "Blake."  In ENGLISH POETRY:  SELECT BIBLIOGRAPHICAL GUIDES.  Ed. A.E. Dyson.  London:  Oxford Univ. Press, 1971, pp. 144-66.

Surveys texts and reproductions of illustrations, critical studies, commentary, biographies, letters, and background materials, as well as listing essential scholarship.  Indispensable.  See no. 63.

596    _____, et al., ed.  A CONCORDANCE TO THE WRITINGS OF WILLIAM BLAKE.  2 vols.  Ithaca, N.Y.:  Cornell Univ. Press, 1967.

Keyed to the Keynes edition, but incorporates textual revisions noted by Blake scholars, most of which appear in the Keynes revised text of 1968.

597    Frye, Northrop.  Revised by Martin T. Nurmi.  "William Blake."  In ENGLISH ROMANTIC POETS AND ESSAYISTS:  A REVIEW OF RESEARCH AND CRITICISM.  Rev. ed.  C.W. Houtchens and L.H. Houtchens.  New York:  New York Univ. Press, 1966, pp. 3-35.

Helpful bibliographical essay describing both the history of and trends in the criticism.

598    Keynes, Geoffrey.  A BIBLIOGRAPHY OF WILLIAM BLAKE.  New York: Grolier Club, 1921.  Illus.

Early attempt to compile a comprehensive list of works by and about Blake.  An important source for later bibliographical studies with a number of plates and illustrations.

599 Keynes, Geoffrey, and Edwin Wolf, II. WILLIAM BLAKE'S ILLUMI-
NATED BOOKS: A CENSUS. New York: Grolier Club, 1953.

Still a valuable accounting of illuminated materials, although dating, sequences, and locations of the books are
sometimes in error.

600 "Recent Studies in the Nineteenth Century." SEL, Nineteenth Century
issue, 1961-- . Annual.

This bibliographical essay often provides valuable commentary
on recent Blakean scholarship and criticism.

601 "The Romantic Movement: A Selective and Critical Bibliography." ELH,
vols. 4-16 (1937-49); PQ, vols. 29-33 (1950-54); ELN, vols. 3-16
(1965-79).

602 THE ROMANTIC MOVEMENT: A SELECTIVE AND CRITICAL BIBLIOG-
RAPHY FOR 1979. Ed. David V. Erdman. New York: Garland Publishing, 1980-- . Annual.

Published as a separate volume, the best bibliography of
the period with excellent annotations and reviews. A
continuation of no. 601.

602A THE ROMANTIC MOVEMENT BIBLIOGRAPHY: 1936-1970. Ed. A.C.
Elkins, Jr., and L.J. Forstner. 7 vols. Ann Arbor: Pierian Press and
R.R. Bowker, 1973.

A comprehensive survey of "all books and articles of substantial interest to scholars of English and Continental
Romanticism." A valuable and useful compilation of the
bibliography as it appeared over the years in ELH, PQ,
and ELN.

## D. COLLECTIONS AND FESTSCHRIFTEN

603 Erdman, David V., and John E. Grant, eds. BLAKE'S VISIONARY
FORMS DRAMATIC. Princeton, N.J.: Princeton Univ. Press, 1970.

Twenty essays, some previously published, covering the
whole range of Blake's achievement.

604 Essick, Robert N., ed. THE VISIONARY HAND: ESSAYS FOR THE
STUDY OF WILLIAM BLAKE'S ART AND AESTHETICS. Los Angeles:
Hennessey and Ingalls, 1973.

Essays from 1917 to 1973, many previously published, devoted to, among other things, Blake's techniques of illumi-

nated printing and etching and to essays on his theories
of art and aesthetics.

605     Frye, Northrop, ed. BLAKE: A COLLECTION OF CRITICAL ESSAYS.
        Englewood Cliffs, N.J.: Prentice-Hall, 1966.

        Collection of previously printed modern critical essays on
        Blake, striving for "some distribution over the whole of
        Blake's output and outlook."

606     Grant, John E., ed. DISCUSSIONS OF WILLIAM BLAKE. Boston:
        Heath, 1961.

        Mostly reprints of articles on Blake, some revised and
        some extracted.

607     Keynes, Geoffrey. BLAKE STUDIES: ESSAYS ON HIS LIFE AND
        WORKS. 2nd ed. Oxford: Clarendon Press, 1971.

        Twenty-nine essays, many printed previously, but indica-
        tive of Keynes's incredible range and depth of scholarship
        and criticism.

608     O'Neill, Judith, ed. CRITICS ON BLAKE: READINGS IN LITERARY
        CRITICISM. Coral Cables, Fla.: Univ. of Miami Press, 1970.

        Prints excerpts from a number of reactions to Blake from
        around 1800 through 1940. A section on modern criticism
        includes a range of essays representing a number of ap-
        proaches to Blake's art.

609     Paley, Morton D., ed. TWENTIETH CENTURY INTERPRETATIONS OF
        SONGS OF INNOCENCE AND OF EXPERIENCE: A COLLECTION OF
        CRITICAL ESSAYS. Englewood Cliffs, N.J.: Prentice-Hall, 1969.

        Good selection of essays (mostly chapters from books)
        representing a variety of approaches to Blake's comple-
        mentary poems.

610     Paley, Morton D., and Michael Phillips, eds. WILLIAM BLAKE:
        ESSAYS IN HONOUR OF SIR GEOFFREY KEYNES. Oxford: Claren-
        don Press, 1973.

        A variety of Blake experts and generally sensitive critics
        of the period, both experienced and new, provide a wide-
        ranging book of essays, making use of varied approaches
        to Blake's earliest art and the relationship between the
        work and the visual context, as well as furnishing informa-
        tion about his final years and his posthumous reputation.

611    Phillips, Michael, ed. INTERPRETING BLAKE. Cambridge: Cambridge
       Univ. Press, 1978.

       Mostly essays revised for publication that were originally
       presented at the 1974 symposium on Blake held at the
       Institute for Advanced Studies in the Humanities at the
       University of Edinburgh, ranging from close analysis of
       single poems to assessments of Blake's influence on the age.

612    Pinto, Vivian De Sola, ed. THE DIVINE VISION: STUDIES IN THE
       POETRY AND ART OF WILLIAM BLAKE. London: Victor Gollanz,
       1957.

       Selected essays, some original, some reprints, by eminent
       Blakeans sponsored and published by the Blake Bicentenary
       Committee. Two essays deal with where Blake might have
       found information about India.

613    Rosenfeld, Alvin H., ed. WILLIAM BLAKE: ESSAYS FOR S. FOSTER
       DAMON. Providence, R.I.: Brown Univ. Press, 1969.

       Impressive essays by first-rate critics, discussing Blake as
       graphic artist and poet, his philosophical and religious
       transmutations, his place in literary history and aesthetics;
       also provides rationalizations for modern scholarly practices.

E. BIOGRAPHY

614    Bentley, Gerald E., Jr., ed. BLAKE RECORDS. Oxford: Clarendon
       Press, 1969. Index.

       Invaluable exhaustive compilation of documents relating to
       Blake as man and artist, arranged in chronological order.
       Fully annotated.

615    Gilchrist, Alexander. LIFE OF WILLIAM BLAKE. Ed. Ruthven Todd.
       London: Dent, 1942; rev. 1945.

       Credited with establishing Blake's literary reputation, this
       biography, originally published in 1863, is still regarded by
       many as the best, but is based mostly on oral information
       that although seemingly accurate is unverifiable.

616    Robinson, Henry Crabb. DIARY, REMINISCENCES, AND CORRESPON-
       DENCE. Ed. Thomas Sadler. 3 vols. London: Macmillan, 1869.

       The best contemporary record of Blake's opinions, statements,
       and attitudes, ranging from politics to mysticism.

617   Wilson, Mona. THE LIFE OF WILLIAM BLAKE. Ed. and rev. Geoffrey
      Keynes. Oxford: Oxford Univ. Press, 1971. Footnotes.

      Contains verified quotations, notes, and references omitted
      in the 1927 and 1932 editions, as well as new footnotes
      to account for recent scholarship. Considered a scrupulously
      researched and thoughtfully composed life exposing some
      persistent legends about Blake, especially regarding his al-
      leged madness. Standard modern biography.

## F. JOURNALS

618   BLAKE: AN ILLUSTRATED QUARTERLY, Department of English, Univer-
      sity of New Mexico, 1977-- .

      A continuation of BLAKE NEWSLETTER. Long articles on
      Blake, especially concerning his art. Comprehensive
      checklist of scholarship.

619   BLAKE NEWSLETTER, Vols. 1-10, 1967-77.

      Brief articles on all aspects of Blake scholarship. Long
      book reviews and annual index of articles and books re-
      viewed.

620   BLAKE STUDIES (BlakeS), American Blake Foundation, Department of
      English, Memphis State University, Tennessee, 1968-- . Biannual.

      A source of much excellent criticism and comment, espe-
      cially of an interdisciplinary nature. Lengthy book reviews
      and brief annotations on publications related to Blake.

## G. CRITICISM

621   Adams, Hazard. WILLIAM BLAKE: A READING OF THE SHORTER
      POEMS. Seattle: Univ. of Washington Press, 1963.

      Employs the vocabulary of new criticism to analyze point
      of view, irony, personification, and other poetic devices,
      but in the context of Blake's archetypal method of organiz-
      ing his world of poetic symbolism. Contains a valuable
      annotated list of criticism of Blake's lyrics, poem by poem.

622   Altizer, Thomas J. THE NEW APOCALYPSE: THE RADICAL CHRISTIAN
      VISION OF WILLIAM BLAKE. East Lansing: Michigan State Univ.
      Press, 1967.

      Presents Blake as "the most original prophet and seer in the
      history of Christendom," and as a poet who created a new

form of vision that to be understood requires of the reader a "new form of theological understanding."

623    Ault, Donald. VISIONARY PHYSICS: BLAKE'S RESPONSE TO NEW-
TON. Chicago: Univ. of Chicago Press, 1974.

Drawing on the history and philosophy of science, mathe-
matics, logic, phenomenology, as well as on Blake's poetry,
discusses Blake's attraction to Newton as surrogate for an
"imaginative organization" and his transformation of New-
tonian materials by "re-creating a new imaginative counter-
vision."

624    Baine, Mary R., and Rodney M. Baine. "Blake's Other Tigers, and
'The Tiger.'"    SEL, 15 (1975), 563-78.

"Blake consistently used the tiger in the fallen world as a
symbol of cruelty, destructiveness, and bastiality" and the
questioner's reaction implies recognition that man has "inverted eternal values" by his pride and selfhood only to
be redeemed by "asserting his Christlike, divine Humanity."

625    Baine, Rodney M. "Blake's 'Tyger': The Nature of the Beast." PQ,
46 (1967), 488-98.

Views the poem in the context of SONGS OF INNOCENCE
AND SONGS OF EXPERIENCE and of its analogs and its
sources as the "shocked and fascinated reaction of an observer imaginatively visualizing the creation of brutal  ·
cruelty in nature and in man."

626    Beer, John. BLAKE'S VISIONARY UNIVERSE. Manchester, Engl.:
Manchester Univ. Press, 1969.

An attempt to deal with Blake's creation of artistic myth
on a grand scale as well as account for the artistic energy
expended in the "minute particulars" of word, image, and
poetic form.

627    Bentley, Gerald E., Jr. WILLIAM BLAKE: THE CRITICAL HERITAGE.
London: Routledge and Kegan Paul, 1975. Illus.

Because Blake was known to his contemporaries as a painter
and engraver, not as a writer, parts 1-4 deal with his artistic
career. Part 5 includes general comments on Blake the
man; and part 6 chronologically arranges references to
Blake. Based on manuscript documents published in BLAKE
RECORDS. See no. 614.

628    Blackstone, Bernard. ENGLISH BLAKE. Cambridge: Cambridge Univ.
Press, 1949.

Conscious attempt to place Blake within the tradition of English thought, both the rationalist and antirationalist strains, and within the milieu of English history, society, and culture.

629    Bloom, Harold. BLAKE'S APOCALYPSE: A STUDY IN POETIC ARGU-MENT. Garden City, N.Y.: Doubleday, 1963.

Chronological treatment of the poems, emphasizing elements that make them more than mere documents tracing a poet's intellectual or spiritual history, and thus focusing on style of presentation, continuities of imagery, and matters of tone. Considers Blake's poems, especially the epics, "the best poetry in English since Milton."

630    _____. "Blake's JERUSALEM: The Bard of Sensibility and the Form of Prophecy." ECS, 4 (1970), 6-20.

As his definitive poem, Blake structures JERUSALEM on the model of the Book of Ezekiel, and imitates this "prophetic form" and its "priestly orator" whose circumstance and sorrow he most resembles.

631    _____. "Dialectic in THE MARRIAGE OF HEAVEN AND HELL." PMLA, 73 (1958), 501-04.

A close and complex reading, showing among other things the unity of structure as dialectical; the necessity for creative opposition in the reading of philosophy, politics, art, and religion; and the ending as an outcry against the imposition of any code of uniformity upon contrary individualities.

632    _____. THE VISIONARY COMPANY: A READING OF ENGLISH ROMANTIC POETRY. New York: Doubleday, 1963.

A justly famous consideration of the theme of the imagination in romantic poetry, finding in such diverse poets as Blake and Byron a "quality of passion and largeness, in speech and in response to life" and a belief in the myth-making function of art. Contains a chapter on Blake.

633    Blunt, Anthony. THE ART OF WILLIAM BLAKE. New York: Columbia Univ. Press, 1959.

Based on the Bampton Lectures, a general introduction contending that Blake's art has much in common with his contemporaries and that he learned much from the traditions and practices of his predecessors.

634    Bogen, Nancy W. "The Problem of Blake's Early Religion." PERSON-
       ALIST, 49 (1968), 509-22.

       Discusses Blake's religious views at the beginning of his
       life and concludes that his alleged Anglican faith is highly
       problematical.

635    Borck, Jim S. "Blake's 'The Lamb': The Punctuation of Innocence."
       TSL, 19 (1954), 163-75.

       Emendations of his eccentric punctuation (or lack of it)
       runs the risk of obscuring his real intention and meaning
       since Blake's point is to depict the pure and unified
       consciousness of an innocent, unimpeded by the artificial
       imposition of modern grammatical practice.

636    Brisman, Leslie. "Re: Generation in Blake." In his ROMANTIC
       ORIGINS. Ithaca, N.Y.: Cornell Univ. Press, 1978, pp. 224-75.

       Considers Blake's central myth of origin "and how the
       successive retellings of this story of generation--the way
       things first came to be the way they are in this world of
       Generation--move to regeneration." Stresses later prophetic
       works.

637    Bronowski, Jacob. WILLIAM BLAKE AND THE AGE OF REVOLUTION.
       Rev. ed. New York: Harper and Row, 1965.

       Discusses the impact of contemporary economic and political
       background on Blake's art, demonstrating how it shaped as
       well as inhibited his work. A revision of WILLIAM BLAKE
       A MAN WITHOUT A MASK (1943).

638    Chayes, Irene H. "Little Girls Lost: Problems of a Romantic Arche-
       type." BNYPC, 67 (1963), 579-92.

       Treats the recurring figure of Lyca, the heroine of the
       two companion poems "The Little Girle Lost" and "The
       Little Girl Found," as belonging to the archetype de-
       scribed by both Jung and Kerényi as Kove, the primordial
       maiden of Greek mythology.

639    Damon, S. Foster. A BLAKE DICTIONARY: THE IDEAS AND SYM-
       BOLS OF WILLIAM BLAKE. Providence, R.I.: Brown Univ. Press,
       1967.

       Contains highly interpretive and personalized notes and
       short essays on a wide variety of Blake topics.

640    _____. WILLIAM BLAKE: HIS PHILOSOPHY AND SYMBOLS. Boston:
       Houghton Mifflin, 1924.

Damon applies his immense knowledge about the occult
and about mysticism to Blake's poetry and painting and
establishes important connections and analogies within
his art that have singularly influenced later treatments.
Damon is considered one of the major twentieth-century
commentators.

640A    Damrosch, Leopold, Jr.  SYMBOL AND TRUTH IN BLAKE'S MYTH.
Princeton, N.J.:  Princeton Univ. Press, 1980.

An ambitious treatment of Blake's "ideas about God and
man, the psychological theology with which he sought to
solve the age-old dilemmas and to achieve the longed-for
regeneration from division into unity." Concludes that
Blake's myth and theory of the imagination on which it
is based are not "philosophically coherent," and contain
"serious inconsistencies" he constantly tried to resolve.

641    Davies, T.G.  THEOLOGY OF WILLIAM BLAKE.  Oxford:  Clarendon
Press, 1948.

Argues that Blake was an orthodox Anglican, and in the
process illuminates his relations with the Swedenborgians,
establishing that Blake's family did not belong to the New
Church.

642    Digby, George Wingfield.  SYMBOL AND IMAGE IN WILLIAM BLAKE.
Oxford:  Clarendon Press, 1957.

Applies modern theories of psychology to explain Blake's
art, but also interprets the suggested juxtaposition of
picture with image and word.

643    Dike, Donald A.  "The Difficult Innocence: Blake's Songs and Pastoral."
ELH, 28 (1961), 353-75.

The innocence and experience sequences look "simultaneously
in the same direction, so taken together, as superimposed
visions, they have the effect of a kind of transparent over-
lay"; for Blake innocence and experience inhere in one
another, reminding the reader "that pastoral, as a way of
relating the human realities, can be toughly honest."

644    Doyno, Victor.  "Blake's Revision of 'London.'"  EIC, 22 (1972), 58-
63.

A close sequential study of both first version and holograph
revision, which creates greater respect for Blake's poetic
craftsmanship and sense of artistic coherence, as well as a
deeper understanding of the poem's meaning.  An interesting

editorial comment by F.W. Bateson takes partial issue with
Doyno while arguing for a more Aristotelean dramatic structure.

645     Eaves, Morris. "Blake and the Artistic Machine: An Essay on Decorum
        and Technology." PMLA, 92 (1977), 903-27.

        Discusses Blake's use of the term machine in his aesthetic
        system as involving the simultaneous processes of conception
        and execution and also notes his attack on neoclassical
        artists who "atomized" and compartmentalized an essentially
        organic creative process.

646     Eliot, T.S. "Blake." In his THE SACRED WOOD. London: Methuen,
        1920, pp. 137-43.

        Regards Blake's poetry as exhibiting the quality of all great
        poetry--"a peculiar honesty, which, in a world too fright-
        ened to be honest, is peculiarly terrifying. It is an honesty
        against which the whole world conspires, because it is un-
        pleasant. . . .This honesty never exists without great techni-
        cal accomplishment."

647     Erdman, David V. BLAKE: PROPHET AGAINST EMPIRE: A POET'S
        INTERPRETATION OF THE HISTORY OF HIS OWN TIME. 2nd ed.,
        rev. Princeton, N.J.: Princeton Univ. Press, 1969.

        A brilliant historical approach to Blake, locating and
        analyzing his references to contemporary history and poli-
        tics and demonstrating as well that he was a man of his
        times. A careful, intelligent analysis generally considered
        second only to that in Frye's FEARFUL SYMMETRY (below).

648     Essick, Robert N. "Blake's Newton." BlakeS, 36 (1971), 149-62.

        Close analysis of the print, discussing the various motifs
        present in the image and concluding that although Newton
        is portrayed in a fallen state, redemption is possible in
        that the scientist sees only abstractions, but the visionary
        artist can perceive and create the "human form divine in
        the rude youth's magnificent body."

649     _____. WILLIAM BLAKE, PRINTMAKER. Princeton, N.J.: Princeton
        Univ. Press, 1980.

        An attempt to compensate for the lack of consideration given
        Blake's activities as a printmaker, studying his graphic en-
        deavors--such as commercial copy prints, original line en-
        gravings, special method of color printing, invention of
        relief processes for publishing pictures and words on the

same plates--and viewing his engraving art in historical
context.

650    Fisher, Peter F.    "Blake's Attacks on the Classical Tradition."  PQ,
       40 (1961), 1-18.

       Blake's attacks on the classics serve to clarify his own
       symbolic system, revealing that although he acknowledged
       that a genuine vision existed in classical myth and philos-
       ophy, he believed it limited by the ends it was to serve,
       by the restricted condition of man's fallen state and by
       the Enlightenment's indication of the tradition through such
       terms as reason and nature.

651    _____.  THE VALLEY OF VISION:  BLAKE AS PROPHET AND REVO-
       LUTIONARY.  Toronto:  Univ. of Toronto Press, 1961.

       A general account of Blake in a historical context of
       Enlightenment philosophy, arguing that the enlightenment
       temperament did not exclude the mystical and prophetic
       dimension of existence and that Blake is "typically prophet
       and seer in the priority that he gives to experience over
       all mental constraints derived from it."

652    See no. 1464.

653    Frosch, Thomas R.  THE AWAKENING OF ALBION: THE RENOVATION
       OF THE BODY IN THE POETRY OF WILLIAM BLAKE.  Ithaca, N.Y.:
       Cornell Univ. Press, 1973.

       Lucid analyses of such difficult Blakean concepts as spectre,
       emanation, idea of line, and auditory style and helpful
       explications of crucial passages on the various renovations
       and transformations affecting fallen man, the body, and
       the senses.

654    Frye, Northrop.  "Blake After Two Centuries."  UTQ, 27 (1957), 10-
       21.

       Excellent introduction to the history of Blake's reputation,
       elucidating his special lyrical, metaphysical, and mythic
       practices and viewing him as a representative of important
       philosophic and literary traditions in English culture:  the
       "combination of Protestant, radical, and Romantic qualities"
       existing side-by-side with a "Catholic, Tory, and Classical
       tradition."

655    _____.  "Blake's Introduction to Experience."  HLQ, 21 (1957), 57-67.

       Warns against the tendency to compartmentalize Blake as

lyric poet and as author of prophecy, demonstrating that the "Introduction" to SONGS OF EXPERIENCE contains the main principles of Blake's thought revealed during his whole career, especially the unifying act of imagination.

656 _____. FEARFUL SYMMETRY: A STUDY OF WILLIAM BLAKE. Rev. ed. Princeton, N.J.: Princeton Univ. Press, 1969.

Originally published in 1947, this edition contains a new preface. A learned and profound treatment of Blake's mythological system, especially the Orc Cycle, in the tradition of archetypal symbolism and of Frye's own critical and interpretive mythological cycles. A lucid, plain-spoken approach to a difficult subject. Generally considered the best work of the century on Blake.

657 Gallant, Christine. BLAKE AND THE ASSIMILATION OF CHAOS. Princeton, N.J.: Princeton Univ. Press, 1978.

A psychological reading of the poetry with a Jungian orientation designed to explore Blake's conscious preoccupation with the process of mythmaking and to explain the function that mythmaking had for him as a poet.

658 Gardner, Stanley. INFINITY ON THE ANVIL: A CRITICAL STUDY OF BLAKE'S POETRY. Oxford: Basil Blackwell, 1954.

Focuses on the poetry, arguing that the poems are self-sufficient and the symbolism understandable within individual structures.

659 Gillham, D.G. BLAKE'S CONTRARY STATES: THE SONGS OF INNOCENCE AND OF EXPERIENCE AS DRAMATIC POEMS. Cambridge: Cambridge Univ. Press, 1966.

Opposes the assumption that Blake's "unusual manner of writing" requires familiarity with his complicated mythology and chooses instead "a patient reading of the poems themselves" without forcing on to them "assistance that only a specialized knowledge can give."

660 Gleckner, Robert F. "Blake and the Senses." SIR, 5 (1965), 1-15.

The sharp distinction between "perishing body" and "eternal soul" in Blake and his contrast between the senses and imagination have led readers to ignore the fact that Blake's theory of vision involves an integration of both senses and imagination into a total perception involving "a fourfold integration of the whole man."

661 _____. "Blake's Miltonizing of Chatterton." BLAKE NEWSLETTER, 11 (1977), 27-29.

Interesting discussion of allusion and verbal echo in Blake, showing how often he wrenches and perverts the sense of the original to suit his own purposes--in many cases turning the allusion or quotation against itself.

662 _____. "Blake's Seasons." SEL, 5 (1965), 533-51.

In POETICAL SKETCHES Blake deliberately alters, shapes, and inverts poetic traditions inherited from Spenser, Milton, and his own eighteenth-century predecessors; and this transformation process later became central to his imaginative habit of mind.

663 _____. "Irony in Blake's 'Holy Thursday I.'" MLN, 71 (1956), 412-15.

Blake's ironic treatment of charity children is profound and pervasive, taking into account not only the schools but also the entire concept of professional charity symbolized by the beadles directing the procession, the regimentation of the children, and by "the wise guardians of the poor."

664 _____. "Most Holy Forms of Thought: Some Observations on Blake and Language." ELH, 41 (1974), 555-77.

Discusses the role of language in Blake's prophetic art and concludes that his verbal configurations are symbols of the world of cosmic regeneration and rehabilitation his poetry presents.

665 _____. THE PIPER AND THE BARD: A STUDY OF WILLIAM BLAKE. Detroit: Wayne State Univ. Press, 1959.

Studies the earlier poetry (to 1794), stressing the importance of narrative point of view, tone, and context in understanding Blake. Combines new critical methodology and mythic interpretations.

666 _____. "Point of View and Context in Blake's SONGS." BNYPL, 61 (1957), 531-38.

"Off-the-mark commentary" on Blake's SONGS is largely the result of ignoring the importance of a central group of related symbols--child, father, Christ, representing the segmented states of innocence, experience, and a higher innocence--and of neglecting to determine the point of view from which the poem is written.

667     _____. "William Blake and the Human Abstract." PMLA, 76 (1961), 373-79.

> Man's own thinking processes are the real cause of human misery, and Blake's own poetic image of the human represents the destructive effects of the mind's rational abstractions.

668     Grant, John E. "Apocalypse in Blake's 'Auguries of Innocence.'" TSLL, 5 (1964), 489-508.

> Discusses the title, the four-line motto, and the final eight lines of "one of the great English poems" in the context of Blake's comprehensive epistemology and his conception of prophecy and eschatology.

669     _____. "The Art and Argument of 'The Tyger.'" TSLL, 2 (1960), 38-60.

> Argues that the poem's "mighty questions" exclude the possibility of affirmation and that "The Tyger" is not "a vehicle for positive thinking, but a study in perplexity and metaphysical rebelliousness," the result, however, of a positive artistic action on Blake's part.

670     _____. "The Fate of Blake's Sun-Flower: A Forecast and Some Conclusions." BlakeS, 5 (1974), 7-64.

> Laments the "methodological license and insufficiently based" assertions about the lyric and proposes to improve the critical readings by noting the traditions of myth and symbolism informing Blake's work, attending to the form and tones, and carefully considering the design.

671     _____. "Interpreting Blake's 'The Fly.'" BNYPL, 67 (1963), 593-612.

> Reviews wrong interpretations of one of Blake's most popular lyrics, and argues that attention to the poem's literal meaning, dramatic circumstance, design or illustration, its place both in SONGS and in Blake's entire work, and its affinities with other writers will finally yield Blake's meaning.

672     Grant, John E., and Fred C. Robinson. "Tense and the Sense of Blake's 'The Tyger.'" PMLA, 81 (1966), 596-603.

> Interesting exchanges between two critics over the tense of the crucial verb "dare" and over other usages in this poem, and in Blake generally, that demonstrate the complexity of this lyric and the breadth and depth of disagreement as to its actual meaning.

673    Hagstrum, Jean H. "Blake's Blake." In ESSAYS IN HISTORY AND LITERATURE. Ed. Heinz Bluhm. Chicago: Newberry Library, 1965, pp. 169-78.

A study of Blake as dramatis personae in his own works, namely in his role as artist and poet, pilgrim and plowman, and traveller.

674    _____. WILLIAM BLAKE: POET AND PAINTER: AN INTRODUCTION TO THE ILLUMINATED VERSE. Chicago: Univ. of Chicago Press, 1964.

Provides a context which will help define Blake's distinctive union of word and design and approaches his art in a generic way, viewing his productions in themselves as illuminations and emblems, not as contributions to wider historical or aesthetic patterns.

675    _____. "William Blake Rejects the Enlightenment." SVEC, 25 (1963), 811-28.

Points out that Blake's loyalty to such preromantics as Macpherson, Chatterton, Gray, Thomson, and Collins cannot explain "the intensity nor the content" of Blake's rejection of neoclassical culture and that in fact his psychological, ethical, and religious vision even found the conventionalities and artificialities of preromanticism inadequate. Yet, what he rejected had in fact "invaded the deepest recesses of his being."

676    _____. "William Blake's 'The Clod and the Pebble.'" In RESTORATION AND EIGHTEENTH-CENTURY LITERATURE: ESSAYS IN HONOR OF ALAN DUGALD McKILLOP. Ed. Carroll Camden. Chicago: Univ. of Chicago Press, 1963, pp. 381-88.

Contrary to predominant interpretations of the poem's symbolism, "the Pebble, not the Clay, is Blake's raisonneur," appropriately expressing his militant and combative religious vision. See no. 103.

677    _____. "'The Wrath of the Lamb': A Study of William Blake's Conversions." In FROM SENSIBILITY TO ROMANTICISM: ESSAYS PRESENTED TO FREDERICK A. POTTLE. Ed. Frederick W. Hilles and Harold Bloom. New York: Oxford Univ. Press, 1965, pp. 311-30.

Discusses Blake's artistic forging of a metaphysical unity from cosmic and philosophic dichotomies in his search for a faith combining "forgiveness of sins with 'mental fight'" and uniting "the prophetic anger and the Innocent meekness that a corrupt society had put asunder." See no. 110.

678    Helmstadter, Thomas H.  "Blake and the Age of Reason:  Spectres in
       the NIGHT THOUGHTS."  BlakeS, 5 (1973), 105-39.

       Investigates portrayals of the faculty of reason in Young's
       poem, showing that Blake often depicts his own antirational
       ideas in the process of illustrating the poem and expanding
       on Young's meaning to the point of destroying the falsehood
       of his age.

679    Hilton, Nelson.  "Blake in the Chains of Being."  ECent, 21 (1980),
       212-35.

       Key formations or assertions relating to the intelligibility
       of world in the eighteenth century are manifest "under the
       sign of the chain," and Blake "seizes" on this construct
       in order to explore its nature and finally to subvert "cul-
       tural fetters" and restraint through the freeing act of the
       imagination.

680    Hirsch, E.D., Jr.  INNOCENCE AND EXPERIENCE:  AN INTRODUC-
       TION TO BLAKE.  New Haven, Conn.: Yale Univ. Press, 1964.

       A study of Blake's "central major work" as intrinsically
       valuable as poetry and as an introduction to the later
       prophetic works, taking into account bibliographical facts,
       textual evidence, and varying interpretations of the poem.
       Part 2 contains poem-by-poem commentary.

681    Hollander, John.  "Blake and the Metrical Contract."  In FROM SENSI-
       BILITY TO ROMANTICISM:  ESSAYS PRESENTED TO FREDERICK A.
       POTTLE.  Ed. Frederick W. Hilles and Harold Bloom.  New York:
       Oxford Univ. Press, 1965, pp. 293-310.

       Discusses Blake's choice of conventional or formal, rather
       than expressive, metrical styles as a key to his broader
       poetic intentions and meaning.  See no. 110.

682    Johnson, Mary Lynn.  "Beulah, 'More Seraphim,' and Blake's THEL."
       JEGP, 69 (1970), 258-78.

       Difficult and complex argument contending that the poem
       is not description of an ethereal state and that although
       the setting and characters are "brilliantly fanciful," Thel's
       problem is "down to earth," the poem ending abruptly
       because she is no longer self-deluded however uncertain
       of her fate.

683    _____.  "Emblem and Symbol in Blake."  HLQ, 37 (1974), 151-70.

       Learned discussion of differences between the emblematic
       and symbolic, allegory and myth, juxtaposing seventeenth-

century emblem literature with Blake's practices to indicate his manner of creating a self-sustaining symbolic world and to show that his images are not merely private but indebted to traditional readings of emblematic literature.

684     Jones, Ben. "Blake on Gray: Outlines of Recognition." In FEARFUL JOY: PAPERS FROM THE THOMAS GRAY BICENTENARY CONFERENCE AT CARLETON UNIVERSITY. Ed. James Downey and Ben Jones. Montreal: McGill-Queen's Univ. Press, 1974, pp. 127-35.

Blake's illustrations of Gray show his close and discerning readings of the poem, but his re-creation and improvising method emphasizes his own sense of human joy and sympathy, whereas Gray's sensibility records pain. See. no. 1290.

685     Keith, William J. "The Complexities of Blake's 'Sunflower': An Archetypal Speculation." In BLAKE: A COLLECTION OF ESSAYS. Ed. Northrop Frye. Englewood Cliffs, N.J.: Prentice-Hall, 1966, pp. 56-64.

Reverses the "current critical fashion" by arguing that the apparent simplicity of such a lyric is really suggestive of "deeper significances and possibilities." See no. 605.

686     Leader, Zachary. READING BLAKE'S SONGS. London: Routledge and Kegan Paul, 1981.

A reading of the texts in conjunction with the celebrated designs, treating the interdependence of these two aspects as a single coherent work of visual and verbal art.

687     Lister, Raymond. INTERNAL METHODS: A STUDY OF WILLIAM BLAKE'S ART TECHNIQUES. London: G. Bell and Sons, 1975.

A book avoiding interpretation of Blake's symbolic and philosophic content and focusing instead on the fundamentally important techniques used by him in creating his visual art.

688     Lowery, Margaret R. WINDOWS OF THE MORNING: A CRITICAL STUDY OF WILLIAM BLAKE'S "POETICAL SKETCHES, 1783." New Haven, Conn.: Yale Univ. Press, 1940.

Pioneer study of the sources of Blake's early poetry, locating them mostly in the eighteenth century, rather than in the Elizabethan period.

689     Margoliouth, Herschel M. WILLIAM BLAKE. Oxford: Oxford Univ. Press, 1961.

A well-known scholar and literary historian traces the
development of thought and myth in Blake through a study
of the individual poems.  A good introduction.

690 Mitchell, W.J. Thomas.  BLAKE'S COMPOSITE ART:  A STUDY OF THE
ILLUMINATED POETRY.  Princeton, N.J.:  Princeton Univ.  Press, 1978.

A major book examining Blake's wedding of the poetic and
pictorial in his scenes of illuminated poems, defining the
nature of this composite art, its relationship to the ut
pictura poesis tradition, and indicating ways he transforms
these traditions into his own visionary art form.  Closely
examines THE BOOK OF THEL, THE BOOK OF URIZEN,
and JERUSALEM.

691 _____.  "Poetic and Pictorial Imagination in Blake's THE BOOK OF
URIZEN."  ECS, 3 (1969), 83-107.

Both the pictorial and poetic Urizens indicate Blake's conscious departure from ut pictura poesis and eighteenth-
century theories about the analogies between painting and
poetry.

692 Murry, John Middleton.  WILLIAM BLAKE.  London:  T. Cape, 1933.

Provocatively claims that Blake was a profound Christian
and at the same time "a great Communist" even before
Marx.

693 Nurmi, Martin K.  BLAKE'S MARRIAGE OF HEAVEN AND HELL:  A
CRITICAL STUDY.  Bulletin Research Series 3.  Kent, Ohio:  Kent
State Univ. Press, 1957.

Views the poem as part satire on Swedenborg and part
theoretical treatise on epistemological and ontological
doctrines necessary for a visionary view of existence,
finding it "a shapely masterpiece" designed to change
man's normal perceptions of things by arguing that good
and evil do not exist in the traditional sense, but rather
as creative contraries necessary for human existence.

694 _____.  "Blake's Revisions of 'The Tyger.'"  PMLA, 71 (1956), 669-
85.

Traces Blake's revisions through all of his drafts to clarify
his intentions and the poem's meaning, and conjectures as
to its occasion, based on the evolving pattern.

695 _____.  "Fact and Symbol in 'The Chimney Sweeper' of Blake's SONGS
OF INNOCENCE."  BNYPL, 68 (1964), 249-56.

Contends that a knowledge of the living and working conditions of London's climbing boys (which Blake assumes of
his readers) helps in understanding their general humanitarian and symbolic significance and Blake's oblique and
ironic approach to the subject.

696     \_\_\_\_. "Joy, Love, and Innocence in Blake's 'The Mental Traveller.'"
SIR, 3 (1964), 109-17.

Critical of previous attempts to view the paradigm of the
Ove cycle as the key to the poem's meaning, and argues
that no single key or pattern unlocks the meaning.

697     \_\_\_\_. WILLIAM BLAKE. London: Hutchinson, 1975.

Attempts to make Blake's poetry accessible to the modern
reader and provides the groundwork for the more demanding
studies by Frye, Erdman, and others. Good general introduction.

698     Ostriker, Alicia. VISION AND VERSE IN WILLIAM BLAKE. Madison:
Univ. of Wisconsin Press, 1965.

Pragmatic and sensitive approach to Blake's prosody, con-
centrating on the connections between imagination and
expression and relating technique to an understanding of
poetic essence. Interesting appendix on the influence of
Isaac Watts's hymns on Blake's SONGS OF INNOCENCE
and SONGS OF EXPERIENCE.

699     Paley, Morton D. "Cowper as Blake's Spectre." ECS, 1 (1968), 236-
52.

Direct and indirect references by Blake to Cowper suggest
certain sympathies for his religious-inspired madness and
despair in the guise of the Spectre.

700     \_\_\_\_. ENERGY AND THE IMAGINATION: A STUDY OF THE DE-
VELOPMENT OF BLAKE'S THOUGHT. Oxford: Clarendon Press, 1970.

Comprehensive examination of Blake in relation to certain
intellectual and literary traditions of his past in order to
establish the uniqueness of his rigorous artistic mind, focusing on the twin concepts of energy and imagination as
manifest in several phases of Blake's early and late thought.

701     \_\_\_\_. "The Female Babe and 'The Mental Traveller.'" SIR, 1
(1962), 97-104.

Concentrates on the implications of the female babe as a

symbolic crux, elucidating the poem's pessimistic philosophy of eternal flux through reference to the Lambeth prophecies and THE FOUR ZOAS.

702 _____. "Tyger of Wrath." PMLA, 80 (1966), 540-51.

Traces the history of interpretations of "The Tyger" and explores still further its meaning by connecting it with the Bible, the sublime, and Jacob Boehme and concluding that it is "an apostrophe to wrath" both in the prophetic sense and in what Boehme calles the First Principle.

703 _____. WILLIAM BLAKE. Oxford: Phaidon Press, 1978. Illus.

An introductory essay to the composite art of Blake, "published in a large format with a sufficient number of plates," designed to indicate the rich variety of his productions and the different modes and various media in which he worked. Some reproductions in color. Folio size.

704 Percival, Milton O. WILLIAM BLAKE'S CIRCLE OF DESTINY. New York: Columbia Univ. Press, 1938.

Comprehensive examination of Blake's mythology and symbolism, connecting his usage with their sources in alchemical and biblical, literature and tradition, as well as in the Kabbalistic or Jewish tradition of mystical interpretation of scripture.

705 Raine, Kathleen. BLAKE AND THE NEW AGE. London: George Allen and Unwin, 1979.

Studies Blake's thought in terms of its bearing on changes taking place in the contemporary mind and views him as especially relevant to a modern age that has reversed the premises upon which a materialist world order was built and instead considers the mind as "the first principle of the universe."

706 _____. BLAKE AND TRADITION. 2 vols. Princeton, N.J.: Princeton Univ. Press, 1968.

An attempt to show the influence of Plato and neo-Platonism on Blake's idealism, despite his strong condemnation of Greek philosophy and a lack of evidence that he knew the work of Thomas Taylor, the chief proponent of neo-Platonism in his age.

707 Rose, Edward J. "Blake's Fourfold Art." PQ, 49 (1970), 400-423.

Discusses Blake's symbolism of the body as commentary on his theory of art.

708    Saurat, Denis. BLAKE AND MODERN THOUGHT. London: Constable and Co., 1929.

Examines Blake against the background of the eighteenth century, concluding that he was abreast of late eighteenth-century philosophy, anthropology, and political thought, even in all of its "absurdity," and that his ideas were "perfectly coherent and reasonable."

709    Schorer, Mark. WILLIAM BLAKE: THE POLITICS OF VISION. New York: Henry Holt, 1946.

Studies Blake's mixture of genial and angry temperaments as an important aspect of personality and the peculiar intellectual and aesthetic qualities resulting from this para-doxical temperament against the background of eighteenth-century radical thought, which his poetry both expresses and corrects, concluding that Blake's poetic evolution was a consequence of personal and political factors.

710    Schulz, Max F. "Point of View in Blake's 'The Clod & The Pebble.'" PLL, 2 (1966), 217-24.

Dismisses previous interpretations and presents a case for a "Bardic point of view, which directs our response to the opinions of the Clod and the Pebble."

711    Singer, Jure K. THE UNHOLY BIBLE: A PSYCHOLOGICAL INTER-PRETATION OF WILLIAM BLAKE. New York: G.P. Putnam's Sons, 1970.

Elaborate analysis of Blake's mythological works by a Jungian analyst who deduces from the art an interpretation of his sexual life.

712    Sutherland, John H. "Blake: A Crisis of Love and Jealousy." PMLA, 87 (1972), 424-31.

Closely examines "William Bond," "My Spectre Around Me," and "The Crystal Cabinet," concluding that before the 1790s Blake viewed sexual love as leading to the four-fold vision of eternity, whereas later he associated sexual love with pity and compassion.

713    _____. "Blake's 'Mental Traveller.'" ELH, 22 (1955), 136-47.

Makes use of two complementary approaches to this diffi-

cult poem, first viewing it against parallel figures and
situations in other Blake poems, and second, paying literal
attention to background, situation, and point of view.

714   Swinburne, Algernon Charles. WILLIAM BLAKE: A CRITICAL ESSAY.
      London: John Camden Hotten, 1868.

      Rhapsodic treatment of Blake, ranking THE MARRIAGE OF
      HEAVEN AND HELL "as about the greatest [work] produced
      by the eighteenth century" and asserting that POETICAL
      SKETCHES are "better than any [other] man could do then."

715   Tannenbaum, Leslie. "Blake's News from Hell: THE MARRIAGE OF
      HEAVEN AND HELL and the Lucianic Tradition." ELH, 43 (1976),
      74-99.

      Places Blake in the underworld satiric tradition of Lucian
      to explain his "fusion of classical satire and the Christian
      prophetic tradition," viewing THE MARRIAGE as a Blakean
      version of Renaissance and Miltonic "prophetic satire."

716   Tayler, Irene. BLAKE'S ILLUSTRATIONS TO THE POEMS OF GRAY.
      Princeton, N.J.: Princeton Univ. Press, 1971. Illus.

      Excellent commentary on the genesis, background, and
      realization of these interpretive illustrations of Gray's
      poems, highlighting the qualities and characteristics in
      Gray's verbal art to which Blake responded. The 116
      designs are reproduced in monochrome.

717   Todd, Ruthven. WILLIAM BLAKE: THE ARTIST. London: Studio Vista,
      1971.

      Brief introduction to Blake's work as both a creative and
      commercial artist.

718   Wagenknecht, David. BLAKE'S NIGHT: WILLIAM BLAKE AND THE
      IDEA OF PASTORAL. Cambridge, Mass.: Harvard Univ. Press, 1973.

      Treats Blake's poetical career in terms of a single unifying
      theme and charts his career according to Virgil's program,
      proceeding from pastoralism to the epic by way of Spenser's
      SHEPHERDS CALENDAR and Milton's LYCIDAS and PARA-
      DISE LOST. A fascinating and convincing study.

719   Warren, Leland E. "Poetic Vision and the Natural World: The Spider
      and his Web in the Poetry of William Blake." EnlE, 6, i (1975), 50-
      62.

      Despite Georges Poulet's statement that the idea of a spider in a web produced pleasure in the eighteenth century, Blake interprets this image as pleasurable only in its transcendence by means of the poetic imagination.

720     White, Helen. MYSTICISM OF WILLIAM BLAKE. Madison: Wisconsin Studies in Language and Literature, no. 23, 1927; rpt. New York: Russell and Russell, 1964.

Compares Blake's works and life with texts from the mystical tradition, concluding that he is "not a great mystic in any sense that means anything."

721     Wicksteed, Joseph H. BLAKE'S INNOCENCE AND EXPERIENCE: A STUDY OF THE SONGS AND MANUSCRIPTS, "SHOWING THE TWO CONTRARY STATES OF THE HUMAN SOUL." London: J. Dent, 1928. Illus.

Comprehensive reading of the poems (with reproductions of etchings and manuscript drafts), but often written in a simplistic, personalized, almost confessional style.

722     Wilkie, Brian, and Mary Lynn Johnson. BLAKE'S FOUR ZOAS. Cambridge: Harvard Univ. Press, 1978.

Intended for readers familiar with and those new to the poem. Approaches this encyclopedic work as allegory, verbal structure, narrative, and myth.

723     Witke, Joanne. "Blake's Tree of Knowledge Grows Out of the Enlightenment." EnlE, 3, ii (1972), 71-84.

With reference to JERUSALEM, demonstrates that Blake's doctrine of ideas and knowledge derives not from Platonism, but from both Berkeley's and Hume's skeptical estimation of reason combined with their reliance on the senses and the imagination.

724     Wittreich, Joseph A., Jr. ANGEL OF APOCALYPSE: BLAKE'S IDEA OF MILTON. Madison: Univ. of Wisconsin Press, 1975.

Fully documents the literature of prophecy in the Renaissance and seventeenth century, as well as accounting for the eighteenth-century reaction to Milton, to argue that for Blake, Milton epitomized betrayed radicalism, the timidities of orthodoxy, and, most important, the use of tradition to subvert tradition.

725     _____. "Blake's Milton: 'To Immortals, . . . A Mighty Angel.'" In THE PRESENCE OF MILTON. Ed. B. Rajan. MiltonS, 11 (1978), 51-82.

Points out that Blake was attentive not to the Satanic, but the visionary books of PARADISE LOST, and that his MILTON both criticizes and celebrates, focusing on the moment when natural man rises up against spiritual man and when spiritual man triumphs and becomes the visionary and all-imaginative Jesus.

# SAMUEL BUTLER (1612-80)

## A. MAJOR EDITIONS

726    HUDIBRAS. Ed. Alfred R. Waller. Cambridge: Cambridge Univ. Press, 1905.

> No annotations, but some variants and alternate readings noted.

727    HUDIBRAS. Ed. John Wilders. Oxford: Clarendon Press, 1967.

> Excellent commentary stressing historical and philosophical contexts, along with notes and textual apparatus. Standard edition. See no. 728.

728    HUDIBRAS PARTS I AND II AND SELECTED OTHER WRITINGS. Ed. John Wilders and Hugh de Quehen. Oxford: Clarendon Press, 1973.

> Includes short satires and some of the prose characters. Fully annotated and contains analytical index. See no. 727.

729    CHARACTERS AND PASSAGES FROM NOTEBOOKS. Ed. Alfred R. Waller. Cambridge: Cambridge Univ. Press, 1908.

> Basis of modern texts, but not fully annotated.

730    CHARACTERS. Ed. Charles W. Daves. Cleveland: Press of Case Western Reserve, 1970.

> Based on Waller edition (1908), but fully annotated with textual and explanatory notes that incorporate findings of recent scholarship. Standard edition.

731    PROSE OBSERVATIONS. Ed. Hugh de Quehen. Oxford: Clarendon Press, 1979.

Standard edition of Butler's surviving manuscripts and William
Longueville's Commonplace Book, a collection of Butler's
manuscripts and transcriptions made by his literary heir.
Meticulously annotated and accompanied by a full commentary. Complements Wilders' edition of HUDIBRAS (above).

## B. CORRESPONDENCE AND JOURNALS

732     Quintana, Ricardo. "The Butler-Oxenden Correspondence." MLN, 48
        (1933), 1-11.

        Concerned with the possible identification of the real-life
        model for Sir Hudibras and with the dating of part 1 of
        the poem.

733     Poynter, F.N.L., ed. THE JOURNAL OF JAMES YONGE. London:
        Longmans, 1963.

        Contains a vivid account of Butler's psychological mixture
        of vitality and gloom, both important qualities in his verse,
        by a shrewd contemporary physician.

## 3. BIBLIOGRAPHY AND TEXTUAL STUDIES

734     Thorson, James L. "The Publication of HUDIBRAS." PBSA, 60 (1966),
        418-38.

        Discusses in detail problems establishing an authoritative
        and reliable text and lists editions published during Butler's
        lifetime.

735     _____. "Samuel Butler (1612-1680): A Bibliography." BB, 30 (1973),
        34-39.

        Aims at comprehensiveness and is organized into four
        sections: biography, bibliography, notable editions, and
        criticism.

## D. CRITICISM

736     Curtiss, Joseph Toy. "Butler's Sidrophel." PMLA, 44 (1929), 1066-78.

        Revisions, additions, and references to a spurious continu-
        ation of the Sidrophel episode, all would suggest that
        Butler viewed this astrologer more as a composite figure
        than as a specific individual.

737    Engler, Balz.   "HUDIBRAS and the Problem of Satirical Distance."
       ES, 60 (1979), 436-43.

       Argues that the poem lacks unity and consistency of char-
       acterization, stemming from Butler's failure to resolve con-
       flicts between the satiric mode and "burlesque ridicule,"
       the argument and narrative.

738    Gibson, Day.   "Samuel Butler."   In SEVENTEENTH CENTURY STUDIES.
       Ed. Robert Shafer.   Princeton, N.J.:   Princeton Univ. Press, 1933,
       pp. 279-335.

       Discusses Butler's views on Restoration society, politics,
       the church, and the new science, summarizing his position
       as that of a "rational empiricist" of "censorious disposition"
       who distrusted mankind, "lending a kind of desperate in-
       tensiveness to his practicality."

739    Granger, Bruce Ingham.   "Hudibras in the American Revolution."   AL,
       27 (1956), 499-508.

       Though not generally successful as poetry, the seventy-
       seven Hudibrastic imitations produced in America between
       1765 and 1783 show the impact of the Butler tradition of
       satire up through revolutionary times.

740    Horne, William C.   "Butler's Use of the RUMP in HUDIBRAS."   LI-
       BRARY CHRONICLE, 37 (1971), 126-35.

       RUMP, an anthology of Royalist satiric verse published in
       1662, provides many stock conventions of abuse that Butler
       incorporates into his poem, especially to one involving a
       Roundhead character.

741    Leyburn, Ellen Douglass.   "HUDIBRAS Considered as Satirical Allegory."
       HLQ, 16 (1953), 141-60.

       The sense of "unwarranted confusion" in HUDIBRAS results
       from shifts in the focus of the speeches from allegory to straight
       satire and back again; thus consideration of the poem as
       allegory helps to explain the feeling of critics that it is a
       collection of brilliant parts, not a whole.

742    Miller, Ward S.   "The Allegory in Part I of HUDIBRAS."   HLQ, 21
       (1957-58), 323-43.

       Argues that part 1 is a purposeful allegorical representation
       of historical forces in conflict during the 1640s, and repre-
       sentative of Butler's early antiroyalist sentiments.

743   Nelson, Nicolas H. "Astrology, HUDIBRAS, and the Puritans." JHI, 37 (1976), 521-36.

Scholarly account of the debate over astrology during 1646 to 1661, suggesting that the Sidrophel episode (part 2) satirizes judicial astrology that posits the influence of the stars on specific human events.

744   Quintana, Ricardo. "Samuel Butler: A Restoration Figure in a Modern Light." ELH, 18 (1951), 7-31.

Behind his satire lies Butler the theorist who "succeeded in devising for himself a reasonably comprehensive and self-consistent philosophic system," the character of which clarifies his true intent as satirist.

745   Richards, Edward Ames. HUDIBRAS IN THE BURLESQUE TRADITION. New York: Columbia Univ. Press, 1937.

Accounts for literary particularities characterizing Hudibrastic expression of the Tory or conservative point of view in Butler's social and political poetry and the continuance of this literary tradition up to 1830, in both England and America.

746   Seidel, Michael A. "Patterns of Anarchy and Oppression in Samuel Butler's HUDIBRAS." ECS, 5 (1971-72), 294-314.

Butler's satire does not reflect the usual positive ideals, but rather satiric energy directed at tyrannizer and tyrannized alike, attacking a wide range of social decay ranging from anarchy to authoritarian intimidation.

747   Wasserman, George R. "HUDIBRAS and Male Chauvinism." SEL, 16 (1976), 351-61.

Views the poem in the tradition of "satires on mankind," attacking reason as the primary source of man's pride in part 1, but in parts 2 and 3, ironically kind to his feminine characters as "testimony of his awareness of the presumptive ignorance of rational man, rather than the virtues of women."

748   _____. SAMUEL "HUDIBRAS" BUTLER. Boston: Twayne, 1976.

A good balanced introductory discussion of Butler's background, beliefs, and his satiric vision as reflected in both the poetry and in the prose CHARACTERS, and also a consideration of HUDIBRAS as a general satire against mankind in the tradition of Swift's GULLIVER'S TRAVELS. Incorporates recent criticism.

749 _____. "'A Strange CHIMAERA of Beasts and Men': The Argument and Imagery of HUDIBRAS, Part I." SEL, 13 (1973), 405-21.

> Imagery involving the brutalizing of men and the human-izing of animals suggests that Butler was writing a tradi-tional satire of mankind in which reason becomes the cause of human folly and vice, rather than the mark of man's superiority.

750 Wilding, Michael. "The Last of the Epics: The Rejection of the Heroic in PARADISE LOST and HUDIBRAS." In RESTORATION LITERATURE: CRITICAL APPROACHES. Ed. Harold Love. London: Methuen, 1972, pp. 91-120.

> Informative study of the rejection of literary images of heroic grandeur in the classical epic. See no. 118.

# THOMAS CHATTERTON (1752-70)

## A. MAJOR EDITIONS

751  THE POETICAL WORKS OF THOMAS CHATTERTON.  Ed. Walter W.
Skeat. 2 vols.  London:  George Bell and Sons, 1875.

> Modernized spelling edition which contains an introduction
> asserting that the Rowley poems demonstrate a phraseology
> and diction "no human ingenuity can translate into fifteenth-
> century English."  Interesting account by an eminent
> Chaucerian.

752  THE ROWLEY POEMS.  Ed. Maurice F. Hare.  Oxford:  Oxford Univ.
Press, 1911.

> Reprint of the famous Tyrwhitt edition of 1777.

753  THE COMPLETE WORKS OF THOMAS CHATTERTON.  Ed. Donald S.
Taylor. 2 vols.  Oxford:  Clarendon Press, 1971.

> Includes letters to Chatterton, and makes four particular
> contributions to studies of the poet:  establishment of the
> canon; dating of the Rowley poems; full-scale commentary
> relating to circumstances of composition; a glossary of
> Rowleyan words with possible sources.  Standard edition.

754  MISCELLANIES IN PROSE AND VERSE, 1778.  Menston, Yorkshire,
Engl.:  Scolar Press, 1972.

> Facsimile reprint of this important edition containing poems
> of questionable authenticity.

## B. CORRESPONDENCE

756  Watkins, Jones A.  "Bishop Percy, Thomas Warton, and Chatterton's
Rowley Poems (1773-1790)."  PMLA, 50 (1935), 769-84.

Prints the full text of three letters written by Percy addressing the question of the authenticity of the Rowley poems, which also show that despite their skepticism both antiquarians respected Chatterton's genius.

## C. BIBLIOGRAPHY AND TEXTUAL STUDIES

757    Lamoine, Charles. "Thomas Chatterton: Bicentenary Studies 1770–1970. Unpublished Material in His Life. A Short Unpublished Text by Th. Chatterton." CALIBAN, 8 (1971), 13–37.

Discusses a manuscript life of Chatterton, by one Orton Smith, an obscure biographer who seems to have had friends knowledgeable about Chatterton's life, but who offered incomplete and erroneous information. Also includes a letter to Chatterton by Mary Newton.

758    Mathew, E.R. Norris. BRISTOL BIBLIOGRAPHY, CITY AND COUNTY OF BRISTOL MUNICIPAL PUBLIC LIBRARIES. A CATALOGUE OF BOOKS, PAMPHLETS, COLLECTANEA. Bristol, Engl.: Libraries Committee, 1916.

Exhibition of materials relating to Chatterton.

759    Taylor, Donald S. "The Authenticity of Chatterton's MISCELLANIES IN PROSE AND VERSE." PBSA, 55 (1961), 289–96.

Points out that because John Broughton, the editor and possibly Chatterton's collaborator, had little feeling for Chatterton's non-Rowley poems, the authenticity of all but a few pieces that Chatterton had already identified is in question.

760    _____. "Chatterton: The Problem of the Rowley Chronology and Its Implications." PQ, 46 (1967), 268–77.

Argues that the Rowley poems occupied Chatterton from summer 1768 to spring 1769, and shows by both external and internal evidence the careful ordering of the poems intended for new readers and patrons.

## D. BIOGRAPHY

761    Dix, John. THE LIFE OF THOMAS CHATTERTON. London: Hamilton, Adams, and Co., 1837.

An early version of what became the romantic myth of the helpless, starving poet who was alienated from a hostile society.

762    Ingram, John H. THE TRUE CHATTERTON: A NEW STUDY FROM THE
       ORIGINAL DOCUMENTS. London: T.F. Unwin, 1910.

       An early twentieth-century exposition, representing Chatter-
       ton as the unrecognized and much maligned figure of the
       romantic tradition.

763    Kelly, Linda. THE MARVELLOUS BOY: THE LIFE AND MYTH OF
       THOMAS CHATTERTON. London: Weidenfeld and Nicolson, 1971.

       Sees the life and works of Chatterton as more than symbolic
       of the powerful preoccupation of Romanticism with suicide,
       the cult of youth, and the idea of neglected poetic genius,
       and finds his poetic achievement as deserving of objective
       praise.

764    Meyerstein, Edward H.W. A LIFE OF THOMAS CHATTERTON. Lon-
       don: Ingpen and Grant, 1930.

       An early twentieth-century attempt to analyze and appraise
       the Rowley poems as English poetry and to view Chatterton
       as part of his environment by careful attention to con-
       temporary evidence.

765    Nevill, John Cranstown. THOMAS CHATTERTON. London: Frederick
       Muller, 1948.

       Popular biography; includes letters and discussion of the
       poems.

766    Russell, Charles E. THOMAS CHATTERTON, THE MARVELOUS BOY:
       THE STORY OF A STRANGE LIFE, 1752-1770. New York: Moffat,
       Yard, 1908.

       A later perpetuator of the poor boy myth characterizing
       most nineteenth-century accounts of Chatterton's life and
       art.

767    Taylor, Donald S. "Chatterton's Suicide." PQ, 31 (1952), 63-69.

       Argues that the memorandum book notations and other
       available documents concerning Chatterton's financial
       situation eliminate poverty as a motive for suicide.

768    Wasserman, Earl R. "The Walpole-Chatterton Controversy." MLN,
       54 (1939), 460-62.

       Points to a little-known account by Isaac Reed of the
       controversy surrounding Horace Walpole's refusal of assis-
       tance to Chatterton, which predates the accusations con-
       cerning Walpole's responsibility for Chatterton's failure and

death, and argues that this account, as told to Reed,
tends to verify Walpole's version of the dispute and that
he feared for his reputation and the possibility of ridicule
of his "feeble antiquarianism."

# E. CRITICISM

769    Bronson, Bertrand H. "Chattertoniana." MLQ, 11 (1950), 417-24.

Disagrees with the opinion that the Rowley poems were
inspired by Thomas Percy's RELIQUES OF ANCIENT
ENGLISH POETRY (1765), and argues that passages in
Elizabeth Cooper's THE MUSES LIBRARY (1737) are
strikingly similar to the tone, temper, metrical patterns,
and subject matter of Chatterton's poems.

770    _____. "Thomas Chatterton." In THE AGE OF JOHNSON: ESSAYS
PRESENTED TO CHAUNCEY BREWSTER TINKER. Ed. Frederick W.
Hilles. New Haven, Conn.: Yale Univ. Press, 1949, pp. 239-55.

Chatterton's circumstances as a posthumous child gave rise
to an indissoluble bond between his father, the past, and
death, and thus the Rowleian hoax was a response to "the
deepest promptings of his being," providing his "imaginative faith." See no. 109.

771    Ellinger, Esther Parker. THOMAS CHATTERTON: THE MARVELOUS
BOY, TO WHICH IS ADDED THE EXHIBITION, A PERSONAL SATIRE.
Philadelphia: Univ. of Pennsylvania Press, 1930.

A psychoanalytic study of Chatterton the man and poet.
Transcribes the original manuscript of the satire THE
EXHIBITION as an appendix.

772    See no. 1464.

773    Friedman, Martin B. "Vigny's Use of Chatterton." REVUE DE LITTÉRA-
TURE COMPARÉE, 38 (1964), 262-63.

Chatterton was more than a name and symbol to Vigny,
and his dramatic portrait indicates that he was familiar
with the poet's work.

774    Greenacre, Phyllis. "The Impostor." PSYCHOANALYTIC QUARTERLY,
27 (1958), 359-82.

A detailed Freudian and psychoanalytic account of motivations behind this special type of liar, stressing the importance of the Oedipal phase in the subject's attempt to

achieve a sense of reality and understanding of self. Uses
case method.

775     Guthke, Karl S. "The Rowley Myth in Eighteenth-Century Germany."
        PBSA, 51 (1957), 238-41.

        Discusses the repercussions of Chatterton's "dashing forgeries"
        on the German literary scene, especially as they related
        to the age's growing historical awareness, antiquarianism,
        and preromanticism.

776     Keith-Smith, Brian. "The Chatterton Theme in Modern German Litera-
        ture." In AFFINITIES: ESSAYS IN GERMAN AND ENGLISH LITERA-
        TURE. Ed. R.W. Last. London: Wolff, 1971, pp. 126-38.

        Germans have admired the genius of the wonder boy, but
        have mainly understood him as a victim of society whose
        influence and incomprehension drove him to despair and
        suicide, a symbol of the dangers of rampant individualism.

777     Kroese, Irvin B. "Chatterton's AELLA and Chatterton." SEL, 12
        (1972), 557-66.

        Chatterton is not really different from Aella, who is blind
        to his flaw; but although the poet is aware of the flaw in
        both himself and his hero, Chatterton embraces, not de-
        stroys, his flaw. Yet, both hero and poet refuse to face
        themselves, choosing rather to assert their final selves
        through suicide, thus avoiding the "painful process of
        self-discovery."

778     Lund, Mary Graham. "The Sources of Chatterton's Genius." UKCR,
        25 (1959), 209-17.

        The reality of Chatterton's unconscious mind was formed
        through definite stages of growth: early childhood when
        objects took on a sense of life; two years of reading and
        wandering about Bristol; a subsequent life in Colston School
        where he both imagined a fifteenth-century age of faith
        and lived in the actual eighteenth-century age of reason;
        and three years in which he could not reconcile the con-
        flicts between illusion and reality except in death.

779     Meyerstein, Edward H.W. "Chatterton: His Significance Today."
        In ESSAYS BY DIVERSE HANDS. BEING THE TRANSACTIONS OF
        THE ROYAL SOCIETY OF LITERATURE OF THE UNITED KINGDOM.
        NS, 16 (1937), 61-91.

        A general overview of Chatterton's life, career, and art
        against the background of some "alarums and excursions"
        of this particular decade.

780    Miles, Josephine. "The Language of Ballads." ROMANCE PHILOLOGY, 7 (1953), 1-9.

      General discussion of the structural features and narrative design of ballads, indicating ways in which Chatterton altered and modified the Percy ballads in terms of diction, prosody, and sentiment.

781    Miller, Frances Schouler. "The Historic Sense of Thomas Chatterton." ELH, 11 (1944), 117-34.

      Chatterton's historic sense has four features: it was achieved through self-education; it was a product of a dream world peopled by his own imagination; it was a fabricated world located in real Bristol; and it was spontaneous, not the result of formal training or travel.

782    Northup, Clark S. "Gray and Chatterton." MARK TWAIN QUARTERLY, 5 (1943), 17-18.

      Compares and contrasts these two poets in general terms, showing similarities of background but differences in temperament, and pointing out that Chatterton confused the truth of physical fact with the truth of the imagination.

783    Potter, G.R. "Thomas Chatterton's Epistle to the Reverend Mr. Catcott." MLN, 39 (1924), 336-38.

      Reads the poem as a satire directed against Catcott's TREATISE ON THE DELUGE (1761) and attempts to explain scientifically the religious account of creation as an indication of Chatterton's religious heterodoxy.

784    Powell, C.F. "Thomas Tyrwhitt and the Rowley Poems." RES, 7 (1931), 314-26.

      A reading of the introduction of Tyrwhitt's anonymous publication of the Rowley poems (1777) reveals that his intention was not exposure of fraud and that he made the effort to edit the poems, not to deceive his readers but because he originally thought they were authentic.

785    Price, J.B. "Thomas Chatterton, the Hoaxer." CONTEMPORARY REVIEW, 185 (1954), 95-99.

      A general treatment of Chatterton's power of ventriloquism that cites his original style, his broadening of taste and sentiments through his passionate attachment to medievalism, and his historical importance to the romantic movement.

786     Sypher, Wylie. "Chatterton's AFRICAN ECLOGUES and the Deluge."
        PMLA, 54 (1939), 246-60.

        The geological elements in Chatterton's setting produce a
        kind of imaginative magic similar to the shaping spirit of
        Coleridge's "Kubla Khan" and account for the poem's
        curious imagery of water, sea, mountains, caverns, and
        strange animals.

787     Taylor, Donald S. "Chatterton: Insults and Gifts to the Rev. Mr.
        Catcott." L&P, 22 (1972), 3-43.

        His ambivalent relationship with Reverend Catcott had
        psychic components that help explain persistent themes
        and motifs, his gratuitous satirical attacks, and the
        generally personal nature of much of Chatterton's poetry.

788     _____. THOMAS CHATTERTON'S ART: EXPERIMENTS IN IMAGINED
        HISTORY. Princeton, N.J.: Princeton Univ. Press, 1978.

        Exhaustive account of a difficult poetic achievement stress-
        ing three major problems: the characters of the individual
        poems, the overall tendencies of his widely divergent
        career, and the evaluation of the internal essence of his
        poetic art. Superb study.

789     Ting, Nai-Tung. "The Influence of Chatterton on Keats." KEATS-
        SHELLEY JOURNAL, 5 (1956), 103-08.

        Chatterton's influence on Keats was more considerable than
        has been thought, and lines in "To Autumn" and in "Fancy,"
        among other poems, attest to Keats's extensive borrowings.

# CHARLES CHURCHILL (1731-64)

## A. MAJOR EDITIONS

790     THE POEMS OF CHARLES CHURCHILL.  Ed. James Laver.  2 vols.
        London:  Eyre and Spottiswade, 1933.

> An expensive addition with extensive annotations, but not
> directed toward a scholarly or knowledgeable audience.

791     POETICAL WORKS OF CHARLES CHURCHILL.  Ed. Douglas Grant.
        Oxford:  Clarendon Press, 1956.

> Standard edition with introduction and notes.  Provides
> accurate documentation of Churchill's life-style and draws
> on contemporary newspapers and periodicals for text and
> annotations.

## B. CORRESPONDENCE

792     THE CORRESPONDENCE OF JOHN WILKES AND CHARLES CHURCHILL.
        Ed. Edward H. Weatherly.  New York: Columbia Univ. Press, 1954.

> Introduction treats biographical and historical background
> material pertinent to the political propaganda of THE
> NORTH BRITON.  The sixty or so letters are painstakingly
> edited.

## C. BIBLIOGRAPHY AND TEXTUAL STUDIES

793     Butterfield, Lyman H.  "Charles Churchill and A FRAGMENT OF AN
        EPIC POEM."  HARVARD STUDIES AND NOTES IN PHILOLOGY AND
        LITERATURE, 15 (1933), 313-27.

> Discusses John Hall-Stevenson's political associations with
> Churchill as the probable cause for the mistaken presence

of A FRAGMENT, a nearly-complete mock-heroic poem by
"the most eminent satirist of the time," in the three-volume
Hall-Stevenson WORKS (1795).

794    Van Domelen, John E.   "Charles Churchill's 'Epistle to William Hogarth':
       A Note."   SNL, 8 (1970), 8-10.

       A note in THE WORKS OF CHARLES CHURCHILL (1774)
       contains information that, if authentic and authoritative,
       would suggest Churchill was considering an attack on
       Hogarth prior to his famous caricature of John Wilkes, a
       friend and political ally of the satirist's, but that their
       relation around 1762 was still amicable.

795    Waldhorn, Arthur.   "Charles Churchill and 'Statira.'"   MLN, 63 (1948),
       114-18.

       The nine editions of THE ROSCIAD (1761-64), marked by
       numerous additions and emendations, have caused problems
       for editors of Churchill and "editorial misinterpretation,"
       and the evidence suggests that Statira is George Anne-
       Bellamy.

796    Whitford, Robert C.   "Gleanings of Churchill's Bibliography."   MLN,
       43 (1978), 30-34.

       Identifies a number of authors of anonymous pamphlets
       omitted in the Beatty listing of minor writers influenced
       by Churchill. See no. 803.

797    See no. 72.


# D. BIOGRAPHY

798    Brown, Wallace Cable.   CHARLES CHURCHILL: POET, RAKE, AND
       REBEL.   Lawrence: Univ. of Kansas Press, 1953.

       Critical biography of a writer whose life was a "bundle
       of contradictions," who was the subject of rumor and
       prejudice and a literary unknown.

799    Nobbe, George.   THE "NORTH BRITON": A STUDY IN POLITICAL
       PROPAGANDA.   New York: Columbia Univ. Press, 1939.

       Important study of the Wilkes-Churchill collaboration as
       an important contribution to the history of political liberty,
       analyzing themes, methods, and the impact of the NORTH
       BRITON in comparison to other periodicals of the age and
       in the context of political thinking of the leading figures.

800    Weatherly, Edward H.  "The Personal and Literary Relationship of
       Charles Churchill and David Garrick."  In STUDIES IN HONOR OF
       A.H.R. FAIRCHILD.  Ed. Charles T. Prouty.  Univ. of Missouri
       Studies, 21.  Columbia: Univ. of Missouri Press, 1946, pp. 153-60.

       Discusses the personal relationships between the two men
       and explains Churchill's unexpected attack on Garrick
       (after profusely praising him in THE ROSCIAD [1761]) as
       due to the production of Samuel Foote's TASTE (1752), a
       broad satire directed against Churchill and Robert Lloyd
       and appearing at Drury Lane, Garrick's theatre.

## E. CRITICISM

801    Beatty, Joseph M.  "The Battle of the Players and Poets, 1761-1776."
       MLN, 35 (1919), 449-62.

       Discusses Churchill's attacks on actors and acting techniques
       in THE ROSCIAD (1761) and notes his sympathy for Garrick's
       efforts to develop a natural acting technique.

802    _____.  "Charles Churchill's Treatment of the Couplet."  PMLA, 34
       (1919), 60-69.

       In his general mode of thought and expression Churchill
       is a conservative--"in revolt, to be sure, against the
       school of Pope, yet an imitator of it at every turn," and
       thus his effort to return to Dryden because in him "genius
       and judgment were joined."

803    _____.  "Churchill's Influence on Minor Eighteenth-Century Satirists."
       PMLA, 42 (1927), 162-76.

       Traces the extent of Churchill's influence on third-rate
       satirists, providing a long and useful list of the writers
       and poems that praised or condemned his satire.  See no.
       796.

804    _____.  "Political Satires of Charles Churchill."  SP, 16 (1919), 303-
       33.

       Outlines the political milieu of the 1760s as a setting for
       Churchill's political poetry, especially THE EPISTLE TO
       WILLIAM HOGARTH (1763) and THE DUELLIST (1763[?]),
       the latter characterized by righteous indignation and un-
       relieved polemics in the defense of Wilkes.

805    Brown, Wallace Cable.  "Charles Churchill: A Revaluation."  SP, 40
       (1943), 405-24.

By means of close analysis of the language and style of Churchill's satires, concludes that he is closer to Pope's mode of expression than to Dryden's and that his verse is generally of high quality, especially the satirical portraits.

806    _____. "Charles Churchill and Criticism in Transition." JEGP, 43 (1944), 163-69.

Although he never wrote an essay on criticism or a progress poem, Churchill's views on poetry, revealed in a number of his poems, reflect the transitional state that caught up literary and critical opinion in the mid-century.

807    _____. "Churchill's Mastery of the Heroic Couplet." JEGP, 44 (1945), 12-23.

Argues that although he was beholden to Dryden and Pope, the acknowledged masters of couplet rhetoric, Churchill was an individual craftsman who altered certain technical aspects of the couplet while maintaining the practices of his two predecessors. Views Churchill's norm as the non-epigrammatic couplet.

808    Cunningham, William Francis. "Charles Churchill and the Satiric Portrait." In ESSAYS AND STUDIES IN LANGUAGE AND LITERATURE. Ed. Hubert H. Petit. Pittsburgh: Duquesne Univ. Press, 1964, pp. 110-32.

The Johnson-Boswell exchanges over the matter of Churchill's poetry focused, among other things, on the success of the satirical portrait or character as both a gesture of local and topical satire and an image with universal meaning.

809    Fisher, Alan S. "The Stretching of Augustan Satire: Charles Churchill's 'Dedication' To Warburton." JEGP, 72 (1973), 360-77.

A full-scale study of this masterpiece of Churchill's, showing how he extends the Augustan satiric mode, on what thematic grounds he does so, and the results of this extension in a poem that retains the objective moral imperative--the "must" at the heart of satire--but relocates it in the subjective "personal integrity" of the satirist.

810    See no. 894.

811    Golden, Morris. "Sterility and Eminence in the Poetry of Charles Churchill." JEGP, 66 (1967), 233-46.

Argues that Churchill's inferior status as a satirist was the result of "thematic preoccupations" that "sapped his vigor" and prevented him from being "a seminal revolutionary" and that concerns with and a fascination for power were undermined by profound doubts and nihilism, a situation fatal to the need for positive norms in satire.

812    Hopkins, Kenneth. PORTRAITS IN SATIRE. London: Barrie Books, 1958.

Chapter on Churchill provides a biocritical approach to the life and art of Churchill, emphasizing contemporary opinions, reactions to the poet, and the literary and political implications of his poems.

813    Jefferson, Douglas W. "'Satirical Landscape': Churchill and Crabbe." YES, 6 (1976), 92-100.

Churchill provides linkage between Crabbe and the Augustan satirists, sharing with Pope some of the satirical wit of the Augustans and with Crabbe's descriptions of nature some of the realism and satire.

814    Lockwood, Thomas. POST-AUGUSTAN SATIRE: CHARLES CHURCHILL AND SATIRICAL POETRY, 1750-1800. Seattle: Univ. of Washington Press, 1979.

Using Churchill as a pivotal point in eighteenth-century satire, analyzes distinctions between the method and content of earlier Augustan satire and those of later satire in terms of traditional generic conventions, individual talent, and audience expectation, and concludes that the special characteristic of the later satire is an increasing self-absorption and inwardness.

815    McAdams, William L. "Monstrous Birth: Charles Churchill's Image Cluster." SNL, 8 (1971), 101-04.

Drawing their force from literary allusions as well as from moral and iconographic traditions in pictorial caricature, Churchill's sensuous image clusters of monstrous birth give to his rhetoric the positive values often found missing from his satire.

816    Quaintance, Richard E., Jr. "Charles Churchill as Man of Feeling: A Forgotten Poem by Mackenzie." MLN, 56 (1961), 73-77.

Responding to James Beattie's virulent attack on Churchill's satire of the Scots and Scotland was Henry Mackenzie, whose clichéd sympathetic defense is of interest to students of eighteenth-century sentiment.

817   Simon, Irène. "An Eighteenth-Century Satirist: Charles Churchill."
      REVUE BELGE DE PHILOLOGIE ET D'HISTORIE, 37 (1959), 645-82.

      Essentially a rebuttal of Ivor Winters' unabashed praise of
      Churchill's poetic achievement, especially in THE DEDICA-
      TION (1765); but also a thorough biographical and critical
      review which concludes with a favorable though qualified
      evaluation of Churchill's art. See no. 822.

818   Smith, Raymond J. CHARLES CHURCHILL. Boston: Twayne, 1977.

      Describes, analyzes, and evaluates the writings of Churchill,
      treating the major poems (and also some contributions to
      THE NORTH BRITON) as independent artistic structures
      and, in the literary and political context of the age, re-
      marking on Churchill's single-mindedness, his nonconformity,
      and vigorous opposition to political or literary tyranny in
      any form.

819   Wasserman, Earl R. "The Return of the Enjambed Couplet." ELH, 7
      (1940), 244-45.

      The theory of versification in the eighteenth century was
      founded on the classical ideal of variety in uniformity,
      but in the poetry of Churchill are found some early pro-
      tests against the constraints of this verse form. Thus, when
      he expresses emotional or dramatic ideas that demand move-
      ment and a sense of progress, Churchill imitates the en-
      jambment of Dryden.

820   Weatherly, Edward H. "Charles Churchill: Neo-Classic Master."
      UKCR, 20 (1954), 266-71.

      General overview of Churchill's achievement, both in
      political and literary satire, noting that unlike the usual
      case of contemporary indifference, Churchill was instan-
      taneously successful and was lionized in literary circles.

821   _____. "Churchill's Literary Indebtedness to Pope." SP, 43 (1946),
      59-69.

      Critics have long overestimated Dryden's influence on
      Churchill, but a detailed study of his poetry reveals that
      he shares with Pope the frequent use of his own "narrowly
      personal interests as a theme of his poetry."

822   Winters, Ivor. "The Poetry of Charles Churchill." In his FORMS OF
      DISCOVERY: CRITICAL AND HISTORICAL ESSAYS ON THE FORMS
      OF THE SHORT POEM IN ENGLISH. Denver: Alan Swallow, 1967,
      pp. 121-45.

Although dogmatic and assertive, provides many insights
into Churchill's employment of an "associative structure" from
his early satiric-didactic poems to the "truly cohesive" and
unified study of evil in "THE DEDICATION, the greatest
English poem of the eighteenth century." See nos. 817 and
132.

# WILLIAM COLLINS (1721-59)

## A. MAJOR EDITIONS

823     THE POETICAL WORKS OF GRAY AND COLLINS.   Ed. Austin Lane
Poole and Christopher Stone.   3rd ed. rev.   London:   Oxford Univ.
Press, 1937.

       Original 1917 publication corrected and revised by Leonard
Whibley (Gray's poems) and Frederick Page (Collins' poems).
Basis for modern editions.

824     THE POEMS OF THOMAS GRAY, WILLIAM COLLINS AND OLIVER
GOLDSMITH.   Ed. Roger Lonsdale.   London:   Longman, 1969.

       Valuable comprehensive edition designed for modern compre-
hensibility, and thus sensibly modernized in spelling and
uniform in accidentals.   Provides extensive biobibliographi-
cal and historical commentary, as well as extensive annotation and helpful identification of the extensive borrowings
(especially Gray and Collins) from other writers.

825     THE POETICAL WORKS OF THOMAS GRAY AND WILLIAM COLLINS.
Ed. Roger Lonsdale.   Oxford:   Oxford Univ. Press, 1977.

       Arranges Gray's poems in order of composition and prints
the Eton manuscript of the ELEGY as an appendix.   Follows
Poole edition regarding arrangement of poems, but adds
"Drafts and Fragments" from the Warton manuscripts and the
recovered "Ode on the Popular Superstitions of the Highlands."   Text, apparatus, and variants supplied and revised
in light of recent scholarship; brief headnotes provide full
information about the poems.

826     THE WORKS OF WILLIAM COLLINS.   Ed. Richard Wendorf and
Charles Ryskamp.   Oxford:   Clarendon Press, 1979.

       Provides an old-spelling text with full reference to manu-

scripts and early printings, as well as complete textual
and critical commentary. Establishes a text "faithful to
the contemporary texts which Collins 'intended.'" Standard
modern edition.

## B. CORRESPONDENCE

827    White, A.O. "The Letters of William Collins." RES, 3 (1927), 12-21.

        Discusses the literary characteristics of Collins' two extant
letters, remarking on their similarity to the techniques and
concerns of his poetry.

## C. BIBLIOGRAPHY AND TEXTUAL STUDIES

828    Cunningham, Joseph S., ed. DRAFTS AND FRAGMENTS OF VERSE.
Edited from the Manuscripts. Oxford: Clarendon Press, 1956.

        Contains valuable material pertaining to Collins' creative
process and principles of textual revision.

829    Lamont, Claire. "William Collins's 'Ode on the Popular Superstitions
of the Highlands of Scotland'--A Newly Recovered Manuscript." RES,
NS 19 (1968), 137-47.

        One of the few manuscripts of Collins' extant and therefore
of considerable interest.

830    See no. 73.

## D. BIOGRAPHY

831    Ainsworth, Edward G., Jr. POOR COLLINS: HIS LIFE, HIS ART,
AND HIS INFLUENCE. Ithaca, N.Y.: Cornell Univ. Press, 1937.

        A full account of Collins as man and poet, discussing his
life, stressing literary sources of his poetry, and assessing
his influence on the younger romantics.

832    Carver, P.L. LIFE OF A POET: A BIOGRAPHICAL SKETCH OF
WILLIAM COLLINS. New York: Horizon Press, 1967.

        A detailed study of Collins' life and poetry, correcting
biographical inaccuracies and identifying as apocryphal
some accounts of the textual history of his poems.

833    Steward, Mary Margaret. "William Collins and Thomas Barrow." PQ,
       48 (1969), 212-19.

>    The "cordial youth" of line 5 in his "Ode on the Popular
>    Superstitions of the Highlands of Scotland" has been identi-
>    fied, since the first publication of the ode in 1785, as
>    Thomas Barrow; and new biographical materials and legal
>    records help to clarify the confusing last lines in the ode,
>    to identify the "destin'd bride," and to shed light on
>    Collins' friendship with John Blair and his Scottish circle
>    in London.

834    Wendorf, Richard. "'Poor Collins' Reconsidered." HLQ, 42 (1979),
       91-116.

>    A valuable corrective of the tendency of critics to romanti-
>    cize Collins as mad poet, pointing out that though he may
>    have suffered periods of psychosis and though his poetry
>    manifests irrational elements often associated with madness,
>    Collins wrote his poetry at a time when he was lucid and
>    free from physical or mental illness.

## E. CRITICISM

835    Brooks, E.L. "William Collins' 'Ode on the Poetical Character.'"
       CE, 17 (1956), 403-04.

>    Focuses on the disputed passage about the weaving of the
>    Cestus of Poethood and shows parallels between Collins'
>    creation of the myth of the poetical character and the
>    creation myth in the Bible.

836    Brown, Mark E. "On William Collins' 'Ode to Evening.'" EIC, 11
       (1961), 136-53.

>    Not merely conventionalized personification of nature nor
>    feeling devoid of thought, the ode demonstrates Collins
>    using nature while completing its meaning through an ef-
>    fective fusion of reason and imagination.

837    Collins, Martha. "The Self-Conscious Poet: The Case of William
       Collins." ELH, 42 (1975), 362-94.

>    Argues that Collins' "self-conscious awareness of his poetic
>    role" stands between his depersonalized moralizing on art
>    in the early period and his later unrestrained use of the
>    poetic self, a theme in romantic poetry.

838    Crider, John R. "Structure and Effect in Collins' Progress Poems." SP,
       60 (1963), 57-72.

Analyzes the translatio studii tradition behind these poems and shows how structural features indicate Collins' paradoxical position on the matter of artistic progress: genuine literary renewal depends on individual inspiration but inspiration must derive from the example of past poetic achievement.

838A    Eversole, Richard. "Collins and the End of the Shepherd Pastoral." In SURVIVALS OF PASTORAL. Ed. Richard F. Hardin. Lawrence: Univ. of Kansas Publications, 1979, pp. 19-32.

Interesting account of the changing attitudes toward pastoral fictions in the eighteenth century, finding in Collins' PERSIAN ECLOGUES (1742) an aspiring young poet attempting to find "a new means for an idealized shepherd pastoral that referred to objective conditions" and "credible circumstances." See no. 371.

839    Garrod, Heathcote William. COLLINS. Oxford: Oxford Univ. Press, 1928.

Generally negative treatment by a sensitive reader who combines textual commentary with critical analysis, noting faults in Collins' syntax and ear for poetry.

840    Hartman, Geoffrey. "Romantic Poetry and the Genius Loci." In his BEYOND FORMALISM: LITERARY ESSAYS, 1958-1970. New Haven, Conn.: Yale Univ. Press, 1970, pp. 321-26.

Identifies in Collins' poetry, especially "Ode to Evening," the genius loci or local spirit that presides over and is immanent in his concept of nature.

841    Johnston, Arthur. "The Poetry of William Collins." PBA, 59 (1973), 321-40.

Overview of Collins' accomplishment, stressing the occasional nature of even his most visionary pieces and his original use of poetic tradition.

842    Kallich, Martin. "'Plain in Thy Neatness': Horace's Pyrrha and Collins' Evening." ELN, 3 (1966), 265-71.

Despite the "clearly defined differences in meaning and tone" between the "Ode to Evening" and Milton's literal version of Horace, Collins, who viewed his predecessor as the true "poetical character," borrowed not only prosody, but also words, phrases, and tonal features from Milton's translation.

843    Mackail, John W. "Collins and the English Lyric." In his STUDIES
OF ENGLISH POETS. London: Longmans, Green, 1926, pp. 137-56.

> Appreciation of Collins' lyric gift, foreshortened and under-
> developed as it was, in an age not noted for its gift of
> song.

844    McKillop, Alan D. "Collins' 'Ode to Evening'--Background and Structure." TSL, 5 (1960), 73-83.

> Argues for the importance of the pictorial traditions of the
> period as a possible explanation for Collins' forging of
> natural description, allegory, and private meditations into
> a unified whole.

845    _____. "The Romanticism of William Collins." SP, 70 (1923), 1-16.

> Points out that Collins' allegorical abstractions and other
> conventions place him squarely in the eighteenth-century
> poetical tradition, but that a sense of the inadequacy of
> these traditional forms of expression infuses his ardor,
> sincerity, and imaginative passion.

846    Murry, John Middleton. "The Poetry of William Collins." In his
COUNTRIES OF THE MIND: ESSAYS IN LITERARY CRITICISM. New
York: E.P. Dutton, 1922, pp. 81-99.

> Pictures Collins' poetry (excepting "Ode to Evening") as
> lacking the technical mastery and style necessary to free
> and shape a rich poetic sensibility.

847    Ober, William B. "Madness and Poetry: A Note on Collins, Cowper,
and Smart." BULLETIN OF THE NEW YORK ACADEMY OF MEDI-
CINE, 2nd ser., 46 (1970), 203-66.

> Exhaustive biocritical study of these three poets, stressing
> the idea "that they wrote the kind of poetry they did and
> used the language of poetry in a particular fashion because
> their mental condition enabled them to perceive reality in
> a fashion different from the ordinary run of men"; concludes
> that Collins and Cowper were both overtly psychotic, but
> that Smart's case is "debatable," the most suitable diagnosis
> being "religious monomania without intellectual deteriora-
> tion."

848    Pettit, Henry. "Collins' 'Ode to Evening' and the Critics." SEL, 4
(1964), 361-69.

> Helpful discussion of the critical tradition growing up
> around Collins in general and the ode in particular over
> the centuries. Argues that his success is marked by

"originality within perfectly traditional patterns" and that in the second and third sections of the ode the thematic connections between nature's influence and human values in a chaotic world are felt in the very images and abstractions so often maligned.

849    Quintana, Ricardo. "The Scheme of Collins's ODES ON SEVERAL . . . SUBJECTS." In RESTORATION AND EIGHTEENTH-CENTURY LITERATURE: ESSAYS IN HONOR OF ALAN DUGALD McKILLOP. Ed. Carroll Camden. Chicago: Univ. of Chicago Press, 1963, pp. 371-80.

Like all eighteenth-century poetry, this volume, as well as the twelve individual poems that compose it, is "organized around a core of compositional logic, showing in this respect a kind of ordering that is close to that given in rhetoric," and its basic aesthetic purpose is to explore "the resources of poetry" and to express "the hopes and desires of a civilized community." See no. 103.

850    Sherwin, Paul S. PRECIOUS BANE: COLLINS AND THE MILTONIC LEGACY. Austin: Univ. of Texas Press, 1977.

Argues that Collins' inventiveness, originality, and daring experimentations in the sublime and visionary modes are made possible by his imaginative accommodation with the legacy of Milton "as epochless being who drew his inspiration from deeper and older sources than any other poet."

851    Sigworth, Oliver F. WILLIAM COLLINS. New York: Twayne, 1965.

Collins' importance does not lie so much with his influence on the romantics or his place in literary history as with the considerable technical resources with which he shaped and conveyed a unique and intense vision of reality. Good general introduction by a sensitive critic.

852    Spacks, Patricia Meyer. "Collins' Imagery." SP, 62 (1965), 719-36.

Imagery provides for Collins a means to fuse the literal and metaphoric, the real and imaginery, and such a process of poetic self-discovery belongs to "a grand poetic tradition."

853    Stitt, Peter A. "William Collins' 'Ode to Evening.'" CP, 5, i (1972), 27-33.

Example of Collins' "lyrical talent," whereby the poet consciously emphasizes his meaning by skillfully using such poetic devices as assonance, consonance, metrical variation, and alliteration, as well as a syntax complementary to the subject matter and structure of the poem.

854    Sypher, Wylie.  "The MORCEAU DE FANTAISIE in Verse:  A New
       Approach to Collins."  UTQ, 15 (1945), 65-69.

       Considers the poetical character of Collins' imagery, sym-
       bols, and psychic representations in which he "cast into
       fantastic derangement the plastic visions that had better
       be called genre pittoresque than romantic."

855    Tillyard, E.M.W.  "William Collins's ODE ON THE DEATH OF THOM-
       SON."  REL, 1, iii (1960), 30-38.

       Excellent close analysis of language and style in the poem,
       showing that the much-maligned conventions of the period
       are functional and alive.

856    Tompkins, J.M.S.  "'In Yonder Grave a Druid Lies.'"  RES, 22 (1946),
       1-16.

       Not a flawed choice of words, the term druid in Collins'
       ode appropriately refers to Thomson as the modern Druid,
       "poet-priest of nature, the patriot glorifying liberty, the
       devout enthusiast of a benevolent Creative Spirit."

857    Van Der Weele, Steve J.  "Proverbs 8 and William Collins's 'Ode on
       the Poetical Character.'"  PLL, 12 (1976), 197-200.

       The ode resembles the Proverbs chapter in the following
       ways:  both writers create a fictional subject whose signifi-
       cance is obliquely conveyed through certain characterizing
       details; the subject of each passage claims timelessness;
       each subject boasts that the deity is infatuated with imagi-
       native creation; and the poet of the ode and the writer of
       Proverbs share the sense "that poetry and wisdom are fused
       into one aesthetic and intellectual vision."

858    Vivante, Leone.  "The Concept of a Creative Principle in the Poems
       of Collins and Gray."  COMPARATIVE LITERATURE STUDIES (Cardiff),
       8 (1942), 12-17.

       Discusses rhapsodically the principle of simplicity that "dis-
       engages the intrinsic, the primal, and the eternal character
       of self-activity" (Collins), and of "the essential, radically
       ontological character of the truths in which Gray's life and
       mind are centered."

859    Wasserman, Earl R.  "Collins's 'Ode on the Poetical Character.'"  ELH,
       34 (1967), 92-115.

       The essential energy of the ode derives not from Collins'
       candid delineation of levels of poetic accomplishment, but
       rather from the presence of the poet caught up in a tension

between divine aspirations and sense of human limitations which paradoxically dissolves at the moment he achieves a Godlike visionary state and resigns himself to "merely human talents."

860    Wendorf, Richard.   "Collins's Elusive Nature."   MP, 76 (1979), 231-39.

Studies the largely neglected ode entitled "The Manners" as giving a fresh perspective on Collins' conception of nature and, like his other major odes of 1745 to 1746, as providing a complex definition of nature, celebrating its objective and external features, but questioning "our ability to perceive that world in all its shapes and colors," while still affirming "our reliance on the reflections of art."

860A       .   WILLIAM COLLINS AND EIGHTEENTH-CENTURY ENGLISH POETRY.   Minneapolis:   Univ. of Minnesota Press, 1981.

Demonstrates that Collins' gift for myth-making places him in the tradition of mythic poetry ranging from Shakespeare and Spenser to that of the Romantics, and argues that his confrontation with such predecessors as Spenser, Milton, and Pope helped produce his best work. A major study.

861    Woodhouse, Arthur S.P.   "Collins and the Creative Imagination: A Study in the Critical Background of his Odes (1746)."   In STUDIES IN ENGLISH BY MEMBERS OF UNIVERSITY COLLEGE TORONTO.   Ed. M.W. Wallace.   Toronto:   Univ. of Toronto Press, 1931, pp. 59-130.

A seminal and lengthy account of the emergence of the concept of the creative imagination in the eighteenth century and the poet's passionate desire for its transcendent power implicit in the literary themes of Joseph Warton and revealed in the poetry of Collins, especially the "Ode on the Poetical Character." See no. 862.

862       .   "The Poetry of Collins Reconsidered."   In FROM SENSIBILITY TO ROMANTICISM: ESSAYS PRESENTED TO FREDERICK A. POTTLE.   Ed. Frederick W. Hilles and Harold Bloom.   New York:   Oxford Univ. Press, 1965, pp. 93-137.

A comprehensive account (supplementing and correcting his earlier effort) of Collins' debt to neoclassical aesthetics and his exploitation of feeling, imagination, and sentiment artistically fused with allegory, description, and other familiar poetic techniques in a new aesthetic context. See no. 861.

# WILLIAM COWPER (1731-1800)


## A. MAJOR EDITIONS

863 THE LIFE AND WORKS OF WILLIAM COWPER. Ed. Robert Southey. 14 vols. 1835; rpt. New York: AMS, 1971.

864 THE POETICAL WORKS OF WILLIAM COWPER. Ed. Humphrey S. Milford. Oxford: Oxford Univ. Press, 1907.

> Standard modern text, but will be superseded by new Clarendon Press edition, below.

865 THE POEMS OF WILLIAM COWPER. Ed. John D. Baird and Charles Ryskamp. Vol. 1: 1748-1782. Oxford: Clarendon Press, 1980-- .

> Meant to "stand in place" of projected Povey edition; incorporates recent discoveries of manuscripts and other biobibliographical materials. A superbly edited, annotated, and indexed edition, utilizing the best modern editing practices.

866 THE TASK (1785). London: Scolar, 1973.

> A facsimile reproduction of a well-known edition, with a new introduction.


## B. CORRESPONDENCE

867 Danchin, Pierre. "William Cowper's Poetic Purpose as Seen in His Letters." ES, 46 (1965), 235-44.

> Utilizes a "strictly historical approach" to the correspondence of Cowper's "authentic and plainly sincere letters," never intended for publication, in order to show their "literary and critical interest."

868    THE CORRESPONDENCE OF WILLIAM COWPER.  Ed. Thomas Wright.
       4 vols.  London:  Hodder and Stoughton, 1904.

          Standard edition, but incomplete and at times inaccurate
          in certain details.  Will be superseded by King-Ryskamp
          edition, below.

869    THE UNPUBLISHED AND UNCOLLECTED LETTERS OF WILLIAM COWPER.
       Ed. Thomas Wright.  London:  C.J. Farncombe, 1925.

          Supplements four-volume edition of 1904.  See no. 868.

870    THE LETTERS AND PROSE WRITINGS OF WILLIAM COWPER.  Ed. James
       King and Charles Ryskamp.  Vol. 1:  ADELPHI AND LETTERS 1750-1781.
       Oxford:  Clarendon Press, 1979.

          Restores the textual accuracy of the "very best letters that
          were ever published" (Blake) to their original length and
          adds newly discovered correspondence.  Will be standard
          edition when completed.  Three more volumes of corres-
          pondence projected and a fifth will contain the prose (in-
          cluding essays and reviews).

## C. BIBLIOGRAPHY AND CONCORDANCES

871    Eaves, T.C. Duncan, and Ben D. Kimpel.  "Cowper's 'An Ode on
       Reading Mr. Richardson's HISTORY OF SIR CHARLES GRANDISON."
       PLL, 2 (1966), 74-75.

          On the basis of the copy of the poem in the Forster Col-
          lection, speculates that the poem was written after Cowper
          read the novel, published in 1753, and that when he later
          met Richardson he made the drastic revisions in the last
          stanza that omit direct mention of the author.

872    Hartley, Lodwick C.  WILLIAM COWPER: THE CONTINUING RE-
       VALUATION; AN ESSAY AND BIBLIOGRAPHY OF COWPERIAN
       STUDIES FROM 1895 TO 1960.  Chapel Hill:  Univ. of North Carolina
       Press, 1960.

          An annotated bibliography combined with a helpful dis-
          cussion of recent trends in Cowper scholarship, and some
          interesting remarks on his poetic art.

873    Neve, John.  A CONCORDANCE TO THE POETICAL WORKS OF
       WILLIAM COWPER.  1887; rpt.  New York:  Burt Franklin, 1969.

          Keyed to the Aldine Edition of the British Poets.

874 Povey, Kenneth. "Notes for a Bibliography of Cowper's Letters." RES, 7 (1931), 182-87.

> Lists additional letters and some corrections of the Thomas Wright (1904) edition of the correspondence.

875 Ringler, Richard N. "The Genesis of Cowper's 'Yardley Oak.'" ELN, 5 (1967), 27-32.

> Discusses evidence, both major and minor, for redating the composition of the poem, and explains that Cowper's interest in Erasmus Darwin's ECONOMY OF VEGETATION, which seems to have influenced the language and imagery of this "magnificent fragment," makes 1792 the more likely year of composition than 1791.

876 Russell, Norma. A BIBLIOGRAPHY OF WILLIAM COWPER, TO 1837. Oxford: Clarendon Press, 1963.

> Lists all that was published by Cowper during his life and items published about him that appeared during his life and after his death up to the date of Robert Southey's WORKS, 1835-37.

877 Zall, Paul M. "A Variant Version of Cowper's 'The Rose.'" HLQ, 25 (1962), 253-56.

> Two versions, one in the hands of Cowper's cousin John Johnson and the other an autograph copy, reveal that Cowper preferred his revised version over Johnson's because he was trying at this point of his career to depersonalize the references to Mary Unwin.

## D. BIOGRAPHY

878 Cecil, David. THE STRICKEN DEER; OR, THE LIFE OF COWPER. Indianapolis: Bobbs-Merrill, 1930.

> Sensitive, but often discursive, appreciation of Cowper's life and art against his eighteenth-century background, portraying him as tragic figure for whom religion gave no solace.

879 Fausset, Hugh I. WILLIAM COWPER. London: Jonathan Cape, 1928.

> Makes a case for the harmful effects of Evangelicalism on Cowper's mind and art.

880 Gregory, Hoosag K. "The Prisoner and His Crimes: Summary Comments

on a Longer Study of the Mind of William Cowper." L&P, 6 (1956), 53-59.

> Freudian approach to Cowper's relationship with his clergy-man father, arguing for its impact on and explanation for his religious fears, mental health, and poetic themes.

881 Hartley, Lodwick. "Cowper and the Polygamous Parson." MLQ, 16 (1955), 137-41.

> Argues that Mary Unwin's capacity for poetically inspiring Cowper has been overrated and that his letters between 1780 and 1781 convincingly show that Cowper turned to writing verse on a larger scale than ever before because of "a tempest in the Evangelical teapot involving his cousin, the Reverend Martin Modan, and his friend John Newton, whose removal to London had by no means dis-placed him as an important influence."

882 _____. "Cowper and the Evangelicals: Notes on Early Biographical Interpretation." PMLA, 65 (1950), 719-31.

> Discusses some of the early documentation connected with the ongoing controversy over the part Evangelicalism or Methodism played in causing Cowper's insanity.

883 _____. WILLIAM COWPER, HUMANITARIAN. Chapel Hill: Univ. of North Carolina Press, 1938.

> Argues persuasively that, despite his reclusive personality, Cowper was a man of his age, speaking out on a wide variety of humanitarian concerns, among them the fate of the poor and enslaved, the horrors of war, and corrupt educational practices.

884 Hayley, William. THE LIFE AND POSTHUMOUS WRITINGS OF WILLIAM COWPER, ESQ. 3 vols. Chichester, Engl.: J. Johnson, 1803.

> Contains biographical information and some writings collected by Cowper's frequent correspondent.

885 MacLean, Kenneth. "William Cowper." In THE AGE OF JOHNSON: ESSAYS PRESENTED TO CHAUNCEY BREWSTER TINKER. Ed. Frederick W. Hilles. New Haven, Conn.: Yale Univ. Press, 1949, pp. 257-67.

> The presence of psychic terror in Cowper's autobiographical MEMOIR, his letters, and the nature imagery in his poems should be not merely of sensationalist interest to the modern reader but a record of a sincere but painful truth of charac-ter. See no. 109.

886  Nicholson, Norman. WILLIAM COWPER. London: Lehmann, 1951.

A critical life that stresses Cowper's popularity as "the conscience of the middle classes," his influence on politics and society in England, and his complex relationship with the Evangelical revival, at once stimulating his verse as well as repressing his love of nature for its own sake.

887  Quinlan, Maurice. WILLIAM COWPER: A CRITICAL LIFE. Minneapolis: Univ. of Minnesota Press, 1953.

Argues that Cowper is best understood when studied in relation to his life and to the changing intellectual milieu of the late eighteenth century, and notes his constant fear of damnation and subsequent fits of insanity as well as his role in espousing a new Evangelicalism, his interest in the natural world, and the highly lyrical and personalized effects in his poetry.

888  Ryskamp, Charles. WILLIAM COWPER OF THE INNER TEMPLE, ESQ.: A STUDY OF HIS LIFE AND WORKS TO THE YEAR 1768. Cambridge: Cambridge Univ. Press, 1959.

"A comprehensive early life" conceived as a demythologizing corrective to earlier biographical preoccupation with Cowper's religious problem and psychological disorders, emphasizing "facts and problems" through newly discovered letters, poems, and evidence about his early career.

889  Thomas, Gilbert Oliver. WILLIAM COWPER AND THE EIGHTEENTH CENTURY. 2nd ed. rev. London: George Allen and Unwin, 1948.

Deals with the claim that Evangelicalism caused Cowper's insanity, insisting that his mental disease was congenital and not the result of a conflict in his consciousness between Calvinism and Arminianism.

## E. CRITICISM

890  Boyd, David. "Satire and Pastoral in THE TASK." PLL, 10 (1974), 363-77.

The pastoral sections are merely a vehicle for Cowper's negative judgments on the urban world, a "flight, not only from the corruption of the world, but also from the boredom of its moral responsibilities."

891  Brown, Marshall. "The Pre-Romantic Discovery of Consciousness." SIR, 17 (1978), 387-412.

At times a dense and difficult structuralist-deconstructionist approach to. Cowper's style and poetic consciousness, focusing on THE TASK; "the force of Cowper's style . . . is reconstructive as well as deconstructive. If it undermines the urban sublime, it does so in order to establish a new synthesis. Cowper's poetry is engaged in a search for a unified origin and stable foundation for experience."

892    See no. 468.

893    Free, William N. WILLIAM COWPER. New York: Twayne, 1970.

Attempts to refocus previous interest in Cowper's life, mental health, religious faith, and literary influence to account for his poetic achievement, showing how "the residue of his experiences appears in such formal aspects of his poetry as theme, structure, tone, and metaphor." Good introduction.

894    Golden, Morris. "Churchill's Literary Influence on Cowper." JEGP, 58 (1959), 655-65.

Compares passages from the two poets to show the extent of Churchill's influence on Cowper's satiric themes, targets, and rhetorical strategies.

895    _____. IN SEARCH OF STABILITY: THE POETRY OF WILLIAM COWPER. New York: Bookman Associates, 1960.

Main focus of this study is "the nature of Cowper's mental preoccupations [especially with authority, society, and stability] . . . and the ways in which these preoccupations intrude themselves upon and shape some of the poems, notably THE TASK."

896    Hartley, Lodwick. "Harlequin Intrudes: William Cowper's Venture into the Satiric Mode." In THE DRESS OF WORDS: ESSAYS ON RESTORATION AND EIGHTEENTH-CENTURY LITERATURE IN HONOR OF RICHMOND P. BOND. Ed. Robert B. White, Jr. Lawrence: Univ. of Kansas Libraries, 1978, pp. 127-37.

Cites "Anti-Thelyphtora: A Tale in Verse" as an example of Cowper's amusing merger of the religious movement of Methodism with the traditions of the mock-heroic poem, representing the short-lived intrusion of the "Harlequin" mode into his poetic sensibility between 1780 and 1781.

897    _____. "'The Stricken Deer' and His Contemporary Reputation." SP, 36 (1939), 637-50.

A consideration of the particular social, religious, and moral preoccupations of the late eighteenth century is essential for understanding the wide popularity of Cowper's writings.

898    See no. 872.

899    _____. "The Worm and the Thorn: A Study of Cowper's OLNEY HYMNS." JOURNAL OF RELIGION, 29 (1949), 220-29.

Reads Cowper's lyrics in the order in which they appear in OLNEY HYMNS, arguing that though such a procedure does some violence to the exact chronology of individual pieces, it increases perception of the essential unity of the series and enhances appreciation of their "literary effectiveness as a spiritual record."

900    Huang, Ts'ui-en (Roderick). WILLIAM COWPER, NATURE POET. London: Oxford Univ. Press, 1977.

Finds in Cowper's nature poetry a fusion of moral didacticism (Methodism, in this case) with depictions of country and rural life in the tradition of Thomson, Young, and Goldsmith.

901    Kroitor, Harry P. "The Influence of Popular Science on William Cowper." MP, 61 (1964), 281-87.

A man of the eighteenth century, Cowper sought both scientific precision and philosophical accuracy in his art, but he often went beyond fact, and even theory, to rearrange imaginatively detailed accounts of scientific phenomena for poetic purposes.

902    Long, Ada W. "Quantitative Stylistics: A New Look at the Poetry of William Cowper." STYLE, 12 (1978), 319-25.

The old distinctions between natural and rhetorical (spontaneous and self-conscious) style in Cowper's verse misrepresent the true reasons for his stylistic differences, and computer-assisted quantification reveals that figures such as synedoche, repetition, and enumeration predominate the natural style while syllepsis and inversion characterize the rhetorical style.

903    Musser, Joseph F., Jr. "William Cowper's Rhetoric: The Picturesque and the Personal." SEL, 19 (1979), 515-31.

Both aesthetic predilections toward the picturesque and acute self-consciousness produce in THE TASK "a rhetoric that demands the active engagement of the reader."

904 _____. "William Cowper's Syntax as an Indication of His Relationship to the Augustans and Romantics." STYLE, 11 (1977), 284-302.

Closely compares syntactical formulations in Cowper's and Pope's rhetoric, arguing that the frequency of compound phrases and clauses in his couplets suggests that for Pope there can be "shared perception of truth based on accumulation of external detail," whereas in Cowper's complex syntax "the perception of truth depends on his adopting the appropriate mode of thought which is externally determined."

905 See no. 847.

906 Quinlan, Maurice J. "Cowper's Imagery." JEGP, 47 (1948), 276-85.

An account of certain recurring biblical images and diction in Cowper's highly subjective poetry and prose as an indication of deep-seated religious fear and acute melancholia.

907 _____. "An Intermediary between Cowper and Johnson." RES, 24 (1948), 141-47.

A discussion of evidence suggesting that Samuel Johnson specifically encouraged a critic to review Cowper's poems, concluding that the volume was so "genuinely moral and religious in tone" that the pious Johnson would have inevitably been pleased.

# GEORGE CRABBE (1754-1832)

## A. MAJOR EDITIONS

908 THE WORKS OF THE REV. GEORGE CRABBE. 8 vols. London: John Murray, 1823.

> Edited by Crabbe for Murray. This is the best-known collected edition of his works in the nineteenth century.

909 THE POETICAL WORKS OF THE REV. GEORGE CRABBE, WITH HIS LETTERS AND JOURNALS, AND HIS LIFE, BY HIS SON. 8 vols. London: John Murray, 1834.

> Includes POSTHUMOUS TALES, miscellaneous poems, a detailed life of the poet, notes, and extensive commentary.

910 POEMS BY GEORGE CRABBE. Ed. Adolphus W. Ward. 3 vols. Cambridge: Cambridge Univ. Press, 1905-07.

> Standard complete edition.

911 THE POETICAL WORKS OF GEORGE CRABBE. Ed. A.J. Carlyle and R.M. Carlyle. Oxford: Oxford Univ. Press, 1914.

> Useful.

912 NEW POEMS BY GEORGE CRABBE. Ed. Arthur Pollard. Liverpool, Engl.: Liverpool Univ. Press, 1960.

> Poems published from the notebooks, mostly dating from his later years, although a few titles are found in Crabbe's correspondence. Edited in order to allow Crabbe to speak for himself (thus preserving eccentricities of spelling and punctuation), as well as to make him intelligible to the modern reader (thus some occasional emendations for clarity's sake).

913    GEORGE CRABBE: AN ANTHOLOGY. Ed. Frank L. Lucas. Cambridge:
Cambridge Univ. Press, 1933.

> Introduced by a comprehensive and far-reaching discussion
> of Crabbe's poetic deficiencies as well as virtues, summing
> up his poetic qualities by the following paradoxes: "naive,
> yet shrewd, straightforward, yet sardonic; blunt, yet tender;
> quiet, yet passionate; realistic, yet romantic."

914    THE BOROUGH OF GEORGE CRABBE (1810). Ilkley, Yorkshire, Engl.:
Scolar Press, 1973.

> Facsimile (original size) of J. Hatchard edition (1810).

915    TALES, 1812 AND OTHER SELECTED POEMS. Ed. Howard Mills.
Cambridge: Cambridge Univ. Press, 1967.

> Aims to provide a larger, more substantial selection of
> Crabbe than is normally provided in anthologies, printing
> nearly a thousand of his poems, including all of the TALES
> (1812), two-thirds of THE PARISH REGISTER, and one-half
> of THE BOROUGH. Helpful general introduction.

## B. CORRESPONDENCE

916    THE LEADBEATER PAPERS. 2 vols. London: Bell and Daldy, 1862.

> Volume 2 contains correspondence between Crabbe and Mrs.
> Leadbeater, an Irish writer who admired his poetry, cover-
> ing a wide range of topics and interests.

917    Wecter, Dixon. "Four Letters from George Crabbe to Edmund Burke."
RES, 14 (1938), 298–309.

> These letters provide a larger framework in which to under-
> stand Burke's relationship with Crabbe, one in which the
> great British statesman generously provided Crabbe patronage,
> a printer, a chance to study for the priesthood, and a ducal
> chaplaincy.

918    THE TENBURY LETTERS. Ed. Edmund H. Fellowes and Edward Pine.
London: Golden Cockrell Press, 1942.

> Prints a previously unpublished letter from the collection
> in the library of St. Michael's College, Tenbury, England,
> that refers to Crabbe's TALES OF THE HALL.

919    Pollard, Arthur. "Two New Letters of Crabbe." RES, NS 2 (1951),
375–77.

These two newly discovered letters help to establish more precisely the composition date of the poem "The Newspaper."

920    Link, Frederick M.   "Three Crabbe Letters."   ELN, 2 (1965), 200–206.

Three hitherto unknown letters of Crabbe discovered at the library of the Massachusetts Historical Society, one of which was marked by his son for possible inclusion in his LIFE, annotated and described.

## C. BIBLIOGRAPHY

921    Bareham, Terence, and S. Gatrell.   A BIBLIOGRAPHY OF GEORGE CRABBE.   Folkestore, Kent, Engl.: Dawson, 1978.   Appendix.

A comprehensive listing of works published in Crabbe's lifetime (collation of at least five of each copies); subsequent editions after his death (includes British and American); bibliographical notes and articles; other Crabbe bibliographies; contemporary reviews of the works; full-length critical and bibliographical studies; and a critical article appearing after his death.   An appendix contains translations and foreign reaction to his poetry.

922    Batdorf, Franklin P.   "The Murray Reprints of George Crabbe:   A Publisher's Record."   SIB, 4 (1951), 192–99.

Records of the printing and sales of the John Murray publishing house attest to Crabbe's popularity and success and also provide additional data valuable to bibliographers.

923    _____.   "Notes on Three Editions of George Crabbe's TALES."   PBSA, 44 (1950), 276–79.

Descriptive bibliography of editions of Crabbe's TALES not generally known to early twentieth-century scholars and found in this country.

924    _____.   "An Unrecorded Early Anthology of Crabbe."   SIB, 3 (1951), 266–67.

The discovery of this collection of the tales and miscellaneous poems of Crabbe, now in the New Orleans Public Library, testifies to the popularity of Crabbe's works in nineteenth-century America.

925    GEORGE CRABBE, 1754-1832.   BICENTENARY CELEBRATIONS:   EXHIBITION OF WORKS AND MANUSCRIPTS HELD AT MOOT HALL,

ALDEBURGH. Aldeburgh, Suffolk, Engl.: Festival Committee and
Suffolk Institute of Archaeology, 1954.

Bibliographical accounts of Crabbe books and manuscripts
exhibited.

926    See no. 936.

927    Pollard, Graham. "The Early Poems of George Crabbe and THE LADY'S
       MAGAZINE." BODLEIAN LIBRARY RECORD, 5 (1955), 149-56.

       Attempts to determine just what early pieces Crabbe con-
       tributed to this periodical.

## D. BIOGRAPHY

928    Ainger, Alfred. CRABBE. London: Macmillan, 1903.

       Contains a number of interesting critical insights into
       Crabbe's poetic mode.

929    Blackburne, Neville. THE RESTLESS OCEAN: THE STORY OF GEORGE
       CRABBE, THE ALDEBURGH POET, 1754-1832. Lavenham, Suffolk,
       Engl.: Terrence Dalton, 1972.

       Concerned with Crabbe the man, seeking to sift, select,
       and rearrange the facts of Crabbe's life according to the
       chronological order, reinterpreting such materials "to throw
       more light on the single life of a writer" who is still an
       enigma.

930    Brewster, Elizabeth. "Two Friends: George Crabbe and Sir Walter
       Scott." QUEEN'S QUARTERLY, 78 (1971), 602-13.

       This unusual friendship was based on "their common interest
       in narrative verse, respect for tradition and authority and
       in a shared sense of humour."

931    Broadley, A.M., and Walter Jerrold. THE ROMANCE OF AN ELDER-
       LY POET: A HITHERTO UNKNOWN CHAPTER IN THE LIFE OF
       GEORGE CRABBE REVEALED BY HIS TEN YEARS' CORRESPONDENCE
       WITH ELIZABETH CHARTER, 1815-1825. London: Stanley Paul, 1913.

       Studies of Crabbe often slight his letter-writing interests,
       and the correspondence reveals not a stern painter of
       nature but a humane and sensitive personality.

932    Hatch, Ronald B. "George Crabbe, the Duke of Rutland, and the
       Tories." RES, NS 24 (1973), 429-43.

The usual assumption--that Crabbe's liberalism was distaste-
ful to the Duke of Rutland--is incorrect, because the Duke
believed in fair economic returns and sympathized with the
laborers. Such misrepresentations of the political world of
the 1780s have led critics to blame politics instead of
personal reasons for the poet's difficult situation at Belvoir
Castle, caught between the fortunes of Rutland and devotion to Edmund Burke.

933    Hazlitt, William. "Mr. Campbell and Mr. Crabbe." In THE SPIRIT
       OF THE AGE, THE COMPLETE WORKS OF WILLIAM HAZLITT. Ed.
       P.P. Hone. Vol. 2. London: J.M. Dent, 1932, pp. 159-69.

       A fascinating insight into the darker side of Crabbe, char-
       acterizing him as "repulsive" and "morbid" and giving only
       "the mean, the little, the disgusting, the distressing" part
       of nature. Highly influential but biased opinion.

934    Hodgart, Patricia, and Theodore Redpath, eds. ROMANTIC PERSPEC-
       TIVES: THE WORK OF CRABBE, BLAKE, WORDSWORTH, AND
       COLERIDGE, AS SEEN BY THEIR CONTEMPORARIES AND BY THEM-
       SELVES. New York: Barnes and Noble, 1964.

       Reprints letters and reviews pertaining to Crabbe's works,
       as well as relevant critiques and biographical data bearing
       on the poet's life and art.

935    Hubble, Douglas. "Opium Addiction and English Literature." MEDI-
       CAL HISTORY, 1 (1957), 323-35.

       Studies Crabbe's (among that of other English poets) opium
       addiction from the medical standpoint, concluding that there
       is no evidence he hoped for poetic inspiration by its use,
       although some dream-scenery passages, especially in "Sir
       Eustace Grey," reveal drug-induced distortions of time
       and space.

936    Huchon, René L. GEORGE CRABBE AND HIS TIMES, 1754-1832:  A
       CRITICAL AND BIOGRAPHICAL STUDY. Trans. Frederick Clarke.
       London: John Murray, 1907. Bibliog.

       The standard biography of Crabbe and the source of much
       valuable information about his life and times.

937    THE LIFE OF GEORGE CRABBE BY HIS SON. Ed. Edmund Blunden.
       London: Cresset Press, 1947.

       Valuable for an introduction stressing Crabbe's psychology,
       love of the Suffolk area, and evocation of the sea.

938    Shepherd, T.B. "George Crabbe and Methodism." LONDON QUAR-
       TERLY AND HOLBORN REVIEW, April 1941, pp. 166-74.

       Discusses Crabbe's attitudes toward Methodism (a "spiritual
       influence") and some of the theology on which he based
       his faith, but senses a covert sympathy with its noncon-
       formist qualities.

## E. CRITICISM

939    Abrams, Meyer H. THE MYTH OF PARADISE: THE EFFECT OF OPIUM
       VISIONS ON THE WORKS OF DEQUINCEY, CRABBE, FRANCIS THOMP-
       SON, AND COLERIDGE. Cambridge, Mass.: Harvard Univ. Press,
       1934.

       Discusses the effects of opium use on Crabbe, the references
       in his journals, and his son's knowledge of his father's
       habits; moreover, "like a true eighteenth-century man of
       letters," Crabbe most feared the Gothic. Reprints "The
       World of Dreams" and "Sir Eustace Grey."

940    Bareham, Terence. "Crabbe's Studies of Derangement and Hallucination."
       ORBIS LITTERARUM, 24 (1969), 161-81.

       Thorough examination of Crabbe's references to and analysis
       of delusion, derangement, and hallucinations that reveals
       a writer who is a "shrewd and sympathetic student" of man-
       kind, desperately believing in rationality, but manifesting
       a deep melancholia and doubt.

941    _____. GEORGE CRABBE. New York: Barnes and Noble, 1977.

       An attempt to place Crabbe within the context of the
       church he served as ordained clergyman for fifty years; to
       discuss the political uncertainties and controversies he
       witnessed and tried to influence between 1780-1830; and
       to treat him also as "a writer making a substantial con-
       tribution to the investigation of the human mind."

942    Bowers, Clementian Francis, F.S.C. CHARACTERIZATION IN THE
       NARRATIVE POETRY OF GEORGE CRABBE. Washington, D.C.:
       Catholic Univ. Press, 1959.

       A study designed to document the favorable opinion and
       enthusiasm associated with Crabbe's characterizations by
       analyzing his characters as "verbal constructs, substructures
       of meaning within general narrative structures."

943    Brewster, Elizabeth. "George Crabbe and William Wordsworth." UTQ,
       42 (1973), 142-56.

Contends that Jeffrey's famous reviews have influenced later
critics to view Wordsworth and Crabbe as hostile to one
another, but that Crabbe avoided poetic diction in his later
works because of the strictures in the "Preface" to LYRICAL
BALLADS and also Wordsworth appreciated Crabbe's character
portrayal.

944   Broman, Walter E.   "Factors in Crabbe's Eminence in the Early Nineteenth Century."  MP, 51 (1953), 42-49.

Takes issue with traditional views of Crabbe in literary
history as an obscure late eighteenth-century realist and
argues that in "the most basic poetic desiderata of the
period--passion, pathos, terror, force"--he is as typical
as Byron and Scott.

945   Chamberlain, Robert L.  GEORGE CRABBE.  New York: Twayne, 1965.

Defines and illustrates Crabbe's "particular claims to greatness as a poet" and establishes his place in English literary
history through a chronological approach to his life and
work:  the early Crabbe, an original poet impeded by
Augustan poetic convention and acute disillusionment; the
Crabbe of middle years finding his own voice and style,
yet still tainted by pessimism; and the mature Crabbe com-
ing into his own as an innovator in the heroic couplet and
creator of strikingly realistic people and stories.

946   Cruttwell, Patrick.   "The Last Augustan."  HudR, 7 (1955), 533-44.

An important essay pointing out that the cast of Crabbe's
mind and his literary affinities were "true Augustan" in
their combination of classical stoicism, rational piety,
abhorrence of "enthusiasm," and use of the heroic couplet.
His Johnson-like background and his sense of alienation
and fears for the disintegration of culture created tension
in his work between the neoclassical demand for restraint
and decorum and the intensity of feeling and psychological
and social realism characterizing Romanticism.

947   Diffey, Carole T.   "Journey to Experience:  Crabbe's 'Silford Hall.'"
DUJ, NS 30 (1969), 129-34.

Views the poem in archetypal terms, as a serioironic quest
of the youthful hero journeying from a state of innocence
to experience.

948   Edwards, Gavin.   "The Grimeses."  EIC, 27 (1977), 127-40.

Combines the techniques of psychoanalysis and linguistics

to approach PETER GRIMES as a way to explain the various
concepts of time, the conflation of past and present in the
narrator's voice, and the ambivalences in Grimes's psyche.

949    Forster, E.M.   "George Crabbe and Peter Grimes (1948)."   In TWO
       CHEERS FOR DEMOCRACY.  London: Edward Arnold, 1951, pp. 166-
       80.

       A shrewd and insightful discussion by a modern writer,
       finding novelistic qualities in Crabbe's PETER GRIMES
       and pointing out that his love-hate relationship with
       Aldeburgh produced an uncertain and troubled mind.

950    Gallon, D.N.   "'Silford Hall' or the Happy Day."  MLR, 61 (1966),
       384-94.

       A close reading of the poem's imagery, tone, and structure,
       remarking on its oblique nature and lack of explicit moral-
       izing, features that make it uncharacteristic of Crabbe.

951    Graham, W.H.   "George Crabbe, Poet of Penury."  CONTEMPORARY
       REVIEW, 179 (1951), 57-103.

       General overview of Crabbe's life and poetic career,
       stressing his realistic depictions of the misery of poverty
       and his desire for social reform in calling attention to
       the plight of the indigent.

952    Gregor, Ian.   "The Last Augustan:  Some Observations on the Poetry
       of George Crabbe (1775-1832)."   DUBLIN REVIEW, 229 (1955), 37-50.

       Crabbe's VILLAGE remains within the decorum and style
       of the English Augustans, making use of traditional pastoral
       and elegiac motifs blended with a realistic description of
       his native region.

953    Haddakin, Lilian.  THE POETRY OF CRABBE.  London: Chatto and
       Windus, 1955.

       An examination of the poetry from a nonhistorical perspec-
       tive, attempting to explain some of Crabbe's psychological
       procedures and poetic techniques in order to establish his
       poetic importance and achievement, especially in the use
       of verse as a vehicle for narrative.

954    Hatch, Ronald B.  CRABBE'S ARABESQUE:  SOCIAL DRAMA IN THE
       POETRY OF GEORGE CRABBE.  Montreal:  McGill-Queen's Univ.
       Press, 1976.

       Even more crucial to the understanding of Crabbe than his
       writing in the couplet of Pope is his way of handling con-

flicting social, moral, and religious matters within a dramatic framework where ideas and attitudes are not inte-
grated but rather are separate entities, each with its own
degree of truth and claim to reality.

955      _____. "George Crabbe and the Tenth Muse." ECS, 7 (1974), 274-
94.

Like many post-Augustan writers, Crabbe embodies "alter-
nate or antithetic visions of the world which result from a
conflict between consciously held ideas and those created
under the pressure of creative practice." Thus, the classical form at the beginning of THE VILLAGE operates as an
inner device to contain anticlassical ideas, and the partly
ironic classical elegiac ending of Book 2 informs the poem
with "those transcendental ideals" Crabbe found missing in
the world of the village.

956      _____. "George Crabbe and the Workhouses of the Suffolk Incorpora-
tions." PQ, 54 (1975), 689-98.

Different from his artistic and moral intentions of the
famous description of the poorhouse in his VILLAGE (1783),
Crabbe's poorhouse in THE BOROUGH (1810) represents his
attack on herding the poor into a single building, cut off
from friends and relatives; thus his real objection lay in
the prison-like features of the workhouse, not in sociologi-
cal issues raised by such institutions.

957      Hibbard, George R.   "Crabbe and Shakespeare." In RENAISSANCE
AND MODERN ESSAYS PRESENTED TO VIVIAN DE SOLA PINTO IN
CELEBRATION OF HIS SEVENTIETH BIRTHDAY. Ed. George R. Hibbard.
London:  Routledge and Kegan Paul, 1966, pp. 83-93.

Unlike the "great Romantics" who rashly tried to resurrect
the black verse tragedy of Shakespeare in their own dramatic offerings, Crabbe successfully utilized the material
of Shakespeare and profitably adapted it to his own age
and to the heroic couplet, in the process laying himself
open to "larger influences," namely, something of Shakespeare's humanity and profound probing of human character.

958      Hsia, Chih-tsing.   "Pope, Crabbe, and the Tradition." TAMKANG
REVIEW, 2 (1971), 51-97.

Compares Crabbe with Pope to indicate ways in which the
later poet transforms the heroic couplet of Augustan didactic,
pastoral, and topographical verse into a new, vital narrative mode, an achievement not often found in the narrative
poems of the Romantics.

959    See no. 813.

960    Jeffrey, Francis. CONTRIBUTIONS TO THE EDINBURGH REVIEW.
       Philadelphia, Pa.: Carey and Hart, 1846.

       Several reviews present a fulsome appreciation by Crabbe's
       critical admirer of the early nineteenth century, welcoming
       the naturalness and common sense of his poetry at the same
       time disparaging, by comparison, Wordsworth's productions
       for their "bad or false taste."

961    Lang, Valery. "Crabbe and the Eighteenth Century." ELH, 5 (1938),
       305-33.

       A detailed description of Crabbe's roots in eighteenth-
       century literature, showing his relationship to the changing
       practices in pastoral, satire, and the humanistic ethic, as
       well as to neoclassical poetic theory.

962    Mercier, Vivian. "The Poet as Sociologist--George Crabbe." DUBLIN
       MAGAZINE, 22 (1947), 19-27.

       The sociological aspects of Crabbe's work, his ability to
       give insight into the social conditions of late eighteenth
       century, are the areas in which his mastery of the heroic
       couplet (in the manner of Dryden) shows itself most ad-
       vantageously.

963    More, Paul Elmer. "A Plea for Crabbe." In his SHELBURNE ESSAYS
       II. New York: G.P. Putnam, 1907, pp. 126-44.

       Argues from the humanist perspective in praise of the moral
       realism and antiromantic tendencies of Crabbe, finding in
       his poetry no trace of "mystic longings toward the infinite."

964    Nelson, Beth. GEORGE CRABBE AND THE PROGRESS OF EIGHTEENTH-
       CENTURY NARRATIVE VERSE. Lewisburg, Pa.: Bucknell Univ. Press,
       1976.

       As the last of the Augustan satirists writing into the nine-
       teenth century, Crabbe was isolated, but undertook a series
       of "ingenious experiments in the service of literary values
       that he accepted early in his apprenticeship to the satirist
       Pope," the most radical and inventive of which was the
       fusing of the novel of the 1790s with the short verse tales
       of the eighteenth century to produce a literary product
       looking toward the yet unwritten works of Eliot, Trollope,
       and James.

965    New, Peter. GEORGE CRABBE'S POETRY. London: Macmillan, 1976.

Discusses paradoxical aspects of Crabbe's sensibility to
make him more accessible to the twentieth-century reader
and concludes that the major interest in Crabbe's best
work concerns process, a focus that connects him with
the leading minds of the nineteenth century and with the
most vital form of that period, the novel.

966    Pollard, Arthur, ed. CRABBE: THE CRITICAL HERITAGE. London:
Routledge and Kegan Paul, 1972.

Contains a helpful and comprehensive introductory essay
on the critical problems facing the reader of Crabbe and
also charts the contemporary reactions to this realist who
"recognizes universality in ordinary everyday life." Selections from periodical and magazine reviews are arranged
according to the sequence of published volumes of poetry,
along with a number of brief critical comments originating
in diaries and in other informal sources.

967    Pound, Ezra. "The Rev. G. Crabbe, L.L.D." In THE LITERARY
ESSAYS OF EZRA POUND. Ed. T.S. Eliot. Norfolk, Conn.: New
Directions, 1954, pp. 276-79.

Pound greatly admired Crabbe's realism and sense of "the
value of writing words that conform precisely with fact,"
and viewed his poetry as a welcome antidote to Words-
worthian "slobber."

968    Sale, Arthur. "The Development of Crabbe's Narrative Art." CAM-
BRIDGE JOURNAL, 5 (1952), 490-98.

Traces the changes in techniques of narrative poetry from
the early THE PARISH REGISTER to TALES and concludes
that Crabbe holds a high place in the pantheon of narrative poets.

969    Sigworth, Oliver F. NATURE'S STERNEST PAINTER: FIVE ESSAYS
ON THE POETRY OF GEORGE CRABBE. Tucson: Univ. of Arizona
Press, 1965.

Five essays on various aspects of Crabbe's art, focusing on
the qualities of his nature poetry, his use of the narrative
mode, and the critical reaction, as well as devoting two
chapters to his dual relationships with both the eighteenth
and nineteenth century literary worlds.

970    Spingarn, Lawrence P. "George Crabbe as Realist." UKCR, 17 (1950),
60-65.

Though he modelled his style on the "orderliness and precision" characterizing Pope's couplet rhetoric, Crabbe

broke with the artificialities of neoclassicism and introduced a new realism, an "attitude of common sense toward
common things, drawing from them an unvarnished and
universal truthfulness."

971  Swingle, L.J.  "Late Crabbe in Relation to the Augustans and Romantics:
the Temporal Labyrinth of his TALES IN VERSE, 1812."  ELH, 42
(1975), 580-94.

What most concerns Crabbe in his verse tales is "the
phenomenon of change, the temporal condition of human
life"; and the persistent Augustan emphasis on how to live
gives way to Crabbe's pressing concern to analyze human
actualities.

972  Thale, Rose Marie.  "Crabbe's VILLAGE and Topographical Poetry."
JEGP, 55 (1956), 618-23.

Despite Samuel Johnson's description of THE VILLAGE as
"original, vigorous, and elegant," the poem is not original
at all, but rather a "topographical poem" in the tradition
of hundreds of other eighteenth-century productions, a
fact that accounts for its structural formlessness and "combination of discordant elements."

973  Thomas, W.K.  "Crabbe's BOROUGH:  The Process of Montage."  UTQ,
36 (1967), 181-92.

Views the poems as a "composite" drawn from many different sources, giving a "montage" effect that is produced
by the memory of observed facts imaginatively transformed.

974  _____.  "Crabbe's Workhouse."  HLQ, 32 (1969), 149-61.

Crabbe employs a number of rhetorical devices in the
portrayal of the workhouse in THE VILLAGE (1783) for
the purpose of moving his readers toward a sympathy for
the poor; and thus he edited out some of what he observed
to reinforce these ethical and artistic goals.

975  _____.  "The Flavour of Crabbe."  DR, 40 (1961), 489-504.

The poetry of Crabbe has something distinctive to offer
not found in other writers--"the love for nature . . . as
it exists in its cold dreariness and vain fruition, and a
love for man, for man as he too exists, even in his folly
and stupidity."

976  _____.  "George Crabbe:  Not Quite the Sternest."  SIR, 7 (1968),
166-75.

Challenges the accuracy of characterizing Crabbe as "nature's sternest painter," and concludes that Crabbe was not stern and was in fact indebted to John Langhorne for much that he supposedly originated.

977    Wilson, P.B.    "Crabbe's Narrative World."    DUJ, 37 (1976), 135-43.

Analyzes certain difficulties of structure caused by Crabbe's attempt to utilize the narrative device of omniscient narrator, but finds in TALES a more successful employment of a character's point of view, dramatization of moral processes, and depiction of the dilemmas of the human condition.

# JOHN DRYDEN (1631-1700)

## A. MAJOR EDITIONS

978 THE WORKS OF JOHN DRYDEN. Ed. Sir Walter Scott. Rev. George
Saintsbury. 18 vols. Edinburgh: Constable, 1882-92.

> Valuable scholarly edition and the basis of all modern
> editions. The biographical essay in the first volume sets
> the stage for modern critical approaches.

979 THE WORKS OF JOHN DRYDEN. Ed. Edward Niles Hooker, H.T.
Swedenberg et al. 20 vols. (projected). Berkeley: Univ. of California Press, 1956-- .

> Will be the standard edition of the works when completed.
> Meticulously edited and aided by the resources of the fine
> collections at the Huntington Library and the William
> Andrews Clark Library of UCLA. Twelve volumes have
> been published, three of which cover poetry from 1649 to
> 1696.

980 THE POETICAL WORKS OF JOHN DRYDEN. Ed. George R. Noyes.
Rev. ed. Boston: Houghton Mifflin, 1950.

> First published in 1909. Revisions included an expanded
> introduction, additional works, and a few new poems, all
> reflecting scholarly advances. Valuable in making avail-
> able early translations from Virgil included in SYLVAE
> (1685) that were later revised for the AENEIS (1697).
> Commentary an early contribution to Dryden criticism,
> but texts are modernized and sometimes faulty.

981 THE POEMS OF JOHN DRYDEN. Ed. James Kinsley. 4 vols. Oxford:
Oxford Univ. Press, 1958.

> Standard edition of the poems based on early printings.

982     FABLES, ANCIENT AND MODERN.  Ed. James Kinsley.  Ilkley, York-
        shire, Engl.: Scolar Press, 1973.

>       Facsimile (original size) from Bodleian Library copy.  Con-
>       tains the famous preface, an exemplary exercise in compara-
>       tive criticism.

983     SYLVAE:  OR, THE SECOND PART OF POETICAL MISCELLANIES.  Ed.
        James Kinsley.  Menston, Yorkshire, Engl.:  Scolar Press, 1973.

>       Facsimile (original size) of Tonson printing of 1685 from
>       Bodleian Library copy.  Bibliographical material contained
>       in introduction.

984     ESSAYS OF JOHN DRYDEN.  Ed. William P. Ker.  2 vols.  Oxford:
        Clarendon Press, 1900.

>       Introductory material provides a valuable overview of Dryden's
>       critical principles.  The complete texts of the essays are
>       printed.  Superseded by Watson edition, below.

985     "OF DRAMATIC POESY" AND OTHER CRITICAL ESSAYS.  Ed. George
        Watson.  2 vols.  London:  Dent, 1962.

>       An excellent, although sometimes excerpted, edition of the
>       criticism with annotations and commentary.  Standard modern
>       edition.

986     THE PROLOGUES AND EPILOGUES OF JOHN DRYDEN:  A CRITICAL
        EDITION.  Ed. William B. Gardner.  New York:  Columbia Univ.
        Press, 1951.

>       Brings together in a single volume these poems important
>       both as a poetic genre and as dramatic criticism.

987     THE SONGS OF JOHN DRYDEN.  Ed. Cyrus L. Day.  Cambridge,
        Mass.:  Harvard Univ. Press, 1932.

>       Standard modern edition of this important part of Dryden's
>       literary achievement, with a helpful discussion of his lyrical
>       gift and a facsimile reproduction of the musical notation of
>       the extant original airs.

## B.  CORRESPONDENCE

988     THE LETTERS OF JOHN DRYDEN.  Ed. Charles E. Ward.  Durham,
        N.C.:  Duke Univ. Press, 1942.

>       Standard edition.  Includes letters addressed to Dryden.

## C. BIBLIOGRAPHY, TEXTUAL STUDIES, CONCORDANCES, AND REFERENCE MATERIALS

989    Aden, John M. THE CRITICAL OPINIONS OF JOHN DRYDEN: A DICTIONARY. Nashville: Vanderbilt Univ. Press, 1963.

    Alphabetically arranged by topic in order to note Dryden's conflicting views on the same subject. Useful treatment of a difficult subject.

990    Brooks, Harold. "When did Dryden Write MACFLECKNOE?: Some Additional Notes." RES, 11 (1935), 74-78.

    On the basis of several parallels and verbal echoes in Oldham's poems, whose dates are secure, argues that 1678 is "the natural place of the poem in the evolution of Restoration satire and of Dryden's art." See no. 1006.

991    Jensen, H. James. A GLOSSARY OF JOHN DRYDEN'S CRITICAL TERMS. Minneapolis: Univ. of Minnesota Press, 1969.

    Explains the terminology of the criticism by placing it in context.

992    Kinsley, James. "Dryden." In ENGLISH POETRY: SELECT BIBLIO-GRAPHICAL GUIDES. Ed. A.E. Dyson. London: Oxford Univ. Press, 1971, pp. 111-27.

    Surveys texts, critical studies and commentary, biographies and letters, bibliographies, and background reading, as well as listing major articles and books. Indispensable. See no. 63.

993    Latt, David J., and Samuel Holt Monk, eds. JOHN DRYDEN: A SURVEY AND BIBLIOGRAPHY OF CRITICAL STUDIES, 1895-1974. Minneapolis: Univ. of Minneapolis Press, 1976. Indexed.

    An updating and extension of the original Monk bibliography, 1895-1948.

994    Macdonald, Hugh. JOHN DRYDEN: A BIBLIOGRAPHY OF EARLY EDITIONS AND DRYDENIANA. Oxford: Clarendon Press, 1939.

    Includes editions and criticism of Dryden's work published during his lifetime; also notes Tonson's miscellanies of 1709, 1716, 1727, collected editions of poems and plays through 1767, and miscellanies printing Dryden's poems for the first time.

995    Monk, Samuel Holt. "Dryden Studies: A Survey, 1920-1945." ELH, 14 (1947), 46-63.

Describes Dryden's recent critical reputation, especially
since Van Doren's study of 1920, and concludes that although not entirely neglected since the eighteenth century,
his writings have been the subject of "intelligent, sympathetic, and at times brilliant critical and scholarly studies."
See no. 1006.

996    Montgomery, Guy, and Lester A. Hubbard, eds. CONCORDANCE
TO THE POETICAL WORKS OF JOHN DRYDEN. Berkeley:  Univ. of
California Press, 1957.

Based on the Noyes edition (no. 980).  Includes original
poems and translations.  Complete, but of limited use
because of the modernized spelling text.

997    Osborn, James M.   "Macdonald's Bibliography of Dryden."  MP, 39
(1942), 313-19.

Handsome tribute to the care and industry of this author
for his contributions to the understanding of Dryden and
his age, although noting that the book is less successful
as a bibliography than as a reference tool.  See no. 1006.

998    Saslow, Edward L.   "Shaftesbury Cursed:  Dryden's Revision of the
ACHITOPHEL Lines."  SB, 28 (1975), 276-83.

The most recent in a number of attempts to explain the
addition to the third edition of ABSALOM AND ACHI-
TOPHEL of twelve lines praising the Earl of Shaftesbury's
political career.

999    Vieth, David M.   "The Discovery of the Date of MAC FLECKNOE."
In EVIDENCE IN LITERARY SCHOLARSHIP:  ESSAYS IN MEMORY OF
JAMES MARSHALL OSBORN.  Ed. René Wellek and Alvaro Ribeiro.
Oxford:  Clarendon Press, 1979, pp. 63-87.

A valuable summary and clarification of the generally
accepted arguments Vieth previously advanced as to the
composition of Dryden's lampoon in response to the publication of Shadwell's play THE VIRTUOSO in 1676.  See
no. 129.

1000    _____.   "Dryden's MAC FLECKNOE:  The Case Against Editorial Confusion."  HLB, 24 (1976), 204-45.

An elaborate and exhaustive study of the manuscripts,
attacking editorial procedures of the California edition
(no. 979) and employing the genealogical method of reconstructing a family tree of the existing manuscripts.

1001    Zamonski, John A., ed. AN ANNOTATED BIBLIOGRAPHY OF JOHN
        DRYDEN: TEXTS AND STUDIES, 1949-1973. New York: Garland,
        1975.

> Designed to supplement the original Monk bibliography.
> Cites many book reviews. See no. 993.

## D. COLLECTIONS

1002    King, Bruce, ed. DRYDEN'S MIND AND ART. London: Oliver and
        Boyd, 1969.

> Essays on various aspects of Dryden's literary career, most
> previously printed.

1003    McHenry, Robert, and David G. Longee, eds. CRITICS ON DRYDEN:
        READINGS IN LITERARY CRITICISM. London: George Allen and
        Unwin, 1973.

> Important essays (reprinted) covering all aspects of Dryden's
> writing. Good representation of nineteenth-century com-
> mentary.

1004    Miner, Earl, ed. JOHN DRYDEN: WRITERS AND THEIR BACKGROUND.
        Athens: Ohio Univ. Press, 1972.

> Ten essays by outstanding Drydenists, some concerned with
> the poetry.

1005    Schilling, Bernard N., ed. DRYDEN: A COLLECTION OF CRITICAL
        ESSAYS. Englewood Cliffs, N.J.: Prentice-Hall, 1963.

> Previously published critical essays, many relevant to
> Dryden's poetry.

1006    Swedenberg, H.T., Jr., ed. ESSENTIAL ARTICLES FOR THE STUDY
        OF JOHN DRYDEN. Hamden, Conn.: Archon Books, 1966.

> Previously published essays useful alike to the young
> scholar, graduate students, and undergraduates. Includes
> supplementary list of studies not included.

## E. BIOGRAPHY

1007    Osborn, James M. JOHN DRYDEN: SOME BIOGRAPHICAL FACTS
        AND PROBLEMS. Rev. ed. Gainesville: Univ. of Florida Press, 1965.

> Invaluable discussion of facts and fictions concerning
> Dryden's biography as it has evolved from an early eigh-

teenth-century account and also from independent "collateral investigations" of cruxes facing his biographers.

1008    Scott, Sir Walter. THE LIFE OF JOHN DRYDEN. Ed. Bernard Kreiss-man. Lincoln: Univ. of Nebraska Press, 1963.

> Reproduces Scott's LIFE in volume 1 of the 1834 edition in order to include the contemporary notes of James G. Lockhart.

1009    Ward, Charles E. THE LIFE OF JOHN DRYDEN. Chapel Hill: Univ. of North Carolina Press, 1961.

> Factual account. Standard biography.

# F. CRITICISM

## Major Satires

1010    Alssid, Michael W. "Shadwell's MAC FLECKNOE." SEL, 7 (1967), 387-402.

> Dryden's MAC FLECKNOE subverts Shadwell's critical theories and dramatic practices, portrays him as a self-incriminating "humors" character, and attacks his Whig politics.

1011    Barbeau, Anne T. "The Disembodied Rebels: Psychic Origins of Re-bellion in ABSALOM AND ACHITOPHEL." STUDIES IN EIGHTEENTH-CENTURY CULTURE, 9 (1979), 489-501.

> The rebels' violation of "the bonds and obligations" of their own physical nature directly affects the corresponding body of the nation, its laws and traditions; and their of-fense to God, law, and order is contrasted with Barzillai's son, whose disembodied soul brings aid to Charles, symbol-izing obedience and courage, not rebellious fear and cowardice.

1012    Black, James. "Dryden on Shadwell's Theater of Violence." DR, 54 (1974), 298-311.

> MAC FLECKNOE is the best key to its occasion, extending the Dryden-Shadwell controversy over the propriety of violence in heroic drama as well as providing Dryden the opportunity to exchange insults with Shadwell through a poetic version of THE REHEARSAL.

1013 Cable, Chester H. "ABSALOM AND ACHITOPHEL as Epic Satire."
In STUDIES IN HONOR OF JOHN WILCOX. Ed. A. Dayle Wallace
and Woodburn O. Ross. Detroit: Wayne State Univ. Press, 1958.

Argues that the poem gains its real and persuasive force
as satire by the particular arrangement of narrative, treatment of characters, singleness of action, and causal relationships between character and action according to recognizable epic theory of the period.

1014 Chambers, A.B. "ABSALOM AND ACHITOPHEL: Christ and Satan."
MLN, 74 (1959), 592-96.

Political application of the story of Absalom and Achitophel
established a tradition in which Achitophel was a type for
a rebellious and wily politician; but for earlier, nonpoliti-
cal interpretations, from medieval exegetes to Bishop Hall,
he was a Judas to the shepherd David's Christ.

1015 Conlon, Michael J. "The Passage on Government in Dryden's ABSALOM
AND ACHITOPHEL." JEGP, 78 (1979), 17-32.

Reads the essay on government passage in a highly political
rather than mythic context and concludes that "it is the
political and doctrinal terminus for Dryden's partisan interpretation of Exclusion as revival of a commonwealth model
of government and a fiduciary interpretation of kingship."

1016 Davies, Godfrey. "The Conclusion of Dryden's ABSALOM AND ACHI-
TOPHEL." HLQ, 10 (1946), 69-82.

An attempt to explain the king's speech (11. 939-1025)
by reference to the particular historical circumstances
involving Charles' connection with the poem and the
date of composition and publication, concluding that
Dryden astutely appeals to the moderates by emphasizing
the Whig threat to constitutional government and rein-
forcing the argument of HIS MAJESTIES DECLARATION
DEFENDED. See no. 1006.

1017 de Beer, E.S. "ABSALOM AND ACHITOPHEL: Literary and Historical
Notes." RES, 17 (1941), 298-309.

The key of 1716 has misled commentators into idle speculation about the specific historical identities of Dryden's
characters, whereas the poem should be approached as a
measure of his poetic wit, artistic control, technical
accomplishment, and vigor.

1018 Donnelly, Jerome. "Movement and Meaning in Dryden's MAC FLECKNOE."
TSLL, 12 (1971), 569-82.

Like the plot of Pope's DUNCIAD, Dryden's poem has a similar dominant feature of structural design: an opposition of vertical, horizontal, and downward movements sustained by wit, irony, and contrasting images.

1019   Freedman, Morris. "Dryden's Miniature Epic." JEGP, 57 (1968), 211-19.

Important argument relating Dryden's ABSALOM AND ACHITOPHEL to Milton's PARADISE LOST and PARADISE REGAINED to show that not only does it incorporate details and strategies from Milton, but also fits the Restoration formulation of true epic action, including concepts of grandeur, finality, authority, and thematic universality.

1020   Griffin, Dustin. "Dryden's Charles: The Ending of ABSALOM AND ACHITOPHEL." PQ, 52 (1978), 359-82.

Attempts to justify the poem's ending have ignored both the wit and theatricality of the final scene and the seriousness of the argument Dryden makes for retaining Charles, even though somewhat dictated by political expediency.

1021   Guilhamet, Leon M. "Dryden's Debasement of Scripture in ABSALOM AND ACHITOPHEL." SEL, 9 (1969), 395-413.

Dryden departs from familiar seventeenth-century typological interpretations of the David story to represent more faithfully his own rational, classical ideal of a new age based on reason and law and presided over by a monarch.

1022   Jones, Harold W., ed. ANTI-ACHITOPHEL, 1682: THREE VERSE REPLIES TO "ABSALOM AND ACHITOPHEL." Gainesville: Scholars' Facsimiles and Reprints, 1961.

Facsimile reprints of answers to Dryden's poem introduced by brief discussion of the form, authors, and details of publication. Identifies names and places in the allegory.

1023   Jones, Richard F. "The Originality of ABSALOM AND ACHITOPHEL." MLN, 46 (1931), 211-18.

The fact that the biblical story figures so prominently in sermons, speeches, treatises, and poems of the seventeenth century to represent political revolt against a monarch and the disloyalty of political advisers does not detract from Dryden's original, vigorous, and energetic treatment of the story. See no. 1006.

1024    Joost, Nicholas. "Dryden's MEDAL and the Baroque in Politics and the Arts." MODERN AGE, 3 (1959), 148-55.

>    Despite overt acceptance of the "Baroque ideal" of monarchy and rejection of the "democratic, liberal ideal," Dryden himself was a sensitive man of divided allegiances, part Puritan gentry in background but finally aligning himself with the Church, part beholden to old literary forms but championing many new methods.

1025    King, Bruce. "ABSALOM AND ACHITOPHEL: A Revaluation." In DRYDEN'S MIND AND ART. Ed. Bruce King. London: Oliver and Bond, 1969, pp. 65-83.

>    Excessive concern with political occasion and personalities has obscured the careful structuring of Dryden's poem and its main theme: "the dangers of the imagination" organized around a series of contrasts between ambition, restlessness, pride, intolerance and tolerance, moderation, order, humility. See no. 1002.

1026    Kinsley, James. "Historical Allusions in ABSALOM AND ACHITOPHEL." RES, NS 6 (1955), 291-97.

>    Discusses problems of identification and misidentification of persons and events in the poem, providing some supplementary information and fact.

1027    Korn, A.L. "MAC FLECKNOE and Cowley's DAVIDEIS." HLQ, 14 (1951), 99-127.

>    Dryden's numerous references to Cowley suggest the influence of his well-known epic DAVIDEIS on MAC FLECKNOE; a comparison of the two poems reveals Dryden's imaginative integration of diverse styles, genres, and conventions as well as his superior artistry. See no. 1006.

1028    Levine, George R. "Dryden's 'Inarticulate Poesy': Music and the Davidic King in ABSALOM AND ACHITOPHEL." ECS, 1 (1967-68), 291-312.

>    Objects to the influence of painting analogies on interpretations of the poem and argues for Dryden's use of the "figura" of David as psalmist and musician and "his symbolic use of music as an abstract harmonizing principle."

1029    Lewalski, Barbara K. "The Scope and Function of Biblical Allusion in ABSALOM AND ACHITOPHEL." ELN, 3 (1965), 29-35.

>    Biblical allusion in the poem goes beyond historical-religious allegory and Miltonic temptation scenes and

creates a "unifying framework" for viewing the episode of
Absalom's rebellion and David's final speech against the
whole panorama of biblical history.

1030    Lord, George de F.  "ABSALOM AND ACHITOPHEL and Dryden's
Political Cosmos."  In JOHN DRYDEN: WRITERS AND THEIR BACK-
GROUND.  Ed. Earl Miner.  Athens:  Ohio Univ. Press, 1972, pp.
156-90.

An exploration of Dryden's use of the "cosmogoric myth
of restoration, recovery, or renewal after exile, defeat,
or destruction" in a variety of shapes and forms throughout
his poetic career, concluding that ABSALOM AND ACHI-
TOPHEL marks the end of serious use of religious myth in
English political poetry and the emergence instead of the
"myth of secular authority."  See no. 1004.

1031    McFadden, George.  "Elkanah Settle and the Genesis of MAC FLECK-
NOE."  PQ, 43 (1964), 55-72.

Argues that MAC FLECKNOE was circulating in manuscript
long before Shadwell's THE MEDAL OF JOHN BAYES
(1682) and that it is not merely an outburst of satiric
pique against Shadwell but represents a "long-matured"
product of Dryden's conception of the true poet, a conception violated by Settle's pretentious style and toadying
to audience pleasure.  Famous minority report on the
genesis and compositional circumstances of the poem.

1032    Maresca, Thomas E.  "The Context of Dryden's ABSALOM AND ACHI-
TOPHEL."  ELH, 41 (1974), 340-58.

Dryden's "imaginative reordering" of history, both English
and biblical, combines with various ideas of creation--
God's, David's, and the Word--in a final vindication of
all poetry and fiction "as a true image of reality."

1033    Marshall, W. Gerald.  "Classical Oratory and the Major Addresses in
Dryden's ABSALOM AND ACHITOPHEL."  RESTORATION, 4 (1980),
71-80.

Examines the speeches of Achitophel, Absalom, and David
as formal classical orations, showing that although they
meticulously follow the divisions devised by ancient rhe-
toricians, with the exception of David's true oration, they
are ironically aligned with the classical model in their
violation of its ethical purpose.

1034    Maurer, A.E. Wallace.  "The Design of Dryden's THE MEDALL."  PLL,
2 (1966), 293-304.

Dryden employs the features of emblematic art, structuring his poem in order to mock the design of the Shaftesbury medal struck on November 24, 1681, and by thus "roguishly" altering that design in his own scenes and description exposes "the inadequacy and the distortion of the two sides of the Whig medal."

1035    Mother Mary Eleanor, S.H.C.J.    "'Anne Killigrew' and MAC FLECK-NOE." PQ, 43 (1964), 47-54.

Sees these two "secure masterpieces" as essentially treatments of the theme of "the fall and restoration of poetry" and analyzes their structural and thematic similarities from this point of view.

1036    Oden, Richard L.    DRYDEN AND SHADWELL: THE LITERARY CONTROVERSY AND "MAC FLECKNOE." Delmar, N.Y.: Scholars' Facsimiles and Reprints, 1977.

Discusses the nature of the controversy and assembles the pertinent documents bearing on the famous quarrel.

1037    Ricks, Christopher.    "Dryden's Absalom." EIC, 11 (1961), 273-89.

Achitophel is obviously Dryden's villain, but knowledge of the historical situation and sensitivity to language and tone will indicate that Absalom, too, is "culpably vulnerable" and the object of condemnation.

1038    Robinson, K.E.    "A Reading of ABSALOM AND ACHITOPHEL." YES, 6 (1976), 53-62.

Views the genuine virtues Charles exhibits in the closing speech as suspect when shown as belonging to the wittily ridiculed Charles of opening lines, especially given that the credibility of the poem depends on the existence of a stable political and moral norm symbolized by the monarch.

1039    Roper, Alan.    "Dryden's MEDAL and the Divine Analogy." ELH, 29 (1962), 396-417.

A full-length rhetorical and philosophical treatment of the royalist assumption of a correspondence existing between ethics, politics, and theology which argues that in dramatizing the dangers of an attempted overthrow of the hereditary monarchy of England, Dryden is analogously viewing this assault as a more fundamental threat to reason, king, and God.

1040    Schilling, Bernard N.  DRYDEN AND THE CONSERVATIVE MYTH:
        A READING OF ABSALOM AND ACHITOPHEL.  New Haven, Conn.:
        Yale Univ. Press, 1961.

> An exhaustive study of a highly topical poem in the con-
> text of a mythology of order and a set of connected myths,
> drawing on the literary tradition from Rome through the
> Renaissance, on the Bible as read in the seventeenth
> century, on the political and religious experiences of the
> mid-century civil war, and on the assumption of rule and
> control that dominate neoclassical literary theory.

1041    Sutherland, William Owen Sheppard, Jr.  "Dryden's Use of Popular
        Imagery in THE MEDAL."  UNIVERSITY OF TEXAS STUDIES IN
        ENGLISH, 35 (1956), 123-34.

> Identifies popular images found in the political pamphlets
> of the period of 1681 to 1682, shows how minor polemicists
> used these materials, and then analyzes Dryden's artful
> adaptation of such materials for satirical purposes.

1042    Tanner, James E.  "The Messianic Image in MAC FLECKNOE."  MLN,
        76 (1961), 220-23.

> The motif is not only complementary to the primary pattern
> of the poem--the presentation of Shadwell as new king of
> the dunces--but acts to unify the images of prophet, priest,
> and king in the unlikely person of the dramatist.

1043    Thomas, W. Keith.  THE CRAFTING OF ABSALOM AND ACHITOPHEL:
        DRYDEN'S "PEN FOR A PARTY."  Waterloo, Ontario: Wilfrid Laurier
        Univ. Press, 1978.

> Comprehensive treatment of historical and political back-
> grounds, leading to a reading of the poem as Varronian
> satire organized as Ciceronian oration.

1044    Towers, Tom H.  "The Lineage of Shadwell:  An Approach to MAC
        FLECKNOE."  SEL, 3 (1963), 323-34.

> Dryden's purpose is best understood by noticing "the
> company he forces Shadwell to keep" and by his constant
> pitting of Shadwell against Jonson.  Dryden, like his
> predecessor, reveals his concern with the possibility that
> theatrical aspects of a play may well obscure the meaning
> and thematic impact.

1045    Vieth, David M.  "Shadwell in Acrostic Land:  The Reversible Meaning
        of Dryden's MAC FLECKNOE."  STUDIES IN EIGHTEENTH-CENTURY
        CULTURE, 9 (1979), 503-16.

Argues that the most enjoyable and fruitful reading of
MAC FLECKNOE is "as a work of the Absurd in the
twentieth-century sense" and that therefore its structure
is not organic or Aristotelian, nor its norms explicit, but
rather open-ended and discontinuous, the metaphysical
and allusive machinery taking on an hilarious life of its
own and ending on a note of fantasy. Provides a helpful
account of recent critical opinion.

1046   Wallerstein, Ruth. "To Madness Near Allied: Shaftesbury and His
       Place in the Design and Thought of ABSALOM AND ACHITOPHEL."
       HLQ, 6 (1943), 445-71.

       Classic study of the role of Architophel in terms of the
       ideas and political concepts he embodies, his function in
       the design of the poem, and his relationship to the popu-
       lace of London.

1047   Wendorf, Richard. "Dryden, Charles II, and the Interpretation of
       Historical Character." PQ, 56 (1977), 82-103.

       Argues that Dryden's portraits, while often metaphorical
       and typological, rely equally upon "the semblance of
       historical verisimilitude."

1048   Wilding, Michael. "Dryden and Satire: MAC FLECKNOE, ABSALOM
       AND ACHITOPHEL, THE MEDALL, and JUVENAL." In JOHN DRY-
       DEN: WRITERS AND THEIR BACKGROUND. Ed. Earl Miner. Athens:
       Ohio Univ. Press, 1972, pp. 191-233.

       Especially sensitive to Dryden's ironies, views the satiric
       game in MAC FLECKNOE as involving the incorporation
       of allusion and parody of classical and Miltonic models
       and ideals, but "excluding any images of light that might
       be contained, either excising them or substituting images
       of dullness." Describes ABSALOM AND ACHITOPHEL as
       polemical and propagandistic, relieved at times by wit and
       subtle characterizations, and THE MEDALL as devoid of
       literary allusion and parody in its direct Juvenalian denunci-
       ation of a specific political act. See no. 1004.

## Religious Poems

1049   Armistead, J.M. "The Narrator as Rhetorician in Dryden's THE HIND
       AND PANTHER." JNT, 3 (1973), 208-18.

       Both narrative technique and allegorical drama are parts
       of a larger poetic strategy, a "lyrically rhetorical" point
       of view, which involves the reader in Dryden's newly
       acquired vision of religious truth.

1050    Atkins, G. Douglas. "Dryden's RELIGIO LAICI: A Reappraisal."
        SP, 75 (1978), 347-70.

        Not a defense of Anglicanism, Dryden's poem reflects the
        age's ambivalence about authority and individualism by
        attacking all forms of religious authority, whether mani-
        fested in the church or in the individual spirit; the poem
        argues for a simple lay approach to Scripture where God's
        might and mercy and man's insufficiency are reconciled.

1051    Budick, Sanford. DRYDEN AND THE ABYSS OF LIGHT: A STUDY
        OF RELIGIO LAICI AND THE HIND AND THE PANTHER. New
        Haven, Conn.: Yale Univ. Press, 1970.

        Comprehensive examination of Dryden's philosophical and
        religious thought, showing that a coherent set of opinions
        informs the poetic structures of these two important poems.

1052    Chiasson, Elias J. "Dryden's Apparent Scepticism in RELIGIO LAICI."
        HARVARD THEOLOGICAL REVIEW, 54 (1961), 207-21.

        Dryden's brand of skepticism is not specifically pyrrhonistic
        or fideistic, but rather in the tradition of Christian human-
        ism common to patristic, medieval, and Renaissance Chris-
        tianity which distinguishes between the order of nature and
        the order of grace, with nature as finally perfected by
        grace. See nos. 1005 and 1006.

1053    Corder, Jim W. "Rhetoric and Meaning in RELIGIO LAICI." PMLA,
        82 (1967), 245-49.

        By utilizing the "recognized rhetorical structure" featured
        in handbooks of oratory, "whether Ciceronian, Ramist, or
        whatever," Dryden addresses himself to the "necessities of
        faith by rhetorically and poetically rendering the inefficacy
        of the common versions of religious truth."

1054    Empson, William. "A Deist Tract by Dryden." EIC, 25 (1975), 74-
        100.

        Continues previous argument, below, concerning deistic
        tendencies in RELIGIO LAICI, but cites as support, works
        known to have influenced Dryden's thinking and in circula-
        tion among the avant-garde during the period of 1672 to
        1679. See no. 1055.

1055    _____. "Dryden's Apparent Scepticism." EIC, 20 (1970), 172-81.

        Argues that Dryden is "consistent and plain" about his
        main doctrine in RELIGIO LAICI: God gave mankind
        basic moral law at creation, regardless of what has

occurred throughout history, including revelation.  See
no. 1054.

1056    Fujimura, Thomas H.  "Dryden's RELIGIO LAICI:  An Anglican Poem."
PMLA, 76 (1961), 205-17.

Argues that Dryden's poem is "not a half-way house to
Catholicism but a conventional work of Anglican apologetics," its doctrine advocating reasonableness, moderate
faith, and the via media of the Church of England.

1057    _____.  "The Personal Drama of Dryden's THE HIND AND THE
PANTHER."  PMLA, 87 (1972), 406-16.

Concern with such matters as theology, the beast fable,
and the argumentative style has obscured the personal
struggle of the poet to achieve faith and charity, and
the poem's final achievement is to transform Dryden's
personal drama into the pattern of the universal Christian
drama.

1058    Gransden, K.W.  "What Kind of Poem is RELIGIO LAICI."  SEL, 17
(1977), 397-406.

An examination of the literary classicism behind the poem
as a key to Dryden's conservatism, quietism, emphasis on
conformity, and avoidance of extremes, showing that
RELIGIO LAICI owes not only its form and structure, but
its rhetorical techniques to the Latin poems Dryden knew
and translated.

1059    Hamm, Victor M.  "Dryden's RELIGIO LAICI and Roman Catholic
Apologetics."  PMLA, 80 (1969), 190-98.

Disagrees that RELIGIO LAICI gives no hint of Dryden's
later conversion to Catholicism, by considering important
Catholic theological and apologetic works well known in
England and echoed in the poem and by noting the de-
fensiveness of the prose apology for Anglicanism.

1060    _____.  "Dryden's THE HIND AND THE PANTHER and Roman Catholic
Apologetics."  PMLA, 83 (1968), 400-415.

Scholarly inquiry into Dryden's acquaintance with the
theological arguments of the day, concluding that rather
than succumbing to authority he was widely read and
knowledgeable about the Church's doctrine, standing "in
the very center of Counter-Reformation orthodoxy."

1061    Hooker, Edward N.  "Dryden and the Atoms of Epicurus."  ELH, 24
(1957), 177-90.

Argues that RELIGIO LAICI is less a religious poem or one about religion than a work responding to a specific debate on the scope and limitations of human reason and the implications of that debate for the political crisis of 1678 to 1682. See nos. 1005 and 1006.

1062    McHenry, Robert W. "Dryden's RELIGIO LAICI: An Augustan Drama of Ideas." EnlE, 4, i (1973), 60–64.

Stresses the idea that Dryden entertains, rather than holds, religious positions in the poem and therefore sees the opposition between rational religion and revelation as dramatic.

1063    Myers, William. "Politics in THE HIND AND THE PANTHER." EIC, 19 (1969), 19–33.

Faulting Dryden for using the beast fable as a vehicle to argue about theology is misdirected in that the bulk of the poem addresses serious political issues of the day, and Dryden's "apparent frivolity" in parts of the poem only underscores the seriousness of the political theme.

1064    Parkin, Rebecca Price. "Heroic and Anti-Heroic Elements in THE HIND AND THE PANTHER." SEL, 12 (1972), 459–66.

The skillful mixing of heroic and antiheroic elements in part 1 simulates both positive and negative, glorious and inglorious, actualities of the religious dilemmas facing Dryden and his age.

1065    Saslow, Edward L. "Angelic 'Fire-Works': The Background and Significance of THE HIND AND THE PANTHER, II, 649-62." SEL, 20 (1980), 373–84.

Argues against those who date Dryden's conversion to Catholicism on the basis of this "personal and confessional" passage, and points out that Dryden's other poems, as well as his theory of poetry, would indicate that the imagery in question is public and traditional in nature and refers to his wish for reunion of the English church with Rome.

1066    Ward, Charles E. "RELIGIO LAICI and Father Simon's HISTORY." MLN, 61 (1946), 407–12.

Study of the publication history of Dickinson's translation of the HISTORY suggests that Dryden knew of the work fully a year before publication of RELIGIO LAICI and thus had the time to familiarize himself with Simon's arguments and other religious treatises. See no. 1006.

1067    Welcher, Jeanne K. "The Opening of RELIGIO LAICI and its Virgilian
        Associations." SEL, 8 (1968), 391-96.

>    The imagery at the beginning of the poem echoes Virgil's
>    AENEID (6. 268-272) where Aeneas enters the underworld
>    to converse with his dead father and also reinforces the
>    theological point about the inadequacy of reason's dim
>    light by playing off the classical pagan against the Chris-
>    tian supernatural in Dante's version of the incident.

## Other Individual Poems

1068    Brennecke, Ernest, Jr. "Dryden's Odes and Draghi's Music." PMLA,
        49 (1934), 1-34.

>    Argues that Dryden's poetical accomplishment in the musi-
>    cal ode tradition is best understood by reference to his
>    own musical collaborators and by analysis of the settings
>    he actually knew and heard. See no. 1006.

1069    Buck, John Dawson Carl. "The Ascetic's Banquet: The Morality of
        ALEXANDER'S FEAST." TSLL, 17 (1975), 573-89.

>    Rather than viewing the poem as an occasional piece
>    commemorating St. Cecilia on her feast day and the
>    power of music generally, sees it as an ironic performance
>    in light of Dryden's pessimism and sense of general corrup-
>    tion which included the sister arts by the year 1697.

1070    Canfield, J. Douglas. "The Image of the Circle in Dryden's 'To My
        Honour'd Kinsman.'" PLL, 11 (1975), 168-76.

>    The circle image, standing for perfection of the soul in
>    the retirement poem tradition, is the central motif of the
>    poem, implying that his cousin John Driden had achieved
>    "transcendence of mutability."

1071    Griffin, Dustin. "Dryden's 'Oldham' and the Perils of Writing." MLQ,
        37 (1976), 133-50.

>    Takes issue with readings of the poem as a model classical
>    expression of restrained and controlled feeling, and in-
>    terestingly stresses the self-implicating nature of the perils,
>    obstacles, and failures of the life of writing for Dryden.

1072    Hoffman, Arthur W. "Dryden's Panegyrics and Lyrics." In JOHN
        DRYDEN: WRITERS AND THEIR BACKGROUND. Ed. Earl Miner.
        Athens: Ohio Univ. Press, 1972, pp. 120-55.

>    Discursive but helpful analysis of Dryden's political

panegyrics in the context of his providential view of
history, as well as a sensitive reading of his commenda-
tory poems of praise, both groups manifesting an essentially
lyric impulse found also in Dryden's songs and odes. See
no. 1004.

1073    Hooker, Edward N. "The Purpose of Dryden's ANNUS MIRABILIS."
HLQ, 10 (1946), 49-67.

Views the poem as an "eloquent panegyric," a "noble
proclamation of Britain's manifest destiny." See no. 1006.

1074    Hope, Alec D. "'Anne Killigrew,' or the Art of Modulating." In
DRYDEN'S MIND AND ART. Ed. Bruce King. London: Oliver and
Bond, 1969, pp. 99-113.

Choosing "a rhetorical and baroque style," Dryden effects
a careful modulation of tones with the skill of a trained
musician in a poem that challenges accepted tastes, pro-
prieties, and often common sense. See no. 1002.

1075    King, Bruce. "'Lycidas' and 'Oldham.'" EA, 19 (1966), 60-63.

Short but instructive comparison of these two elegies,
indicating similarities in phrasing, diction, imagery, and
use of classical allusion (especially Virgilian echoes), but
also pointing out major differences between Milton's Christian conceptualization and Dryden's classicism.

1076    Kinsley, James. "Dryden and the Art of Praise." ES, 34 (1953),
57-64.

Ties Dryden's panegyrical mode to the classical and Renaissance traditions of praise and shows that the heightening
and idealizing procedures of compliment constitute the
imaginative freedom that characterizes all good art. See
no. 1006.

1077    Levine, Jay Arnold. "John Dryden's 'Epistle to John Driden.'" JEGP,
62 (1964), 450-74.

Comprehensive study of this verse epistle, exploring the
contributions of history, politics, the Horatian model, the
body-politic imagery, religious themes, and biographical
fact to its rhetorical organization and effects. See no.
1002.

1078    McKeon, Michael. POLITICS AND POETRY IN RESTORATION
ENGLAND: THE CASE OF DRYDEN'S ANNUS MIRABILIS. Cambridge,
Mass.: Harvard Univ. Press, 1975.

A difficult and sometimes overly schematic study attempting
to fuse the familiar poetic and political approaches to the
poem into a new fully rhetorical reading of the poem that
better accounts for a variety of particular concerns pre-
occupying Dryden at the time.

1079    MacLean, G.M.  "Poetry as History: The Argumentative Design of
        Dryden's ASTRAEA REDUX."  RESTORATION, 4 (1980), 54-64.

        Argues that Dryden's poem presents contemporary history
        "opportunistically," constructing an argument that con-
        trols his use of ideas of history and his shaping of his-
        torical events.

1080    Maurer, A.E. Wallace.  "The Structure of Dryden's ASTRAEA REDUX."
        PLL, 2 (1966), 13-20.

        At this critical beginning for Dryden of a new political
        era and a new poetic career, his organizational pattern
        follows the master plan of the classical oration as defined
        in England by Renaissance and neoclassical commentators
        concerning the establishment of authoritative speech.

1081    Mell, Donald C., Jr.  "Dryden and the Transformation of the Classical."
        PLL, 17 (1981), 146-63.

        For Dryden, ideal imitation "necessarily involves returning
        to the classical past by means of the present imaginative
        act," the process of creation affirming the past in the
        present and reinforcing the importance of "individual
        talent" in redeeming the "tradition." Treats especially
        "To the Earl of Roscommon," "To Sir Godfrey Kneller,"
        and "To the Memory of Mr. Oldham."

1082    Miner, Earl.  "Chaucer in Dryden's FABLES."  In STUDIES IN CRITI-
        CISM AND AESTHETICS, 1660-1800: ESSAYS IN HONOR OF SAMUEL
        HOLT MONK.  Ed. Howard Anderson and John S. Shea.  Minneapolis:
        Univ. of Minnesota Press, 1967, pp. 58-72.

        An excellent account of the purposes guiding Dryden's
        numerous alterations of Chaucer's text (as he knew it)
        in terms of his historical conception and the processes
        of mimetic transformation of Chaucer into permanent
        status as a classic. See no. 93.

1083    _____.  "Dryden's EIKON BASILIKE: TO SIR GODFREY KNELLER."
        In SEVENTEENTH-CENTURY IMAGERY: ESSAYS ON THE USES OF
        FIGURATIVE LANGUAGE FROM DONNE TO FARQUHAR.  Ed. Earl
        Miner.  Berkeley: Univ. of California Press, 1971, pp. 151-67.

Close analysis of the poem's themes, structure, and patterns of imagery, focusing on the sister arts motif, on the temporal division into sections dealing with past, present, and future, and on images equating historical and artistic progress and fulfillment in the continuities of time.

1084    See no. 1035.

1085    Peterson, R.G. "The Unavailing Gift: Dryden's Roman Farewell to Mr. Oldham." MP, 66 (1969), 232-36.

Discusses Dryden's uses of the conventions of Latin poetry and Roman life, especially in Virgil, Catullus, and the technique of conclamatio, the final tribute to the dead.

1086    Proffitt, Bessie. "Political Satire in Dryden's ALEXANDER'S FEAST." TSLL, 11 (1970), 1307-16.

Contends that this famous ode celebrating the expressive powers of music is actually a subtle attack on William III, developing its political theme not through image patterns, but rather through the ideas of illegitimacy and illegality that run through the poem.

1087    Roper, Alan. "Dryden's SECULAR MASQUE." MLQ, 23 (1962), 29-40.

Considers the emblematic reading of the masque as inadequate and points out the many assumptions underlying its use of mythology and masque structure, concluding that Momus' famous final lines are highly ambiguous, simultaneously prophesying the beginning of a new golden age and a repetition of the "foolish, frivolous" historical process.

1088    Sloman, Judith. "Dryden's Originality in SIGISMONDA AND GUIS-CARDO." SEL, 12 (1972), 445-57.

Dryden's changes from the original Boccaccio version reveal how much FABLES (1700) expresses his conception of psychological complexity also found in earlier plays; the pattern of light imagery enforces the themes and intentions of his poetic art.

1089    _____. "An Interpretation of Dryden's FABLES." ECS, 4 (1970-71), 199-211.

Deals with the disillusionment revealed by Dryden's design of the volume which grew out of the clash between his notion of progressive spiritual and religious ideals since Christianity and his recognition of human limitations shared with his classical and Renaissance predecessors.

1090    Smith, Ruth. "The Argument and Contexts of Dryden's ALEXANDER'S
        FEAST." SEL, 18 (1978), 465-90.

>    Dryden treats Alexander as both a humbling figure and as
>    an object of ridicule who is used not only to symbolize
>    human frailty against a background of human achievement
>    but also as a figurative means of questioning both frailty
>    and heroism, a satirical method of ironic qualification
>    reminiscent of Dryden's plays.

1091    Swedenberg, H.T. "England's Joy: ASTRAEA REDUX in its Setting."
        SP, 50 (1953), 30-44.

>    Considered in its historical perspective and as a tract of
>    the times, Dryden's panegyric transcends personal or party
>    matters and celebrates a traditional English attitude toward
>    government and monarchy in terms of the myth of Astraea,
>    the return of law and order.

1092    Tillyard, E.M.W. "Ode on Anne Killigrew." In FIVE POEMS.
        London: Chatto and Windus, 1948. pp. 49-65.

>    An account of the poem analyzing its form and structure
>    and demonstrating its embodiment of seventeenth-century
>    metaphysics, traditions of poetic decorum, classicism,
>    and high valuation of the arts. See no. 1005.

1093    Vieth, David M. "Irony in Dryden's ODE TO ANNE KILLIGREW."
        SP, 62 (1965), 91-100.

>    Not just a display of literary convention or a compendium
>    of Renaissance literary forms designed for praise and lament,
>    the ode employs an irony latent in the hyperbole of praise
>    and is a "vital expression of the Augustan sensibility,"
>    communicating affection but not at the expense of realism.

1094    _____. "Irony in Dryden's Verses to Sir Robert Howard." EIC, 22
        (1972), 239-43.

>    Argues that underlying irony gives depth and added interest
>    to Dryden's praise of his friend and future brother-in-law's
>    translations and that the loose organization of images is
>    made coherent by the tone of qualified praise.

1095    Wallerstein, Ruth. "On the Death of Mrs. Killigrew: The Perfecting
        of a Genre." SP, 44 (1947), 519-28.

>    Classic generic study of Dryden's poem, showing by means
>    of its invention, imagery, versification, and formal design
>    that it artistically unites thought and feeling while re-
>    constituting the tradition of the formal ode. See no. 1006.

## General Critical Studies

1096    Amarasinghe, Upali. DRYDEN AND POPE IN THE EARLY NINETEENTH
        CENTURY: A STUDY OF CHANGING LITERARY TASTE. Cambridge:
        Cambridge Univ. Press, 1962.

> Detailed study of the complex forces affecting the repu-
> tations of Dryden, Pope, and Johnson during the early
> nineteenth century, showing that pro-Augustan and anti-
> Augustan attitudes often existed together in the same
> critic.

1097    Atkins, G. Douglas. THE FAITH OF JOHN DRYDEN: CHANGE
        AND CONTINUITY. Lexington: Univ. Press of Kentucky, 1980.

> Treats the entire range of his work, not just the two
> major religious poems, exploring the tensions between
> Dryden and the priesthood and the church, as well as
> the conflicting impulses within his mind and heart that
> reflect "his own evolution from a modernistic viewpoint
> to a much more traditional understanding" in his process
> of formulating a layman's faith.

1098    Blair, Joel. "Dryden's Ceremonial Hero."  SEL, 9 (1969), 379-93.

> Dryden's early poems of praise transform particular histori-
> cal subjects into symbols involved in the ritualistic process
> of overcoming threats and danger. In the late panegyrics,
> this ceremonial treatment fails because of Dryden's skepti-
> cal view of individual destiny as separate from political
> role.

1099    Bottkol, J.M.  "Dryden's Latin Scholarship."  MP, 40 (1942-43),
        241-54.

> Refutes charges that Dryden was a careless translator irre-
> sponsibly using his originals, by demonstrating that his de-
> partures or alterations are either aesthetic or stylistic.
> See no. 1006.

1100    Bredvold, Louis I. THE INTELLECTUAL MILIEU OF JOHN DRYDEN:
        STUDIES IN SOME ASPECTS OF SEVENTEETH-CENTURY THOUGHT.
        Ann Arbor: Univ. of Michigan Press, 1934.

> Classic study of the influence of the traditions of skepti-
> cism on Dryden's intellect, political and religious thought,
> and artistic consciousness.

1101    Brower, Reuben A.  "An Allusion to Europe:  Dryden and the Poetic
        Tradition."  ELH, 29 (1952), 38-48.

Emphasizes Dryden's public, classical, and allusive qualities as reaffirming Europe in English poetry and culture,
by imitating and making use of the resources of other
poets and poetic modes and at the same time displaying
an originality and establishing an individual style. Lays
the groundwork for three decades of Dryden criticism.
See no. 1005.

1102 _____. "Dryden's Epic Manner and Virgil." PMLA, 55 (1940), 119-
38.

Seminal essay exploring Dryden's use of Virgilian allusions
to create the heightened tones of the heroic mode. See
no. 1006.

1103 _____. "Visual and Verbal Translation of Myth: Neptune in Virgil,
Rubens, Dryden." DAEDALUS, 101 (1972), 155-82.

Discusses three versions of the Quos ego (Neptune calming
the tempest) scene as rendered by Virgil, Rubens, and
Dryden to explain the special visual-verbal complexity
of Dryden's rendition.

1104 Cameron, W.J. "John Dryden's Jacobitism." In RESTORATION LITERA-
TURE: CRITICAL APPROACHES. Ed. H. Love. London: Methuen,
1972, pp. 277-308.

Locates in Dryden's poetry and translations certain ideological conflicts resulting from his adherence to the lost cause
of Jacobitism; but views his making of the revolutionary
settlement "passively acceptable to Jacobites," through
the postscript to his AENEIS, a positive contribution to
his country. See no. 118.

1105 Ehrenpreis, Irvin. "Continuity and Coruscation: Dryden's Poetic
Instincts." In his JOHN DRYDEN II. Intro. Maximillion E. Novak.
Los Angeles: William Andrews Clark Memorial Library, 1978, pp. 3-26.

Characterizes Dryden's poetry as remarkable for its lack
of continuity and describes his genius as essentially
dualistic, playing off tones and modes against one another
as well as manipulating neoclassical rules and categories
for ironic purposes.

1106 Eliot, T.S. "John Dryden." In his SELECTED ESSAYS OF T.S. ELIOT.
New York: Harcourt, Brace, 1932, pp. 264-74.

Influential essay of appreciation, stressing Dryden's use
of the denotative qualities of language and his "unique

merit" in transforming prosaic matters into poetry and
making the trivial grand for satiric purposes.

1107 _____. JOHN DRYDEN: THE POET, THE DRAMATIST, THE CRITIC.
New York: Terence and Elsa Holliday, 1932.

Appreciative but perceptive essay signaling Dryden's importance to the modern writer-critic as both stylist and
transitional figure in the history of English poetry.

1108 Emslie, Macdonald. "Dryden's Couplets: Wit and Conversation." EIC,
11 (1961), 264–73.

Full appreciation of Dryden's "new range of colloquial
inflexions" requires not only sensitivity to the quality
and variety of tones and attitudes, but also a familiarity
with the audience Dryden addresses and the values of
the society of his age.

1109 Erskine-Hill, Howard. "John Dryden: The Poet and Critic." In THE
HISTORY OF LITERATURE IN THE ENGLISH LANGUAGE. Ed. Roger
Lonsdale. Vol. 4. London: Barrie and Jenkins, 1971, pp. 23–59.

Sees Dryden's greatness as "a poet of public life," en-
dowing affairs of state with "excitement, dignity, and
splendor" while at the same time developing a uniquely
personal expression that gave rise to tensions between the
heroic and comic, the lofty and plain, the lyrical and
prosaic. See no. 32A.

1110 Feder, Lillian. "John Dryden's Use of Classical Rhetoric." PMLA, 69
(1954), 1258–78.

Despite his reputation for colloquial diction and rhetorical
simplicity, Dryden often employed Ciceronian and Quintil-
ian oratorical style and practice from his earliest panegyrics
in such later poems as THE HIND AND THE PANTHER.
See no. 1006.

1111 Ferry, Anne Davidson. MILTON AND THE MILTONIC DRYDEN.
Cambridge, Mass.: Harvard Univ. Press, 1968.

Views the traditional separation of these two poets as
misleading and emphasizes Dryden's assimilation of the
design, heroic manner, and language of PARADISE LOST
into his ABSALOM AND ACHITOPHEL.

1112 French, A.L. "Dryden, Marvell and Political Poetry." SEL, 8 (1968),
397–413.

Unlike Marvell's "Horatian Ode," in which classical and Old Testament parallels provide positive standards of value, Dryden's ABSALOM AND ACHITOPHEL uses such imagery in a more perfunctory way, revealing his age's loss of faith in classical and biblical values.

1113    Frost, William. DRYDEN AND FUTURE SHOCK. ELS Monograph Series, no. 5. Victoria, B.C.: English Literary Studies, 1976.

An innovative and bizarrely organized discussion of Dryden (with some attention to Rochester) as a writer deeply involved in and influenced by his age, an influence on his age as well, and, finally, an artist whose perceptions and style continually provide "future shocks."

1114    _____. DRYDEN AND THE ART OF TRANSLATION. New Haven, Conn.: Yale Univ. Press, 1955.

Discusses Dryden's themes and practice of translation as well as the age's complex attitudes toward the heroic past. Final two chapters focus on Dryden's use of heroic materials in his original poetry and make a number of critical comparisons with Pope. Best book on the topic.

1115    _____. "English Persius: The Golden Age." ECS, 2 (1968), 77-101.

Surveys well-known translations of Persius and explores the linguistic, literary, moral, and psychological qualities of the original that inspired a number of imaginative renditions, especially Dryden's, in the period of 1660 to 1800.

1116    Fujimura, Thomas H. "Dryden's Poetics: The Expressive Values in Poetry." JEGP, 74 (1975), 195-208.

Excessive concern for political-religious background and figurative language obfuscates the expressive potentialities of music, harmony, and sound in Dryden's poetic creation of a "vision of a golden civilization on the par with the great Augustan world."

1117    _____. "John Dryden and the Myth of the Golden Age." PLL, 11 (1975), 149-67.

Discusses various manifestations of the golden age concept and cultural primitivism in selected poems of Dryden.

1118    _____. "The Temper of John Dryden." SP, 72 (1975), 348-66.

Argues that Dryden was not a representative figure of his age and that his personality was "essentially vigorous, aggressive, and independent."

1119    Garrison, James D.  DRYDEN AND THE TRADITION OF PANEGYRIC.
        Berkeley:  Univ. of California Press, 1975.

> Investigates the connections between Dryden's panegyrical
> verse and the literary traditions and conventions of the
> mode in the classics as well as in the seventeenth century,
> and shows how Dryden shapes these practices to celebrate
> a turning point in British history and to remind the rulers
> of their political responsibilities and limitations.  Excellent
> discussion.

1120    Guibbory, Achsah.  "Dryden's Views of History."  PQ, 52 (1973),
        187-204.

> Dryden's historical perspective combines three distinct
> themes of history assimilating a classical cyclic theory
> with the modern deterministic and Christian-providential
> views through a skeptical modification which eliminates
> their seeming mutual exclusiveness.

1121    Hamilton, Kenneth G.  JOHN DRYDEN AND THE POETRY OF STATE-
        MENT.  East Lansing:  Michigan State Univ. Press, 1969.

> By close analysis of structure, technique, and the craft
> of poems mainly from the years 1682 to 1687, explains
> the special poetic life of Dryden's direct and discursive
> poetry of statement.

1122    Harth, Phillip.  CONTEXTS OF DRYDEN'S THOUGHT.  Chicago:
        Univ. of Chicago Press, 1968.

> Fine scholarly study of Dryden's religious views and his
> attitudes toward the competing claims of reason and reve-
> lation, especially in RELIGIO LAICI and THE HIND AND
> THE PANTHER, against the background of the specific
> historical contexts in which he wrote.  This best study
> of the intellectual milieu to date supersedes Bredvold.

1123    Hemphill, George.  "Dryden's Heroic Line."  PMLA, 72 (1957), 803-
        79.

> Studies metrical variations from the norm of the heroic line,
> accounting for the "patterning of stresses" and distribution
> of syllables in order to show Dryden's careful prosodic
> control and craftsmanship.  See no. 1006.

1124    Hoffman, Arthur W.  JOHN DRYDEN'S IMAGERY.  Gainesville:  Univ.
        of Florida Press, 1962.

> A fine new critical approach to image patterns and meta-
> phorical systems in selected poems.  An important applica-

tion of close analysis to Dryden's poetry, and the best
example of this approach to date.

1124A    Hume, Robert D. DRYDEN'S CRITICISM. Ithaca, N.Y.: Cornell
Univ. Press, 1970.

A full-scale study of Dryden's literary opinions. Assesses
Dryden's critical aims and methods, places them in the
context of his age, and demonstrates the unity and stability of his critical principles as part of "a coherent
and sophisticated view of literature." The best book-
length treatment.

1125     Jefferson, Douglas W. "Aspects of Dryden's Imagery." EIC, 4 (1954),
20-41.

Believes that Dryden's imagery at its best encompasses,
rather than rejects, the distinct features of metaphysical
poetry of wit, namely the juxtapositioning of grandeur
with absurdity, the exalted with the petty, the serious
with comic deflation, and the possibility of imaginative
transcendence with a sense of human limitations. See
no. 1002.

1126     Kinsley, James, and Helen Kinsley, eds. DRYDEN: THE CRITICAL
HERITAGE. London: Routledge and Kegan Paul, 1971.

Includes extracts from early (THE REHEARSAL, 1671) and
late attacks (Blake) on Dryden; but since he was often
"his own best critic," also prints excerpts from his dedi-
cations, critical essays on the theater, and the great
tributes ranging from Congreve's and Pope's to Johnson's
and Walter Scott's.

1127     Love, Harold. "Dryden's 'Unideal Vacancy.'" ECS, 12 (1978), 74-89.

Treats Dryden's (and others') use of imagery and metaphor
in the context of Cartesian and Lockean language theories
and argues that tropes, conceits, and metaphysical wit
were "conscious and calculated features of style," rather
than truly representative of the "Augustan ideals of clarity
and decorum."

1128     Macdonald, Hugh. "The Attacks on Dryden." ESSAYS AND STUDIES
BY THE MEMBERS OF THE ENGLISH ASSOCIATION, 21 (1936), 41-74.

Surveys the inveterate and often abusive attacks throughout
his literary career, marvelling that, unlike the much maligned Pope, Dryden remained even-tempered, modest,
often generous, and possessed a noncontroversial personality. See no. 1006.

1129   McFadden, George.  DRYDEN: THE PUBLIC WRITER 1660-1685.
       Princeton, N.J.: Princeton Univ. Press, 1978.

       Careful discussion of the artistic continuity marking Dry-
       den's response to "contingent events and circumstances"
       characterizing the often chaotic reign of Charles II.

1130   Mell, Donald C.  "Art Versus History:  Dryden's Ambivalence Toward
       the Idea of Artistic Progress."  EnlE, 5, iii-iv (1974), 49-70.

       Discussion of Dryden's complex attitudes toward time,
       change, and history as treated in the images of artistic
       permanence and recurring cycles of human experience
       found in the poems of praise.  Treats ASTRAEA REDUX
       and the poems addressed to Howard, Roscommon, Oldham,
       and Congreve.

1131   Miner, Earl.  "Dryden and the Issue of Human Progress."  PQ, 40
       (1961), 120-29.

       Examines the sharpening of Dryden's critical sense as a
       result of his "heightened awareness of the relation of
       the past to the present" and his witty and complex use
       of imagery to depict simultaneously development and
       growth, achievement and process, and accomplishment
       lying outside temporal perfection.

1132   _____.  "Dryden's Admired Acquaintance, Mr. Milton."  In THE
       PRESENCE OF MILTON.  Ed. B. Rajan.  MiltonS, 11 (1978), 3-27.

       Takes issue with critics who suggest that Dryden felt
       Freudian anxiety toward a "poetic father" or an intellec-
       tual "burden of the past" and argues persuasively that
       the Milton-Dryden relationship predates the romantic view
       of literary history and originality and that Dryden spent
       thirty years being original through indebtedness to earlier
       writers, emerging finally into full maturity with FABLES.

1133   _____.  DRYDEN'S POETRY.  Bloomington: Indiana Univ. Press,
       1967.

       A comprehensive study of Dryden's poetic art, locating
       the creative force in his characteristic expressiveness of
       unified themes, his Christian humanism yet progressivist
       faith and modernity, his personalized religious beliefs
       and thought, and the still essentially public nature of his
       expression.  Best full-length study since Van Doren's (no.
       1147).

1134   _____.  "Forms and Motives of Narrative Poetry."  In JOHN DRYDEN:

209

WRITERS AND THEIR BACKGROUND. Ed. Earl Miner. Athens: Ohio
Univ. Press, 1972, pp. 234-66.

> Discusses the influence of the heroic mode and narrative
> practice on Dryden's career, citing his critical writings
> for theoretical justification and the variety of narrative
> actions manifest in his panegyrical mode, political satire,
> religious poems, and FABLES. See no. 1004.

1135 _____. "On Reading Dryden." In JOHN DRYDEN: WRITERS AND
THEIR BACKGROUND. Ed. Earl Miner. Athens: Ohio Univ. Press,
1972, pp. 1-26.

> Excellent overview of Dryden's reputation and a commentary
> on his artistic strengths and weaknesses, concluding with an
> analysis of his new version of the ancient concept of dis-
> cordia concors as reflected in the creative force of his
> comparative method, his sense of separateness yet identity
> in both his poetry and criticism. Good introduction to
> Dryden. See no. 1004.

1136 _____. "The Poetics of the Critical Act: Dryden's Dealings with
Rivals and Predecessors." In EVIDENCE IN LITERARY SCHOLARSHIP:
ESSAYS IN MEMORY OF JAMES MARSHALL OSBORN. Ed. René
Wellek and Alvaro Ribeiro. Oxford: Clarendon Press, 1979, pp. 45-62.

> Valuable and suggestive discussion of Dryden's situation in
> the history of English literature as someone uniquely aware
> "that he was prosecuting a critical career in which poetic
> practice and critical precept were counterparts." See no.
> 129.

1137 _____. "In Satire's Falling City." In THE SATIRIST'S ART. Ed.
H. James Jensen and Malvin R. Zirker, Jr. Bloomington: Indiana
Univ. Press, 1972, pp. 3-27.

> Far-reaching and speculative analysis contending that
> satire's central concern with "the process of the ruin of
> an ideal city" and, conversely, panegyric's idealizing
> vision and procedures of celebration are both extreme
> views of reality that depend on one another for their
> meaning. See no. 113.

1138 _____. "Some Characteristics of Dryden's Use of Metaphor." SEL,
2 (1962), 309-20.

> Close analysis of selections primarily from ABSALOM AND
> ACHITOPHEL and MAC FLECKNOE, showing how various
> types of metaphoric action control the structure, tone, and
> values of the whole poem. See no. 1005.

1139   Myers, William. DRYDEN. London: Hutchinson, 1973.

Seeks to demonstrate how "completely and impressively Dryden deployed a limited and perhaps debased poetic idiom" to the examination of human problems created by the particular historical circumstances in which he wrote. Good general study.

1140   See no. 1864.

1141   Proudfoot, L.D. DRYDEN'S AENEID AND ITS SEVENTEENTH CENTURY PREDECESSORS. Manchester, Engl.: Univ. of Manchester Press, 1960.

Still the standard and best study of Dryden's knowledge and use of earlier translations and renderings of Virgil's poem, as well as a careful assessment of his superior translation.

1142   Ramsey, Paul. THE ART OF JOHN DRYDEN. Lexington: Univ. of Kentucky Press, 1969.

The nature Dryden imitates is a "life-giving power that derives from the ordered, vigorous whole of the universe" and, thus, his poetry continually reflects order, energy, design, and imagination.

1143   Ricks, Christopher. "Allusion: The Poet as Heir." In STUDIES IN THE EIGHTEENTH CENTURY III: PAPERS PRESENTED AT THE THIRD DAVID NICHOL SMITH MEMORIAL SEMINAR, CANBERRA, 1973. Ed. R.F. Brissenden and J.C. Eade. Toronto: Univ. of Toronto Press, 1976, pp. 209-40.

Explores the literal and metaphoric use of familial succession motifs in Dryden's poetry, touching on the political ramification of the succession idea and on his relationship with such fellow poets as Milton. A brilliant discussion fusing literary history, psychological motivation, and a detailed knowledge of the times. See no. 99.

1144   Roper, Alan. DRYDEN'S POETIC KINGDOMS. London: Routledge and Kegan Paul, 1965.

Dryden's special contribution to English poetry is his successful celebration of the public values of peace, security, authority, and political orders; and this royalism transcends politics by shaping and controlling his whole interpretation of human experience. Excellent study.

1145   Sutherland, James. JOHN DRYDEN: THE POET AS ORATOR. Glasgow: Jackson, Son and Co., 1963.

Generalized tribute to Dryden's belief in "the power of writing" and to his faith in the capacity of language to move people, no matter what literary form he chose.

1146    Swedenberg, H.T., Jr.  "Dryden's Obsessive Concern with the Heroic."  In ESSAYS IN ENGLISH LITERATURE OF THE CLASSICAL PERIOD, SP, Extra Series, 4 (1967), 12-26.

The heroic mode was "the métier toward which his genius naturally leaned," especially in Dryden's panegyrics and historical and satirical poems.

1147    Van Doren, Mark.  JOHN DRYDEN: A STUDY OF HIS POETRY.  Bloomington: Indiana Univ. Press, 1960.

Originally published in 1920, this pioneering study of Dryden's poetry attracted important reviews by T.S. Eliot, among others.  Seminal critical study of the century.

1148    Verrall, Arthur W.  LECTURES ON DRYDEN.  Cambridge:  Cambridge Univ. Press, 1914.

Famous series of lectures assessing Dryden's achievement as poet, playwright, and critic; markedly judicious and sympathetic in evaluations of his art.

1149    Vieth, David M.  "Concept as Metaphor:  Dryden's Attempted Stylistic Revolution."  LANGUAGE AND STYLE, 3 (1970), 201-03.

Well known as a period of linguistic and stylistic innovation, the Restoration in the person of John Dryden repeatedly tried to make abstract concepts or principles perform the function of metaphor, operating simultaneously as idea and image.  Brief references to ABSALOM AND ACHITOPHEL, ALEXANDER'S FEAST, ELEONORA, and THE MEDAL.

1150    Wasserman, George R.  JOHN DRYDEN.  New York: Twayne, 1964.

General analysis of major areas of Dryden's career, synthesizing new discoveries and enthusiasms in the early panegyrics, political and literary satires, religious poems, and later lyrics.

1151    West, Michael.  "Shifting Concepts of Heroism in Dryden's Panegyrics."  PLL, 10 (1974), 378-93.

Argues that Dryden moves from hero worship to a profound mistrust of heroism, the earlier poems of praise celebrating heroic virtue, the later redefining the heroic in Christian

terms, and holds that this ambivalent view toward the
heroic reveals itself in his mock-heroic masterpieces.

1152    Wykes, David.  A PREFACE TO DRYDEN.  New York:  Longman,
        1977.  Illus.

        Intended "for those needing modern and authoritative
        guidance."  Useful survey of Dryden's life, thought,
        political and historical milieu, and art.  Includes in-
        teresting illustrations and short biographies of various
        political figures.

1153    Zwicker, Steven N.  DRYDEN'S POLITICAL POETRY: THE TYPOLOGY
        OF KING AND NATION.  Providence, R.I.: Brown Univ. Press, 1972.

        Argues that Dryden's political poems appeal to the modern
        reader mostly because of his attempt "to forge a sacred
        history" for England through the association of political
        events with biblical prophecy and sacred history.

# STEPHEN DUCK (1705-56)

## A. MAJOR EDITIONS

There is no modern edition of Duck's poetry.

1154    POEMS ON SEVERAL OCCASIONS. London: W. Bickerton, 1736.

        Includes Joseph Spence's famous account (1730) of Duck's career, background, acquisition of taste, and reading habits, pointing out that Milton's PARADISE LOST was to Duck what the Greek and Roman classics were to the better known Augustans and provided his inspiration to write poetry.

1155    Southey, Robert. "Steven Duck." In LIVES AND WORKS OF THE UNEDUCATED POETS. Ed. J.S. Childers. London: H. Milford, 1925, pp. 88-113, 182-91.

        An appreciation of Duck, pointing out that he was conscious that his talents for poetry were imitative rather than inventive and also that he was incapable of imitating what he clearly saw was best; thus, he could not really have developed into a great poet.

1156    POEMS ON SEVERAL OCCASIONS, 1736. Intro. John Lucas. 1736; Facs. rpt. Menston, Yorkshire, Engl.: Scolar Press, 1973.

## B. BIBLIOGRAPHY AND TEXTUAL STUDIES

1157    See no. 1160.

## C. BIOGRAPHY

1158    Blunden, Edmund. "The Farmer's Boy: S. Duck and R. Bloomfield."

In his NATURE IN ENGLISH LITERATURE.  New York:  Harcourt, Brace, 1929, pp. 106-31.

> Views Duck as a misguided, almost tragic, figure, whose talents lay in a realistic native style rooted in the experiences of his rural years, and asserts that neither his contemporaries nor he really believed that "the voice of Nature" was possible in poetry.

1159    Peel, J.H.B.  "From Farm Labourer to Court Poet."  LISTENER, 68 (1962), 616, 619.

> A biographical account of Duck's literary successes as well as failures, the latter partly the result of his attempts to ape contemporary poetic fashions uncongenial to his native talents.

# D.  CRITICISM

1160    Davis, Rose Mary.  STEPHEN DUCK, THE THRESHER-POET.  Orono: Univ. of Maine Press, 1926.  Bibliog.

> Extensively documented critical biography that explains the fascination for Duck in socioliterary terms: as the romantic interest of the literary establishment of the 1730s in a truly proletarian-peasant-poet.

1161    Furnival, R.G.  "Stephen Duck:  The Wiltshire Phenomenon, 1705-1756."  CAMBRIDGE JOURNAL, 6 (1953), 486-96.

> Duck may not have written "what we now would designate as great poetry.  He created something else.  He created a sensation."  He should be remembered as "singularly unfitted" to enter the "most brilliant and exacting literary societies."

1162    Osborn, James M.  "Spence, Natural Genius, and Pope."  PQ, 45 (1966), 123-44.

> A discussion of the concept of the natural genius in the early part of the century and of the interest shown by Spence and Pope in such untutored writers of promise and talent as Duck.

1163    Paffard, Michael.  "Stephen Duck, The Thresher Poet."  HISTORY TODAY, 27 (1977), 467-72.

> Describes the rise to poetic fame of this unlikely "common Thresher" from obscure rural beginnings to contender for the poet laureateship in 1730.

# JOHN DYER (1699-1758)

## A. MAJOR EDITIONS

1164    POEMS BY JOHN DYER. 1761; Facs. rpt. Menston, Yorkshire, Engl.: Scolar Press, 1971.

       Reprints first edition of Dodsley printing of 1761.

1165    MISCELLANEOUS POEMS AND TRANSLATIONS. Ed. Richard Savage. London: S. Chapman, 1726.

       Includes the Pindaric version of "Grongar Hill," among other poems. Also prints poems of Savage and Aaron Hill.

1166    See no. 552.

1167    POEMS BY JOHN DYER. Ed. Edward D. Thomas. London: T.F. Unwin, 1903.

       Best known early twentieth-century edition.

1168    GRONGAR HILL. Ed. Richard C. Boys. Baltimore: Johns Hopkins Press, 1941.

       Examines the successive stages of GRONGAR HILL, from Pindaric structure to the more familiar tetrameter version, treating the sequence of texts and complex textual evidence.

## B. BIBLIOGRAPHY AND TEXTUAL STUDIES

1169    Greever, Garland. "The Two Versions of GRONGAR HILL." JEGP, 16 (1917), 274-81.

       Gives in full the first version of GRONGAR HILL as it appeared in Richard Savage's MISCELLANEOUS POEMS

AND TRANSLATIONS (1776)--consisting of a mixture of the styles of Dryden and Pope, the lilting measures of Milton's L'ALLEGRO and IL PENSEROSO, and iambic pentameter variously rhymed--but judges the final tetrameter version superior in respect to meter, handling of imagery, and tone.

1170   Hughes, Helen S. "John Dyer and the Countess of Hertford." MP, 27 (1930), 311-20.

A transitional version of GRONGAR HILL is found copied in the opening pages of Lady Hertford's manuscript MISCELLANY, written in its final octosyllabic couplets with some phrases preserved from the earlier Pindaric ode form and with some experimental lines omitted in the later Dodsley edition of 1761.

1171   Tillotson, Geoffrey. "GRONGAR HILL: An Introduction and Texts." In his AUGUSTAN STUDIES. London: Athlone Press, 1961, pp. 184-203.

Discusses the textual history and prints several versions of the poem--all prefaced by a commentary on Dyer's modernity in choosing such a place as a poetic setting and combining natural description with reflective and meditative modes. See no. 126.

1172   Williams, Ralph M. "The Publication of Dyer's RUINS OF ROME." MP, 44 (1946), 97-101.

Dyer's careful and compulsive revising practices account, in part, for the small quantity of verse he published, and his wide variety of interests often impelled him into new projects before he had finished the poem at hand.

## C. BIOGRAPHY

1173   Parker, Edward A., and Ralph M. Williams. "John Dyer, The Poet as Farmer." AGRICULTURAL HISTORY, 22 (1948), 134-41.

Fascinating account, derived from Dyer's notebooks, of his first year as a farmer (1734), discussing ways in which his records possibly reflect contemporary farming practices of his locality and their value as resources for the writing of an agricultural history of the period.

1174   Williams, Ralph M. "John Dyer's Degree from Cambridge." MLN, 61 (1946), 172-75.

Dyer received a mandated degree of Bachelor of Laws from

Cambridge University in 1751 through the good offices of
his patron Philip Yorke, and the motivations behind this
action explain some of the methods employed in awarding
degrees per literas regias.

1175 _____. POET, PAINTER, AND PARSON: THE LIFE OF JOHN DYER.
New York: Bookman Associates, 1956.

A biography using material from family papers and other
manuscript sources in order to fill in gaps about the life
and career of this versatile man.

## D. CRITICISM

1176 See no. 468.

1177 Reichert, John F. "GRONGAR HILL: Its Origin and Development."
PLL, 5 (1969), 123-29.

Although scholars have long noted the influence of Denham's
"Cooper's Hill" and Dyer's study of landscape painting in
his poem GRONGAR HILL, the early Pindaric version
(1726) is remarkably close to the structure of ideas in
Addison's SPECTATOR papers 411 and 412. The revised
version, however, features the novel idea of ordering the
descriptions from the speaker's point of view as he climbs
the hill, thus "fusing the landscape with the emotions of
a precisely located observer."

1178 Spate, O.H.K. "The Muse of Mercantilism: Jago, Grainger, and
Dyer." In STUDIES IN THE EIGHTEENTH CENTURY I: PAPERS PRE-
SENTED AT THE DAVID NICHOL SMITH MEMORIAL SEMINAR,
CANBERRA, 1966. Ed. R.F. Brissenden. Toronto: Univ. of Toronto
Press, 1968, pp. 119-31.

Discusses Dyer's treatment of wool trade in THE FLEECE
as exemplifying a patriotic celebration of the city,
science, and commerce that constitutes an emerging "Whig
tradition" pronouncing the values of modernity in the eighteenth century. See no. 97.

1179 Williams, Ralph M. "Coleridge's Parody of Dyer's GRONGAR HILL."
MLR, 41 (1946), 61-62.

Identifies "Inside the Coach" (1791) as a parody of Dyer,
burlesquing especially the opening lines of GRONGAR
HILL, but points out that it also exemplifies Coleridge's
principle of parody: mocking a silly poem by writing a
sillier one.

1179A    See no. 2179.


1180     Wordsworth, William.   "Sonnet XVII, To the Poet, John Dyer."
         ("Miscellaneous Sonnets," pt. 1).   In THE POETICAL WORKS OF
         WILLIAM WORDSWORTH.   Ed. Ernest de Selincourt and Helen Darbi-
         shire.   Vol. 3.   Oxford:  Clarendon Press, 1946, p. 10.

              A glowing tribute addressed to Lady Beaumont in a letter
              of November 20, 1811:  "In point of imagination, and
              purity of style, I am not sure that [Dyer] is not superior
              to any writer in verse since the time of Milton."

# SIR SAMUEL GARTH (1661-1719)

## A. MAJOR EDITIONS

1181    THE DISPENSARY. In POEMS ON AFFAIRS OF STATE: AUGUSTAN
        SATIRICAL VERSE 1660-1704. Vol. 6, 1697-1704. Ed. Frank H.
        Ellis. New Haven, Conn.: Yale Univ. Press, 1970, pp. 58-128.

> This carefully edited second edition of THE DISPENSARY,
> contained in volume 6 of the above, is the standard text
> of Garth's major poem. See no. 41.

## B. CORRESPONDENCE

1182    THE LETTERS OF SAMUEL GARTH. Ed. John F. Sena. BNYPL, 78
        (1974), 69-94.

> Surviving correspondence.

## C. BIBLIOGRAPHY AND TEXTUAL STUDIES

1183    Rogers, Pat. "The Publishing History of Garth's DISPENSARY: Some
        'Lost' and Pirated Editions." TRANSACTIONS OF THE CAMBRIDGE
        BIBLIOGRAPHICAL SOCIETY, 5 (1971), 167-77.

> Reviews the publication history of the poem, noting the
> presence of heretofore unauthorized or missing editions
> that show important artistic modifications by Garth.

1184    Schneider, Duane B. "Dr. Garth and Shakespeare: A Borrowing."
        ELN, 1 (1964), 200-202.

> A similar ordering of objects in their descriptions of
> apothecary shops suggests that Garth was familiar with
> Shakespeare's ROMEO AND JULIET.

## D. BIOGRAPHY

1185    Boyce, Benjamin. "THE DISPENSARY, Sir Richard Blackmore, and the
Captain of the Wits." RES, 14 (1938), 453-58.

> Garth and Blackmore took opposing sides in the ongoing
> dispute between pro- and antidispenserians, Garth the
> physician attacking Blackmore's verse and associating him
> with conspiring apothecaries.

1186    Cornog, William H. "Sir Samuel Garth, A Court Physician of the
Eighteenth Century." ISIS, 29 (1938), 29-42.

> A comprehensive account of Garth's career as a famous
> physician as recorded in the many references to him by
> writers and politicians of importance during the eighteenth
> century.

1187    McCue, Daniel L. "Samuel Garth, Physician and Man of Letters."
BULLETIN OF THE NEW YORK ACADEMY OF MEDICINE, 53 (1976),
368-402.

> General treatment of Garth's medical career, the impact
> of THE DISPENSARY, and his association with the "wits,"
> reviewing recent scholarship while lamenting that no
> definitive biography or complete modern edition exists.

1188    Roberts, Philip E. "The Background and Purpose of Garth's DISPEN-
SARY (1659)." JOURNAL OF THE ROYAL COLLEGE OF PHYSICIANS
OF LONDON, 2 (1968), 154-60.

> Discusses Garth's role in the quarrel over the creation of
> dispensaries and concludes that apart from its literary
> success, the poem failed "in its attempt to reconcile the
> [College of Physicians of London] with the apothecaries
> to the extent of preventing their practising of medicine
> or to undermine the habitual recourse of the people to
> the apothecaries for advice."

## E. CRITICISM

1189    Ackerman, Stephen J. "The 'Infant Atoms' of Garth's DISPENSARY."
MLR, 74 (1979), 513-23.

> A carefully organized work of art, this satire achieves
> unity from the themes and topoi or forms through which
> Garth presents his satirical view of the scientific atomist,
> or "Epicurean," at the end of the century; and examina-
> tion of the structure and philosophical context of the poem
> attests to its artistic integrity.

1190    Cook, Richard I.   "Garth's DISPENSARY and Pope's RAPE OF THE
        LOCK."  CLA JOURNAL, 6 (1962), 107-16.

> Although both Garth and Pope employ the mock-heroic
> genre and other similar techniques of satire, THE DIS-
> PENSARY and THE RAPE OF THE LOCK differ in tone
> and outlook, Garth an involved participant, Pope an
> amused observer.

1191    _____.  SIR SAMUEL GARTH.  Boston: Twayne, 1980.

> A lucid and highly informative account of Garth's life
> as a physician and author, giving the historical and
> literary backgrounds of THE DISPENSARY, an analysis
> of this major poem and of some minor works, and noting
> his influence on later poets, especially Pope. Demonstrates
> Garth's literary sophistication and utilization of comic and
> serious styles.

1192    Sena, John F.   "Samuel Garth and THE DISPENSARY: The Project
        and the Poem."  In MEDICINE AND LITERATURE.  Ed. Enid Rhodes
        Peschel.  Intro. by Edmund D. Pellegrino.  New York:  Neale Wat-
        son, 1980, pp. 28-34.

> General discussion of the "paper-and-pill war" over medi-
> cal treatment of the poor, which culminates in THE DIS-
> PENSARY, a satiric attack on apothecaries and other
> opponents of the dispensing concept and "one of the most
> compelling examples in English history of the manner in
> which literature and medicine can complement one another."

1193    _____.  "Samuel Garth's THE DISPENSARY."  TSLL, 15 (1974), 639-
        48.

> Discusses Garth's satiric strategies and thematic interests,
> concluding that despite a number of fine descriptive
> passages, Garth's personal prejudices, predilections, and
> his consuming commitment to the subject of free medical
> care for the poor preclude the playful, witty, and comic
> approach to subject matter associated with Pope and the
> Augustans.

# JOHN GAY (1685-1732)

## A. MAJOR EDITIONS

1194    THE POETICAL WORKS OF JOHN GAY.  Ed. Geoffrey C. Faber.
        London:  Oxford Univ. Press, 1926.

>       Useful edition, but superseded by Dearing-Beckwith (below).

1195    POETRY AND PROSE OF JOHN GAY.  Ed. Vinton A. Dearing and
        Charles E. Beckwith.   2 vols.  Oxford:  Clarendon Press, 1974.

>       Authoritative modern edition based on first editions of
>       works published during Gay's lifetime and on manuscripts
>       with emendations and authorial changes noted.  Full com-
>       mentary provided and problems of the canon assessed.

## B. CORRESPONDENCE AND JOURNALS

1196    Benjamin, Lewis S. [Lewis Melville].  LIFE AND LETTERS OF JOHN
        GAY (1685-1732).  London:  Daniel O'Connor, 1921.

>       Contains some correspondence and an incomplete chronologi-
>       cal list of the letters.

1197    Rawson, Claude J.  "Some Unpublished Letters of Pope and Gay; and
        Some Manuscript Sources of Goldsmith's LIFE OF THOMAS PARNELL."
        RES, NS 10 (1959), 371-87.

>       Unpublished letters by Gay and Pope to Parnell and copies
>       of six letters, previously published with omissions or variants
>       in Sherburn's edition of Pope's correspondence from other sources,
>       contain information about the lives of Pope and Gay and
>       affairs of the Scriblerus Club from 1714 to 1716.

1198    THE LETTERS OF JOHN GAY.  Ed. Chester F. Burgess.  Oxford:
        Clarendon Press, 1966.

Provides a convenient single source for all letters known
to be extant. Excludes letters to Gay because of the
complete Pope and Swift collections. Standard modern edition.
See the correspondence of Pope and Swift, nos. 1518 and
1990.

## C. BIBLIOGRAPHY AND TEXTUAL STUDIES

1199    Aden, John M. "The 1720 Version of RURAL SPORTS and the Georgic
Tradition." MLQ, 20 (1959), 228-32.

        Gay's changes in versions reflect his interest in aligning
the poem with the georgic tradition, and in so doing he
alters theme, structure, tone, and style.

1200    Klein, Julie Thompson. JOHN GAY: AN ANNOTATED CHECKLIST
OF CRITICISM. Troy, N.Y.: Whitston, 1974.

        Lists articles; books (with their scholarly reviews) on the
poems and plays; and chapters and passing references in
general studies.

## D. BIOGRAPHY

1201    Gaye, Phoebe Fenwick. JOHN GAY: HIS PLACE IN THE EIGH-
TEENTH CENTURY. London: Collins, 1938.

        Popular appreciation written in highly impressionistic style.

1202    Irving, William Henry. JOHN GAY: FAVORITE OF THE WITS.
Durham, N.C.: Duke Univ. Press, 1940.

        Views Gay as representative of his age: urbane, friendly,
and refusing "to disturb the balanced symmetries of life."

## E. CRITICISM

1203    Ames, Dianne S. "Gay's TRIVIA and the Art of Allusion." SP, 75
(1978), 199-222.

        Discusses Gay's "complementary powers" as an allusive poet
and satirist of the decline of culture and remarks on his
sophistication, wit, and ardent advocacy of Scriblerian
causes equal to that of Pope and Swift.

1204    Armens, Sven. JOHN GAY: SOCIAL CRITIC. New York: King's
Crown Press, 1954.

Notes the seriousness of Gay's poetry achieved by relocating the pastoral genre in the realistic setting of Devonshire, and by mildly burlesquing his shepherds' pretensions and foibles at the same time exposing the follies of town life and showing concern for social injustice.

1205    Battestin, Martin C. "Menalcas' Song: The Meaning of Art and Artifice in Gay's Poetry." JEGP, 65 (1966), 662-79.

Gay is a clear representative of the Augustan aesthetic and world view expressed in the controlling aesthetic paradox that "in the poem, as indeed in life, Nature must be made to imitate Art, and thus form and artifice are the distinguishing features of his verse."

1206    Brown, Wallace Cable. "Gay's Mastery of the Heroic Couplet." PMLA, 61 (1946), 114-25.

Gay's handling of this form, along with Pope's, is "closest of all approximations to the norm of the heroic couplet," and from both a technical and poetic standpoint he was always skillful and sometimes excellent.

1207    Bull, John. "'Business Calls Me from the Plains': John Gay's RURAL SPORTS as a Version of Eighteenth-Century Pastoral." Delta, 50 (1972), 22-35.

Reads the 1713 version as reflecting urban middle-class energies and as an expression of Gay's personal doubts; and sees the 1720 text as an impersonal, decorous pastoral that plays down anticourt sentiments in order not to offend the aristocracy.

1208    Ellis, William D., Jr. "Thomas D'Urfey, The Pope-Philips Quarrel, and THE SHEPHERD'S WEEK." PMLA, 74 (1959), 203-12.

Argues that Gay's overall intention in this squabble was to hinder the growth of the native and realistic pastoral by ironically citing D'Urfey's rustic versions as models by which to judge this new and decidedly unclassical pastoral.

1209    Fischer, John Irwin. "Never on Sunday: John Gay's THE SHEPHERD'S WEEK." STUDIES IN EIGHTEENTH-CENTURY CULTURE, 10 (1980), 191-203.

By way of classical pastoral, modern theories of the absurd, and St. Paul, argues skillfully that although Gay's poem depicts rural actuality and parodies contemporary pastoralists, it more exactly celebrates the pleasures of discovering the lack of orderly systems of language and religion while further delighting in the very contemplation of civilization's concrete particularities.

1210 Forsgren, Adina. "Gay Among the Defenders of the Faith." STUDIA NEOPHILOLOGICA 38 (1966), 301-13.

Despite moments of comic idealization, "A Contemplation on Night" and "A Thought on Eternity" concern themselves with contemporary religious issues and champion orthodox Christian beliefs about the rewards of virtue.

1211 _____. JOHN GAY: POET "OF A LOWER ORDER." Stockholm: Natur och Kultur, 1964.

Examines Gay's early poems against their social, political, and aesthetic backgrounds and concludes that his early cheerful depiction of the realistic details of rural life became a dominant part of his comic aesthetic that mixes traditional modes and contemporary realism.

1212 _____. "Some Complimentary Epistles by John Gay." STUDIA NEOPHILOLOGICA 36 (1964), 82-100.

Gay characteristically creates a mild tone of burlesque by depicting "low" realistic subject matter and human psychological concerns through a mixture of classical (Horatian) models.

1213 Graham, Edwin. "John Gay's Second Series, The CRAFTSMAN in FABLES." PLL, 5 (1969), 17-25.

Read in light of Gay's life and of opposition pamphleteering, the FABLES (written 1731-32) appears aimed at Walpole by utilizing the diction and emphasizing themes found in the CRAFTSMAN.

1214 Heuston, Edward F. "Gay's Bowzybeus and Thomas D'Urfey." SCRIBLERIAN, 1 (1968), 30-31.

Argues that the caricature of D'Urfey as a vulgar entertainer reflects his reputation as a good-natured buffoon and is a fitting climax to the pattern of ridicule throughout "Saturday" in THE SHEPHERD'S WEEK.

1215 See no. 478.

1216 Mack, Maynard. "Gay Augustan." YALE UNIVERSITY LIBRARY GAZETTE, 21 (1946), 6-10.

A bibliographical-critical discussion of fourteen pieces of

a collection of Gay given to the Yale Library by Chauncey
B. Tinker, representing first editions of Gay's works that
exhibit his strengths and weaknesses as a poet.

1217    Moore, John Robert. "Gay's Burlesque of Sir Richard Blackmore's
Poetry." JEGP, 50 (1951), 83-89.

Two of Blackmore's better pieces, the song of Mopas from
PRINCE ARTHUR and his CREATION, were the object of
Gay's subtle burlesque technique in the song of Bowzybeus
in "Saturday" of THE SHEPHERD'S WEEK.

1218    Rees, Christine. "Gay, Swift, and the Nymphs of Drury-Lane." EIC,
23 (1973), 1-21.

Swift's wariness of the artifice of nymph fiction and Gay's
contrary embracing of theatrical and pastoral illusions
paradoxically represent serious treatment of the "complex
relation of the truth and fiction."

1219    Rogers, Pat. "Satiric Allusion in John Gay's 'Welcome to Mr. Pope.'"
PLL, 10 (1974), 427-32.

Convincingly argues that the "sharp political satire" mocks
George I's triumphant entry into London in 1714 and his
ill-timed sojourn (1716) in Hanover, thus accounting for
the poem's long suppression (it was first published in 1776).

1220    Sherbo, Arthur. "Virgil, Dryden, Gay, and Matters Trivial." PMLA,
85 (1970), 1063-71.

Many faults attributed to Gay's TRIVIA would disappear
if sufficient attention were paid to the variety of ways
Gay reinforces its mock-georgic features by continual
allusion to Virgil's GEORGICS via Dryden's translation
and actual phrasing, all of which establish the poem's
mock dignity and demonstrate Gay's supreme artistry.

1221    Spacks, Patricia Meyer. JOHN GAY. New York: Twayne, 1965.

Best general survey to date, employing a critical vocabulary helpful in tracing Gay's varied attempts to find an
appropriate poetic stance and voice and in demonstrating
his sophisticated control of aesthetic distance and perspective through wit and irony.

1222    _____. "John Gay: A Satirist's Progress." EIC, 14 (1964), 156-70.

Focuses on Gay's apparent difficulties in establishing
"satiric authority" when choosing a persona much like

himself. When he writes about his own literary problems
through the device of a fable or tale, his sharp charac-
terizations and comic wit emerge.

1223    Sutherland, James. "John Gay." In POPE AND HIS CONTEMPO-
RARIES: ESSAYS PRESENTED TO GEORGE SHERBURN. Ed. James L.
Clifford and Louis A. Landa. New York: Oxford Univ. Press, 1949,
pp. 701-14.

Gay's poetic art has suffered from his fate as a minor
Scriblerian and friend of Pope and Swift and should be
considered on its own terms--as "delicate and sophisticated craftsmanship" rendering "the thing perfectly said."
See no. 107.

1224    Trowbridge, Hoyt. "Pope, Gay and THE SHEPHERD'S WEEK." MLQ,
5 (1944), 79-88.

Even-handed treatment of Pope's assertions about Gay's
real aims in this pastoral cycle, indicating that burlesque
of Philips was his basic motive and that the poem's meaning is best understood in light of that purpose.

1225    Winton, Calhoun. "John Gay and a Devon Jug." WINTERTHUR
PORTFOLIO, 2 (1965), 62-64.

The inscription on this jug (1698), which most likely found
its way into southern Delaware as part of prerevolutionary
trade from Barnstable, displays the sprightly humor and
robust exuberance of the ballads and pastorals of John
Gay, North Devon resident where the jug was manufac-
tured.

# OLIVER GOLDSMITH (1730?-74)

## A. MAJOR EDITIONS

1226    THE POEMS AND PLAYS OF OLIVER GOLDSMITH. Ed. Austin
Dobson. 2 vols. London: J.M. Dent, 1889.

> Most accurate nineteenth-century edition and the one on
> which the Goldsmith concordance is based.

1227    COLLECTED WORKS OF OLIVER GOLDSMITH. Ed. Arthur Friedman.
5 vols. Oxford: Clarendon Press, 1966.

> The most accurate determination of the canon, with close
> attention to all relevant editions and manuscripts in order
> to present a text faithful to Goldsmith's final intentions.

1228    See no. 824.

## B. CORRESPONDENCE AND JOURNALS

1229    NEW ESSAYS BY OLIVER GOLDSMITH. Ed. Ronald S. Crane. Chicago:
Univ. of Chicago Press, 1927.

> Eighteen essays written between January 1760 and June
> 1762, never before ascribed to Goldsmith.

1230    THE COLLECTED LETTERS OF OLIVER GOLDSMITH. Ed. Katharine C.
Balderston. Cambridge: Cambridge Univ. Press, 1928.

> Introduction contains material pertinent to Goldsmith's
> family life, the Fiddlebach adventure, his abandonment
> of the East India voyage, the composition of THRENODIA
> AUGUSTALIS, and the production of SHE STOOPS TO
> CONQUER. Standard edition.

## C. BIBLIOGRAPHY, TEXTUAL STUDIES, AND CONCORDANCES

1231    Friedman, Arthur. "The Problem of Indifferent Readings in the Eigh-
        teenth Century, with a Solution from THE DESERTED VILLAGE." SB,
        13 (1960), 143-47.

> A classic theory of textual editing that discusses printing
> procedures in the later eighteenth century, noting the
> care usually taken in textual composition generally and
> the compositional and editing habits of Goldsmith and
> his printers to explain the textual history of THE DESERTED
> VILLAGE from the first edition of 1770 on.

1232    _____. "The Time of Composition of Goldsmith's EDWIN AND
        ANGELINA." In RESTORATION AND EIGHTEENTH-CENTURY LITERA-
        TURE: ESSAYS IN HONOR OF ALAN DUGALD McKILLOP. Ed.
        Carroll Camden. Chicago: Univ. of Chicago Press, 1963, pp. 155-59.

> Careful investigation of the dating of EDWIN AND
> ANGELINA from textual evidence suggesting that a
> version of the ballad appeared in the manuscript of the
> VICAR OF WAKEFIELD of 1762. See no. 103.

1233    Paden, William D., and Clyde K. Hyder. A CONCORDANCE TO
        THE POEMS OF OLIVER GOLDSMITH, 1940; rpt. Gloucester, Mass.:
        Peter Smith, 1966.

> Based on the Austin Dobson edition (1906), but notes
> occasional variants and additions to the canon since Dobson.

1234    Scott, Temple. OLIVER GOLDSMITH BIBLIOGRAPHICALLY AND
        BIOGRAPHICALLY CONSIDERED. Intro. A. Edward Newton. London:
        Maggs, 1928.

> Refers to the W.M. Wilkins' library collection. Not com-
> plete and superseded by NCBEL and Friedman edition of
> Goldsmith.

1235    Todd, William B. "The 'Private Issues' of THE DESERTED VILLAGE."
        SB, 6 (1954), 24-44.

> Challenges the two theories concerning private or trial
> issues of Goldsmith's poem--the Bishop Percy-Countess
> Northumberland explanation and the one involving Gold-
> smith's alleged desire to experiment with different punctu-
> ation--and elaborately describes the circumstances surround-
> ing publication of the poem.

1236    _____. "Quadruple Imposition: An Account of Goldsmith's TRAVELLER."
        SB, 7 (1955), 103-11.

Discusses the earliest version of Goldsmith's poem in its various quarto and half-sheet state, theorizing about the reasons for the regressive text and other oddities.

1237 See no. 73.

1238 Woods, Samuel H., Jr. "The Goldsmith 'Problem.'" SBHT, 19 (1978), 47-60.

A valuable survey and critique of recent scholarship devoted to Goldsmith in all his literary aspects, lamenting the indifference of students of the period to Goldsmith's art and explaining the neglect as the result of Goldsmith's versatility.

## D. BIOGRAPHY

1239 Balderston, Katharine C. THE HISTORY AND SOURCES OF PERCY'S MEMOIR OF GOLDSMITH. Cambridge: Cambridge Univ. Press, 1926.

Studies the genesis of this important early account of Goldsmith to facilitate revaluation of contemporary sources of information and to prepare the way for a modern biography. See no. 1230.

1240 Forster, John. THE LIFE OF OLIVER GOLDSMITH. 2 vols. London: Bradbury and Evans, 1854.

Adds new material about Goldsmith in London.

1241 Ginger, John. THE NOTABLE MAN: THE LIFE AND TIMES OF OLIVER GOLDSMITH. London: Hamish Hamilton, 1977.

Biography for the general reader, which disputes Friedman's datings at times.

1242 Gwynn, Stephen. OLIVER GOLDSMITH. New York: Henry Holt, 1935.

Popular life.

1243 Harp, Richard L. "New Perspectives for Goldsmith's Biography." ECent, 21 (1980), 162-75.

A satisfactory biography of Goldsmith will be written only when "two things are done": (1) identifying and rejecting romantic influences in modern biographical methodology as a means of assessing characters; (2) directing attention from idiosyncrasies that dominate previous accounts and recogniz-

ing how well Goldsmith was liked and accepted during
his life.

1244    Lucas, Frank L. THE SEARCH FOR GOOD SENSE. London: Cassell,
        1958.

        Sensitive and sympathetic treatment of important literary
        figures of the period, especially Johnson and Goldsmith,
        as interesting in and of themselves and as exemplary
        figures for our own age.

1245    MacLennan, Munro. THE SECRET OF OLIVER GOLDSMITH. New
        York: Vantage Press, 1975.

        Suggests that the key to Goldsmith's social eccentricities
        and constant references to color in his works is color
        blindness of some form. Delightfully bizarre.

1246    Prior, James. THE LIFE OF OLIVER GOLDSMITH. 2 vols. London:
        J. Murray, 1837.

        A worthy biography.

1247    Sells, A. Lytton. OLIVER GOLDSMITH: HIS LIFE AND WORKS.
        London: George Allen and Unwin, 1974.

        Acknowledges the difficulties of writing a competent life
        of Goldsmith, whose friendships, attitudes, and thought
        were often "wrapped in mystery," and proceeds to address
        six problematic areas for the biographer. Valuable on the
        French influences.

1248    Sherwin, Oscar. THE LIFE AND TIMES OF OLIVER GOLDSMITH.
        New York: Collier Books, 1962.

        Popular biography.

1249    Wardle, Ralph M. OLIVER GOLDSMITH. Lawrence: Univ. of Kansas
        Press, 1957.

        The first modern attempt to publish a scholarly biography
        on Goldsmith, taking into account newly discovered
        Boswell materials and the work of Crane, Balderston, and
        Friedman. Claims Goldsmith would have been "a leader
        in the Romantic Revival in English Literature" had he
        possessed confidence in his own convictions.

1250    Wibberley, Leonard. THE GOOD-NATURED MAN: A PORTRAIT OF
        OLIVER GOLDSMITH. New York: William Morrow, 1979.

Highly subjective account of Goldsmith's life and works, making "deductions about Goldsmith that are denied the scholar."

# E. CRITICISM

1251    Andrews, William L. "Goldsmith and Freneau in THE AMERICAN VILLAGE." EAL, 5 (1970), 14-23.

> Emphasizes ways in which Freneau capitalizes on "sense of loss" in THE DESERTED VILLAGE in order to praise America as inheritor of the rural ideal and to warn readers of threats to this ideal.

1252    Bell, Howard J., Jr. "THE DESERTED VILLAGE and Goldsmith's Social Doctrines." PMLA, 59 (1944), 747-72.

> Goldsmith's arguments against luxury as the cause of rural depopulation and, eventually, national ruin were based on classical precedent and was an aspect of contemporary Tory thinking, not personal nostalgia.

1253    Davie, Donald. "THE DESERTED VILLAGE: Poem as Virtual History." TWENTIETH CENTURY, 156 (1954), 161-74.

> Discusses Suzanne Langer's response to E.M.W. Tillyard's contention that Goldsmith's poetry is directly concerned with actual villages as a springboard to a comparison of Blake's "The Echoing Green," characterized as an oblique dramatization of the idea of fruition; although disagreeing with Langer's reading of Goldsmith, accepts her basic concept of "symbolic form."

1254    Eisinger, Chester E. "Land and Loyalty: Literary Expressions of Agrarian Nationalism in the Seventeenth and Eighteenth Centuries." AL, 21 (1949), 160-78.

> Notes that Goldsmith's DESERTED VILLAGE was highly influential in America and played an important role in the agrarian nationalism of the country. Cites, especially, Timothy Dwight's GREENFIELD HILL and Philip Freneau's poetry in general.

1255    Eversole, Richard. "The Oratorical Design of THE DESERTED VILLAGE." ELN, 4 (1966), 99-104.

> Reads Goldsmith's poem as a traditional seven-section classical oration intended for political persuasion.

1256     Fielding, K.J.   "THE DESERTED VILLAGE and Sir Robert Walpole."
         ENGLISH, 12 (1958), 130-32.

>    Argues that Walpole's Houghton, and the dispossession of
>    surrounding lands accompanying its construction, helped
>    inspire a literary tradition that began with Tory pamphle-
>    teers, included such poems as THE DESERTED VILLAGE
>    and THE TRAVELLER, and led to the ruined cottage motif
>    of the romantics.

1257     Fraser, George S.   "Johnson and Goldsmith: The Mid-Augustan Norm."
         ESSAYS AND STUDIES, 23 (1970), 51-70.

>    "The only two poets, after Pope, who can be considered
>    to have added something to what Pope had done in heroic
>    couplets" was Johnson, who contributed "weightiness,"
>    and Goldsmith, who brought "mellowness"; and thus from
>    a stylistic viewpoint they were both central figures of
>    the mid and late eighteenth century.

1258     Golden, Morris.   "The Broken Dream of THE DESERTED VILLAGE."
         L&P, 10 (1959), 41-44.

>    Examines the motif of female innocence.

1259     _____.   "The Family-Wanderer Theme in Goldsmith."   ELH, 25 (1958),
         181-93.

>    Considers the contrast between the family circle and the
>    wandering son of major thematic importance, affecting
>    Goldsmith's thinking of such matters as literary criticism
>    and political theory in THE TRAVELLER and THE DESERTED
>    VILLAGE, among other works.

1260     Goldstein, Laurence.   "The Auburn Syndrome: Change and Loss in
         THE DESERTED VILLAGE and Wordsworth's Grasmere."   ELH, 40 (1973),
         352-71.

>    Goldsmith's understanding that "a continuity of self depends
>    not upon memory but continuity of place" generates the
>    sense of failure and loss at the end of the poem, an artis-
>    tic and moral predicament Wordsworth responds to by find-
>    ing some faith that would protect both himself and nature
>    from the extinction Goldsmith records in his poem.

1261     Halgerson, Richard.   "The Two Worlds of Oliver Goldsmith."   SEL,
         13 (1973), 516-34.

>    During the 1760s, Goldsmith's works were governed by
>    an opposition between the worlds of village and city,
>    which he does not reconcile; but as one who has left

the village, he views it with both condescension and awe, while recognizing both the material superiority and spiritual lack of the city.

1262    Hopkins, Robert H. THE TRUE GENIUS OF OLIVER GOLDSMITH. Baltimore: Johns Hopkins Press, 1969.

In the course of assessing Goldsmith's art, Hopkins reads THE TRAVELLER not as autobiography, but as political statement, employing a variety of rhetorical and persuasive devices. A curiously incomplete study.

1263    Jaarsma, Richard J. "Ethics in the Wasteland: Image and Structure in Goldsmith's THE DESERTED VILLAGE. TSLL, 13 (1971), 447-59.

Not sentimental indulgence, nor yearning for bygone innocence, but rather a protest against the demise of humanistic values.

1264    Kirk, Clara M. OLIVER GOLDSMITH. New York: Twayne, 1967.

Stresses Goldsmith's complex personality, at once sociable and solitary, happy and melancholic, sincere and a player of roles. Short sections on the poems.

1265    Lonsdale, Roger. "'A Garden, and a Grave': The Poetry of Oliver Goldsmith." In THE AUTHOR IN HIS WORK: ESSAYS ON A PROBLEM IN CRITICISM. Ed. Louis L. Martz and Aubrey Williams. Intro. Patricia Meyer Spacks. New Haven, Conn.: Yale Univ. Press, 1978, pp. 3-30.

An important corrective of the view of Goldsmith as a role-playing poetic manipulator, arguing that the collapse of the poetic conventions which his imagination finds inadequate reflects genuine self-expressive intentions. Fine study. See no. 119.

1266    Mahony, Robert. "Lyrical Antithesis: The Moral Style of THE DESERTED VILLAGE." ArielE, 8, ii (1977), 33-47.

The lyrical elements of Goldsmith's style evoke the personal pain of the author, but also communicate "the moral dimensions of the speaker's argument for traditional values which Auburn represents and which luxury threatens."

1267    Miner, Earl. "The Making of THE DESERTED VILLAGE." HLQ, 22 (1958-59), 125-41.

Discusses the economic changes occurring in England put in focus by Goldsmith's ambivalence toward luxury as expressed in the poem through a series of contrasts between traditional rural and moral values and the evils created by trade and depopulation and also his successful blending of Tory beliefs, poetic charm, and pastoral ideals, all gently qualified by irony.

1268    Quintana, Ricardo. "THE DESERTED VILLAGE: Its Logical and Rhetorical Elements." CE, 26 (1964), 204-14.

Important essay which questions interpretations stressing the self-expressive aspects of the poem and argues for the rhetorical nature of the authorial "I."

1269    _____. OLIVER GOLDSMITH: A GEORGIAN STUDY. New York: Macmillan, 1967.

Chapter dealing with the poetry focuses on THE TRAVELLER, RETALIATION, and THE DESERTED VILLAGE, pointing out in the latter the carefully contrived rhetorical effects and patterns. Good general introduction.

1270    _____. "Oliver Goldsmith: Ironist to the Georgians." In EIGHTEENTH-CENTURY STUDIES IN HONOR OF DONALD F. HYDE. Ed. William H. Bond. New York: Grolier Club, 1970, pp. 297-310.

Generalizes on some ironic practices of the eighteenth century and describes specific techniques displayed in the poems, especially those involving the motif of the naive traveller. See no. 94.

1271    Rousseau, George S. GOLDSMITH: THE CRITICAL HERITAGE. London: Routledge and Kegan Paul, 1974.

Covers reactions from contemporary anonymous reviews to Harrison's article on his prose (1912), treating the major works in categories separate from general commentary on Goldsmith's literary career and personality.

1272    Schwegel, Douglas M. "The American Couplets in THE DESERTED VILLAGE." GEORGIA REVIEW, 16 (1962), 148-53.

The nine couplets describing the region of the Altamaha River in Georgia reveal Goldsmith's interest in America from his youth and present a striking contrast in the poem between a dangerous and formidable America wilderness and a comfortable and inviting English countryside for the purpose of generating sympathy for the lot of the American immigrants.

1273    Seitz, R.W. "The Irish Background of Goldsmith's Social and Political Thought." PMLA, 52 (1937), 405-11.

His nurturing in Ireland led Goldsmith to the conviction "that society was made for man and not man for society," and he thus opposed the new commercialism and material- istic philosophy of progressive Whigs and Tories.

1274 Storm, Leo. "Conventional Ethics in Goldsmith's THE TRAVELLER." SEL, 17 (1977), 463-76.

Depreciation of Goldsmith's intellectual capacity should not blind readers to his skillful poetic execution of a "small stock of ideas and those ideas he found in the conventional literary genres of the eighteenth century." However, the poem is flawed by allowing descriptive materials and a personal note to overpower the ethical theme and by the conventional Augustan structure of ideas.

1275 _____. "Literary Convention in Goldsmith's DESERTED VILLAGE." HLQ, 33 (1970), 243-56.

Goldsmith consciously manipulates reader response by means of familiar poetic genres and stock poetic conventions to deplore cultural degeneration and affirm "a conservative social order."

1276 Wills, Jack C. "THE DESERTED VILLAGE, Ecclesiastes, and the En- lightenment." EnlE, 4, iii-iv (1973), 15-19.

Biblical and other source materials of the poem move it beyond the local, topical, and personal level, making it an emphatic statement of general truth, paralleling the "sober strains" and imagery of darkness characterizing Ecclesiastes.

# THOMAS GRAY (1716-71)

## A. MAJOR EDITIONS

1277    THE WORKS OF THOMAS GRAY. Ed. Edmund Gosse. 4 vols. London: Macmillan, 1884.

>    Best known nineteenth-century edition. Cook concordance (no. 1283) keyed to this edition.

1278    See no. 823.

>    Superseded by Starr-Hendrickson edition (below), but a convenient resource for comparing Gray and Collins.

1279    THE COMPLETE POEMS OF THOMAS GRAY: ENGLISH, LATIN AND GREEK. Ed. Herbert W. Starr and John R. Hendrickson. Oxford: Clarendon Press, 1966.

>    Standard edition with textual apparatus, notes, and annotations.

1280    SELECTED POEMS OF THOMAS GRAY AND WILLIAM COLLINS. Ed. Arthur Johnston. London: Edward Arnold, 1967.

>    Extensive interpretive commentary and helpful identification of allusions and references.

1281    See no. 824.

## B. CORRESPONDENCE AND JOURNALS

1282    CORRESPONDENCE OF THOMAS GRAY. Ed. Paget Toynbee and Leonard Whibley. 3 vols. 1935; rpt. with additions and corrections by Herbert W. Starr. Oxford: Clarendon Press, 1971.

Standard text; the 1971 edition contains minor corrections
and letters discovered since 1935. Contains copious notes.

## C. BIBLIOGRAPHY, TEXTUAL STUDIES, AND CONCORDANCES

1283    Cook, Albert S.  CONCORDANCE TO THE ENGLISH POEMS OF
        THOMAS GRAY.  1908; rpt.  Gloucester, Mass.:  Peter Smith, 1967.

>   Based on Gosse edition (1884) with normalized spellings
>   for consistency.

1284    Garrod, Heathcote W.  "Note on the Composition of Gray's ELEGY."
        In ESSAYS ON THE EIGHTEENTH CENTURY PRESENTED TO DAVID
        NICHOL SMITH IN HONOUR OF HIS SEVENTIETH BIRTHDAY. Ed.
        James Sutherland and F.P. Wilson.  Oxford:  Clarendon Press, 1945,
        pp. 111–16.

>   Discusses the controversial dating of the poem, arguing
>   for an early date (1742) on the basis of Richard West's
>   death and the similarity of the verse to the accurately
>   dated sonnet to West.  See no. 124.

1285    Johnston, Arthur.  "Gray's 'The Triumphs of Owen.'"  RES, NS 11
        (1960), 275–85.

>   The original Welsh version of this poem was sent to Gray
>   translated into literal Latin; and this translation, not
>   Evan's English prose version published six years after the
>   height of Gray's interest (1758–61), was probably his
>   source.

1286    Macdonald, Alastair, ed.  AN ELEGY WROTE IN A COUNTRY
        CHURCH YARD: THE ETON MS. AND FIRST EDITION, 1751.  Ilkley,
        Yorkshire, Engl.:  Scolar Press, 1976.

>   Facsimile reproduction of the working draft of the poem,
>   discussion of text, and transcriptions.  An important ex-
>   ample of Gray's creative process.

1287    Northup, Clark S.  A BIBLIOGRAPHY OF THOMAS GRAY.  New
        Haven, Conn.:  Yale Univ. Press, 1917.

>   A complete record through 1916 of editions, reviews,
>   critical commentary, and related studies of Gray.

1288    Starr, Herbert W.  A BIBLIOGRAPHY OF THOMAS GRAY, 1917–1951.
        Philadelphia:  Univ. of Pennsylvania Press, 1953.

>   A detailed continuation of Clark S. Northup's bibliography,

covering continental, English, and American materials.
See no. 1287.

1289    Stokes, Francis Griffin, ed. AN ELEGY WRITTEN IN A COUNTY
        CHURCH YARD. Oxford: Clarendon Press, 1929.

        Prints the differing manuscript versions and the bibliograph-
        ical circumstances surrounding the poem's first publication.

## D. COLLECTIONS

1290    Downey, James, and Ben Jones, eds. FEARFUL JOY: PAPERS FROM
        THE THOMAS GRAY BICENTENARY CONFERENCE AT CARLETON
        UNIVERSITY. Montreal: McGill-Queen's Univ. Press, 1974.

        Excellent essays devoted to Gray's literary and scholarly
        career.

1291    Starr, Herbert W., ed. TWENTIETH-CENTURY INTERPRETATIONS OF
        GRAY'S ELEGY. Englewood Cliffs, N.J.: Prentice-Hall, 1968.

        Brings together a number of excellent readings of the poem,
        especially some concerned with the stonecutter controversy,
        the poem's ending, and the epitaph.

## E. BIOGRAPHY

1292    Jones, William Powell. THOMAS GRAY, SCHOLAR: THE TRUE
        TRAGEDY OF AN EIGHTEENTH-CENTURY GENTLEMAN. Cambridge,
        Mass.: Harvard Univ. Press, 1937.

        Useful study of Gray's immense learning and knowledge,
        an accomplishment inextricably intertwined with his
        creative life as poet.

1293    Ketton-Cremer, Robert W. THOMAS GRAY: A BIOGRAPHY. Cam-
        bridge: Cambridge Univ. Press, 1955.

        Standard biography in English.

1294    Martin, Roger. ESSAI SUR THOMAS GRAY. Paris: Les Presses
        Universitaires, 1934.

        Notable psychologically oriented reading of Gray, and
        the source of much interesting speculation.

# F. CRITICISM

1295    Berry, Francis. "The Sound of Personification in Gray's ELEGY." EIC, 12 (1962), 442-45.

> Views the question of abstract and concrete diction in relative terms and defends Gray's personifications and employment of initial capital letters in the ELEGY as contributing to the desired sonority of the lines and to the slow, emphatic pace of the poem.

1296    Brady, Frank. "Structure and Meaning in Gray's ELEGY." In FROM SENSIBILITY TO ROMANTICISM: ESSAYS PRESENTED TO FREDERICK A. POTTLE. Ed. Frederick W. Hilles and Harold Bloom. New York: Oxford Univ. Press, 1965, pp. 177-89.

> Finds difficulty with previous readings and argues that consideration of the poem's revisions (from the "Stanza's" version to the final ELEGY) throws light on the self-reflexive theme of the "Narrator and his limited fulfillment." See no. 110.

1297    Bronson, Bertrand H. "On the Special Decorum in Gray's ELEGY." In FROM SENSIBILITY TO ROMANTICISM: ESSAYS PRESENTED TO FREDERICK A. POTTLE. Ed. Frederick W. Hilles and Harold Bloom. New York: Oxford Univ. Press, 1965, 171-76.

> Gray's willingness to experiment and challenge certain established poetic conventions and stylistic practices is carefully balanced by his observance of Cicero's "special decorum" in the "handling of the poem's inescapable egocentricity." See no. 110.

1298    Brooks, Cleanth. "Gray's Storied Urn." In his THE WELL-WROUGHT URN: STUDIES IN THE STRUCTURE OF POETRY. New York: Harcourt, Brace, 1947, pp. 96-113.

> Warns against reading the ELEGY as a direct statement of conventional truths and gives a detailed reading of ironic contrasts between the villagers and those buried in the abbey church and the paradoxical language and phrasings applied to such figures as Milton and Cromwell. Deservedly famous essay. See no. 1291.

1299    Carper, Thomas R. "Gray's Personal Elegy." SEL, 17 (1977), 451-62.

> Both versions of the ELEGY--the Eton manuscript and the published one--are intensely personal, and a brief survey of Gray's earlier verse shows how much his role as a contemplative man behaving in the manner of a pastoral poet was natural and habitual.

1300    Cecil, Lord David. "The Poetry of Thomas Gray." In EIGHTEENTH-
        CENTURY ENGLISH LITERATURE: MODERN ESSAYS IN CRITICISM.
        Ed. James L. Clifford. New York: Oxford Univ. Press, 1959, pp.
        233-50.

> An overview of Gray's poetry stressing the paradox at the
> heart of his achievement: a highly conventional, academic,
> and literary style that expresses a uniquely individualized
> poetic consciousness. See no. 105.

1301    Doherty, Francis. "The Two Voices of Gray." EIC, 13 (1963), 222-
        30.

> Argues that Gray alternates between a public and highly
> rhetorical voice and a private, sincere voice when directly
> expressing personal emotion.

1302    Dyson, A.E. "The Ambivalence of Gray's ELEGY." EIC, 7 (1957),
        257-61.

> Gray's basic attitude toward the plight of the rustics is
> contradictory: they are at once the happiest of men and
> the victims of society and the nature of things. See no.
> 1291.

1303    Ehrenpreis, Irvin. "The Cistern and the Fountain: Art and Reality
        in Pope and Gray." In STUDIES IN CRITICISM AND AESTHETICS,
        1660-1800: ESSAYS IN HONOR OF SAMUEL HOLT MONK. Ed.
        Howard Anderson and John S. Shea. Minneapolis: Univ. of Minneap-
        olis Press, 1967, pp. 156-75.

> Argues that the "structural integrity" and "deepest appeal"
> of "Epistle to a Lady" depends not on impersonal literary
> coherence, but rather on allusions to Pope's experience
> with portrait painting and reference to historical reality.
> Conversely, Gray's "The Bard" fails as a poem by evading
> appeals to reality outside of the "limits of literature" and
> by self-consciously asserting Gray's own "impotence" as poet.
> See also nos. 93 and 1534.

1304    Ellis, Frank H. "Gray's ELEGY: The Biographical Problem in Literary
        Criticism." PMLA, 66 (1951), 971-1008.

> Forceful essay on the topic of the "biographical fallacy,"
> demonstrating that interpretations of this poem have often
> suffered from attempts to establish biographical fact from
> the poems at the expense of image, tone, and structure.
> See no. 1291.

1305    _____. "Gray's Eton College Ode: The Problem of Tone." PLL, 5
        (1969), 130-38.

An elaborate analysis of tone and voice in the poem,
pointing out a number of nonserious features of the poem
that produce a "mixed or unpure tone" enabling the
"distanced" speaker to "confront for a moment the real
desolations of mankind, without hope and yet not without
humor."

1306    Empson, William. SOME VERSIONS OF PASTORAL. London: Chatto
and Windus, 1935.

Regardless of one's political ideology--bourgeois or
Marxist--Gray's ELEGY evokes "permanent truths": no
matter to what extent improvements occur in society,
human powers and potential as well as life itself are
tragically wasted.

1307    See no. 1914.

1308    Foerster, Donald M. "Thomas Gray." In THE AGE OF JOHNSON:
ESSAYS PRESENTED TO CHAUNCEY BREWSTER TINKER. Ed. Frederick
W. Hilles. New Haven, Conn.: Yale Univ. Press, 1949, pp. 217-26.

Gray's correspondence would suggest his indifference
toward his own poems and exhibits a lackluster life resulting in discontent, melancholia, and a curious lack
of interest in the human affairs that inspire great art.
See no. 109.

1309    Foladare, Joseph. "Gray's 'Frail Memorial' to West." PMLA, 75
(1960), 61-65.

Argues that Gray's allusion in the "Sonnet on the Death
of Richard West" to PARADISE LOST, 5.1-25, evokes in
a pastoral context a sense of loss and desolation similar to
that depicted in Milton as well as raising the issue of the
nature of true fame, a theme explored later in the ELEGY.
See no. 1291.

1310    Gilmore, Thomas B., Jr. "Allusion and Melancholy in Gray's ODE
ON A DISTANT PROSPECT OF ETON COLLEGE." PLL, 15 (1979),
52-58.

Recognition of three "striking" allusions (to COMUS, the
Crenacus passage in Statius, and the AENEID, Book 6)
in the ode invites consideration of the contexts they im-
port, extending and deepening the poem's "desolate
melancholy."

1311    Glazier, Lyle. "Gray's ELEGY: 'The Skull Beneath the Skin.'" UKCR,
19 (1953), 174-80.

Argues that class-consciousness is absent from the poem and that the all-pervasive fact of mortality underscores Gray's theme of equality of all men.

1312    Golden, Morris. THOMAS GRAY. New York: Twayne, 1964.

Discusses Gray's personality, his poetic themes, and examines all of his English poems "freshly" as works of literature, bringing to bear recent critical views of his transitional position in English literary history.

1313    Greene, Donald. "The Proper Language of Poetry: Gray, Johnson, and Others." In FEARFUL JOY: PAPERS FROM THE THOMAS GRAY BICENTENARY CONFERENCE AT CARLETON UNIVERSITY. Ed. James Downey and Ben Jones. Montreal: McGill-Queen's Univ. Press, 1974, pp. 85-102.

Interesting discussion of the question of poetic diction and changing poetic tastes in the eighteenth century, which concludes that, with perhaps the exception of a few satirical poems, Gray did not usually express human sentiments in the language really used by men, unlike practice advocated by both Johnson and Wordsworth. See no. 1290.

1314    Griffin, Dustin. "Gray's Audiences." EIC, 28 (1978), 208-15.

In his best poems, Gray is preoccupied with the indifference of audience as a measure of his "characteristic stance" of alienation; "but this sense of alienation, and a corresponding sense of poetic failure, is overcome when in some few poems Gray speaks in effect to two different audiences, one uncomprehending, and one sympathetic." Treats the "Sonnet on West," the "Eton College Ode," and the ELEGY.

1315    Guilhamet, Leon. "Imitation and Originality in the Poems of Thomas Gray." In PROCEEDINGS OF THE MODERN LANGUAGE ASSOCIATION: NEOCLASSICISM CONFERENCES, 1967-1968. Ed. Paul J. Korshin. New York: AMS, 1970, pp. 33-52.

Gray's best poems "present an inward colloquy between the personated or imitative voices of Gray and that single, serious voice which Plato thought everyone should have, the voice we use to speak to God and the person we love."

1316    Hagstrum, Jean H. "Gray's Sensibility." In FEARFUL JOY: PAPERS FROM THE THOMAS GRAY BICENTENARY CONFERENCE AT CARLETON UNIVERSITY. Ed. James Downey and Ben Jones. Montreal: McGill-Queen's Univ. Press, 1974, pp. 6-19.

Responsible and probing analysis of the psychological complexities of "Gray Agonistes," reconstructing the "pangs of
Passion" lying behind the "cool lapidary statement." See
no. 1290.

1317    Hartog, Curt. "Psychic Resolution in Gray's ELEGY." L&P, 25 (1975),
5-16.

An interesting psychoanalytical study of the poem, arguing
that, unlike Milton's "Lycidas" which successfully involves
the reader in the experience of loss at the primitive level
of childhood, as well as the reintegration of self beyond
acceptance of that loss, Gray's ELEGY fails to return us
to the real world of adult relationships, and thus "for all
its richness and all its acclaim" remains flawed.

1318    Hutchens, Eleanor N. "Gray's Cat and Pope's Belinda." TSL, 6
(1961), 103-08.

The enduring success of Gray's "Ode on the Death of a
Favorite Cat" is in large measure owing to the "double
charm" of basing his verse on the model of Pope's RAPE,
which is comic, but in effect a serious work of art; so that
Gray's own poem has the dual advantage of simultaneously
identifying its subject with the comically absurd (Pope's
subject matter) but also with something substantial (Pope's
poem).

1319    Jack, Ian. "Gray's ELEGY Reconsidered." In FROM SENSIBILITY TO
ROMANTICISM: ESSAYS PRESENTED TO FREDERICK A. POTTLE. Ed.
Frederick W. Hilles and Harold Bloom. New York: Oxford Univ.
Press, 1965, pp. 139-69.

A combination of controlled technique, careful planning,
and the "spontaneous power" of the creative imagination
characterizes the structure of this famous poem whose theme
is "the nostalgia of mankind aware of morality." See no.
110.

1320    Johnston, Arthur. "Gray's Use of the Gorchesty Beirdd in THE BARD."
MLR, 59 (1964), 335-38.

Discusses Gray's note calling attention to his use of Welsh
meter in the epodes of the poem and concludes that Gray's
"double cadence" has little resemblance to Welsh prosody
and that he may have wanted to draw attention to the
source of his inspiration to remind the reader of his intention to combine "wildness and variety."

1321    _____. "'The Purple Year' in Pope and Gray." RES, NS 14 (1963), 389-93.

   Argues that from a lexicographical standpoint that the
   phrase in Gray's "Ode on the Spring" and Pope's "Spring,"
   like phrases in Dryden and Milton, is associated with the
   brilliance of spring flowers and not with the light of a
   spring sun.  Believes Gray's context evokes a spring less
   classical and literary and more appropriate to "an English-
   man's naturalistic experience of the season."


1322    _____. "Thomas Gray:  Our Daring Bard." In FEARFUL JOY: PAPERS
   FROM THE THOMAS GRAY BICENTENARY CONFERENCE AT CARLETON
   UNIVERSITY.  Ed. James Downey and Ben Jones.  Montreal: Mc-Gill-
   Queen's Univ. Press, 1974, pp. 50-65.

   The bold language and imagery of Gray's prophetic odes
   that Blake praised and Johnson disliked constitute the
   "element of the extreme" characterizing Gray's poetic
   consciousness.  See no. 1290.


1323    Jones, Myrddin.  "Gray, Jaques, and the Man of Feeling."  RES,
   NS 25 (1974), 39-48.

   Considers the appeal to Gray of a character such as Jaques
   and suggests that in stanza 26 of the ELEGY, Gray refers
   to the scene in Shakespeare's AS YOU LIKE IT in which
   Jaques is observed by the First Lord and that such a connection indicates the increasing acceptance of this melancholic image in the eighteenth century.


1324    Kuist, James M.  "The Conclusion of Gray's ELEGY."  SAQ, 70
   (1971), 203-14.

   The concluding passages employ "heightened sentiment"
   with a careful artistic calculation, avoiding the gratuitous
   displays of emotion Gray so much disliked and thus broad-
   ening the basic themes of the poem, muting the concept
   of human limitations, and appealing to the literary tradition of an ethically significant melancholia.


1325    Lainoff, Seymour.  "Bolingbroke's Deism and Gray's ELEGY."  EnlE, 5,
   iii-iv (1974), 3-6.

   Gray's posthumously published "Essay on the Philosophy of
   Lord Bolingbroke" (composition date ca. 1748) explains
   the warm and personal religious consolation of the epitaph.


1326    Lonsdale, Roger.  "The Poetry of Thomas Gray:  Versions of Self."
   PBA, 59 (1973), 105-23.

Interesting study of the self created and projected in the
poems as a reflection of Gray's personal and political
struggle to find forms and structures to express private
experience, "the real spring of his creativity."

1327    Maclean, Kenneth. "The Distant Way: Imagination and Image in
        Gray's Poetry." In FEARFUL JOY: PAPERS FROM THE THOMAS
        GRAY BICENTENARY CONFERENCE AT CARLETON UNIVERSITY. Ed.
        James Downey and Ben Jones. Montreal: McGill-Queen's Univ. Press,
        1974, pp. 136-45.

        A highly sensitive analysis of the impact of Lockean simple
        sensation on Gray's poetry as imaginatively revealed in
        images of water, color, architectural form, and circularity.
        See no. 1290.

1328    Mandel, Eli. "Theories of Voice in Eighteenth-Century Poetry: Thomas
        Gray and Christopher Smart." In FEARFUL JOY: PAPERS FROM THE
        THOMAS GRAY BICENTENARY CONFERENCE AT CARLETON UNI-
        VERSITY. Ed. James Downey and Ben Jones. Montreal: McGill-
        Queen's Univ. Press, 1974, pp. 103-18.

        Discusses implications of Gray's and Smart's metaphoric
        identification of music and poetry, differentiating between
        Smart's lyrics of celebration and dramatic tones and Gray's
        more tentative, hesitant voice--at once "nostalgic and
        prophetic, elegiac and visionary." See no. 1290.

1329    Mell, Donald C., Jr. "Form as Meaning in Augustan Elegy: A Read-
        ing of Thomas Gray's 'Sonnet on the Death of Richard West.'" PLL,
        4 (1968), 131-43.

        Gray's use of poetic diction to create an intentional con-
        trast between literary feeling and sincere expression of
        grief does not account for the function of the allusions to
        Milton's Eden, which suggest both the ideal world of per-
        manence and the fallen world of mortality, at once attrac-
        tive to the speaker, but finally illusory and inadequate
        except as a mythic defense against time formalized into
        the permanence of art.

1329A   Micklus, Robert. "Voices in the Wind: The Eton Ode's Ambivalent
        Prospect of Maturity." ELN, 18 (1981), 181-86.

        Argues against the popular view of the Eton ode as an
        exposure of youth's illusions and suggests that Gray stages
        a dialog between the voice of fancy and the voice of
        reality in the mind of a man who is ambivalent about his
        role as an adult and whose ambivalence toward maturity
        remains unresolved.

# Thomas Gray

1330    Moore, Judith K.  "Thomas Gray's 'Sonnet on the Death of Richard West': The Circumstances and the Diction."  TSL, 19 (1974), 107-13.

> Studies the circumstances surrounding the poem's composition, analyzes the various kinds of language, and concludes that it enacts its own thesis--"the poet's isolation in the midst of a mating, communicating world."

1331    Pattison, Robert.  "Gray's 'Ode on the Death of a Favourite Cat': A Rationalist's Aesthetic."  UTQ, 49 (1979), 156-65.

> Study of the genesis and history of the poem's composition shows its indebtedness not only to classical Latin and Greek sources for its wit, but to "the prevailing aesthetic of Gray's tone, rationalism."

1332    Peckham, Morse.  "Gray's 'Epitaph' Revisited."  MLN, 71 (1956), 409-11.

> Considers the poem as a dramatic monologue in which the speaker imagines a "local Stone-cutter Poet" in accord with the eighteenth-century practice of creating a fictional narrator to achieve objectivity.  See no. 1291.

1333    Shepard, Odell.  "A Youth to Fortune and to Fame Unknown."  MP, 20 (1923), 347-73.

> An early (but much disputed) theory that Richard West is the subject of the ELEGY's famous epitaph.  See no. 1291.

1334    Snow, Malinda.  "The Gray Parody in BRAVE NEW WORLD."  PLL, 13 (1977), 185-88.

> Recognition of Huxley's parody of the opening stanza of Gray's ELEGY in chapter 5 of his novel "sharpens the reader's satirical perception and enhances his understanding of Huxley's purposes."

1335    Spacks, Patricia Meyer.  "'Artful Strife': Conflict in Gray's Poetry."  PMLA, 81 (1966), 63-69.

> Gray's early poems successfully reveal the theme of conflicting oppositions, but the static pictorial imagery of the later prophetic odes inadequately expresses his theme of poetry as process or creative activity.

1336    _____.  "Statement and Artifice in Thomas Gray."  SEL, 5 (1965), 519-32.

> Awareness of himself as poetic contriver leads Gray to an insight into reality and a further understanding of human (and poetic) limitation.

1337    Starr, Herbert W. "Gray's Craftsmanship." JEGP, 45 (1946), 415-29.

Examines Gray's revisions in the ELEGY, THE PROGRESS OF POETRY, and THE BARD to prove that, though he is possibly deficient in "the highest kind of creative imagination," Gray was a skilled and disciplined poetic craftsman who had a fine sense of critical judgment, especially in respect to his own work.

1338    _____. "'A Youth to Fortune and to Fame Unknown': A Re-Estimation." JEGP, 48 (1949), 97-107.

Carefully analyzes pronoun references and syntax of ll. 93-94 of the ELEGY and concludes that there is no evidence that Gray was referring specifically to West but probably imagining an unappreciated village poet of no historical importance. See no. 1291.

1339    Sugg, Richard P. "The Importance of Voice: Gray's ELEGY." TSL, 19 (1974), 115-20.

Studies the images of sound-silence signifying life-death in which the interweaving of the poem's various voices indicates how man survives death—"the poet survives in the voice of the poem he has created and this survival clearly suggests that man outlives death through the voices he creates."

1340    Sutherland, John H. "The Stonecutter in Gray's ELEGY." MP, 55 (1957), 11-13.

Denies that Gray's epitaph refers outside the poem to a stonecutter and argues that the narrator and subject of the epitaph are the same "educated young gentleman." See no. 1291.

1341    Tillotson, Geoffrey. "Gray's 'Ode on the Death of a Favourite Cat, Drowned in a Tub of Gold Fishes.'" In his AUGUSTAN STUDIES. London: Athlone Press, 1961, pp. 216-23.

Using Johnson's hostile reaction as a springboard, deftly analyzes the humorous effects of Gray's mock-heroic, mock-elegiac allusive mode. See no. 126.

1342    _____. "Gray's Ode on the Spring." In his AUGUSTAN STUDIES. London: Athlone Press, 1961, pp. 204-15.

Discusses the relation of Gray's allusive diction and imagery to both classical and native antecedents and the conscious projection of a responsive self into the scene to produce a coherent and meaningful poetic statement. See no. 126.

1343    Tracy, Clarence. "Melancholy Marked Him For Her Own." In FEAR-
        FUL JOY: PAPERS FROM THE THOMAS GRAY BICENTENARY CON-
        FERENCE AT CARLETON UNIVERSITY. Ed. James Downey and Ben
        Jones. Montreal: McGill-Queen's Univ. Press, 1974, pp. 37-49.

            General treatment of the ELEGY, emphasizing such Augus-
            tan qualities as death's inevitability and man's total de-
            pravity and inclination to evil, as well as Gray's ambiguous
            social consciousness and his "ethic of withdrawal and non-
            commitment." See no. 1290.


1344    Vernon, P.F. "The Structure of Gray's Early Poems." EIC, 15 (1965),
        381-93.

            Study of Gray's early poems reveals an already developing
            "elaborate and original, if unobstrusive, symbolic method,
            a feature characteristic of his later odes."


1345    Wagman, Stephen. "Myth and the Commonplace in Gray's ELEGY."
        EnlE, 5, iii/iv (1974), 7-13.

            Argues against rhetorical readings and furnishes a psycho-
            logical study of the ELEGY as reflecting Gray's plight
            as a failed poet able to find solace only in a "ready-
            made religious formula."


1346    Watson, George. "The Voices of Gray." CRITICAL QUARTERLY, 19
        (1977), 51-57.

            A linguistic approach to uncertainties in Gray's use of
            active and passive voice in the ELEGY, arguing that he
            applies the copulative forms of such verbs as "to be" to
            other noncopulative verbs to effect a blurring of the syn-
            tactical difference between subject and object.


1347    Weinbrot, Howard D. "Gray's ELEGY: A Poem of Moral Choice and
        Resolution." SEL, 18 (1978), 537-51.

            Combines R.S. Crane's arguments (THE LANGUAGES OF
            CRITICISM AND THE STRUCTURE OF POETRY, 1953) re-
            garding the psychological and moral plot of the poem with
            collateral analyses of setting, character, and poetic language
            in order to show that the poem "is concerned not with a
            choice of life or death, but a choice of eternity."


1348    Wright, George T. "Eliot Written in a Country Churchyard: The
        ELEGY and FOUR QUARTETS." ELH, 43 (1976), 227-43.

            Interesting discussion of thematic and structural similarities
            between the two works, concluding that in the handling of
            "the paradox that comprehends both stillness and motion,"
            Eliot is clearly the artistic master.

1349     _____ . "Stillness and the Argument of Gray's ELEGY." MP, 74 (1977), 381-89.

> The central subject of the poem "is not the contrast between the poor and the great, but the nature and meaning of epitaphs," Gray's point being that they are necessary but ultimately futile and superfluous in light of God's "more imageless ground of being."

1350   See no. 858.

# SAMUEL JOHNSON (1709-84)

## A. MAJOR EDITIONS

1351    THE YALE EDITION OF THE WORKS OF SAMUEL JOHNSON. Ed.
Allen T. Hazen, John H. Middendorf, et al. 11 vols. (projected).
New Haven, Conn.: Yale Univ. Press, 1958-- .

> When complete, will supersede all other editions. Vol.
> 6, ed. E. L. McAdam, Jr., with George Milne (1964),
> is the standard edition of the poems. Makes use of new
> information in Boswell papers; gives significant variants
> of textual importance; prints poems in chronological order;
> normally uses as copy text the last version approved by
> Johnson; and furnishes, for comparison, passages from
> Juvenal beneath the corresponding lines in LONDON and
> THE VANITY OF HUMAN WISHES.

1352    THE POEMS OF SAMUEL JOHNSON. Ed. David Nichol Smith and
Edward L. McAdam. 2nd ed. rev. Oxford: Clarendon Press, 1974.

> Includes newly discovered poems since first edition and
> utilizes advancement in Johnsonian scholarship and in
> textual editing, but generally reverts to same original
> documents and photographs used as a basis for the text
> of 1941. Records significant variants, provides commentary,
> and adds a draft of LONDON and a whole version of THE
> VANITY OF HUMAN WISHES.

1353    "LONDON," 1738 AND 1748; "THE VANITY OF HUMAN WISHES,"
1749 AND 1755. Menston, Yorkshire, Engl.: Scolar Press, 1971.

> Facsimile reprint of the four printings.

1354    LIVES OF THE ENGLISH POETS. Ed. George Birkbeck Hill. 3 vols.
Oxford: Clarendon Press, 1905. Index.

> Johnson's critical opinions remain amazingly sound and
> resilient. Annotated.

1355    JOHNSONIAN MISCELLANIES. Ed. George Birkbeck Hill. 2 vols.
Oxford: Clarendon Press, 1897; rpt. New York: Barnes and Noble,
1970.

> Contains the Thrale-Piozzi ANECDOTES, Johnson's
> PRAYERS AND MEDITATIONS, ANNALS of his child-
> hood, and collections of minor information.

## B. CORRESPONDENCE

1356    THE LETTERS OF SAMUEL JOHNSON. Ed. Robert W. Chapman.
3 vols. Oxford: Clarendon Press, 1952.

> Considered a model edition of eighteenth-century corre-
> spondence because of Chapman's principle of giving an
> exact transcription of all peculiarities in the execution
> of the letters as indications of Johnson's state of mind,
> health, attitudes, and writing habits.

## C. BIBLIOGRAPHY, TEXTUAL STUDIES, AND CONCORDANCES

1357    Allen, Robert R.    "Variant Readings in Johnson's LONDON." PBSA,
60 (1966), 214-15.

> Notes a few variants (two textual and two in notes) in
> the Lloyd Francis Nickell copy of the poem that differ
> from the known Harvard, Yale, Donald F. Hyde, and
> Illinois versions, but that seem more like "curiosities"
> than significant contributions to the poem's publication
> history.

1358    Chapman, Robert W., and Allen T. Hazen.    "Johnsonian Bibliography:
A Supplement to Courtney."    OXFORD BIBLIOGRAPHICAL SOCIETY,
5 (1938), 119-66.

> A supplement reflecting additions in the Johnson canon
> and offering a more detailed bibliographical description
> of the books than heretofore provided. See no. 1362.

1359    Clifford, James L.    JOHNSONIAN STUDIES, 1887-1950: A SURVEY
AND BIBLIOGRAPHY.    Minneapolis: Univ. of Minnesota Press, 1951.

> Provides a valuable survey of the critical opinion, as well
> as a list of studies. See no. 1360.

1360    Clifford, James L., and Donald J. Greene.    "A Bibliography of
Johnsonian Studies, 1950-1960 (With Additions and Corrections to
Johnsonian Studies, 1887-1950)."    In JOHNSONIAN STUDIES. Ed.
Magdi Wahba.    Cairo: Oxford Univ. Press, 1962, pp. 203-341.

Extends earlier bibliography and provides a valuable survey of ten years of Johnsonian studies, indicating (in the
editors' judgment) especially important scholarly contributions to the understanding and appreciation of Johnson's
life and art. Also supplements and corrects earlier bibliography. See no. 1359.

1361 _____, eds. SAMUEL JOHNSON: A SURVEY AND BIBLIOGRAPHY
OF CRITICAL STUDIES. Minneapolis: Univ. of Minnesota Press, 1970.

Combines the two major previous surveys, above, and
provides two important additions: (1) recent studies,
1960-68 (Clifford); (2) early studies during Johnson's
lifetime through 1887 (Greene). Principle of selection
provides essays that add to previous knowledge about
Johnson, contribute something original, and also those
that are notoriously "obtuse" or perverse in some way.
Summarizes the changing critical opinions of Johnson
over the years.

1362 Courtney, William Prideaux, and David Nichol Smith. A BIBLIOG-
RAPHY OF SAMUEL JOHNSON. Oxford: Clarendon Press, 1915.

Although a pioneer work, still highly respected for its
accuracy and completeness. See no. 1358.

1363 Flood, W.H. Grattan. "On the Death of Dr. Robert Levet." RES,
4 (1928), 88-89.

Points out that the GENTLEMAN'S MAGAZINE text of
the poem was the basis for a rare edition of the POETICAL
WORKS OF SAMUEL JOHNSON, edited by Thomas Pack
in 1805.

1364 Horne, Colin J. "Johnson's Correction of Lines 137-38 of THE VANITY
OF HUMAN WISHES." PBSA, 69 (1975), 552-60.

Argues that modern editors' emendation of the word "Burns"
for "Spreads," printed in the fourth edition of Dodsley's
COLLECTION OF POEMS (1755), on the strength of
Boswell's report of Johnson's revisions of 1778, is dubious
and that evidence proves these lines "less authoritative"
than the 1755 reading, which Johnson ultimately approved.

1365 Moody, Anthony D. "The Creative Critic: Johnson's Revisions of
LONDON and THE VANITY OF HUMAN WISHES." RES, NS 22
(1971), 137-50.

Inspired by the Yale edition, gives a detailed study of

the editorial changes and revisions of the poems to discover Johnson's "critical impulses in their more vital and
illuminating form, actively at work in his poetic practice"
and to become aware of the critic in the poem, not in
the abstract formulations of his prose.

1366    Nangle, Helen Harrold, and Peter B. Sherry, eds. A CONCORDANCE
TO THE POEMS OF SAMUEL JOHNSON. Ithaca, N.Y.: Cornell
Univ. Press, 1973.

Keyed to the Smith-McAdam Oxford edition of the POEMS with
supplementary material provided from the more recent volume 6
of the Yale edition. Divides the corpus into three separate
sections: poems in English, poems in Latin, and doubtful poems.

1367    Roberts, Sydney C. "'On the Death of Dr. Robert Levet'--A Note on
the Text." RES, 3 (1927), 442-45.

Studies especially the textual variants of the final stanza,
showing the printings in the GENTLEMAN'S MAGAZINE,
the LONDON MAGAZINE, and the ANNUAL REGISTER
and argues that the text in the GENTLEMAN'S MAGA-
ZINE (where the poem first appeared) should be restored,
with the exception of the printer's error in 1.17, for both
authenticity and aesthetic reasons.

1368    Sherbo, Arthur. "Samuel Johnson and Certain Poems in the May 1747
GENTLEMAN'S MAGAZINE." RES, NS 17 (1966), 382-90.

Challenges some of the decisions of the Yale editors in
treating the authenticity of Johnson's poetic canon, arguing
that some poems dropped from the canon deserve reconsideration based on the available evidence.

1369    Weinbrot, Howard. "Samuel Johnson's 'Short Song of Congratulation'
and the Accompanying Letter to Mrs. Thrale: The Huntington Library
Manuscripts." HLQ, 34 (1970), 79-80.

Close examination of the Johnson manuscript and accompanying letter to Mrs. Thrale throws into doubt the authority of the Yale printing: the name Sir John Lade in the
fifth paragraph is clearly in Johnson's handwriting; and the
several corrections in the manuscript, which were accepted
by Mrs. Thrale for the first publication in BRITISH SYN-
ONYMY, would suggest that the Yale text may not represent Johnson's real intentions.

## D. COLLECTIONS AND FESTSCHRIFTEN

1370    Bronson, Bertrand H. JOHNSON AGONISTES AND OTHER ESSAYS.

Berkeley: Univ. of California Press, 1965.

The volume reprints three important essays in the 1946 edition and adds a fourth.

1371 Greene, Donald J., ed. SAMUEL JOHNSON: A COLLECTION OF ESSAYS. Englewood Cliffs, N.J.: Prentice-Hall, 1965.

Excellent collection of previously printed essays representative of the range and insight of the critical opinion. Introduction presents a fine commentary prompted by the range of the various essays.

1372 Hilles, Frederick W., ed. NEW LIGHT ON DR. JOHNSON: ESSAYS ON OCCASION OF HIS 250TH BIRTHDAY. New Haven, Conn.: Yale Univ. Press, 1959.

Widely diverse essays, about one-half never before published and the others either privately printed or revised from periodicals.

1373 JOHNSON, BOSWELL AND THEIR CIRCLE: ESSAYS PRESENTED TO LAWRENCE FITZROY POWELL IN HONOUR OF HIS EIGHTY-FOURTH BIRTHDAY. Oxford: Clarendon Press, 1965.

Essays by sixteen contributors devoted to all aspects of Johnson's literary career.

## E. BIOGRAPHY

1374 Bate, W. Jackson. SAMUEL JOHNSON. New York: Harcourt Brace Jovanovich, 1977.

Widely acclaimed biography stressing Johnson's complicated psychological makeup. Argues for the success of the conventions of literary pastoralism in "London" and considers "The Vanity of Human Wishes" a depiction of "the inner landscape" of Johnson's mind.

1375 Boswell, James. BOSWELL'S LIFE OF JOHNSON. Ed. George Birkbeck Hill and L.F. Powell. 6 vols. Oxford: Clarendon Press, 1934-64.

A rich source of information and critical opinion recorded by this friend and interpreter of Johnson in what is considered the most famous biography in English.

1376 Clifford, James. DICTIONARY JOHNSON: SAMUEL JOHNSON'S MIDDLE YEARS. New York: McGraw-Hill, 1979.

Lucid account of Johnson's life from 1749 to 1763, bringing to bear all the latest scholarship and understanding of this highly productive time of his life.

1377 _____. YOUNG SAM JOHNSON. New York: McGraw-Hill, 1955.

Standard modern biography of Johnson's years from birth to 1749, the time in which his ethical convictions and tastes were being formed. Both a readable and meticulously researched life.

1378 Wain, John. SAMUEL JOHNSON. New York: Viking Press, 1974.

In many ways the best recent biography of Johnson, written with wit, imagination, and a strong affinity for Johnson's view of life and a shared sense of the centrality of his moral vision.

## F. CRITICISM

1379 Aden, John M. "RASSELAS and THE VANITY OF HUMAN WISHES." CRITICISM, 3 (1961), 295-303.

Argues that RASSELAS represents a repudiation of the melancholy and pessimism characterizing the poem and is not a prose extension of these attitudes.

1380 Adler, Jacob. "Notes on the Prosody of THE VANITY OF HUMAN WISHES." SLitI, 5, ii (1972), 101-17.

Johnson's critical utterances on the question of prosodic regularity vary, but his "constitutional desire" for variety balances his "constitutional desire" for regularity and is reflected in his couplet rhetoric.

1381 Alkon, Paul Kent. SAMUEL JOHNSON AND MORAL DISCIPLINE. Evanston, Ill.: Northwestern Univ. Press, 1967.

Refers to Johnson's intellectual background and discusses the "controlling assumptions" of his moral writings, touching on THE VANITY OF HUMAN WISHES.

1382 Ames, George T. "The Style of THE VANITY OF HUMAN WISHES." MLQ, 35 (1974), 16-29.

Attempts to account for the emotional power of the poem apparent because "held in tightest check, so that the detachment and abstractions emerge as personal defenses against despair" and as the result of aspects of structure, prosody, and diction that contribute to tone of "courageous manliness."

1383    Bate, Walter Jackson. THE ACHIEVEMENT OF SAMUEL JOHNSON. New York: Oxford Univ. Press, 1955.

Respected assessment of Johnson's accomplishment as poet, critic, and moralist, taking into account his personal side as well as his faith in the "stability of truth."

1384    Bloom, Edward A. SAMUEL JOHNSON IN GRUB STREET. Providence, R.I.: Brown Univ. Press, 1957.

Well-researched discussion of Johnson's journalistic career and its relationship to his larger literary output, touching on connections between his periodical writings and audience and on the production and intentions of his poetry.

1385    _____. "THE VANITY OF HUMAN WISHES: Reason's Images." EIC, 15 (1965), 181-92.

Contributes to the twentieth-century revaluation of the poem by means of "a comprehensive analysis of the poem's recurrent images, which make up in coherence and functional propriety what they seem to lack in concrete particularity."

1386    Bloom, Edward A., and Lillian D. Bloom. "Johnson's LONDON and Its Juvenalian Texts." HLQ, 34 (1970), 1-23.

Careful consideration of editions of Juvenal's text and their use in eighteenth-century grammar schools leads to a fuller understanding of Johnson's education, the scope of his classical knowledge, and the ways he coped with Juvenal's "grossness" and rendered his "moral profundity."

1387    _____. "Johnson's LONDON and the Tools of Scholarship." HLQ, 34 (1971), 115-39.

Johnson's familiarity with Juvenal's THIRD SATIRE ran together in his mind with post-Renaissance scholarly commentary to produce in the poem a "mixture of gaiety and stateliness, of pointed sentences, and declamatory grandeur," as he wrote in the LIFE OF DRYDEN.

1388    _____. "Johnson's 'Mournful Narrative': The Rhetoric of 'London.'" In EIGHTEENTH-CENTURY STUDIES IN HONOR OF DONALD F. HYDE. Ed. W.H. Bond. New York: Grolier Club, 1970, pp. 107-44.

Describes some of the ways Johnson modifies Juvenal's

rhetorical strategies (and the classical rhetorical tradition)
to fit the tastes and expectations of his audience and his
own "personal piety" according to the long-accepted
rhetorical principle of adjusting old means to new ends.
See no. 94.

1389    Bogel, Fredric V.  "The Rhetoric of Substantiality:  Johnson and the
Later Eighteenth Century."  ECS, 12 (1979), 457-80.

Different from the example of Smart, whose poetic vision
and rhetoric attempt to dissolve distinctions between the
metaphysical and substantial, Johnson in his verse insists
on recognition of the dichotomy between the heavenly
and earthly in order to value each realm of existence
appropriately.

1390    Boulton, James T.  JOHNSON:  THE CRITICAL HERITAGE.  New
York:  Barnes and Noble, 1971.

Extracts ranging from an early reference (1738) to Johnson's
search for a publisher for LONDON to the famous reviews
by Macaulay and Carlyle of the Croker edition of Boswell's
LIFE are chosen on the basis of interest, historical importance, and representativeness and arranged chronologically
under the titles of major publications.

1391    Boyd, D.V.  "Vanity and Vacuity:  A Reading of Johnson's Verse
Satires."  ELH, 39 (1972), 387-403.

Stresses the subversive element in Johnson's satire, but
explains that his sympathies and identification with the
follies and vices of his victims are not preromantic but
rather based on the condition called ontological insecurity,
a result of Johnson's perfectly orthodox religious faith and
his belief in the arbitrary and inexplicable nature of man's
existence.

1392    Butt, John.  "Johnson's Practice in the Poetical Imitation."  In NEW
LIGHT ON DR. JOHNSON:  ESSAYS ON OCCASION OF HIS 250TH
BIRTHDAY.  Ed. Frederick W. Hilles.  New Haven, Conn.:  Yale
Univ. Press, 1959, pp. 19-34.

Compares Johnson's accomplishment in the area of poetic
imitation with that of Pope's, concluding that because his
"genius was toward generalization," "philosophical satire"
seemed more comfortable than Pope's Horatian-styled political contemporaneity.  See no. 1372.

1393    Chapin, Chester F.  THE RELIGIOUS THOUGHT OF SAMUEL JOHN-
SON.  Ann Arbor:  Univ. of Michigan Press, 1968.

Comprehensive account of reasons why orthodox Christian beliefs so appealed to Johnson's consciousness and provided the basis for his art.

1394   Damrosch, Leopold, Jr.  SAMUEL JOHNSON AND THE TRAGIC SENSE.  Princeton, N.J.:  Princeton Univ. Press, 1972.

Chapter 6 focuses on the relationship of the "tragic quality" in Johnson to satiric elements that critics have detected in THE VANITY OF HUMAN WISHES, and concludes that the poem moves in a peculiarly Johnsonian manner beyond tragedy and satire "into a larger and more comprehensive vision."

1395   Eliot, T.S.  "Johnson as Critic and Poet."  In ON POETRY AND POETS.  New York:  Farrar, Straus and Cudahy, 1957, pp. 184-222.

Holds that the study of Johnson's poetry is relevant to his critical opinions (and vice versa), and thus takes a critical approach ranging widely over Johnson's poetic practices, especially in THE VANITY OF HUMAN WISHES, to explain his tastes and sensibility in respect to Thomson, Akenside, Goldsmith, and Milton.

1396   _____.  "Johnson's LONDON and THE VANITY OF HUMAN WISHES."  In ENGLISH CRITICAL ESSAYS: TWENTIETH CENTURY.  Ed. Phyllis M. Jones.  London:  Oxford Univ. Press, 1933, pp. 301-10.

Reprint of the famous introduction to the Haleswood Books Edition (1930) which takes Matthew Arnold at his own word and argues that Johnson's verse is great because it shares the qualities of his best prose and that generally "to have the virtues of good prose is the first and minimum requirement of good poetry."

1397   _____.  "What is Minor Poetry?"  SR, 54 (1946), 1-18.

Argues that Johnson is a major poet by the "single testimony" of THE VANITY OF HUMAN WISHES, which displays both structural unity and a variety of effects and represents a good long poem.

1398   Emslie, Macdonald.  "Johnson's Satires and 'The Proper Wit of Poetry.'"  CAMBRIDGE JOURNAL, 7 (1954), 349-60.

Excellent study of metaphorical effects and manifestations of wit in Johnson, finding characteristically both in Johnson and Pope "an image rich in poetic implication deliberately subdued."

1399   Fussell, Paul.  SAMUEL JOHNSON AND THE LIFE OF WRITING.
       New York:  Harcourt Brace Jovanovich, 1971.

       Demonstrates that, as with his other literary compositions,
       the shape and impact of Johnson's most personal poetry
       depends on literary convention and tradition, serious
       parody, and imitation ranging broadly from classical
       models to the eighteenth-century Anglican hymn.

1400   Gifford, Henry.  "THE VANITY OF HUMAN WISHES."  RES, NS  6
       (1955), 157-65.

       Argues that for Johnson writing poetry (even Latin transla-
       tions) was a vehicle for personal conviction and that his
       alterations of the temper and tone of Juvenal's TENTH
       SATIRE reveals his concern "with the deepest things in
       his experience" that go beyond the satire of manners to
       "the mystery of human existence."

1401   Grant, Douglas.  "Samuel Johnson:  Satire and Satirists."  NEW
       RAMBLER, 3, ser. C (June 1967), 5-17.

       Discusses LONDON and THE VANITY OF HUMAN WISHES
       as illustrative of Johnson's penchant for generality in com-
       parison to the more personal satire of Dryden, Pope, and
       Churchill.

1402   Greene, Donald.  "'An Extempore Elegy.'"  JOHNSONIAN NEWS
       LETTER, 26, i (1966), 11-12.

       Suggests that Fanny Burney's recollection of the structure
       of the "elegy" on "a woman of the town" is faulty and
       that possibly stanzas 3 and 4 should be reversed to make
       better poetic sense.

1403   _____.  "Johnson on Garrick."  JOHNSONIAN NEWS LETTER, 14,
       iii (1954), 10-12.

       Perhaps the extended diatribe against the French in "London"
       is a personal attack on the Garricks, the only family of
       French extraction Johnson ever knew; and although Johnson
       was clearly susceptible to the famous Garrick charm, he
       and the Garricks were never on intimate terms, especially
       after their Lichfield and Edial Hall days.

1404   _____.  "'Pictures to the Mind':  Johnson and Imagery."  In JOHN-
       SON, BOSWELL AND THEIR CIRCLE:  ESSAYS PRESENTED TO
       LAWRENCE FITZROY POWELL IN HONOUR OF HIS EIGHTY-FOURTH
       BIRTHDAY.  Oxford:  Clarendon Press, 1965, pp. 137-58.

       A convincing refutation of the view that Johnson's poetry

(and prose) make ineffective use of concrete imagery and
thus lack poetic suggestiveness.  See no. 1373.

1405 _____. THE POLITICS OF SAMUEL JOHNSON.  New Haven, Conn.:
Yale Univ. Press, 1960.

An important contribution to the understanding of eighteenth-
century politics in general and Johnson's in particular,
demonstrating the inaccuracy of the term reactionary when
applied to Johnson and the ambivalent position he held
in regard to Walpole, the Whigs, theories of monarchy,
and patriotism.

1406 _____. SAMUEL JOHNSON.  New York: Twayne, 1970.

The short section on the verse carefully analyzes Johnson's
precise, original, and suggestive use of language and metaphor, citing his skillful parody and comic experiments and
indirectly answering the complaint (romantic and Victorian
in origin) that the eighteenth century was an age of prose.
Excellent contribution to the often uneven Twayne series.

1407 Griffin, Dustin.  "Johnson's Funeral Writings."  ELH, 41 (1974), 192-
211.

Examines "On the Death of Dr. Robert Levet" in the context of Johnson's attitudes toward death and of the neoclassical genres of epitaph and elegy.

1408 Hagstrum, Jean H.  SAMUEL JOHNSON'S LITERARY CRITICISM.
1952; rev. ed. Chicago:  Univ. of Chicago Press, 1967.

Still the best single book on Johnson as critic, approaching
the criticism topically by employing such terms as nature,
pleasure, wit, among other categories.  The preface to the
1967 edition cites recent scholarship, explores issues raised
in the earlier edition, and underscores Johnson's impact on
twentieth-century criticism.

1409 Hardy, John.  "Hope and Fear in Johnson."  EIC, 26 (1976), 285-99.

Focuses on THE VANITY OF HUMAN WISHES, among
other works, in arguing that Johnson presents "a clear-
eyed perception of man's inhumanity to man" which acknowledges the familiar temptations of pride, power, and
wealth; judges this vision as hardly severe or patient or
hopeful in any sense, but overcome rather with darkness,
fear, and a painful consciousness of the "miseries of the
world."

1410       ____. "Johnson's LONDON: The Country Versus the City." In STUDIES IN THE EIGHTEENTH CENTURY I: PAPERS PRESENTED AT THE DAVID NICHOL SMITH MEMORIAL SEMINAR, CANBERRA, 1966. Ed. R.F. Brissenden. Toronto: Univ. of Toronto Press, 1968, pp. 251-68.

> In contrast to Juvenal's ironic treatment of the city-country antithesis, Johnson imaginatively links the corruption of London with his political objections to the court and ministry of Robert Walpole and thus seriously depicts the country as a desirable alternative. See no. 97.

1411       ____. SAMUEL JOHNSON: A CRITICAL STUDY. London: Routledge and Kegan Paul, 1979.

> Provides a general commentary on the poetry, quoting extensively from Johnson's prose discussions of the nature of imitation, as well as analyzing Johnson's imitative practice in the major poems.

1412    Hilles, Frederick W. "Johnson's Poetic Fire." In FROM SENSIBILITY TO ROMANTICISM: ESSAYS PRESENTED TO FREDERICK A. POTTLE. Ed. Frederick W. Hilles and Harold Bloom. New York: Oxford Univ. Press, 1965, pp. 67-77.

> Discusses the importance of Johnson's "farsighted" literal and moral perspective during his survey of mankind in the establishment of stability and poise that characterizes "Christian stoicism." See no. 110.

1413    Hodgart, Matthew T.C. SAMUEL JOHNSON AND HIS TIMES. New York: Arco Publishing, 1962.

> Short appraisal of Johnson's life and literary career.

1414    Horne, Colin J. "The Roles of Swift and Marlborough in THE VANITY OF HUMAN WISHES." MP, 73 (1976), 280-83.

> Johnson's several portraits of military conquerors also recall indirectly Swift's political writings of 1710-11 in THE EXAMINER and in THE CONDUCT OF THE ALLIES in which he promotes the Tory desire for the end of the War of the Spanish Succession by charging Marlborough with corruption and pride. Thus in lines 255-58 of THE VANITY OF HUMAN WISHES, Swift and Marlborough appear "less as objects of satire than as memento mori" because of Johnson's method of underscoring the "dread pathos" and tragedy associated with their ends.

1415    See no. 1810.

1416    Kolb, Gwin J. "Johnson Echoes Dryden." MLN, 74 (1959), 212-13.

The close resemblance of language and phrasing between
the end of Dryden's STATE OF INNOCENCE (1677) and
Johnson's passage depicting fortunate old age in THE
VANITY OF HUMAN WISHES (11. 290-98) seems to
indicate that Johnson remembered Dryden's lines on the
same subject and spoke in the words of the earlier poet.

1417    Krieger, Murray. "Samuel Johnson: The 'Extensive View' of Mankind
and the Cost of Acceptance." In THE CLASSIC VISION; THE RETREAT
FROM EXTREMITY IN MODERN LITERATURE. Baltimore: Johns Hopkins Press, 1971, pp. 125-45.

Heavily rhetorical, THE VANITY OF HUMAN WISHES
consciously represents "the artificial character of neoclassical poem-making," Johnson avoiding as much as
possible imitation of "life's particularities" and employing
his abstractions to preserve sanity and to protect himself
from reality at the same time that he reminds himself that
actuality must be lived with. See no. 383.

1418    Krutch, Joseph Wood. SAMUEL JOHNSON. New York: Henry Holt,
1944.

A narrative of Johnson's life along with a general appreciation of his literary achievement, devoting several pages to
LONDON and THE VANITY OF HUMAN WISHES and
viewing the latter as superior to the former.

1419    Kupersmith, William. "'More like an Orator than a Philosopher':
Rhetorical Structure in THE VANITY OF HUMAN WISHES." SP, 72
(1975), 454-72.

Johnson's poem does not manifest "logical structure" or
"organic form" in any modern critical sense of those terms,
but rather exhibits a scheme of organization and pattern
derived from classical rhetoric.

1420    Lascelles, Mary. "Johnson and Juvenal." In NEW LIGHT ON DR.
JOHNSON: ESSAYS ON OCCASION OF HIS 250TH BIRTHDAY. Ed.
Frederick W. Hilles. New Haven, Conn.: Yale Univ. Press, 1959,
pp. 35-55.

Argues that Johnson's "London" mutes Juvenal's irony and
lacks "the brillance of its original" and that the mode of
THE VANITY OF HUMAN WISHES is "tragic irony, learnt
in the contemplation of life," rather than the Juvenalian
"satiric irony" of a bitter mind for whom "life has nothing
to give." See no. 1372.

1421    Lipking, Lawrence. "Learning to Read Johnson: THE VISION OF
        THEODORE and THE VANITY OF HUMAN WISHES." ELH, 43 (1976),
        517-37.

        These two seemingly dissimilar works illustrate the single
        purpose for Johnson of all imaginative literature: helping
        men "endure the pain of existence" and achieve self-
        understanding.

1422    See no. 1244.

1423    MacAndrew, Elizabeth. "Life in the Maze--Johnson's Use of Chiasmus
        in THE VANITY OF HUMAN WISHES." STUDIES IN EIGHTEENTH-
        CENTURY CULTURE, 9 (1979), 517-27.

        The rhetorical device of chiasmus with its inverted syntacti-
        cal parallelism underscores Johnson's "dead-end" outlook on
        life which sees the best and worst human aspirations in-
        evitably leading to defeat.

1424    McCutcheon, Roger P. "Samuel Johnson: 1709-1959." TSL, 6 (1961),
        109-17.

        Reviews Johnson's achievement, addressing such matters as
        bibliography, biography, and the developing critical
        opinion and noting that reactions to the poetry have been
        enthusiastic.

1425    McGlynn, Paul D. "Rhetoric as Metaphor in THE VANITY OF HUMAN
        WISHES." SEL, 15 (1975), 473-82.

        Johnson's moral thesis--"people pursue specious goals"--
        cannot be separated from the poem's rhetorical structure;
        its catalog of illustrative examples suggests "exhaustiveness"
        and the futility of the search itself.

1426    Mell, Donald C., Jr. "Johnson's Moral Elegiacs: Theme and Structure
        in 'On the Death of Dr. Robert Levet.'" Genre, 5 (1972), 293-306.

        Surely sincere "by any standard invoked" as well as dis-
        playing Johnson's "massive personality" and "moral con-
        sciousness," this moving tribute to Levet turns out to be
        on close inspection a "variation on familiar literary themes
        and conventions," demonstrating a complex interplay of
        elegiac attitudes toward art and time.

1427    O'Flaherty, Patrick. "Johnson as Satirist: A New Look at THE VANITY
        OF HUMAN WISHES." ELH, 34 (1967), 78-91.

        Argues that Johnson's vision of human life was too dark,

sorrowful, and tragic for the "useless and false mask of
the satirist." Swift, Pope, and Dryden were humanists who
had faith in the capacity of mankind for limited progress and
improvement; Johnson considered misery and vice man's
inevitable condition.

1428  Quinlan, Maurice J.  SAMUEL JOHNSON:  A LAYMAN'S RELIGION.
Madison:  Univ. of Wisconsin Press, 1964.

A study of the impact of the deep religious fervor in the
writings of an age noted for its secularism as well as its
religious fanaticism.

1429  Ricks, Christopher.  "Johnson's 'Battle of the Pygmies and Cranes.'"
EIC, 16 (1966), 281-89.

This youthful translation of Joseph Addison's PROELIUM
INTER PYGAMCOS ET GRUES (1698), although of no
"great intrinsic merit," throws much light on the metaphorical skill by which Johnson revivifies and invigorates
dead metaphors and poetic cliches into "a discriminatingly
relevant prominence, varying their dress and situation so
as to give them fresh grace and more powerful attractions"
(RAMBLER 3).

1430  _____.  "Wolsey in THE VANITY OF HUMAN WISHES."  MLN, 73
(1958), 563-68.

Suggests that Johnson's description of Cardinal Wolsey
(based on Juvenal's Sejanus) reflects certain of the attacks
on Robert Walpole in opposition newspapers that compare
him with Wolsey, a familiar conjoining of the two found
also in Swift's WINDSOR PROPHECY (1711), THE CRAFTS-
MAN (1726), and Pope's EPILOGUE TO THE SATIRES
(1740).

1431  Sachs, Arieh.  PASSIONATE INTELLIGENCE:  IMAGINATION AND
REASON IN THE WORK OF SAMUEL JOHNSON.  Baltimore: Johns
Hopkins Press, 1967.

Lucid, brief discussion of the relation of the concepts of
particularity and generality to Johnson's aesthetics and
his view that the poetic art is not an escape from reality,
but a confrontation with the "stability of truth."

1432  Schwartz, Richard B.  SAMUEL JOHNSON AND THE NEW SCIENCE.
Madison:  Univ. of Wisconsin Press, 1971.

Discusses the nature of scientific inquiry in the eighteenth century and demonstrates Johnson's comprehensive knowledge of science and his adaptation of "the Baconian legacy" with its reliance on experience as the test of secular truths.

1433     _____. SAMUEL JOHNSON AND THE PROBLEM OF EVIL. Madison: Univ. of Wisconsin Press, 1975.

Discusses the implication of Johnson's strictures on Pope's and Soame Jenyns' blurring of the orthodox distinctions between natural and moral evil and analyzes his masterful exposure of Jenyns' theodicy.

1434     Selden, R. "Dr. Johnson and Juvenal: A Problem in Critical Method." CL, 22 (1970), 289-302.

Examines THE VANITY OF HUMAN WISHES in the "comparative context" of earlier versions of his Juvenalian model to determine the "stylistic character of the poem as imitation" and to assess the complications that Johnson's Christian perspective introduces to his rendering of Juvenal.

1435     Sitter, John E. "To THE VANITY OF HUMAN WISHES through the 1740's." SP, 74 (1977), 445-64.

Thoughtful and original analysis of the two distinct voices exhibited by Johnson in "London" and in THE VANITY, arguing that these differences depend less on the contrasting tonal characteristics of the Juvenalian models or on Johnson's changed literary and personal circumstances than on the rapidly shifting way in which poems make statements in this decade in which a combative, provocative, and assertive mode of generalizing is replaced by a less certain attitude expressed from a position of solitude reflecting human uncertainties.

1436     Smith, David Nichol. "Johnson's Poems." In NEW LIGHT ON DR. JOHNSON: ESSAYS ON OCCASION OF HIS 250TH BIRTHDAY. Ed. Frederick W. Hilles. New Haven, Conn.: Yale Univ. Press, 1959, pp. 9-17.

Essentially a review of the Clarendon Press edition of 1941, but notes in passing the variety of tones and range of effects in Johnson's poetry, demonstrating the "resonant music" of his "strong mind" in THE VANITY OF HUMAN WISHES. See nos. 1371 and 1372.

1437     Spacks, Patricia Meyer. "From Satire to Description." YR, 58 (1969), 232-48.

A comparison of Johnson's THE VANITY OF HUMAN
WISHES with Robert Lowell's modern version (1967) by
the same title shows how each is a distinctive and representative poem of its age and how poetic values, attitudes
toward satire, and philosophic assumptions have changed
since the time of Juvenal, Johnson's loose imitation
characterized by diversity of imagery and a "sense of
the chaos of human possibility" and Lowell's version bare,
scornful, and concentrated in a manner closer to Juvenal's
tone.

1438    Tucker, Susie I., and Henry Gifford.   "Johnson's Poetic Imagination."
RES, NS 8 (1957), 241-48.

Focuses on the metaphorical force and structure of THE
VANITY OF HUMAN WISHES, concluding that the pleasure of Johnson's poetry is mainly imparted by the images
which "give general truth a most moving personal ring."

1439    Vales, Robert L.   "The Reading of the Basic Images in THE VANITY
OF HUMAN WISHES."   EnlE, 3, ii (1972), 106-12.

Johnson contrasts two basic image configurations, one
temporal and one permanent, leading him to the Christian
consolation of the optimistic, permanent, and realistic
ending.

1440    Vesterman, William.   THE STYLISTIC LIFE OF SAMUEL JOHNSON.
New Brunswick, N.J.: Rutgers Univ. Press, 1977.

Chapter 5 consists of close readings of Johnson's major
poems, finding that although his control of language and
tonal sophistication ("sense of response to one's own terms")
were conspicuously lacking in LONDON (1738), his artistic
skills developed further in THE VANITY OF HUMAN
WISHES (1749), culminating finally in the poetic triumph
of the Levet elegy (1783).

1441    Voitle, Robert.   SAMUEL JOHNSON THE MORALIST.   Cambridge,
Mass.: Harvard Univ. Press, 1961.

Argues that the fatalism and determinism of THE VANITY
OF HUMAN WISHES probably reflects momentary disillusionment and depression during the period of composition,
especially in light of Johnson's otherwise professed faith
in human reason and dignity.

1442    Watkins, Walter B.C.   JOHNSON AND ENGLISH POETRY BEFORE
1660.   Princeton, N.J.: Princeton Univ. Press, 1936.

Uses material gathered from the first revised edition of the
DICTIONARY (1755), the Shakespeare notes, and other
relevant works to determine the nature and extent of
Johnson's knowledge of English poetry before 1660.

1443    See no. 439.

1444    Weinbrot, Howard.  "Johnson's LONDON and Juvenal's Third Satire:
        The Country as 'Ironic' Norm."  MP, 73 (1967), 556-65.

Questions critics who read Johnson's praise of country life
as ironic and proposes a proper reading of this imitation
in light of Juvenal's poetic practices and in the context
of classical commentators where the country is treated as
a "clear, positive" norm.

1445    White, Ian.  "THE VANITY OF HUMAN WISHES."  CQ, 6 (1973),
        115-25.

Argues that the inevitable thematic comparisons of the
poem and RASSELAS distort both works, and through a
close analysis of language and tone of THE VANITY OF
HUMAN WISHES concludes that its personal and poetic
power is a matter of force not weight, motivated by
Johnsonian savage indignation, bitterness, and frustrated
ambition.

1446    Wilson, Gayle Edward.  "Poet and Moralist:  Dr. Johnson's Elegiac
        Art and 'On the Death of Dr. Robert Levet.'"  EnlE, 4, i (1973),
        29-38.

Johnson faced a problem of decorum as a moralist seeking
to praise Christian virtue, and he effectively chose the
"epideictic oration" as the best way to praise the obscure
physician and "assert the efficacy of old truths."

# JAMES MACPHERSON (1736-96)

## A. MAJOR EDITIONS

1447    THE POEMS OF OSSIAN, CONTAINING THE POETICAL WORKS OF
        JAMES MACPHERSON IN PROSE AND RHYME.  Ed. Malcolm Laing.
        2 vols.  Edinburgh:  James Ballantyne, 1805.

> Definitive early nineteenth-century edition with introduction
> and Macpherson's 1773 notes on translation.

1448    THE POEMS OF OSSIAN TRANSLATED BY JAMES MACPHERSON,
        WITH NOTES AND WITH AN INTRODUCTION.  Ed. William Sharp.
        Edinburgh:  Patrick Geddes, 1896.

> Reprints Centenary Edition, edited by Hugh Campbell
> (1822), with further annotation.

1449    FRAGMENTS OF ANCIENT POETRY COLLECTED IN THE HIGHLANDS
        OF SCOTLAND, AND TRANSLATED FROM THE GALLIC OR ERSE
        LANGUAGE (1760).  Ed. Otto L. Jiriczek.  Heidelberg, W.Ger.:
        Carl Winters, 1915.

> Standard edition of this volume.  Introduction in German.

## B. BIBLIOGRAPHY AND TEXTUAL STUDIES

1450    Black, George F.  "Macpherson's Ossian and the Ossianic Controversy:
        A Contribution Towards a Bibliography."  BNYPL, 30 (1976), 424-39,
        505-24.

> Records printings in English and foreign languages of frag-
> ments, Ossianic poems, selections, and other materials
> pertaining to the Ossianic controversy during the eighteenth
> and nineteenth centuries.

1451    Chapman, Robert W.  "Blair on OSSIAN."  RES, 7 (1931), 80-83.

Several letters connected with the publication of OSSIAN, emphasizing the skill of the translation but also the merit of the originals.

1452    Hudson, Wilson M.   "The Homer of the North Translates Homer." LIBRARY CHRONICLE OF THE UNIVERSITY OF TEXAS, 4 (1950), 25-42.

Study of the genesis, publication, and reception of Macpherson's translation of the ILIAD leads to a fuller understanding of his Ossianic approach to the epic, theory of translation, and successes of FINGAL (1762) and TEMORA (1763).

1453    Todd, William B.   "Macpherson's FINGAL and TEMORA."  BOOK COLLECTOR, 8 (1959), 429-30.

Points out discrepancies between William Strahan's ledger and the actual printings of FINGAL in 1761 and TEMORA in 1763.

## C. BIOGRAPHY

1454    Keith, Christina.  "Second Thoughts on Ossian."  QUEEN'S QUARTERLY, 58 (1951), 551-57.

Biographical account of Macpherson's life and a general commentary on the reception of the Ossianic poems, delighting Continental Europe but enraging both London and Dublin.

1455    Saunders, Thomas Bailey.  THE LIFE AND LETTERS OF JAMES MAC-PHERSON, CONTAINING A PARTICULAR ACCOUNT OF HIS FAMOUS QUARREL WITH DR. JOHNSON, AND A SKETCH OF THE ORIGIN AND INFLUENCE OF THE OSSIANIC POEMS.  1894; rpt. New York: Haskell House, 1968.

An account of the origin, reception, and extraordinary effect of the Ossianic poems in eighteenth-century English literary history, approached from the standpoint of Macpherson's "actual proceedings," character, personality, attainments, and biography.

1456    Walsh, W.E.  "Macpherson's OSSIAN."  QUEEN'S QUARTERLY, 45 (1938), 366-76.

Impressionistic discussion of Macpherson's poetic appeal that characterizes the poet as "proud, romantic and gifted, but unfortunately devoid of moral sense" and describes his poems as contributing to the Scottish revival.

## D. CRITICISM

1457    Barratt, Glynn R.  "The Melancholy and the Wild:  A Note on Mac-
        pherson's Russian Success."  STUDIES IN EIGHTEENTH-CENTURY CUL-
        TURE, 3 (1973), 125–35.

>   Ossian's legacy in Russia was "the expression of diffuse
>   but powerful emotions," often blunted and softened by
>   the familiar and standard French translations.

1458    Blair, Hugh.  A CRITICAL DISSERTATION ON THE POEMS OF OSSIAN,
        THE SON OF FINGAL (1765).  New York:  Garland, 1970.

>   A famous treatise arguing that the fragments verified the exist-
>   ence of a Highland epic amidst primitive and unsophisticated po-
>   etry. An important example of the vogue of the new primitivism.

1459    Carnie, Robert Hay.  "Macpherson's FRAGMENTS OF ANCIENT POETRY
        and Lord Hailes."  ES, 41 (1960), 17–26.

>   Explains the important "dual roles" Sir David Dalrymple (Lord
>   Hailes) played: in the popularization and success of Macpher-
>   son's collecting and translation of Gaelic poetry, but also in
>   the debunking of his historical work and scholarly abilities.

1460    Carpenter, Frederic I.  "The Vogue of Ossian in America:  A Study of
        Taste."  AL, 2 (1931), 405–17.

>   The vogue of the Ossianic poems manifested itself in Ameri-
>   ca in three distinct phases:  from 1766 to 1775 the poems
>   moved several prominent writers and indicated greater popu-
>   larity to follow; from 1786 to 1800 the poems enjoyed wide-
>   spread newspaper popularity reaching minor poets and liter-
>   ary men.  The third phase is characterized by intermittent
>   nineteenth-century popularity until Whitman, who was
>   strongly influenced by the rhythms and spirit of Ossian
>   and who regarded the poems as classics.

1461    Dunn, John J.  "Coleridge's Debt to Macpherson's OSSIAN."  SSL,
        7 (1969), 76–89.

>   Coleridge made use of Ossianic imagery, especially in his
>   early poetry but also in passages in his best-known poems;
>   and an awareness of this debt reveals his "power to trans-
>   form his reading into something new and rich and strange."

1462    _____.  "James Macpherson's First Epic."  SSL, 9 (1971), 48–54.
>   THE HIGHLANDER (1758) is the work of an inexperienced
>   poet, trying out the neoclassical conventions and practices
>   derived from Dryden's and Pope's translations of the classi-
>   cal epic; but what is evident from the poem is more than

literary opportunism: Macpherson wanted to write an epic
on a Scottish theme before FINGAL and TEMORA.

1463    Fitzgerald, Robert P. "The Style of Ossian." SIR, 6 (1966), 22-33.

The rhythmic prose of Macpherson's FRAGMENTS OF
ANCIENT POETRY, COLLECTED IN THE HIGHLANDS
OF SCOTLAND (1760), with its simple syntax and profusion
of exotic imagery, was novel and partly accounts for the
success of the volume. But his sensibility, knowledge of
authentic ballads, and appreciation of the literary qualities
of Gaelic originals explain not only the faith of his supporters but also his own literary genius.

1464    Folkenflik, Robert. "Macpherson, Chatterton, Blake and the Great
Age of Literary Forgery." CentR, 18 (1974), 378-91.

These great poets represent the burden of the past syndrome
in the eighteenth century, believing that writing poetry
was especially difficult in the age, that the greatest poetry
had been previously written, and that the literary artist's
first task was to create "poets" capable of producing great
art by finding voices not previously sounded or by producing epics as did the great poet-prophets of the past.

1465    Fraser, G.M. "The Truth about Macpherson's OSSIAN." QUARTERLY
REVIEW, 245 (1925), 331-45.

Discussion of the Ossianic controversy and the arguments
on either side of the issue, noting the differences in literary ethics between the eighteenth century and our own
and the common practice of adapting the work of an
earlier poet, but finally applauding the rejection of
Macpherson and his OSSIAN as "one of the most remarkable literary impostures that has happened in Britain in
modern times."

1466    Fridén, Georg. JAMES FENIMORE COOPER AND OSSIAN. Cambridge, Mass.: Harvard Univ. Press, 1949.

The language of Cooper's Indians was more or less modelled
on the style of OSSIAN, a work he undoubtedly read
while in England or became familiar with through the
interest of Byron and Scott. Moreover, Cooper clearly
idealized his Indians as did Macpherson his Celtic heroes.

1467    Gantz, Kenneth F. "Charlotte Brooke's RELIQUES OF IRISH POETRY
and the Ossianic Controversy." UNIVERSITY OF TEXAS STUDIES IN
ENGLISH, 20 (1940), 137-56.

Detailed examination of the effects of Macpherson's attacks
on the literature and traditions of Ireland, demonstrating

that despite Brooke's clear opposition to many dubious and
unwarranted assertions of the Ossianic poet, the publication of RELIQUES "did not materially lessen the faith" of
his supporters and would seem a "lost opportunity" to
have engaged him directly with a formal rebuttal.

1468   Greenway, John L.   "The Gateway to Innocence:  Ossian and the
Nordic Bard as Myth."   STUDIES IN EIGHTEENTH-CENTURY CULTURE,
4 (1975), 161-69.

The Ossianic poems represent a "mythic narrative for a
modern era," providing for a "symbolic apprehension of
reality" by fusing two mutually exclusive universes:  a
nationalistc construct and a classical humanist culture.

1470   Hennig, John.   "Goethe's Translation of Ossian's SONGS OF SELMA."
JEGP, 45 (1946), 77-87.

Examines the translations of SONGS to provide materials
for a more comprehensive account of the techniques and
methods Goethe utilizes in English-language translations.

1471   Leary, Lewis.   "Ossian in America: A Note."  AL, 14 (1942), 305-06.

Joseph Brown Ladd published a poetic adaptation of Ossian
in 1785; in his ambition to become a man of letters, Ladd
failed to mention his model, but was happy to have his
readers believe that he knew the Gaelic originals.

1472   Meyerstein, Edward H.W.   "The Influence of Macpherson."   ENGLISH,
7 (1948), 95-98.

Lists a number of anticipations of the Rowley poems in
OSSIAN and other Ossianic influences, similarities, and
connections involving Yeats, Collins, and Milton.

1473   Moore, John Robert.   "Wordsworth's Unacknowledged Debt to Macpherson's OSSIAN."   PMLA, 40 (1925), 362-78.

Although he dismissed Macpherson as a forger and imposter,
Wordsworth was familiar with Ossianic subject matter, theme,
and phraseology; and he occasionally borrowed words,
phrases, and sentiments from the "blind bard of Selma."

1474   Peers, E. Allison.   "The Influences of Ossian in Spain."  PQ, 4
(1925), 121-38.

Although Ossianism had little direct influence on the
writers of the Spanish Romantic period, "a certain interest"
in his poems seems to have occurred years after in Spain.

1475    Price, J.B. "James Macpherson's OSSIAN." CONTEMPORARY REVIEW, 188 (1955), 404–08.

  Discussion of Macpherson's general appeal and the cult of the Celtic Renaissance, finding his achievement in a "ghostly beauty" that is generated by a "peculiar vein of melancholy," musicality of verse, and the cadences of his phrasing and language.

1476    Saase, H.C. "Michael Denis as a Translator of Ossian." MLN, 60 (1965), 546–52.

  Despite elegiac motifs in the Ossianic poems, the naive artificial diction, and repetitive formulae—never presenting particular linguistic or philological abstractions—the number of doubting German readers was smaller than on the continent generally because of the unfamiliarity of this mode of writing and the resulting reliance on translations.

1477    Snyder, Edward Douglas. THE CELTIC REVIVAL IN ENGLISH LITERATURE, 1760–1800. Cambridge, Mass.: Harvard Univ. Press, 1923.

  Classic study of the diverse and remote sources that shaped the interest in and imitation of Celtic history, language, literature, customs, and rituals by five pioneers—Morris, Evans, Gray, Mason, and Macpherson.

1478    Stewart, Larry L. "Ossian, Burke, and the 'Joy of Grief.'" ELN, 15 (1977), 29–32.

  Though this phrase has been long associated with the Ossianic consciousness, the impetus for the phrase originated from Burke's treatise on the sublime and beautiful, which defines the relationship between joy and grief and suggests to Stewart that Ossianic poems "are solidly grounded in the aesthetic and psychological understanding of the age of sensibility."

1479    Stuart, Dorothy Margaret. "Ossian Macpherson Revisited." ENGLISH, 7 (1948), 16–18.

  The defects of Macpherson's "lays" should not blind us to their virtues: "the rich, rolling cadence of his style, his occasional gleams of authentic poetry, his patches of eloquence, his touches of pathos, and his creation of an uncanny atmosphere, wild, sensitive, and elemental."

1480    Thomson, Derick S. THE GAELIC SOURCES OF MACPHERSON'S OSSIAN. Edinburgh: Oliver and Boyd, 1952.

  Discusses the Gaelic sources of the Ossianic poems and presents the texts in their sometimes corrupted forms as keys to Macpherson's peculiar orthography and translation process.

# JOHN OLDHAM (1653-83)

## A. MAJOR EDITIONS

1481    POEMS OF JOHN OLDHAM. Ed. Bonamy Dobrée. Carbondale: Southern Illinois Univ. Press, 1960.

> General introduction along with a photographic reproduction of the R. Bell edition of 1854. A modern scholarly edition is being prepared by Harold F. Brooks.

## B. CORRESPONDENCE

1482    See no. 1485.

## C. BIBLIOGRAPHY AND TEXTUAL STUDIES

1483    Brooks, Harold. "A Bibliography of John Oldham, The Restoration Satirist." OXFORD BIBLIOGRAPHICAL SOCIETY, PROCEEDINGS AND PAPERS, 5 (1936), 1-38.

> Lists manuscripts and printed books and includes separate works and collections.

1484    _____. "The Chief Substantive Editions of John Oldham's Poems, 1679-1684: Printer, Compositors, and Publication." SB, 27 (1974), 188-226.

> Detailed examination of all important matters pertaining to the editing of Oldham's canon and to a number of resulting biographical problems.

1485    _____. "John Oldham: Some Problems of Biography and Annotation." PQ, 54 (1975), 569-78.

> Raises two problems faced in writing a biography of Oldham and editing his poems: the identity of "L.G." in "Satyr

Upon a Woman" and the person Oldham is addressing in
his conventional love verses of 1676 and 1677.

1486        . "Oldham and Phineas Fletcher: An Unrecognized Source for
SATYRS UPON THE JESUITS." RES, 22 (1971), 410-22.

Argues convincingly, by means of parallel passages, that
Fletcher's THE LOCUSTS, a satire on the Gunpowder Plot,
was a source for some of Oldham's diction, a number of
images, and the overall satiric tone of his own satire on
Jesuits.

1487    Vieth, David M. "John Oldham, the Wits, and A SATYR AGAINST
VERTUE." PQ, 32 (1953), 90-93.

Argues that a brief narrative, headed 1677 on a manuscript copy of the poem (in the Osborn Collection at
Yale University), calls into question the accuracy of an
anecdote to the effect that Oldham composed the poem
"as a trial of skill" to prove to the court wits that he
had written a particular earlier poem. All indications are
that Rochester and the wits probably knew Oldham's verse.

## D. CRITICISM

1488    Brooks, Harold. "The Poetry of John Oldham." In RESTORATION
LITERATURE: CRITICAL APPROACHES. Ed. Harold Love. London:
Methuen, 1972, pp. 177-203.

Discusses Oldham as an earlier practitioner of Augustan
imitation and heroic satire, forms perfected by the major
poets who followed, and as an artist whose poems are "a
source of pure literary pleasure." See no. 118.

1489    Cable, Chester H. "Oldham's Borrowing From Buchanan." MLN, 66
(1951), 523-27.

Takes issue with assertions that Jonson's CATILINE is the
chief influence on the SATYRS UPON THE JESUITS, arguing that "Loyola's Will" in particular makes use of the
form and language of Buchanan's FRANCISCAN. See nos.
1490 and 1494.

1490    Mackin, Cooper R. "The Satiric Technique of John Oldham's Satyrs
upon the Jesuits." SP, 62 (1965), 78-90.

Discusses Oldham's Elizabethanism as manifest in his conventional association of drama and satire, his modeling of

the vir indignatus persona on the practice of Joseph Hall
and others, and his use of materials from Jonson's CATILINE.
See no. 1494.

1491    O'Neill, John H. "Oldham's 'Sardanapalus': A Restoration Mock-
Encomium and Its Topical Implications." Cliol, 5 (1976), 193-210.

Composed for the amusement of the court wits, this "mock-
panegyric" satire ridicules, rather than celebrates, libertin-
ism especially the brand practiced by the "premier libertine," Charles II.

1492    Weygant, Peter S. "Oldham's Versification and the Literary Style of
the English Enlightenment." EnlE, 3, ii (1972), 120-25.

Dryden's censure of Oldham in "To Mr. Oldham" reflects
the older poet's distaste for the tradition of Elizabethan
satire employed in the younger writer's "eccentric" major
work and his failure to appreciate Oldham's maturing
style in other poems.

1493    Williams, Weldon M. "The Genesis of John Oldham's SATYRS UPON
THE JESUITS." PMLA, 58 (1943), 958-70.

Despite arguments emphasizing the influence of Juvenal
and Boileau on his satire, Oldham was not indifferent
to the structures and modes of English political satire,
both new or old, popular or literary, and made use of
current practices, especially the "ghostly monologue."

1494    _____. "The Influence of Ben Jonson's CATILINE upon John Oldham's
SATYRS UPON THE JESUITS." ELH, 11 (1944), 38-62.

Considers the possible impact on Oldham of (1) native
popular satire; (2) Cleveland and his school; (3) Juvenal
and classical satire; and (4) Boileau's practice (on the
milder style). Concludes, however, that the evidence
really points to Jonson (and especially CATILINE) as the
chief influence on the tone and style of Oldham's satire.
See no. 1490.

1495    Wykes, David. "Aspects of Restoration Irony: John Oldham." ES,
52 (1971), 223-31.

Certain poems of Oldham reveal how a writer in the latter
part of Charles II's monarchy employed "verbal irony and
ironic forms" characteristic of the Augustans, allowed vice
to speak in "self-revealing unawareness," yet exerted
authorial control over reader reaction by supplying sub-
titles that indicate content and intention.

# THOMAS PARNELL (1679-1718)

## A. MAJOR EDITIONS

1496 POEMS ON SEVERAL OCCASIONS. WRITTEN BY DR. THOMAS
PARNELL, LATE ARCHDEACON OF CLOGHER: AND PUBLISHED BY
MR. POPE. London: B. Lintot, 1722.

> Once regarded as the only certain, authentic collection
> of Parnell's poems. Includes several SPECTATOR and
> GUARDIAN papers.

1497 WORKS IN VERSE AND PROSE OF DR. THOMAS PARNELL: EN-
LARGED WITH VARIATIONS AND POEMS NOT BEFORE PUBLISH'D.
Glasgow: R. and A. Foulis, 1755.

> Includes seven pieces not previously published and examples
> of original texts of poems edited by Pope.

1498 THE POETICAL WORKS OF THOMAS PARNELL. London: Bell and
Daldy, 1866.

> The Aldine edition of British poets. Includes a dedicatory
> epistle by the Reverend Alexander Dyce and a life by the
> Reverend John Mitford.

1499 THE POETICAL WORKS OF THOMAS GRAY, THOMAS PARNELL,
WILLIAM COLLINS, MATTHEW GREEN, AND THOMAS WARTON.
Ed. Robert A. Willmott. London: George Routledge, 1855.

> Well known nineteenth-century edition.

## B. BIBLIOGRAPHY AND TEXTUAL STUDIES

1500 Rawson, Claude J. "New Parnell Manuscripts." SCRIBLERIAN 1, ii
(1969), 1-2.

> Material in the possession of Lord Congleton adds some
> seventy poems (mostly in autograph) to the canon, bringing
> to light the role of Pope as editor of some poems, estab-
> lishing the authenticity of a number of posthumous editions,
> and giving insight into Parnell's creative process.

1501    See no. 1197.


1502    _____. "Swift's Certificate to Parnell's 'Posthumous Works.'"  MLR,
57 (1962), 179-82.

> Argues from bibliographical evidence that Swift's note
> and the contents of THE POSTHUMOUS WORKS OF DR.
> PARNELL (1758) are genuine.


## C. BIOGRAPHY

1503    Goldsmith, Oliver. LIFE OF THOMAS PARNELL. COMPILED FROM
ORIGINAL PAPERS AND MEMOIRS, IN WHICH ARE INCLUDED
SEVERAL LETTERS OF POPE, GAY, AND ARBUTHNOT. London:
T. Davies, 1770.

> A life based on, among other materials, documents owned
> by Sir John Parnell, nephew of the poet, and recently re-
> discovered by Claude J. Rawson. See no. 1197.


## D. CRITICISM

1504    Cruickshank, A.H. "Thomas Parnell, or What Was Wrong with the
Eighteenth Century." ESSAYS AND STUDIES, 7 (1921), 57-81.

> A general account of Parnell's life and literary associations,
> rather unsympathetically concluding that the poets of the
> early period lacked depth, humanity, and a hold on men's
> "higher aspirations and tendencies," but still judges that
> Parnell deserves our attention.


1505    Havens, Raymond D. "Parnell's 'Hymn to Contentment.'" MLN, 59
(1944), 329-31.

> This "pleasing but confused poem" has little to say about
> the theme of contentment because its real subject lies in
> the joy to be found in nature "when one has subjected
> one's will to God."


1506    Jackson, R. Wyse. "Thomas Parnell, The Poet." DUBLIN MAGA-
ZINE, 20 (1945), 28-35.

A brief discussion of Parnell's life and his friendships "with the great minds of the early eighteenth century," along with a somewhat condescending view of his verse as generally failing to "rise beyond an amiable and slick neatness."

1507  Starr, Herbert W.  "Gray's Opinion of Parnell."  MLN, 57 (1942), 675-76.

Gray's "fastidious temperament" probably impelled him to react negatively to the word "dung" in BACCHUS OR THE DRUNKEN METAMORPHOSIS in the 1758 edition he had read and to describe Parnell as "the dunghill of Irish-Grubstreet."

# ALEXANDER POPE (1688-1744)

## A. MAJOR EDITIONS

1508    THE WORKS OF ALEXANDER POPE. Ed. Whitwell Elwin and W.J.
Courthope. 10 vols. London: John Murray, 1871-89.

> Contains poems, letters, and prose, but is now superseded
> by the Twickenham Edition (below). The great nineteenth-
> century edition of Pope still valuable as a scholarly reference.

1509    THE TWICKENHAM EDITION OF THE POEMS OF ALEXANDER POPE.
Ed. John Butt et al. 11 vols. New Haven, Conn.: Yale Univ.
Press, 1939-69.

> Standard edition of the poetry with especially informative
> and insightful introductions and discussions of textual
> matters. Model edition of an eighteenth-century poet.

1510    ALEXANDER POPE: POETICAL WORKS. Ed. Herbert Davis. Oxford
Standard Authors edition. London: Oxford Univ. Press, 1966.

> Omits translations of Homer and prints the VARIORIUM
> DUNCIAD and the early texts of THE RAPE OF THE LOCK
> in an appendix. Uses both the 1751 (Warburton) text and
> the late quartos of the DUNCIAD (1743); ESSAY ON MAN
> and ESSAY ON CRITICISM of February 1744; and the
> EPISTLES TO SEVERAL PERSONS of May 1744.

1511    Schmitz, Robert M., ed. POPE'S WINDSOR FOREST, 1712: A STUDY
OF THE WASHINGTON UNIVERSITY HOLOGRAPH. St. Louis: Washington Univ. Press, 1952.

> Prints the 1712 manuscript, gives historical background,
> and analyzes the creative process of a developing poet.

1512    Wasserman, Earl R., ed. POPE'S "EPISTLE TO BATHURST": A CRITI-

CAL READING WITH AN EDITION OF THE MANUSCRIPTS. Baltimore: Johns Hopkins Press, 1960.

>Prints the Twickenham text (1744) and the heavily revised first draft (1732), speculating on the rationale for the textual changes. An introduction treats the "climate of attitudes" informing this satiric poem's skillful use of Christian theology, Aristotelian ethics, and Horatian style.

1513    Mack, Maynard. "Pope's PASTORALS." SCRIBLERIAN, 12, ii (1980), 85-161.

>Facsimile (enlarged) of Pope's manuscript of the four poems with an introductory essay. Full bibliographical commentary.

1514    THE PROSE WORKS OF ALEXANDER POPE, 1711-1720. Ed. Norman Ault. Vol. 1: THE EARLIER WORKS, 1711-1720. Oxford: Basil Blackwell, 1936.

>Standard edition of the prose. Relevant as background for historical and social milieu.

1515    MEMOIRS OF THE EXTRAORDINARY LIFE, WORKS, AND DISCOVERIES OF MARTINUS SCRIBLERUS. Ed. Charles Kerby-Miller. New Haven, Conn.: Yale Univ. Press, 1950.

>Valuable edition of the Scriblerian project, documenting crucial cultural and intellectual factors that informed the attitudes and beliefs of this talented group of writers and gave rise to their concerted attack on "false taste in learning."

1516    THE ART OF SINKING IN POETRY. Ed. Edna Leake Steeves. Bibliographical Notes on "The Last Volume" of the Swift-Pope MISCELLANIES by R.H. Griffith and E.L. Steeves. New York: King's Crown Press, 1952.

>Standard edition of this enterprise of the "Scriblerus Club" directed against "undigested and misapplied learning" and "disputatious knowledge and frivolous speculation." Notes and commentary. 1727 text reprinted in facsimile.

1517    LITERARY CRITICISM OF ALEXANDER POPE. Ed. Bertrand A. Goldgar. Lincoln: Univ. of Nebraska Press, 1965.

>Useful collection of Pope's critical pronouncements, including prefaces, poems, and relevant passages from the correspondence. Introduction surveys his whole output.

## B. CORRESPONDENCE

1518    THE CORRESPONDENCE OF ALEXANDER POPE. Ed. George Sherburn.
5 vols. Oxford: Clarendon Press, 1956.

> Superbly edited, standard modern edition of the letters
> known to date of publication. Additional letters turned
> up since 1956 have been noted in a number of journals.

## C. BIBLIOGRAPHY, TEXTUAL STUDIES, AND CONCORDANCES

1519    Abbot, Edwin. A CONCORDANCE TO THE WORKS OF ALEXANDER
POPE. New York: D. Appleton, 1875.

> Keyed to the 1751 Warburton edition. Superseded by Bed-
> ford and Dilligan Gale concordance, below.

1520    Bedford, Emmett G., and Robert T. Dilligan, eds. A CONCORDANCE
TO THE POEMS OF ALEXANDER POPE. 2 vols. Detroit: Gale Research Co., 1974.

> Based on Twickenham text and incorporating (1) optical
> scanning directly from critical edition of text; and (2)
> computer resetting from programmed tape--which repro-
> duce most typographical distinctions and record the pres-
> ence of compounds and word frequencies.

1521    Bloom, Lillian. "Pope as Textual Critic: A Bibliographic Study of
his Horatian Text." JEGP, 47 (1948), 150-55.

> Pope's Latin text of Horace was eclectic, not a single
> text, and he drew on the Dutch scholar Heinsius as well
> as Bentley's well-known scholarly edition, despite his
> hostility toward Bentley the man.

1522    Butt, John. "'A Master Key to Popery.'" In POPE AND HIS CON-
TEMPORARIES: ESSAYS PRESENTED TO GEORGE SHERBURN. Ed.
James L. Clifford and Louis A. Landa. New York: Oxford Univ.
Press, 1949, pp. 41-57.

> A combined bibliographical and attribution study conclud-
> ing that Pope himself wrote the defense of the "Timon's
> Villa" passage in the EPISTLE TO BURLINGTON. The
> document is also reprinted. See nos. 107 and 1533.

1523    \_\_\_\_\_. "Pope's Poetical Manuscripts." PBA, 40 (1957), 23-39.

> Study by the Twickenham editor of editions of Pope's works,
> including the variants and annotations Pope and later edi-
> tors supplied. See no. 1533.

1524    Dearing, Vinton A. "The Prince of Wales's Set of Pope's Works."
        HLB, 4 (1950), 320-38.

>    Compares differing versions of EPISTLE TO A LADY, notes
>    revisions, and in particular speculates on the circumstances
>    surrounding the character of Atossa, including the question
>    of the personal application of the portrait. See no. 1533.

1525    Griffith, Reginald H. ALEXANDER POPE: A BIBLIOGRAPHY. 2
        vols. Austin: Univ. of Texas Press, 1922-27.

>    Lists publication of Pope's own compositions during the
>    period of 1709 to 1751.

1526    Guerinot, Joseph V. PAMPHLET ATTACKS ON ALEXANDER POPE
        1711-1744: A DESCRIPTIVE BIBLIOGRAPHY. New York: New York
        Univ. Press, 1969.

>    Important description of pamphlets, broadsides, and books
>    (also a few newspaper items), identifying the passages
>    and sections pertinent to charges against Pope the man
>    and poet.

1527    Lopez, Cecilia L. ALEXANDER POPE: AN ANNOTATED BIBLIOG-
        RAPHY, 1945-1967. Gainesville: Univ. of Florida Press, 1970.

>    Fully annotated list of critical editions, scholarly works,
>    and articles on Pope from 1945 to 1967 (except foreign
>    items and unavailable materials, which are merely noted);
>    cross-referenced and indexed. Reviews identified.

1528    Tillotson, Geoffrey. "Pope." In ENGLISH POETRY: SELECT BIB-
        LIOGRAPHICAL GUIDES. Ed. A.E. Dyson. London: Oxford Univ.
        Press, 1971, pp. 128-43.

>    Discusses texts, critical studies and commentary, biogra-
>    phies and letters, and lists major bibliographies and rele-
>    vant background readings as well as citing major studies
>    and trends in criticism. Indispensable. See no. 63.

1529    Tobin, James E. A LIST OF CRITICAL STUDIES PUBLISHED FROM
        1895 TO 1944. New York: Cosmopolitan Science and Art, 1945.

>    Checklist of studies, but not complete or annotated.

## D. COLLECTIONS

1530    Dixon, Peter, ed. ALEXANDER POPE: WRITERS AND THEIR BACK-
        GROUND. Athens: Ohio Univ. Press, 1972.

Essays relating to Pope as poet, critic, and translator, as well as to the contexts and historical circumstances in which he wrote.

1531    Erskine-Hill, Howard, and Anne Smith, eds. THE ART OF ALEXANDER POPE. New York: Barnes and Noble, 1979.

Essays incorporating some new perspectives on Pope. Introduction effectively addresses the special problems Pope presents to the modern reader, arguing that his public, satiric, and self-consciously formal mode of writing should not detract from his equally important private, personal voice and self-reflexive mode of expression.

1532    Guerinot, Joseph V., ed. POPE: A COLLECTION OF CRITICAL ESSAYS. Englewood Cliffs, N.J.: Prentice-Hall, 1972.

Selects essays that both illustrate the direction of Pope studies over the previous three decades and offer important critical insights.

1533    Mack, Maynard, ed. ESSENTIAL ARTICLES FOR THE STUDY OF ALEXANDER POPE. Rev. and enlarged. Hamden, Conn.: Archon Books, 1968.

Important previously published essays on all aspects of Pope's literary art. Prints six new essays not included in the 1964 edition, and omits one on the principle that no author is represented by more than a single entry.

1534    Mack, Maynard, and James A. Winn, eds. POPE: RECENT ESSAYS BY SEVERAL HANDS. Hamden, Conn.: Archon, 1980.

Third in the "essential articles" series, printing important essays written since the earlier (1964, 1968) editions.

1535    O'Neill, Judith, ed. CRITICS ON POPE: READINGS IN LITERARY CRITICISM. Coral Gables, Fla.: Univ. of Miami Press, 1968.

Part 1 surveys the changes in taste and critical judgments affecting Pope's reputation by excerpting eighteenth-, nineteenth-, and twentieth-century responses; part 2 reprints (selectively) larger pieces since 1940 covering the major poems.

1536    Rousseau, George S., ed. THE RAPE OF THE LOCK: A COLLECTION OF CRITICAL ESSAYS. Twentieth Century Interpretation Series. Englewood Cliffs, N.J.: Prentice Hall, 1969.

Reprints six important essays (complete) and eight briefer excerpted comments that characterize the range of modern opinion.

1537    Wimsatt, William K. THE PORTRAITS OF ALEXANDER POPE. New
        Haven, Conn.: Yale Univ. Press, 1965.

> Fascinating assemblage of Pope portraits from private
> sources and public institutions fully described and ex-
> plained in terms of cultural milieu and of painting tech-
> niques and method.

## E. BIOGRAPHY

1538    Ault, Norman. NEW LIGHT ON POPE. London: Methuen, 1949.

> Carefully researched account of Pope's life and works,
> describing his relationships with friend and foe alike,
> his dealings with printers, publishers, and fellow artists,
> and assessing the reliability of the canon to help dispel
> lingering prejudices about his character and personal
> morality.

1539    Boyce, Benjamin. "The Poet and the Postmaster: The Friendship of
        Alexander Pope and Ralph Allen." PQ, 45 (1966), 114-22.

> Discusses the genesis and development of the friendship
> between "the nation's leading poet" and a provincial
> businessman of widely differing talents, temperament,
> personality, and interests.

1540    Nicolson, Marjorie H., and G.S. Rousseau. "THIS LONG DISEASE,
        MY LIFE": ALEXANDER POPE AND THE SCIENCES. Princeton, N.J.:
        Princeton Univ. Press, 1968.

> Discusses the effects of science on Pope's poetic imagina-
> tion, especially the field of medicine to which Pope often
> referred and on which he depended as a chronic invalid.
> Contains a detailed medical case history.

1541    Quennell, Peter. ALEXANDER POPE: THE EDUCATION OF GENIUS,
        1688-1728. New York: Stein and Day, 1968.

> Popular biography, at times impressionistic rather than
> factual.

1542    Rogers, Pat. "The Burlington Circle in the Provinces: Alexander Pope's
        Yorkshire Friends." DUJ, 36 (1975), 219-26.

> Interesting account of men living in this northern country
> who were interested in the arts, particularly in Burlington's
> architecture, and who shared in a devotion to Pope and
> his tastes.

1543    Ruffhead, Owen. THE LIFE OF ALEXANDER POPE. 1769; Facs. rpt.
        Hildesheim, W.Ger.:  G. Olms, 1968.

>    Not noted for judicious use of source materials or for
>    originality.

1544    Sherburn, George. EARLY CAREER OF ALEXANDER POPE. Oxford:
        Clarendon Press, 1934.

>    An influential biography of Pope's early years (up to 1726),
>    carefully researched and free of traditional nineteenth-
>    century misconceptions, prejudices, and preverse opinions
>    about Pope and his circle.

1545    Sibley, Agnes Marie. ALEXANDER POPE'S PRESTIGE IN AMERICA,
        1725-1835.  New York:  King's Crown Press, 1949.

>    Goes beyond the fact of the popularity of Pope and the
>    Augustans in America to show that the widespread reprint-
>    ing of his works, especially the ESSAY ON MAN, indicates
>    the deeper significance of Pope's moral and religious
>    beliefs on the shaping of the American mind.

1546    Sitwell, Edith. ALEXANDER POPE. London: Farber and Farber, 1930.

>    Answers the hostile criticism and Arnold's "school inspector"
>    mentality with an ecstatic defense of Pope as a man "of
>    beauty and character" whose life exemplifies the importance
>    of such qualities as loyalty and friendship.

1547    Spence, Joseph. OBSERVATIONS, ANECDOTES, AND CHARACTERS
        OF BOOKS AND MEN. Ed. James Osborn. 2 vols. Oxford: Claren-
        don Press, 1966.

>    Circulated in manuscript and not published until 1820. Valu-
>    able source of a wide range of biographical data arranged into
>    three discussions based on subject matter. Part 1 contains
>    anecdotes about Pope; part 2 deals with other British subjects;
>    and part 3 covers Spence's tours. Full textual apparatus and
>    excellent notes.

1548    Stephen, Leslie. ALEXANDER POPE. London: Macmillan, 1902.

>    Early twentieth-century life often marred by moralizing
>    and uncritical use of the poet's biography to explain his
>    art.

1549    Strachey, Lytton. "Pope." In his LITERARY ESSAYS. London: Chatto
        and Windus, 1948, pp. 79-93.

>    Published in 1925; represents an early appreciation of
>    Pope's poetic art, devoid of the excessive moralizing and

personalizing that often characterized Victorian reactions and unique in recognizing the fun and essential comic element even in Pope's most serious satire.

## F. CRITICISM

### Pastorals and Windsor Forest

1550    Battestin, Martin C.   "The Transforming Power:  Nature and Art in Pope's PASTORALS."  ECS, 2 (1969), 183-204.

Pope's idea of the Virgilian golden age is the controlling conception of his poetry from beginning to end, and in the PASTORALS reveals itself paradoxically.  The most sophisticated art becomes a means of presenting a world of simplicity and perfect naturalness; thus art repudiates Adam's legacy and the fall of man by restoring the harmony between man and nature.  See no. 1534.

1551    Clements, Frances M.   "Lansdowne, Pope, and the Unity of WINDSOR-FOREST."  MLQ, 33 (1972), 44-53.

Takes a less cosmic view of the poem's unity than previous critics and argues for the importance of the dedication to George Granville as indicative of Pope's belief in the future benefits accruing to England from the Peace of Utrecht, even beyond the idyllic condition under Anne.

1552    Durant, David S.   "Man and Nature in Alexander Pope's PASTORALS."  SEL, 11 (1971), 469-85.

Pope's presentation of the changing relationships between man, nature, and art--art reflecting natural beauty in "Spring," compared with art's subservience to man in "Winter"--explains his rejection of the pastoral mode and subsequent study of mankind.

1553    Houser, David R.   "Pope's Lodona and the Uses of Mythology."  SEL, 6 (1966), 465-82.

A well-documented discussion of the classical backgrounds and medieval and Renaissance allegorizing procedures of the Lodona and other myths found in WINDSOR FOREST and the ways Pope transforms and reshapes traditional materials for the poetic purpose of celebrating the new golden age and renewal of society under Queen Anne and the Tory peace.

1554    Melchiori, Georgio.   "Pope in Arcady:  The Theme of ET IN ARCADIA

EGO in his Pastoral." ENGLISH MISCELLANY: A SYMPOSIUM ON HISTORY, LITERATURE, AND THE ARTS, 14 (1963), 83-93.

> Rationalist Pope was "possessed and obsessed" by the fact of mortality in his earliest PASTORALS, and throughout his career an "Arcadian serene composure" runs side by side with the fear of "Universal Darkness." See no. 1533.

1555    Miller, Rachel A. "Regal Hunting: Dryden's Influence on WINDSOR-FOREST." ECS, 13 (1979-80), 169-88.

> Helpful discussion of Dryden's influence on Pope's early work, pointing out that FABLES, with its images of the hunt, concordia discors, and motifs of art and trade, provides an immediate model for WINDSOR FOREST which, like FABLES, also satirizes William III, tyranny, and war, although at the same time celebrating the Stuart monarchy and peace.

1556    Moore, John Robert. "WINDSOR FOREST and William III." MLN, 66 (1951), 451-54.

> Contrary to arguments alleging his nonpartisan stance in 1713, Pope denounced the Glorious Revolution and attacked the person of William III. Lines 43-90 (final version) make his feelings explicit.

1557    Morris, David B. "Virgilian Attitudes in Pope's WINDSOR-FOREST." TSLL, 15 (1973), 231-50.

> From beginning to end, Pope's poetic career was rooted in Virgilian attitudes and convictions about the nature and function of art, and as a civilized and civilizing poet his goal was always the improvement of mankind. See no. 1534.

1558    Rogers, Pat. "'The Enamelled Ground': The Language of Heraldry and Natural Description in WINDSOR-FOREST." STUDIA NEOPHILO-LOGICA, 45 (1973), 356-71.

> Demonstrates how Pope connects physical landscape and moral and political ideals through his "vocabulary of armorial bearings" and describes WINDSOR FOREST as an heraldic emblem further suggesting Pope's Jacobite sympathies. See no. 1534.

1559    _____. "Rhythm and Recoil in Pope's PASTORALS." ECS, 14 (1980), 1-17.

> Hoping to construct an "adequate defense in the 1980s" for Pope's PASTORALS, analyzes the elaborate symmetries,

echoes, and repetitions that constitute the poem's structure and considers the whole sequence as an intricate
and eloquent reanimation of "the dead conceit of the
music of time."

1560 _____. "Time and Space in WINDSOR FOREST." In THE ART OF
ALEXANDER POPE. Ed. Howard Erskine-Hill and Anne Smith. New
York: Barnes and Noble, 1979, pp. 40-51.

Discusses the blending of the descriptive mode and historical focus in the poem and assesses the imaginative
effects generated by the continual alteration of the
perspectives of time and place. See no. 1531.

## An Essay on Criticism

1561 Benson, James D. "Confusion in AN ESSAY ON CRITICISM and
THE DUNCIAD." EnlE, 3, i (1972), 3-6.

The critical confusion mocked in Pope's ESSAY is balanced
by his presentation of the proper methods for conducting
literary evaluation, whereas the obscurantism and darkness in THE DUNCIAD are metaphysical and unrelieved.

1562 Bogue, Ronald L. "The Meaning of 'Grace' in Pope's Aesthetic."
PMLA, 94 (1979), 434-48.

The aesthetic notion informing Pope's famous phrase
"Grace beyond the Reach of Art" (ESSAY ON CRITI-
CISM, 1.155) does not merely involve a contrast between creative inspiration and invention and regular
and proportional art, but suggests a more comprehensive
aesthetic in which artistic energy both reveals and
vitalizes an order inherent in nature.

1563 Empson, William. "Wit in the ESSAY ON CRITICISM." In his THE
STRUCTURE OF COMPLEX WORDS. Norfolk, Conn.: New Directions,
1951, pp. 84-100.

Brilliant analysis of Pope's creation of structures of meaning and a whole work of art around the word wit.

1564 Fenner, Arthur, Jr. "The Unity of Pope's ESSAY ON CRITICISM."
PQ, 39 (1960), 435-56.

Views Pope's poem as more than a collection of critical
judgments and importunings and as "unified poem in its
own right" whose shift in tone from banter to impassioned
plea provides an effective defense of poets against hostile
criticism. See no. 1533.

1565    Fisher, Alan S.   "Cheerful Noonday, 'Gloomy' Twilight: Pope's
        ESSAY ON CRITICISM."  PQ, 51 (1972), 832-44.

>    A searching analysis of Tory "gloom" in Pope, pointing
>    out that even when he appears most hopeful his opti-
>    mistic faith is vulnerable to doubts and pessimism.

1566    Hotch, Ripley.   "Pope Surveys His Kingdom:  AN ESSAY ON CRITI-
        CISM."  SEL, 13 (1973), 474-87.

>    Interesting argument contending that the object of the
>    poem is for Pope to announce himself as a poet, in
>    images relating to law and kingship, and, moreover,
>    as the heir of Roscommon and Walsh who will reestablish
>    the true poetic kingdom without slavishly following the
>    ancients.

1567    Hooker, Edward Niles.   "Pope on Wit: The ESSAY ON CRITICISM."
        In THE SEVENTEENTH CENTURY:  STUDIES IN THE HISTORY OF
        ENGLISH THOUGHT AND LITERATURE FROM BACON TO POPE.
        Ed. Richard Foster Jones.  Stanford, Calif.:  Stanford Univ. Press,
        1951, pp. 225-46.

>    Comprehensive analysis of Pope's equation of critical
>    taste with creative genius, his response to hostilities
>    toward wit as antirational and immoral, and his cham-
>    pioning of Wycherley as poet of wit.  See no. 115.

1568    Morris, David B.   "Civilized Reading: The Act of Judgment in AN
        ESSAY ON CRITICISM."  In THE ART OF ALEXANDER POPE.   Ed.
        Howard Erskine-Hill and Anne Smith.   New York: Barnes and Noble,
        1979, pp. 15-39.

>    Rather than a precocious announcement of himself as
>    poet, or a collection of critical platitudes, Pope's
>    ESSAY is an original contribution to literary theory
>    and criticism.  See no. 1531.

1569    Nierenberg, Edwin.   "Art's Own Reason in an Age of Enlightenment:
        Pope's ESSAY ON CRITICISM."  EnlE, 1, iii/iv (1970), 179-89.

>    The ESSAY is not a "supermarket" of neoclassical literary
>    theories, but a statement of art for art's sake with intrin-
>    sic merit as a coherent structure of meaning.

1570    Ramsey, Paul.   "The Watch of Judgment: Relativism and AN ESSAY
        ON CRITICISM."  In STUDIES IN CRITICISM AND AESTHETICS,
        1660-1800:  ESSAYS IN HONOR OF SAMUEL HOLT MONK.   Ed.
        Howard Anderson and John S. Shea.   Minneapolis:  Univ. of Minne-
        sota Press, 1967, pp. 128-39.

The watch metaphor, especially, does not signify a
pervasive critical relativism in the poem, but is rather
consistent with the poem's central doctrine: "judgment
is necessary and fallible and correctable." See no. 93.

1571    Spacks, Patricia Meyer.  "Imagery and Method in AN ESSAY ON
        CRITICISM."  PMLA, 85 (1970), 97-106.

        Wit operates both as a controlling and creative force,
        providing both content and form in the ESSAY.  See
        no. 1534.

## The Rape of the Lock

1572    Beyette, Kent.  "Milton and Pope's THE RAPE OF THE LOCK."  SEL,
        16 (1976), 421-36.

        Belinda violates "the true character of woman," and
        Pope's satiric comment and moral judgments draw signifi-
        cance from allusions to COMUS, IL PENSEROSO, and
        PARADISE LOST, poems in which the tragic results of
        human pride are demonstrated.

1573    Brooks, Cleanth.  "The Case of Miss Arabella Fermor:  A Re-
        Examination."  In his THE WELL-WROUGHT URN: STUDIES IN
        THE STRUCTURE OF POETRY.  New York: Harcourt, Brace, 1947,
        pp. 74-95.

        Widely reprinted classic essay in new criticism demon-
        strating the rich suggestiveness and complexity of tone
        underlying Pope's paradoxical treatment of Belinda as
        coquette, goddess, and sexual woman.  See nos. 1532,
        1533, and 1536.

1574    Cohen, Murray.  "Versions of the Lock:  Readers of THE RAPE OF
        THE LOCK."  ELH, 43 (1976), 53-73.

        Complicated but important view of the poem interpreting
        its subject as "the nature of meaning" and its method
        as "a careful discrimination among ways of reading,"
        its satiric intention depending therefore on assumptions
        about the relationship between language and reality.

1575    Cohen, Ralph.  "Transformation in THE RAPE OF THE LOCK."  ECS,
        2 (1969), 205-24.

        The poem displays "inevitable natural changes and arti-
        ficial or unnatural changes," the first involving processes
        of time and nature, the second artificial human attempts
        to effect change; but all such changes are cycles where
        "the range of possibilities is fulfilled or distorted."

1576    Cunningham, Joseph S. POPE: THE RAPE OF THE LOCK. London:
        Edward Arnold, 1961.

> An excellent introduction to the complex interplay of
> contrasts characterizing the mock-heroic mode: "the
> gap between the two worlds can . . . be ironically
> exploited to favour either side, or even both sides at
> once." See no. 1536.

1577    Folkenflik, Robert. "Metamorphosis in THE RAPE OF THE LOCK."
        ArielE, 5, ii (1974), 27-36.

> Pope's "most Ovidian poem" in which the idea of
> transformation both informs Clarissa's advice to Belinda
> on the human and moral level and describes Pope's
> method of changing the materials of life into the perma-
> nence of art.

1578    Frost, William. "THE RAPE OF THE LOCK and Pope's Homer."
        MLQ, 8 (1947), 342-54.

> In much more than a successful mock-heroic exercise,
> Pope, in an "unusual poetic proceeding," parodies and
> mimics his early translations of Homer.

1579    Grove, Robin. "Uniting Airy Substance: THE RAPE OF THE LOCK
        1712-1736." In THE ART OF ALEXANDER POPE. Ed. Howard
        Erskine-Hill and Anne Smith. New York: Barnes and Noble, 1979,
        pp. 55-88.

> Traces the many revisions and imaginative maturation
> of the poem by focusing on Pope's sensitive treatment
> of Belinda and the Sylphs. See no. 1531.

1580    Halsband, Robert. THE RAPE OF THE LOCK AND ITS ILLUSTRA-
        TIONS, 1714-1896. Oxford: Clarendon Press, 1980.

> Scholarly presentation of the various illustrations of
> Pope's famous poem, ranging from Louis Du Guerier's
> depiction in 1714 to Aubrey Beardsley's version in
> which the Pope of the famous Kneller portrait is placed
> in the center of his own Cave of Spleen, which exem-
> plify the varying responses of pictorial to great literary
> art as well as the renewing and revivifying quality of
> that literary art.

1581    Hardy, John P. "The Rape of the Lock." In REINTERPRETATIONS:
        ESSAYS ON POEMS BY MILTON, POPE AND JOHNSON. London:
        Routledge and Kegan Paul, 1971, pp. 50-80.

> Sees Belinda as "beautiful, assured, possessed of a proper

daring" in the game of love and therefore "superior
to that world which nevertheless derives such brilliance
from her presence."

1582    Huntley, Frank J. "How Really to Play the Game of Ombre in
Pope's RAPE OF THE LOCK." ECLife, 4, iv (1978), 104-06.

With a certain humorous touch, attempts to connect
card playing with the Sylphs, the sexual war, and
popular associations of certain suits and cards drawn
from ancient cartomancy, concluding that Pope's reading public could see that "hearts" was Belinda's best
suit.

1583    Jackson, James L. "Pope's RAPE OF THE LOCK Considered as a
Five-Act Epic." PMLA, 65 (1950), 1283-87.

From Le Bossu or Davenant, Pope could have found
theoretical justification for substituting dramatic form
for epic structure and seems to have relied consciously
or unconsciously on the conventional five-part dramatic
structure of the Elizabethans as the organizing principle
of his mock epic.

1584    Kinsley, William. CONTEXTS 2: THE RAPE OF THE LOCK.
Hamden, Conn.: Archon, 1979.

Interesting attempt to place Pope's text in the cultural
milieu in which it was written and published, repro-
ducing (in facsimile) periodical essays concerning a
woman's role in society and relevant literary theory
and criticism pertaining to the classical epic.

1585    Krieger, Murray. "'The Frail China Jar' and the Rude Hand of
Chaos." In his THE PLAY AND PLACE OF CRITICISM. Baltimore:
Johns Hopkins Univ. Press, 1967, pp. 53-68.

A "reckless allegorical excursion" into Pope's RAPE
OF THE LOCK and DUNCIAD (by way of AN ESSAY ON
MAN) brilliantly arguing that all of these poems are
concerned with the "power of art" whose "artificiality
testifies to the persistence, the indomitable humanity
of its creator's vision" in a world of time and mortality.
See no. 1533.

1586    Landa, Louis A. "Pope's Belinda, The General Emporie of the
World, and the Wondrous Worm." SAQ, 70 (1971), 215-35.

Interesting account of Belinda as a fashionplate and
embodiment of luxury "who takes some coloration from
her economic milieu." See no. 1534.

1587    Parkin, Rebecca Price. "Mythopoeic Activity in THE RAPE OF THE LOCK." ELH, 21 (1954), 30-38.

Sensitive reading of Pope's oblique and suggestive treatment of a divine presence in the material objects of Belinda's world and in the Homeric, Christian, and Rosicrucian myths constituting the poem's framework. See no. 1532.

1588    Reichard, Hugo. "The Love Affair in Pope's RAPE OF THE LOCK." PMLA, 69 (1954), 887-902.

Extends previous descriptions of the poem as a dramatization of the comedy surrounding premarital rituals of courtship in the age by analyzing the maneuverings of both the Baron and Belinda, "two commanding personalities--an uninhibited philanderer and an invincible flirt."

1589    Rogers, Pat. "Wit and Grammar in THE RAPE OF THE LOCK." JEGP, 72 (1973), 17-31.

Discusses the importance of such grammatical properties of language as tense, mood, and number in creating the poem's comic timing, especially in passages mocking Belinda.

1590    Rudat, Wolfgang E.H. "Another Look at the Limits of Allusion: Pope's RAPE OF THE LOCK and the Virgilian Tradition." DUJ, NS 40 (1978), 27-34.

Complex reading of the coffee-pouring and hair-snipping rituals in the RAPE which concludes that the sexual exuberance reflected in Virgil's GEORGICS is doubly operative in the context of Pope's poem, reflected not only in the mock sex act but also suggestive of a deeper psychosexual compulsion shared by both Pope and Virgil.

1591    _____. "Belinda's 'Painted Vessel': Allusive Technique in THE RAPE OF THE LOCK." TSL, 19 (1954), 49-55.

Strenuous psychosexual interpretation of this "painted vessel" passage in canto II via such figures as Ovid, Virgil, Shakespeare, Freud, and Krafft-Ebing.

1592    Sena, John. "Belinda's Hysteria: The Medical Context of THE RAPE OF THE LOCK." ECLife, 5, iv (1979), 29-42.

Belinda's hysteria, in canto IV of the poem, is a realistic description of this well-known eighteenth-century malady, revealing Pope's knowledge of contemporary medicine and demonstrating his ability to use the symptoms and effects to reinforce satirically the notion that women were erratic and feeble creatures.

1593    _____. "'The wide Circumference around': The Context of Belinda's Petticoat in THE RAPE OF THE LOCK." PLL, 16 (1980), 260-67.

Points out that the significance of Belinda's petticoat goes beyond references to heroic shields from the classical past and brings into the poem a contemporary social, economic, and moral context associated in the eighteenth century with Belinda's undergarment.

1594    Tracy, Clarence. THE RAPE OBSERV'D. Toronto: Univ. of Toronto Press, 1974. Illus.

Valuable edition that sets the poem in the context of the material objects and life-styles of Pope's era. Reproduces many of the objects, vehicles, and situations the poem mentions.

1595    Wasserman, Earl R. "The Limits of Allusion in THE RAPE OF THE LOCK." JEGP, 65 (1966), 425-44.

Brilliant analysis of the subtleties of allusive technique, arguing that a full reading of the RAPE depends on the context imported from classical or biblical sources. An approach recently subject to much controversy. See no. 1536.

1596    Williams, Aubrey. "The 'Fall' of China and THE RAPE OF THE LOCK." PQ, 41 (1962), 412-25.

Study of the vessel imagery, the many parallels with PARADISE LOST, and the Sarpedon speech in Homer's ILIAD leads to a suggestive discussion of the archetypal nature of Belinda's central experience and its parallels with the fall of man. See no. 1533.

1597    Wimsatt, William K. "Belinda Ludens: Strife and Play in THE RAPE OF THE LOCK." NLH, 4 (1973), 357-74.

Learned excursion into Kantian, Wittgensteinian, and Neo-Platonic aesthetics and a fascinating application of play and game theories (homo ludens) to the game of Ombre, "a precise and exquisite miniature of the whole poem." See no. 1534.

1598    _____. "The Game of Ombre in THE RAPE OF THE LOCK." RES, NS 1 (1950), 136-43.

Offered both as a summary of and corrective to the many analyses of the game, from Seymour's COURT-GAMESTER (1719) to recent discussions of specific rules and technical matters; but more important as a consideration of Pope's skill in depicting Belinda's fortune as reflected by the cards.

## Eloisa to Abelard and Elegy to the Memory of an Unfortunate Lady

1599    Ackerman, Stephen J. "The Vocation of Pope's Eloisa." SEL, 19 (1979), 445-57.

Points out links between the formal and dramatic elements of ELOISA TO ABELARD and discusses Pope's artful use of couplet rhetoric to analyze Eloisa's character as well as comment on her passions.

1600    Hooven, Evelyn. "Racine and Pope's Eloisa." EIC, 24 (1974), 368-74.

Racinian tragedy and Pope's heroic epistle share in the celebration of the capacity of the human consciousness to endure "intolerable contradiction, passionate strife, extreme perplexity" and in the transcendence of self into a visionary world.

1601    Jack, Ian. "The Elegy as Exorcism: Pope's VERSES TO THE MEMORY OF AN UNFORTUNATE LADY." In AUGUSTAN WORLDS: ESSAYS IN HONOUR OF A.R. HUMPHREYS. Ed. J.C. Hilson, M.M.B. Jones, and J.R. Watson. Leicester, Engl.: Leicester Univ. Press, 1978, pp. 69-83.

Cites the unfruitful attempts to establish the identity of the unfortunate lady and then focuses on the poem as a simple but audacious "rite of exorcism," incorporating a number of traditional classical themes and procedures. See nos. 111 and 1534.

1602    Kalmey, Robert P. "Pope's ELOISA TO ABELARD and 'Those Celebrated Letters.'" PQ, 47 (1968), 164-78.

Discusses Pope's adaptations of Hughes's translation of the LETTERS between the lovers to form an overall Christian framework in which Eloisa finally achieves a new order of love "that now embraces first God, and then Abelard the sanctified man."

1603    _____. "Rhetoric, Language, and Structure in ELOISA TO ABELARD" and a "REPLY" by Murray Krieger. ECS, 5 (1971), 315-20.

Interesting exchange involving the alleged disjunction between the language of Eloisa's erotic emotions and Pope's rhetorical pattern of argument involving the psychic action of Eloisa's penance. See no. 1604.

1604    Krieger, Murray. "ELOISA TO ABELARD: The Escape from the Body or the Embrace of Body." ECS, 3 (1969), 28-47.

Sees a basic clash between the poem's rhetorical design and the psychological intensity revealed in the diction and imagery expressing Eloisa's erotic torment and physical passion for Abelard. See no. 1603.

1605    Mell, Donald C., Jr. "Pope's Idea of the Imagination and the Design of 'Elegy to the Memory of an Unfortunate Lady.'" MLQ, 29 (1968), 395-407.

The design of the poem depends upon "a complex theory of the imagination" which acknowledges "the limits of art" while proving "the ultimate triumph of art over time" through consolations provided by the poem's elegiac action formalizing feelings of loss into the permanence of art.

1606    Morris, David B. "'The Visionary Maid': Tragic Passion and Redemptive Sympathy in Pope's ELOISA TO ABELARD." MLQ, 34 (1973), 247-71.

Samuel Johnson was correct in his assessment of the poem's effect, and Pope's attitude toward Eloisa indeed "is based ultimately on a deep commitment to the saving value of human affection."

1607    O Hehir, Brendan. "Virtue and Passion: The Dialectic of ELOISA TO ABELARD." TSLL, 2 (1960), 219-32.

Not uncontrolled, chaotic, or undisciplined, Pope's heroic epistle demonstrates his control of poetic materials as well as a deliberate and artful shaping of emotive and romantic language. See no. 1533.

1608    Pettit, Henry. "Pope's ELOISA TO ABELARD: An Interpretation." UNIV. OF COLORADO STUDIES: SERIES IN LANGUAGE AND LITERATURE, 4 (1953), 69-74.

More than portraying a conflict between grace and nature, the poem presents Eloisa's "wavering" between theological demands and a pagan conception of life, both rooted for the eighteenth century in the idea of human passion as a means of emotional and moral transcendence.

1609    Trowbridge, Hoyt.  "Pope's 'Eloisa' and the 'Heroides' of Ovid."  In his FROM DRYDEN TO JANE AUSTEN:  ESSAYS ON ENGLISH CRITICS AND WRITERS, 1660-1818.  Albuquerque:  Univ. of New Mexico Press, 1977, pp. 135-53.

    By analyzing contemporary editions and criticism, reconstructs Restoration and early eighteenth-century attitudes toward Ovid's poem as the key to understanding Pope's artistic intentions.

1610    Weinbrot, Howard D.  "Pope's 'Elegy to the Memory of an Unfortunate Lady.'"  MLQ, 32 (1971), 255-67.

    Rejects recent analyses of the elegy that ignore the "sense of the whole" and argues that Pope is "characteristically moral, Christian, and anti-pagan" in depicting the results of suicide on the lady's soul and on the friend and lover who cannot at first accept the truth of divine justice, but finally reconciles himself to her rejection by Heaven, life, and art.

1611    Winn, James A.  "Pope Plays the Rake:  His Letters to Ladies and the Making of the ELOISA."  In THE ART OF ALEXANDER POPE.  Ed. Howard Erskine-Hill and Anne Smith.  New York:  Barnes and Noble, 1979, pp. 89-118.

    Thoughtful and convincing account of the relation of Pope's letters to the genesis and imaginative realization of ELOISA TO ABELARD.  See no. 1531.

## An Essay on Man

1612    Atkins, G. Douglas.  "Pope and Deism:  A New Analysis."  HLQ, 35 (1972), 257-78.

    Argues that Pope's flexibility in regard to religious doctrine has encouraged critics to view him as a Deist, but that deism was a protean term in the period and that Pope never espoused the "sufficiency" of natural religion, a requirement of the Deist belief.  See no. 1534.

1613    Boyce, Benjamin.  "Baroque into Satire:  Pope's Frontispiece for the ESSAY ON MAN."  CRITICISM, 4 (1962), 14-27.  Illus.

    Discussion of the vogue in Pope's day for pictures featuring classical ruins and the somewhat ironic relationship of this capriccio picture genre to the frontispiece of the 1745 edition, designed by Pope himself.

1614    Cameron, James Munro.  "Doctrinal to an Age:  Notes toward a Re-

valuation of Pope's ESSAY ON MAN." In his THE NIGHT BATTLE.
Baltimore: Helicon Press, 1962, pp. 150-68.

> Concludes that Pope's intentions (stated in his prose intro-
> duction to ESSAY) and the poem he produced are at
> variance and that the poem's imagery represents serious
> "description," not "explanation," from Pope's vantage
> point of poetic "spectator" perusing the philosophical
> scene. See no. 1533.

1615    Choudhuri, A.D. "The Abbé Prevost on the ESSAY ON MAN." ES,
        49 (1968), 534-39.

> Summarizes and traces the chronology of French critical
> opinion, showing the importance of the Abbé Prevost's
> critique to this foreign reaction.

1616    Cunningham, Joseph S. "On Earth as it Laughs in Heaven: Mirth
        and the 'Frigorifick Wisdom.'" In AUGUSTAN WORLDS: ESSAYS
        IN HONOUR OF A.R. HUMPHREYS. Ed. J.C. Hilson, M.M.B.
        Jones, and J.R. Watson. Leicester, Engl.: Leicester Univ. Press,
        1978, pp. 131-51.

> Speculative discussion of the trope of the smiling or laugh-
> ing deity, especially as an index of the Christian concep-
> tion of wisdom and self-knowledge. Focuses on Pope's
> ESSAY ON MAN and Milton's PARADISE LOST. See no.
> 111.

1617    Edwards, Thomas R. "Visible Poetry: Pope and Modern Criticism."
        In TWENTIETH-CENTURY LITERATURE IN RETROSPECT. Ed. Reuben
        A. Brower. Harvard English Studies, no. 2. Cambridge, Mass.:
        Harvard Univ. Press, 1971, pp. 299-321.

> Argues that hostility to Arnold's pronouncement regarding
> Dryden and Pope ("classics of our prose") has caused critics
> to overreact and fabricate ordering features and structural
> coherences which, although congenial to modern organic
> theories of criticism, in fact obscure Pope's nonrational
> and "logically loose" poetic organization of complex and
> conflicting attitudes and feelings. Analyzes passages from
> the ESSAY ON MAN.

1618    French, David P. "Pope, Milton and the ESSAY ON MAN." BuR,
        16, ii (1968), 103-11.

> Pope's alteration of Milton's phrase to read "vindicate the
> ways of God to Man" indicates a changed theological and
> philosophic intent, and instead of explaining the mind of
> God he counters with a pervasively skeptical and secular
> reaction to Milton's theological certainties to establish
> God's presence.

1619    Goldgar, Bertrand A.  "Pope's Theory of the Passions:  The Background of Epistle II of the ESSAY ON MAN."  PQ, 41 (1962), 730-43.

   Pope's eclectic use of different traditions relating to the psychology and ethics of the passions or affections is governed by the artistic and intellectual requirements of his poem.

1620    Hughes, Richard E.  "Pope's ESSAY ON MAN:  The Rhetorical Structure of Epistle I."  MLN, 70 (1955), 177-81.

   The rhetorical structure of Epistle 1 establishes the rational basis for our acceptance of the succeeding arguments of Epistles 2, 3, and 4.

1621    Kallich, Martin.  HEAV'N'S FIRST LAW:  RHETORIC AND ORDER IN POPE'S ESSAY ON MAN.  De Kalb:  Northern Illinois Univ. Press, 1967.

   Essays devoted to analysis of three main stylistic devices and modes of expression--namely, antithesis, repetition of key words and phrases, and patterns of imagery--that "provide overwhelming testimony of the power and variety of Pope's poetic genius."

1622    Lawlor, Nancy K.  "Pope's ESSAY ON MAN:  Oblique Light for a False Mirror."  MLQ, 28 (1967), 305-16.

   Pope's eclecticism in the poem is a serious attempt to establish the "logical foundations" of Christian unity, and his dedication to the deist Bolingbroke is a somewhat comic and subtle method of disagreeing with his friend's theology while at the same time asserting his own brand of Christianity.

1623    Monk, Samuel Holt.  "'Die of a Rose':  ESSAY ON MAN, I, 199-200."  HLQ, 21 (1958), 359-61.

   Although Pope's famous couplet took its structure and phrasing from Lady Winchilsea's THE SPLEEN, its surprising scientific precision owes its origin to his knowledge of Robert Boyle's essay on "effluviums."

1624    Schackleton, Robert.  "Pope's ESSAY ON MAN and the French Enlightenment."  In STUDIES IN THE EIGHTEENTH CENTURY II: PAPERS PRESENTED AT THE SECOND DAVID NICHOL SMITH MEMORIAL SEMINAR, CANBERRA, 1970.  Ed. R.F. Brissenden.  Toronto:  Univ. of Toronto Press, 1973, pp. 1-15.

   Argues that for all its ambivalences and philosophic contradictions, Pope's poem appears to have made him "friend

and ally" of the moderate French philosophes and that
his "constructive deism" appealed to a wide variety of
continental thinkers.  See no. 98.

1625    Simon, Irène.  "AN ESSAY ON MAN, III, 109-146:  Footnote."
ES, 50 (1969), 93-98.

Despite Pope's contention that he takes a middle way between egoistic and benevolistic ethical theories, the poem's
moral system is heavily stoical even while acknowledging
the presence and value of the passions.

1626    Sutherland, John.  "Wit, Reason, Vision, and AN ESSAY ON MAN."
MLQ, 30 (1969), 356-69.

Pope is no system maker or philosopher, and his accomplishment in the ESSAY rests in the process of thinking poeti-
cally and intuitively through the "language of wit" and
"symbolic imagery" on the "fringes of consciousness."

1627    Tuveson, Ernest.  "AN ESSAY ON MAN and 'The Way of Ideas.'"
ELH, 26 (1959), 368-86.

Discusses ways that Locke's new psychology of the mind
affected the fabric of Pope's poetry and his views about
nature and man in nature, using as an example this
philosophically oriented poem.

1628    Varey, Simon.  "Rhetoric and AN ESSAY ON MAN."  In THE ART
OF ALEXANDER POPE.  Ed. Howard Erskine-Hill and Anne Smith.
New York: Barnes and Noble, 1979, pp. 132-43.

The rhetorical strategies of the poem represent an indirect
rationalization of Pope's poetic career, establishing his
relationship as a poet to the reader, to mankind in general,
and to himself.  See no. 1531.

1629    White, Douglas H.  POPE AND THE CONTEXT OF CONTROVERSY:
THE MANIPULATION OF IDEAS IN AN ESSAY ON MAN.  Chicago:
Univ. of Chicago Press, 1970.

Treats Pope's poem within the context of ongoing philosophical and theological controversies of his age to illuminate
the workings of his mind and intellect.

## Epistles to Several Persons

1630    Aden, John M.  "Bethel's Sermon and Pope's EXEMPLUM:  Towards a
Critique."  SEL, 9 (1969), 463-70.

Comparison of the homiletic, stylistic, and political aspects of Bethel's sermon and Pope's own moral statement shows differing purposes, the one dramatized through the image of the Fall, the other through the image of Redemption.

1631    Alpers, Paul J. "The EPISTLE TO BATHURST and the Mandevillian State." ELH, 25 (1958), 23-42.

The formal and rhetorical tensions of the poem are the result of Pope's realistic observation of economic facts and a conflict between his political and moral imaginations. See no. 1533.

1632    Brady, Frank. "The History and Structure of Pope's TO A LADY." SEL, 9 (1969), 439-62.

Bibliographical and interpretive study determining that EPISTLES TO SEVERAL PERSONS was not fully printed during Pope's life, that Warburton gave "To a Lady" its final form, and that a consideration of textual changes suggests some portraits have been omitted or rearranged over the course of the publication process.

1633    Brower, Reuben A. "The Groves of Eden: Design in a Satire by Pope." In his THE FIELDS OF LIGHT: AN EXPERIMENT IN CRITICAL READING. New York: Oxford Univ. Press, 1951, pp. 138-63.

Contains a perceptive close analysis of the allusive mode and total imaginative design of Pope's "Epistle to Burlington."

1634    Davidow, Lawrence Lee. "Pope's Verse Epistles: Friendship and the Private Sphere of Life." HLQ, 40 (1977), 151-70.

Pope's verse epistles share with his letters a concern for the moral ideal of friendship, and do not reinforce institutional norms or affirm the status quo but, rather, place "ultimate value on the vigorous ideals of personal integrity and an open heart."

1635    Erskine-Hill, Howard. "Heirs to Vitruvius: Pope and the Idea of Architecture." In THE ART OF ALEXANDER POPE. Ed. Howard Erskine-Hill and Anne Smith. New York: Barnes and Noble, 1979, pp. 144-56.

Architectural relationship and rhythm were a compelling interest throughout Pope's life, and such patterns helped him to achieve formal and expressive order in individual epistles as well as in the group of the four EPISTLES TO SEVERAL PERSONS. See no. 1531.

1636    _____. THE SOCIAL MILIEU OF ALEXANDER POPE: LIVES, EXAMPLE AND THE POETIC RESPONSE. New Haven, Conn.: Yale Univ. Press, 1975.

> The first section provides a careful and fully researched accounting of the lives and times of Pope's exemplars of virtue--John Kyrle, John Caryll, William Digby, and Ralph Allen--and those symbolic of evil and corruption, Peter Walter and John Blunt. Part 2 discusses the realization of the values these men represent, especially in EPISTLES TO SEVERAL PERSONS and IMITATIONS OF HORACE.

1637    Fox, Christopher. "'Gone as Soon as Found': Pope's 'Epistle to Cobham' and Death-Day as Moment of Truth." SEL, 20 (1980), 431-48.

> Pope does not advocate that man search only by the "ruling passion" for knowledge of human nature, but suggests both when and how we arrive at knowledge of man's character through his poetic use of the classical-Montaignean philosophic tradition of the day of death as moment of truth.

1638    Gibson, William A. "Three Principles of Renaissance Architectural Theory in Pope's EPISTLE TO BURLINGTON." SEL, 11 (1971), 487-505.

> The aesthetic norms underlying Pope's poem derive from architectural themes, especially Renaissance commentaries on Vitruvius' decor, involving relationships between the form and order of a structure, its social function, and the moral dimension provided by its patron or inhabitants. See no. 1534.

1639    Mahaffey, Kathleen. "Timon's Villa: Walpole's Houghton." TSLL, 9 (1967), 193-222.

> The fact that recent scholarship has shown Chandos was not the model for Pope's Timon in no way proves the satire impersonal; in fact, the portrait and setting are given imaginative power and added dimensions by their resemblance to Walpole's Houghton. See no. 1534.

1640    Nussbaum, Felicity A. "Pope's 'To a Lady' and the Eighteenth-Century Woman." PQ, 54 (1975), 444-56.

> The traits of inconstancy, pride, and witty affectation characterize Pope's display of women and the antifeminism of the eighteenth century as well, and his sequence of portraits gains increased detail and immediacy resulting in a "deepening moral seriousness."

1641    Osborn, James M. "Pope, The. 'Apollo of the Arts,' and his Countess."
        In ENGLAND IN THE RESTORATION AND EARLY EIGHTEENTH
        CENTURY: ESSAYS ON CULTURE AND SOCIETY. Ed. H.T. Sweden-
        berg, Jr. Berkeley: Univ. of California Press, 1972, pp. 101-43.

>   Pope's EPISTLE TO BURLINGTON is a fitting poetic tribute
>   to a memorable friendship of three decades with the Boyles
>   carried on through letters, light verse, travel, and intellec-
>   tual compatibility. See no. 125.

1642    Parkin, Rebecca Price. "The Role of Time in Alexander Pope's EPISTLE
        TO A LADY." ELH, 32 (1965), 490-501.

>   Time, a process whose urgency is felt in the gallery of
>   feminine portraits, intersects in the poem with conceptions
>   of timeless moral absolutes, and these "two interpenetrat-
>   ing paradoxes" depict character and good humor, moral
>   ideals in Pope's age. See no. 1533.

## Horatian Poems

1643    Aden, John M. "Another Analogue to Pope's Vice Triumphant."
        MP, 66 (1968), 150-51.

>   An episode in Bolingbroke's "The First Vision of Camiloch,"
>   printed in THE CRAFTSMAN, shares with Pope's Vice
>   Triumphant passage in EPILOGUE TO THE SATIRES I "the
>   theme and image of venal degradation."

1644    _____. "Pope and the Satiric Adversary." SEL, 2 (1962), 267-86.

>   Pope capitalizes on the adversaries formula found in the
>   Roman satura and transforms it into a dialog device that
>   enlivens satiric discourse; diversifies the style, tone, and
>   moral statement; promotes dramatic immediacy; and creates
>   the semblance of objectivity and independence. See no.
>   1533.

1645    _____. SOMETHING LIKE HORACE: STUDIES IN THE ART AND
        ALLUSION OF POPE'S HORATIAN SATIRES. Nashville: Vanderbilt
        Univ. Press, 1969.

>   Discusses the conventions and rhetorical strategies Pope
>   inherits from Horace and analyzes his extension and shap-
>   ing of these practices into a satiric genre flexible enough
>   to combine sacred and secular and colloquial tones.

1646    _____. "That Impudent Satire: Pope's SOBER ADVICE." In ESSAYS
        IN ENGLISH LITERATURE OF THE CLASSICAL PERIOD. SP, Extra
        Series 4 (1967), 88-106.

Questions usual condemnations of the poem as either perverse, pornographic, or just playful and argues that its
satirical ethos is "in keeping with [Pope's] recently
assumed role of moral poet and imitator of Horace."

1646A    Bogel, Fredric V. ACTS OF KNOWLEDGE: POPE'S LATER POEMS.
Lewisburg, Pa.: Bucknell Univ. Press, 1981.

Pope's poems from AN ESSAY ON MAN through THE
DUNCIAD exhibit a thematic and structural unity deriving
from "a continuing dialogue between two modes of knowledge, schematic and substantial, and between the two
kinds of world and knower that each mode implies."
Especially provocative discussion of "An Epistle to Dr.
Arbuthnot" as Pope's effort toward poetic self-knowledge
and self-discovery.

1647    Douglass, Richard H. "More on the Rhetoric and Imagery of Pope's
ARBUTHNOT." SEL, 13 (1973), 488-502.

Pope associates himself with great men as a sign of an
achieved harmony and generosity in clear contrast to
the greed, malice, acquisitiveness, shallowness, and
crudities associated with the dunces, and his character-
izations of them through images of humor obviously suggest his own virtue of self-discipline.

1648    Feder, Lillian. "Sermo or Satire: Pope's Definition of His Art." In
STUDIES IN CRITICISM AND AESTHETICS, 1660-1800: ESSAYS IN
HONOR OF SAMUEL HOLT MONK. Ed. Howard Anderson and
John S. Shea. Minneapolis: Univ. of Minnesota Press, 1967, pp.
140-55.

In his major satires, Pope's blend of the casual and harsh
tones characterizing Horace's sermones is a means of establishing his own persona and defining the goals of his
satiric art. See no. 93.

1649    Gabriner, Paul. "Pope's 'Virtue' and the Events of 1738." SCRIPTA
HIEROSOLYMITANA: FURTHER STUDIES IN ENGLISH LANGUAGE
AND LITERATURE, 25 (1973), 96-119.

Pope's masterful allegorical representation of virtue's defeat in "Dialogue I" of the EPILOGUE TO THE SATIRES
makes clear reference to the political situation in 1738
and the failure of the Tory opposition to Walpole and
marks Pope's final disillusionment with and resignation to
political realities. See no. 1534.

1650    Greene, Donald J. "'Dramatic Texture' in Pope." In FROM SENSI-

BILITY TO ROMANTICISM: ESSAYS PRESENTED TO FREDERICK A.
POTTLE. Ed. Frederick W. Hilles and Harold Bloom. New York:
Oxford Univ. Press, 1965, pp. 31-53.

An excellent corrective (at the time written) to the pejorative view of Pope's poetry, demonstrating from the later
poems the rich drama of voices and tones and feelings present
in poetry mistakenly called "impersonal, objective, dispassionate." See no. 110.

1651    Hardy, John P. "AN EPISTLE TO DR. ARBUTHNOT." In his
REINTERPRETATIONS: ESSAYS IN POEMS BY MILTON, POPE AND
JOHNSON. London: Routledge and Kegan Paul, 1971, pp. 81-102.

The poem is a carefully articulated structure in which the
three satiric portraits characterize by contrast the speaker's
moral purpose.

1652    Hotch, Ripley. "The Dilemma of an Obedient Son: Pope's EPISTLE
TO DR. ARBUTHNOT." ESSAYS IN LITERATURE, 1 (1974), 37-45.

In describing his growth as a satirical poet, Pope creates
a convincing portrait by successfully confronting the
psychological ambivalences and contradictions inherent
in his role as both a satirist and a representative of the
character of a good man. See no. 1534.

1653    Hughes, Richard E. "Pope's IMITATIONS OF HORACE and the
Ethical Focus." MLN, 71 (1956), 569-74.

These poems offer an example of Pope's self-defensiveness
and the care he took to present himself rhetorically in the
best possible light in order to make plausible his attacks
on others.

1654    Hunter, G.K. "The 'Romanticism' of Pope's Horace." EIC, 10
(1960), 390-414.

Despite his urbanity and wit, Pope is "quite un-Horatian"
in his IMITATIONS, substituting for Horace's assured,
public, and socially directed ethos another form emphasizing the passionate awareness of the individual satiric consciousness. See no. 1533.

1655    Hunter, J. Paul. "Satiric Apology as Satiric Instance: Pope's
ARBUTHNOT." JEGP, 68 (1969), 625-47.

More than a personal or professional apology for satire,
the poem's tone and structure exemplifies the "composure,"
"moral balance," and "human compassion" proper to the
satirical perspective. See no. 1534.

1656    Knoepflmacher, U.C.   "The Poet as Physician:  Pope's EPISTLE TO
        DR. ARBUTHNOT."  MLQ, 31 (1970), 440-49.

        With reference to Renaissance distinctions between a
        physician treating physical sickness and a moralist min-
        istering to the soul, shows that Pope's choice of Arbuthnot
        as adversarius was more than a gesture to a dying friend
        and relies instead on the satiric counterpoint between his
        own blunt challenges and the prudent evasions of a physi-
        cian helpless in the grips of a mortal illness.

1657    Lauren, Barbara.  "Pope's 'Epistle to Lord Bolingbroke':  Satire from
        the Vantage of Retirement."  SEL, 15 (1975), 419-30.

        Views the dual postures of "retired man" and "honest
        satirist" as interdependent, reinforcing one another in
        face of the degeneration of public life and politics
        under Walpole.

1658    Levine, Jay Arnold.  "Pope's EPISTLE TO AUGUSTUS, Lines 1-30."
        SEL, 7 (1967), 427-51.

        A full accounting of the historical, literary, and religious
        implications of these opening lines, concluding that Pope,
        writing at the close of the Christian humanist tradition,
        exploits and elaborates its beliefs and artistic modes for
        satiric purposes.

1659    Maresca, Thomas E.  POPE'S HORATIAN POEMS.  Columbus:  Ohio
        State Univ. Press, 1966.

        Brings to bear important information about the practice of
        Renaissance Horatian commentary in support of a thesis
        arguing for the essentially Christian quality of Pope's
        imitations.

1660    Mengel, Elias F., Jr.  "Patterns of Imagery in Pope's ARBUTHNOT."
        PMLA, 69 (1954), 184-97.

        Images of animals, filth, disease, persecution, and human
        virtue are meaningfully related to "give to the whole
        a metaphoric value" and unity of satiric purpose.  See
        no. 1533.

1661    Moskovit, Leonard A.  "Pope and the Tradition of Neoclassical
        Imitation."  SEL, 8 (1968), 445-62.

        Pope's Horatian Imitations utilize not only the trans-
        lational mode, which remains faithful to the original,
        but also freely adapt his models to contemporary needs,
        advancing new meanings and satirizing personal targets.

1662     Osborn, James M.  "Pope, the Byzantine Empress, and Walpole's
         Whore."  RES, NS 6 (1955), 372-82.

         More than "abstract personification," this satiric portrait
         of Vice Triumphant alludes to the biblical whore of Baby-
         lon, Justinian's wife and former prostitute Theodora, and
         the second Lady Walpole.  See no. 1533.


1663     Paulson, Kristoffer F.  "Rochester and Milton: The Sound, Sense,
         and Sources of Pope's Portraits of Bufo, Atticus, and Sporus in AN
         EPISTLE TO DR. ARBUTHNOT."  PLL, 12 (1976), 299-310.

         These famous satiric portraits derive from specific models
         in Rochester and in Milton's PARADISE LOST, and the
         climactic Sporus portrait shows Pope's ability to synthesize
         and imaginatively transform previous materials into "an
         organic whole."


1664     Reverand, Cedric D., II.  "Ut pictura poesis and Pope's 'SATIRE II, i.'"
         ECS, 9 (1976), 553-68.

         Treats Pope's use of the pictorial arts and painting images
         in depicting the theme of virtue in the Horatian imitations
         and contends that his speaker does not capitulate to
         Fortescue's warnings about the dangers of political opposi-
         tion.  See no. 1534.


1665     Schonhorn, Manuel.  "The Audacious Contemporaneity of Pope's
         EPISTLE TO AUGUSTUS."  SEL, 8 (1968), 431-43.

         Discusses the poem as a topical polemic openly referring
         to George II's dislike of his son, Frederick, Prince of
         Wales, and thus as both an attack on the monarch and a
         celebration of his savior-hero son who has aligned himself
         with the anti-Walpole opposition.


1666     _____.  "Pope's EPISTLE TO AUGUSTUS:  Notes Toward a Mythol-
         ogy."  TSL, 16 (1971), 15-33.

         Pope's debased versions of the Merlin and Astraea myths,
         placed in contemporary political and literary contexts,
         vividly show the extent of the "decay of classical values
         for his time."  See no. 1534.


1667     Stack, Frank.  "Pope's EPISTLE TO BOLINGBROKE and EPISTLES I,
         i."  In THE ART OF ALEXANDER POPE.  Ed. Howard Erskine-Hill
         and Anne Smith.  New York: Barnes and Noble, 1979, pp. 169-91.

         Places the original version of Horace side-by-side with
         Pope's adaptation to facilitate close examination of the
         language, imagery, and style of each in order to deter-

mine the character and contours of Pope's originality.
See no. 1531.

1668    Williams, Aubrey L.  "Pope and Horace: THE SECOND EPISTLE OF
THE SECOND BOOK."  In RESTORATION AND EIGHTEENTH-
CENTURY LITERATURE:  ESSAYS IN HONOR OF ALAN DUGALD
McKILLOP.  Ed. Carroll Camden.  Chicago:  Univ. of Chicago
Press, 1963, pp. 309-21.

Pope's "deliberate departures" from Horace (as much as
his similar renderings) signal important themes of these
IMITATIONS, in this particular case the motif of thievery
equated with the losses inflicted on man by time.  See
no. 103.

## The Dunciad

1669    See no. 1561.

1670    Brockbank, J. Philip.  "The BOOK OF GENESIS and the Genesis
of Books: The Creation of Pope's DUNCIAD."  In THE ART OF
ALEXANDER POPE.  Ed. Howard Erskine-Hill and Anne Smith.
New York:  Barnes and Noble, 1979, pp. 192-211.

Stresses the ways the poem evokes and enacts creativity
and views it as a "phantasmagoric territory" in which the
literary creation becomes analogous to the creation of the
natural world.  See no. 1531.

1671    Chambers, Jessie Rhodes.  "The Episode of Annius and Mummius:
DUNCIAD IV 347-96."  PQ, 43 (1964), 185-92.

Scholarly analysis of the theme of the Anti-Christ of wit
and its relation to the spiritual destruction implied by
Pope's satire on these representative virtuosi.

1672    Erskine-Hill, Howard.  "The 'New World' of Pope's DUNCIAD."
RMS, 6 (1962), 47-67.

The DUNCIAD, "while not an impeccable poem," generates exuberant, not solemn, satire through its witty advancement of a coherent and humorous fantasy world of
duncery.  An early challenge to traditional readings
stressing tragic overtones and the prophecy of a universal
darkness blotting out humanistic values.  See no. 1533.

1673    Friedman, Arthur.  "Pope and Deism (THE DUNCIAD, IV. 459-92)."
In POPE AND HIS CONTEMPORARIES:  ESSAYS PRESENTED TO
GEORGE SHERBURN.  Ed. James L. Clifford and Louis A. Landa.
New York:  Oxford Univ. Press, 1949, pp. 89-95.

This passage written late in Pope's career refutes charges that he was really a Deist and shows his awareness of the main issues pertaining to the Deist controversies of his age. See no. 107.

1674    Gneiting, Teona T. "Pictorial Imagery and Satiric Inversion in Pope's DUNCIAD." ECS, 8 (1975), 420-430.

The Goddess of Dulness will not only subvert learning and debase poetry, but also destroy "all areas of human creativity, including the visual arts."

1675    Griffith, Reginald H. "THE DUNCIAD." PQ, 24 (1945), 155-57.

Pope's satire is not "merely a personal brawl" but, rather, advocates cultural tradition, the established order in politics, religion, and the arts in face of the "extinction of learning" and emergence of "the Modern World in England." See no. 1533.

1676    Howard, William J. "The Mystery of the Cibberian DUNCIAD." SEL, 8 (1968), 463-74.

Rather than being primarily a political poem, the 1743 version makes use of a number of controversies centering on the mysteries of Christianity, and Pope's use of religious allusions throughout shows his awareness of the controversies.

1677    Jones, Emrys. "Pope and Dulness." PBA, 54 (1968), 231-63.

An important rejoinder to the reading of Pope's DUNCIAD as a solemn cultural and educational treatise on the demise of Western culture, and a reading which instead emphasizes the poem's energy and vigor in its utilization of both burlesque and mock-heroic traditions. See nos. 1532 and 1534.

1678    Kinsley, William. "The DUNCIAD as Mock-Book." HLQ, 35 (1971), 29-47.

Consideration of the poem as a mock-book highlights what the dunces do as well as don't do and also emphasizes Pope's two satiric purposes: (1) mocking all aspects of bookmaking, the characteristic activity of the dunces; (2) condemning duncery by juxtaposing its products with classical epic and biblical literature. See no. 1534

1679    _____. "Physico-Demonology in Pope's DUNCIAD IV, 71-90." MLR, 70 (1975), 20-31.

Discusses Pope's satiric attacks on the Dunces' conversion
of the European cultural landmark of physico-theology
into its opposite, physico-demonology.

1680    Knuth, Deborah J.  "Pope, Handel, and the DUNCIAD."  MLS, 10,
iii (1980), 22-28.

Comments on Pope's lines in praise of Handel, showing
that the poet was not insensitive to music as often alleged,
and in fact knew the composer's work and admired the
"Drydenic mythmaking" that linked English monarchs and
the Bible, an association impossible for Pope to make
given the reign of Dulness and eternal night of Book 4.

1681    Kropf, Carl R.  "Miscreation:  Another Miltonic Allusion in THE
DUNCIAD."  PLL, 10 (1974), 425-27.

Points out that the creation of Dulness (Book 1, 11.
54-78) parodies Milton's positive description of God's
creative activities in PARADISE LOST (7, 11. 276-81).

1682    Lawler, Traugott.  "'Wafting Vapours from the Land of Dreams':
Virgil's Fourth and Sixth Eclogues and the DUNCIAD."  SEL, 14
(1974), 373-86.

Virgil's twin pastoral poems are sources for and keys to
interpreting the DUNCIAD, and Pope uses Virgil's
pastoral style, as he does Virgil's epic, not only to
ridicule the failure of the dunces to sustain cultural
value, but also to prove that he can "write beautifully
as well as satirically."  See no. 1534.

1683    Mengel, Elias F.  "The DUNCIAD Illustrations."  ECS, 7 (1973-74),
161-78.

The seven plates found in the editions of the DUNCIAD
through 1743, though not of Pope's personal design, are
integral to the poem's meaning and "confirm visually the
satiric mode of the poem."  See no. 1534.

1684    Morris, David B.  "The Kinship of Madness in Pope's DUNCIAD."
PQ, 51 (1972), 813-31.

Studies the dark relationships between the stone statues
depicting madness on the gates above Bedlam and Colley
Cibber, whose father carved them, and concludes that
Pope skillfully expands his satire of hack writers into a
searching examination of the threat of the irrational to
God's creative wisdom.

1685     Peterson, R.G. "Renaissance Classicism in Pope's DUNCIAD." SEL, 15 (1975), 431-45.

> The Renaissance tradition of allegorized myths, symbolic gods, systems of iconography, and reconstructions of an ideal ancient world is an important part of the classical past alluded to in Pope's satire.

1686     Regan, John V. "The Mock-Epic Structure of the DUNCIAD." SEL, 19 (1979), 459-73.

> An elaborate study (with numerous charts) of Pope's use of the basic structure of Virgil's AENEID, in the DUNCIAD, concluding that Book 4 is an integral part of its totality and that the DUNCIAD's "structural harmony" was not in fact fully realized until the 1743 edition, which added Book 4.

1687     _____. "Orpheus and THE DUNCIAD's Narrator." ECS, 9 (1975), 87-101.

> Argues for the thematic importance of the Ovidian epigraph concerning the death of Orpheus, which refers not only to the destruction of poetic powers, but also to the continuing "civilizing influence" and "hopeful core" implicit in the Orphic myth.

1688     Reid, B.L. "Ordering Chaos: THE DUNCIAD." In QUICK SPRINGS OF SENSE: STUDIES IN THE EIGHTEENTH CENTURY. Ed. Larry S. Champion. Athens: Univ. of Georgia Press, 1974, pp. 75-96.

> The poem is not neatly unified, and its very awkwardness and violent energies are "the defects of its virtue"; but an all-consuming "passion" and "intellectual outrage" underlie the four books and merge into a final vision "sufficiently apocalyptic." See nos. 104 and 1534.

1689     Rogers, Pat. "The Critique of Opera in Pope's DUNCIAD." MUSICAL QUARTERLY, 59 (January 1973), 15-30.

> Explicit reference to the operatic scene of his day reveals Pope's knowledge of contemporary musical controversies and provides a source for "the living image of Dulness" in the metaphor of sound without sense.

1690     _____. "The Name and Nature of Dulness: Proper Nouns in the DUNCIAD." ANGLIA, 92 (1974), 79-102.

> Pope exploits certain syntactical and referential ambiguities generated by proper nouns used in idiosyncratic constructions and deliberately confounds their status as

either concrete or abstract words to reinforce thematic and satiric goals, his poem achieving much of its "imaginative density" from this practice.

1691 _____. "Pope, Settle, and the Fall of Troy." SEL, 15 (1975), 447-58.

Elkanah Settle, through his Grub Street dramatic efforts, is the "imaginative relation" between Virgil's AENEID and Smithfield, an ironic version of the legendary burning of Troy and establishment of Rome.

1692 Rosenblum, Michael. "Pope's Illusive Temple of Infamy." In THE SATIRIST'S ART. Ed. H. James Jensen and Malvin R. Zirker, Jr. Bloomington: Indiana Univ. Press, 1972, pp. 28-54.

Interestingly argues that THE DUNCIAD advances not only Pope's dark vision of reality, but also provides him the opportunity for wittily converting duncery and dulness into a self-contained work of the satiric imagination. See no. 113.

1693 Sellery, J'nan. "Language and Moral Intelligence in the Enlightenment: Fielding's Plays and Pope's DUNCIAD." EnlE, 1 (1970), 17-26; 108-19.

The variety of terms used to define and describe literature from 1660 to 1800 would suggest a pluralism of thematic concerns, but Pope's DUNCIAD shares with Fielding's drama an "antipathy to intellectual obscurantism," "pretentious verbosity," and a "nominalistic view of language."

1694 Sherbo, Arthur. "No Single Scholiast: Pope's THE DUNCIAD." MLR, 65 (1970), 503-16.

Annotations of this study contain key lines and couplets to show the extent of Pope's extraordinarily rich allusive texture in the DUNCIAD (and several other poems).

1695 Sherburn, George. "THE DUNCIAD, Book IV." TEXAS STUDIES IN ENGLISH, 24 (1944), 174-90.

Book 4 functions as a significant "intellectual pronouncement" on matters of education, science, religion, and philosophy in the period, and its structural design amalgamates elements from classical epic, PARADISE LOST, and Fielding's dramatic farces to create "diverse complexity." See no. 1533.

1696 Siebert, Donald T. "Cibber and Satan: THE DUNCIAD and Civilization." ECS, 10 (1976-77), 203-21.

This view of Pope's DUNCIAD as a playful exercise in

good fun and of the dunces themselves as trivial, inept, and essentially comic fools represents an important challenge to "School of Deep Intent" readings that have stressed the poem's pessimistic attitude toward the future of Western civilization and its essentially tragic conclusion.

1697    Sitter, John E. THE POETRY OF POPE'S DUNCIAD. Minneapolis: Univ. of Minnesota Press, 1971.

Analyzes the "poetic complexity" of this "anti-epic" dream-vision of Grub Street turned nightmare as designed ironically to reconcile Western culture to the inevitable establishment of Dulness, in a manner much like that in which Virgil positively reconciles the world to Rome.

1698    Tanner, Tony. "Reason and the Grotesque: Pope's DUNCIAD." CRITICAL QUARTERLY, 7 (1965), 145-60.

Brilliant exploration of the "grotesque element" in the DUNCIAD, viewing the poem as a "final heroic gesture" for the principles of order and reason "in a universe given over to perversity and chaos." See no. 1533.

1699    Williams, Aubrey L. POPE'S DUNCIAD: A STUDY OF ITS MEANING. London: Methuen, 1955.

Highly influential study of the differing versions of the poem; analyzes structure, use of metaphor, parodies of Milton and the classical epic, and the conscious inversion of Christian themes and symbols--all employed in the service of satire on hack writing and its perversions of language and meaning.

1700    Williams, Robert W. "Some Baroque Influences in Pope's DUNCIAD." BJA, 9 (1969), 186-94.

Cites Heinrich Wölfflin's definition of baroque art as "the expression of a directed movement within [a] body" and within this framework discusses the images of mass and motion informing the DUNCIAD.

## Other Individual Poems

1701    Erskine-Hill, Howard. "The Medal Against Time: A Study of Pope's EPISTLE TO MR. ADDISON." JWCI, 28 (1965), 274-98.

Treats the epistle against the historical background of the fall of Rome, a subject previously treated in AN

ESSAY ON CRITICISM and later in Book 3 of THE
DUNCIAD, and demonstrates its accomplishment as poetic
art and its importance as an index to Pope's Augustanism.
See no. 1534.

1702    Griffin, Dustin. "Revisions in Pope's 'Ode on Solitude.'" MLQ,
        36 (1975), 369-75.

Textual study of revisions over a thirty-five year period
of Pope's best lyric showing that his small changes, when
considered together, significantly improve the poem's
quality, making it simultaneously more English and more
Latinate.

1703    Jack, Ian. "Pope and 'The Weighty Bullion of Dr. Donne's Satires.'"
        PMLA, 66 (1951), 1009-22.

Comparison of Pope's "versifications" with Donne's SATYRES
reveals fewer differences than normally assumed, especially
in diction, imagery, and tone; prosodic practices actually
constitute the chief difference in their satiric idioms.
See no. 1533.

1704    Rogers, Robert W. "Alexander Pope's UNIVERSAL PRAYER." JEGP,
        54 (1955), 612-24.

Valuable study of the manuscript providing a picture of
the poem's growth and a clarification of Pope's controversial attitudes toward free will and other tenets of
Christianity as expressed in his ESSAY ON MAN.

1705    Tillotson, Geoffrey. "Pope's 'Epistle to Harley': An Introduction
        and Analysis." In POPE AND HIS CONTEMPORARIES: ESSAYS
        PRESENTED TO GEORGE SHERBURN. Ed. James L. Clifford and
        Louis A. Landa. New York: Oxford Univ. Press, 1949, pp.
        58-77.

Describes the occasion and genesis of Pope's poem addressed to Harley, focusing on the skillful blending of
the forms of elegy and verse epistle. See no. 107.

1706    Wasserman, Earl R. "Pope's ODE FOR MUSICK." ELH, 28 (1961),
        163-86.

Finds the poem flawed, despite the "complex intensity
of its art," because the musical metaphor, occasion, and
religious theme fail to achieve a unified artistic whole.
See no. 1533.

## General Studies

1707      Aden, John M. "Pope and Politics: 'The Farce of State.'" In ALEXANDER POPE: WRITERS AND THEIR BACKGROUND. Ed. Peter Dixon. Athens: Ohio Univ. Press, 1972, pp. 172–99.

> Wide-ranging and comprehensive general account of Pope's attraction to politics, singling out his Catholicism, Tory wit, patriotism, and Robert Walpole as the main impetus. See no. 1530.

1708      _____. POPE'S ONCE AND FUTURE KINGS: SATIRE AND POLITICS IN THE EARLY CAREER. Knoxville: Univ. of Tennessee Press, 1978.

> An important study of Pope's career in satire and politics (up to approximately 1728) in the context of his Catholic background and general religious concerns.

1709      Adler, Jacob H. "Pope and the Rules of Prosody." PMLA, 76 (1961), 218–26.

> Documents Pope's "violations" of conventionally held prosodic rules of the period, even those he himself espoused in his letter to Henry Cromwell and in the ESSAY ON CRITICISM.

1710      _____. THE REACH OF ART: A STUDY IN THE PROSODY OF POPE. Gainesville: Univ. of Florida Press, 1964.

> Analyzes Pope's varied prosodic techniques, investigating especially the use of caesura, rhetorical devices, syncope, monosyllabic lines, rhymes, alliteration, and representative metrical practices.

1711      Allen, Robert J. "Pope and the Sister Arts." In POPE AND HIS CONTEMPORARIES: ESSAYS PRESENTED TO GEORGE SHERBURN. Ed. James L. Clifford and Louis A. Landa. New York: Oxford Univ. Press, 1949, pp. 78–88.

> Traces the extent to which Pope was "conscious of and interested in" the techniques of painting and discusses some resulting influences on his poetic imagery. See no. 107.

1712      Altenbernd, A.L. "On Pope's Horticultural Romanticism." JEGP, 54 (1955), 470–77.

> Pope's theory of garden art, calling for abandonment of the artificial and formalized practices of the French and

for adoption of a natural, freer design, led to the widespread popularity of "natural landscape garden." See no. 1533.

1713    Auden, W.H. "Alexander Pope." EIC, 1 (1951), 208-24.

Opinionated but shrewd appreciative account of Pope's genius, asserting that his interests were mainly himself, others opinions of him, his own art, and his social manners and that his best writing stemmed from personal experiences. See no. 1533.

1714    Barnard, John. POPE: THE CRITICAL HERITAGE. London: Routledge and Kegan Paul, 1973.

Necessarily selective account of Pope's reputation as recorded during his lifetime from 1745 through Warton's ESSAY (1782) and Johnson's LIFE. Omits personal attacks and chooses the literary criticism and comment that modified or changed Pope's critical thinking, principles, and actual literary career.

1715    Bluestone, Max. "The Suppressed Metaphor in Pope." EIC, 8 (1958), 347-54.

Interesting discussion that singles out the "dress of thought" passage in AN ESSAY ON CRITICISM and the hog simile in Dialogue 2 of the EPILOGUE TO THE SATIRES to argue that Pope's rhetoric suppresses overt imagery and metaphor contrary to "the metaphysical manner." See no. 1791.

1716    Boyce, Benjamin. THE CHARACTER-SKETCHES IN POPE'S POEMS. Durham, N.C.: Duke Univ. Press, 1962.

In an age addicted to portraiture, Pope's verbal sketches are better understood when viewed in relation to their literary models and to possible living originals in history.

1717    Bracher, Frederick. "Pope's Grotto: The Maze of Fancy." HLQ, 12 (1949), 140-62.

Pope's brilliantly luminous version of a long garden-grotto tradition reflects the romantic and highly imaginative qualities in his poetic art. See no. 1533.

1718    Brower, Reuben Arthur. ALEXANDER POPE: THE POETRY OF ALLUSION. Oxford: Clarendon Press, 1959.

Pope's characteristic allusive mode relates the classical

literary tradition and that of Spenser and Milton to the
world of eighteenth-century London, making him a truly
European poet. A seminal and influential treatment of
allusion in Pope and still the shrewdest from a critical
and analytical standpoint.

1719 _____. "Dryden and the 'Invention' of Pope." In RESTORATION
AND EIGHTEENTH-CENTURY LITERATURE: ESSAYS IN HONOR
OF ALAN DUGALD McKILLOP. Ed. Carroll Camden. Chicago:
Univ. of Chicago Press, 1963, pp. 211-33.

Dryden was Pope's "master" not only for Pope's public
poetry, heroic mode, and role as social and political
satirist, but also for his later Horatian "poetry of retirement" mode. See no. 103.

1720 Brownell, Morris R. ALEXANDER POPE AND THE ARTS OF
GEORGIAN ENGLAND. Oxford: Clarendon Press, 1978. Illus.

Study of Pope's career "as a virtuoso in the Renaissance
tradition" against the background of tastes and artistic
practices of the Georgian period. Successfully demonstrates Pope's cultivation of "an aesthetic sensibility of
his own" in the sister arts. The best book on the subject.

1721 Butt, John. "The Inspiration of Pope's Poetry." In ESSAYS ON
THE EIGHTEENTH CENTURY PRESENTED TO DAVID NICHOL
SMITH IN HONOUR OF HIS SEVENTIETH BIRTHDAY. Ed. James
Sutherland and F.P. Wilson. Oxford: Clarendon Press, 1945,
pp. 65-79.

General treatment of the "three inspirations" of Pope's
art--fancy, morality, and literary tradition. See no.
124.

1722 _____. "Pope: The Man and the Poet." In OF BOOKS AND
HUMANKIND. Ed. John Butt. London: Routledge and Kegan
Paul, 1964, pp. 69-79.

Gracefully written general introduction to Pope's fame
and financially successful career as literary artist, stressing the special qualities his personal relationships lent
to the tone of his poetry. See no. 1534.

1723 Callan, Norman. "Pope and the Classics." In ALEXANDER POPE:
WRITERS AND THEIR BACKGROUND. Ed. Peter Dixon. Athens:
Ohio Univ. Press, 1972, pp. 230-49.

Important contribution to the understanding of the impact
of the classics on Pope and the Augustans generally,

explaining that the process of making Virgil and Horace contemporaries, the assumption that they shared the same literary aims, had its pros and cons artistically and from a scholarly viewpoint, but that what matters essentially is recognition of the classical element and its importance for Pope's poetic consciousness. See no. 1530.

1724    Carruth, Hayden. "Three Notes on the Versewriting of Alexander Pope." MICHIGAN QUARTERLY REVIEW, 15 (1976), 371-81.

Interesting account of Pope's usage of apostrophe marks, elision, syllabification, and diction to produce not regularity, but a natural and free line.

1725    Chapin, Chester. "Alexander Pope: Erasmian Catholic." ECS, 6 (1973), 411-30.

Pope's Catholicism was not mere appearance but sincere religious belief expressed in his best poems in accord with the Erasmian principles of faith and charity.

1726    Clark, David Ridgely. "Landscape Painting Effects in Pope's HOMER." JAAC, 22 (1963), 25-28.

Asserts that Pope's interpretation of Homeric pictures links his conception of classical epic with such contemporary landscape painting techniques as coloration, framing of scenes, and use of perspective. See no. 1533.

1727    Clark, Donald B. ALEXANDER POPE. New York: Twayne, 1967.

Organizes his material on the basis of the major divisions of Pope's literary career and identifies the concept of concordia discors as Pope's guiding philosophy and poetic vision from the early affirmative PASTORALS through the late satires and the final disillusioned DUNCIAD.

1728    Cohen, Ralph. "Pope's Meanings and the Strategies of Interpretation." In ENGLISH LITERATURE IN THE AGE OF DISGUISE. Ed. Maximillian E. Novak. Berkeley: Univ. of California Press, 1977, pp. 101-30.

Complex analysis of continuities, change, and interrelation in Pope's verse leading to a comprehensive theory of meaning for all eighteenth-century poetry described as "combinations of parts associatively connected to achieve particularized generic ends."

1729    Cunningham, Joseph S. "Pope, Eliot, and 'The Mind of Europe.'" In THE WASTE LAND IN DIFFERENT VOICES. Ed. A.D. Moody. London: Edward Arnold, 1974, pp. 67-85.

Compares THE WASTE LAND with Pope's DUNCIAD,
marking these two poets' agreement that "Hell has
London landmarks," that in both poems creativity exists
side-by-side with uncreation, and argues that both poems
make us feel what it would be like "to redeem time by re-
deeming the heritage." Judges Pope's transformation of
the language and style of the classics as more inventive
and energetic than Eliot's "calculating creative economy."

1730    Dixon, Peter. "'Talking Upon Paper': Pope and Eighteenth Century
Conversation." ES, 46 (1965), 36-44.

The conversational mode of Pope's verse, with its effects
of raillery, encompasses the sociable tone, the tone of
a man who writes and converses with ease; these are
qualities that in and of themselves condemn the antisocial activities of the pedants, antiquarians, Timons,
and Atossas.

1731    _____. THE WORLD OF POPE'S SATIRES: AN INTRODUCTION
TO THE EPISTLES AND IMITATIONS OF HORACE. London:
Methuen, 1968.

Discusses some of the rhetorical practices of Pope's
Horatian satires as expressive of the social ideals and
moral values of his age, indicating that though he often
voices representative opinions, his oblique and subtle
approach to Augustan commonplaces makes these poems
memorable as art.

1732    Edwards, Thomas R., Jr. THIS DARK ESTATE: A READING OF
POPE. Berkeley: Univ. of California Press, 1963.

Views Pope's poetic art as a dialectic between the actual
world of time and morality and between idealizations of
the imagination and intellect, balanced in the Augustan
poems but under strain and pressure in the "grotesque"
and disillusioned satire of the later period. A lucid and
sensitive analysis of this controlling idea in Pope's poetry.

1733    See no. 1303.

1734    Ehrenpreis, Irvin. "The Style of Sound: The Literary Value of
Pope's Versification." In THE AUGUSTAN MILIEU: ESSAYS PRE-
SENTED TO LOUIS LANDA. Ed. Henry Knight Miller, Eric Rothstein, and G.S. Rousseau. Oxford: Clarendon Press, 1970, pp.
232-46.

Pope's overzealous concern for "local expressiveness"
and sounds which reinforce the sense at the couplet

level often interferes with larger structural patterns and overall coherence. See no. 120.

1735    Erskine-Hill, Howard. "Pope and the Financial Revolution." In ALEXANDER POPE: WRITERS AND THEIR BACKGROUND. Ed. Peter Dixon. Athens: Ohio Univ. Press, 1972, pp. 200-229.

Focusing on the person of Sir John Blunt as representative of the new moneyed interest of finance capitalism, shows how Pope responds to the financial revolution of the 1720s and 1730s and in the art of the EPISTLE TO BATHURST to the ambiguities generated by the clash between moral principle and historical fact. See no. 1530.

1736    Fraser, Donald. "Pope and the Idea of Fame." In ALEXANDER POPE: WRITERS AND THEIR BACKGROUND. Ed. Peter Dixon. Athens: Ohio Univ. Press, 1972, pp. 286-310.

Explores Pope's complex and sensitive treatment of the perennial theme of literary fame in his correspondence and his verse from the early TEMPLE OF FAME (1715) to the late DUNCIAD. See no. 1530.

1737    Fraser, George. "Pope and Homer." In AUGUSTAN WORLDS: ESSAYS IN HONOUR OF A.R. HUMPHREYS. Ed. J.C. Hilson, M.M.B. Jones, and J.R. Watson. Leicester, Engl.: Leicester Univ. Press, 1978, pp. 119-30.

An appreciation of Pope's "idea of Homer," pointing out how he adapts the Homeric sublime to eighteenth-century concerns and topics and how his translation differs from earlier and later versions. See no. 111.

1738    Goldberg, S.L. "Integrity and Life in Pope's Poetry." In STUDIES IN THE EIGHTEENTH CENTURY II: PAPERS PRESENTED AT THE SECOND DAVID NICHOL SMITH MEMORIAL SEMINAR, CANBERRA, 1970. Ed. R.F. Brissenden. Toronto: Univ. of Toronto Press, 1973, pp. 185-207.

Account of Pope's poetic career emphasizing his dramatic, intensely self-conscious sense that "his destiny, his very self, was essentially that of poet and wit" who embodies ideal possibilities but also makes visible "fascinating actuality." See nos. 98 and 1534.

1739    Goldstein, Malcolm. POPE AND THE AUGUSTAN STAGE. Stanford, Calif.: Stanford Univ. Press, 1958.

Excellent study analyzing the general appeal of early eighteenth-century drama to men of taste and cultivation and discussing in particular the influences of the theater as a cultural institution on Pope's art.

1740    Gordon, I.R.F. A PREFACE TO POPE. Preface Books. London: Longman, 1976.

Intended "for those needing modern and authoritative guidance." Organized by topic (e.g., "The Urban and Rural Setting," "Augustan Literary Tenets") and especially good on the complicated network of important literary friends and enemies.

1741    Griffin, Dustin H. ALEXANDER POPE: THE POET IN THE POEMS. Princeton, N.J.: Princeton Univ. Press, 1978.

An interesting revisionist approach to Pope's poetry, aiming "to recover some of the personal energy that invigorates Pope's greatest poems" and showing him sufficiently self-revelatory in his many creations of self for us to construct an accurate picture of his historical reality. Combines biography and close analysis of poems.

1742    Humphreys, Arthur R. "Pope, God, and Man." In ALEXANDER POPE: WRITERS AND THEIR BACKGROUND. Ed. Peter Dixon. Athens: Ohio Univ. Press, 1972, pp. 60–100.

A study in the history-of-ideas tradition which offers a "scheme of dominant conceptions" available in Pope's works and informing his attempts "to define the world picture, and the social picture, of a whole culture in its aspirations, policies, arts, and conduct." See no. 1530.

1743    Hunt, John Dixon. "Emblem and Expressionism in the Eighteenth-Century Landscape Garden." ECS, 4 (1971), 294–317.

Argues persuasively that developments in eighteenth-century landscape gardening parallel certain developments in literary taste, namely, the displacement of emblematic figures and images by expressive modes of language and art.

1744    Jones, John A. "The Analogy of Eighteenth-Century Music and Poetry: Bach and Pope." CentR, 21 (1977), 211–35.

As "our most concrete and patterned musical poet," Pope's notion of sound echoing sense and his couplet rhetoric parallel J.S. Bach's musical word painting and contrapuntal structures—both "representative of the late Baroque sensibility and mind which attempted to achieve unity and

harmony more by variation of similarity and likeness than
by the resolution of difference and contrast."

1745      \_\_\_\_\_. POPE'S COUPLET ART. Athens: Ohio Univ. Press, 1969.

Careful analysis of Pope's prosody that establishes both
the presence of "couplet norms" or recurring syntactical
patterns and larger configurations of couplets dominating
the structure of whole passages and verse paragraphs.

1746   Keener, Frederick M. AN ESSAY ON POPE. New York: Columbia
Univ. Press, 1974.

Articulate questioning of certain excesses in recent Pope
criticism, offering instead a three-part essay on the major
poems, addressing the question of voice and biographical
matters in an attempt to "perceive coherence and development both accessible and engaging in the works and
other records of a poet too easily regardable as wholly
alien from that posterity he so wished to please."

1747   Kelsall, Malcolm. "Augustus and Pope." HLQ, 39 (1976), 117-31.

Argues that Pope's use of such obvious devices as irony
in the satiric portrait of George II in the IMITATIONS
OF HORACE should not divert readers from a certain
skeptical and ambiguous view of Augustus' Rome and
that, furthermore, his close association with Bolingbroke
and with the publication of THE PATRIOT KING suggests
that he did not necessarily want an Augustus but recognized no political alternative was possible.

1748   Kenner, Hugh. "Pope's Reasonable Rhymes." ELH, 41 (1974),
74-88.

An expert discussion of the metaphysics of Pope's rhyming
practices, showing that congruence of sound is a poet's
intuition of order and reason "as old as human record."
See no. 1534.

1749   Kermode, Frank. THE CLASSIC: LITERARY IMAGES OF PERMA-
NENCE AND CHANGE. New York: Viking Press, 1975.

Further explanation of the implications of T.S. Eliot's
thoughts as expressed in his essay "What is a Classic?"
touches on the function of Virgil's imperial theme in
the late seventeenth century and Augustan period and
on Pope's parody of this "antique ideal" in THE DUN-
CIAD.

1750    Knight, Douglas. POPE AND THE HEROIC TRADITION: A CRITICAL
        STUDY OF HIS "ILIAD." New Haven, Conn.: Yale Univ. Press,
        1951.

>    Thinks Pope had an understanding of Homer and an appre-
>    ciation of the heroic tradition as a mediating concept be-
>    tween classical antiquity and his own Augustan age. Pope's
>    HOMER is an "original" poem providing him a system of
>    values, a living heroic style, and an artistic inspiration
>    that both shaped his own poetic career and was in turn
>    shaped by his moral and aesthetic principles.

1751    Knight, G. Wilson. LAUREATE OF PEACE: ON THE GENIUS OF
        ALEXANDER POPE. London: Routledge and Kegan Paul, 1954.

>    Highly impressionistic treatment of Pope's doctrine and
>    diction, of six particular works, and of Byron's remarks
>    praising his poetry as "great literature" that "radiates
>    living meanings" and speaks to us "with a living voice."

1752    Krutch, Joseph Wood. "Pope and Our Contemporaries." In POPE
        AND HIS CONTEMPORARIES: ESSAYS PRESENTED TO GEORGE
        SHERBURN. Ed. James L. Clifford and Louis A. Landa. New York:
        Oxford Univ. Press, 1949, pp. 251-59.

>    Appreciation of Pope's poetic sensibility and genius and
>    discussion of his relevance to modern poetry and criticism.
>    Dated but sensitive. See no. 107.

1753    Leranbaum, Miriam. ALEXANDER POPE'S 'OPUS MAGNUM' 1729-
        1744. Oxford: Clarendon Press, 1977.

>    Comprehensive study of the nature and scope of Pope's
>    projected "opus magnum," his ethic system of which only
>    the preliminary ESSAY ON MAN and what was later to
>    be called the MORAL ESSAYS were completed; also in-
>    vestigates the accretions after 1735 in the DUNCIAD IV
>    and the manuscript plan for BRUTUS.

1754    Lewalski, Barbara K. "On Looking into Pope's Milton." In THE
        PRESENCE OF MILTON. Ed. B. Rajan. MiltonS, 11 (1978), 29-50.

>    Explores the relationship between the two poets to determine
>    what Pope thought of Milton and how stylistically, the-
>    matically, and mythopoeically he uses Milton as well as
>    to suggest in what ways Pope's borrowings and interests
>    may illuminate Milton.

1755    Lonsdale, Roger. "Alexander Pope." In THE HISTORY OF LITERA-
        TURE IN THE ENGLISH LANGUAGE. Vol. 4. Ed. Roger Lonsdale.
        London: Barrie and Jenkins, 1971, pp. 100-143.

A chronological survey of Pope's literary career stressing the discipline of his art as an assertion of the ideals of order, morality, and civilization he saw threatened by materialism, perversions of language, political corruption, and modern duncery. See no. 32A.

1756    MacDonald, William L. POPE AND HIS CRITICS: A STUDY IN EIGHTEENTH CENTURY PERSONALITIES. Seattle: Univ. of Washington Press, 1951.

Investigates the impact of personalities on the criticism of Pope in the eighteenth century and the effects on the critical judgment of those involved. Sections on Owen Ruffhead, Johnson, and Joseph Warton.

1757    Mack, Maynard. THE GARDEN AND THE CITY: RETIREMENT AND POLITICS IN THE LATER POETRY OF POPE. Toronto: Univ. of Toronto Press, 1969.

Skillful blend of biography, intellectual and literary history, and critical analysis showing how his villa and grotto at Twickenham provided Pope a "rallying point for his personal values" and concrete embodiment of a mythopoeic vision. The best book on Pope's later poetry (and perhaps on Pope generally) to date.

1758    _____. "The Muse of Satire." YR, 41 (1951), 80-92.

Highly influential essay distinguishing between the historical Pope and the rhetorical Pope who ordinarily expresses himself in the guise of the naif, vir bonus, and public defender of civilized values. This stress on the rhetorical and fictive quality of satire dominated Pope criticism for more than two decades. See no. 122.

1759    _____. "On Reading Pope." CE, 7 (1946), 263-73.

Seminal essay in the twentieth-century reconsideration of Pope's poetry, focusing on WINDSOR FOREST to demonstrate the complex poetic effects at the couplet level, as well as the larger intimations in Pope of lost Edens and paradises to be regained both artistically and morally.

1760    _____. "'Wit and Poetry and Pope': Some Observations on His Imagery." In POPE AND HIS CONTEMPORARIES: ESSAYS PRESENTED TO GEORGE SHERBURN. Ed. James L. Clifford and Louis A. Landa. New York: Oxford Univ. Press, 1949, pp. 20-40.

Although generated from certain "prose affinities" and relying on "normal and traditional associations," Pope's use of imagery at the couplet level, as well as his irony and allusive and mock-heroic procedures in the poems at large, "obtain the benefits of metaphor without being, in any of the ordinary senses, strikingly metaphoric." An excellent, widely reprinted discussion of Pope's poetic method. See nos. 105 and 107.

1761    MacKillop, I.D. "The Satirist in His Own Person." In THE ART OF ALEXANDER POPE. Ed. Howard Erskine-Hill and Anne Smith. New York: Barnes and Noble, 1979, pp. 157-68.

The practices of Molière and Boileau shed light on similar creative problems Pope faced in the presenting of self in his writings. See no. 1531.

1762    Olson, Elder. "Rhetoric and the Appreciation of Pope." MP, 37 (1939), 13-35.

Famous reading that characterizes Pope as rhetorically professing moral excellence at the same time he establishes himself as a person of such quality to subtly disarm a hostile audience and gain its acceptance of this conception of virtue.

1763    Parkin, Rebecca Price. "Alexander Pope's Use of Biblical and Ecclesiastical Allusions." SVEC, 57 (1967), 1183-1216.

Pope avoided direct use of biblical and religious references and instead approached his subject matter obliquely through a variety of rhetorical devices and strategies, blending Christian and pagan ritual and employing irony and satire through multiple personae.

1764    _____. THE POETIC WORKMANSHIP OF ALEXANDER POPE. Minneapolis: Univ. of Minnesota Press, 1955.

Analysis of rhetorical strategies and practices showing that Pope's poetry has relevance at both the semantic and the technical levels as a reaction against the intellectual, moral, and spiritual disorders of his age.

1765    Paulson, Ronald. "Satire, and Poetry, and Pope." In his ENGLISH SATIRE. Los Angeles: William Andrews Clark Memorial Library, 1972, pp. 55-106.

Analysis of Pope's poetic career, beginning and ending with the fiction of the alienated poet expressing the "discontinuities of the world" and projecting a vision of decline "in the form of something beautiful and lasting which contradicts (or qualifies) the pessimistic conclusion of the vision itself." See no. 1534.

1766    Probyn, Clive T. "Pope's Bestiary: The Iconography of Deviance."
        In THE ART OF ALEXANDER POPE. Ed. Howard Erskine-Hill and
        Anne Smith. New York: Barnes and Noble, 1979, pp. 212-30.

        Discusses Pope's particular shaping of the literary tradition
        that compares man with animals and sees such connections
        as "the nervous system of his ethical concerns," the
        "supreme moral achievement of his imagination." See
        no. 1531.

1767    Reeves, James. THE REPUTATION AND WRITINGS OF ALEXANDER
        POPE. London: Heinemann, 1976.

        A long complaint about the "academic takeover" of Pope,
        whose allusive mode and creation of fictional identities
        make him an attractive target for overzealous annotators
        and scholars. Heavily moralistic and strangely oblivious
        to the possible self-involvement of Pope in the follies he
        often attacks.

1768    Reichard, Hugo M. "Pope's Social Satire: Belles-Lettres and Busi-
        ness." PMLA, 67 (1952), 420-34.

        Exploration of Pope's hostility toward a commercial culture
        where hack, duke, banker, and statesman "all live by the
        same bimetallism of lead and gold, and all thrash about
        in the same darkness and disorder." See no. 1533.

1769    Reverand, Cedric D., II. "Pope and Blackmore: The Not so Nasty
        Wasp of Twit'nam." DUJ, 37 (1975), 55-61.

        Pope's satiric attacks on Blackmore, even after his death,
        would indicate that the hostility was professional rather
        than personal and that Pope was following a well-established
        tradition in attacking this symbol of literary prolixity and
        dullness.

1770    Rogal, Samuel J. "Pope's 'Contribution' to English Hymnody." UNI-
        VERSITY OF DAYTON REVIEW, 10 (1973), 85-97.

        Discusses the editorial alterations and abbreviations
        necessary to fit passages and whole poems of Pope into
        the format of nineteenth- and twentieth-century hymnals
        and also points out certain similarities in phrasing and
        rhyming that would indicate his influence on Charles
        and John Wesley.

1771    Rogers, Pat. AN INTRODUCTION TO POPE. London: Methuen,
        1975. Bibliog.

        Views his book as an "act of sociable courtesy," inviting

his readers to understand and appreciate "the most representative European poet of his age." Literate, insightful, and incorporating recent critical opinions, this discussion goes beyond routine coverage to fully consider
the role of translation, editions, and prose in Pope's
artistic career.

1772       _____. "Pope and the Social Scene." In ALEXANDER POPE:
WRITERS AND THEIR BACKGROUND. Ed. Peter Dixon. Athens:
Ohio Univ. Press, 1972, pp. 101-42.

Though Pope earned a respected position in his society
through poetry accommodated to the social forms and
manners of his age, his Catholicism and deformity made
him an outsider, a threat to society, and therefore a
rebel in the cause. See no. 1530.

1773   Rogers, Robert W. THE MAJOR SATIRES OF ALEXANDER POPE.
Urbana: Univ. of Illinois Press, 1955.

Revaluation of Pope in this century, focusing on the ethical assumptions of the great satires from 1728 to 1744 and
on the manner in which these poems form part of a larger
context of moral and philosophical beliefs.

1774   Root, Robert Kilburn. THE POETICAL CAREER OF ALEXANDER
POPE. Princeton, N.J.: Princeton Univ. Press, 1938.

An early signal of the renewed interest during this century
in Pope's art and the parallel lessening of hostility toward
his personality, his satiric attacks, and the Augustan
poetic sensibility in general.

1775   Rothman, Irving N. "The Quincunx in Pope's Moral Aesthetics."
PQ, 55 (1976), 374-88.

This particular style of planting and arrangement of trees
held considerable importance for Pope, both in his own
gardening efforts and as a symbolic representation in his
poetry of "invention," judgment, taste, and morality
aimed at "a sense of unity and harmony, not division."

1776   Rousseau, George S. "On Reading Pope." In ALEXANDER POPE:
WRITERS AND THEIR BACKGROUND. Ed. Peter Dixon. Athens:
Ohio Univ. Press, 1972, pp. 1-59.

Good introduction to Pope, noticing, among many points,
his intellectual and moral contemporaneity; his unequalled
poetic craftsmanship; his genius that transcends as well as
characterizes his age; and his treatment of the perennial
themes of "virtue, vice, corruption, pride, genuine versus

perfunctory art, freedom, the law"--all of this accomplished with a "poise and subtlety" that is the envy of his readers from Samuel Johnson to Allen Tate. See no. 1530.

1777    Russo, John Paul. ALEXANDER POPE: TRADITION AND IDENTITY. Cambridge, Mass.: Harvard Univ. Press, 1972.

Quasibiographical approach to Pope as man and poet, showing how "tradition served him as a continual and self-renewing source of strength for his progress as an artist."

1778    Sambrook, James. "Pope and the Visual Arts." In ALEXANDER POPE: WRITERS AND THEIR BACKGROUND. Ed. Peter Dixon. Athens: Ohio Univ. Press, 1972, pp. 143-71. Illus.

Discussion of Pope's activities as a painter, his tastes in Continental art, his role in the ut pictura poesis tradition, and his relationship to the Palladian movement and contributions to the running controversy over garden design-- all reflecting a deeply felt belief in the power of art to transform nature. See no. 1530.

1779    Sanders, Charles. "'First Follow NATURE': An Annotation." ES, 49 (1968), 289-302.

This famous injunction represents Pope's own realization of a "Horatian or Roman rhetorical-cautionary tradition," filtered through French and Restoration criticism that produces the neoclassical ideal of balance between reason and imagination, restraint and freedom, judgment and wit.

1780    Sherburn, George. "Pope and 'The Great Shew of Nature.'" In THE SEVENTEENTH CENTURY: STUDIES IN THE HISTORY OF ENGLISH THOUGHT AND LITERATURE FROM BACON TO POPE. Ed. Richard Foster Jones. Stanford, Calif.: Stanford Univ. Press, 1951, pp. 306-15.

Discusses the basic meaning of the term nature in Pope's works and the reverence in which he held this abstract concept of an ordered universe in which man was an integral part of a harmonious whole. See no. 115.

1781    _____. "Pope at Work." In ESSAYS ON THE EIGHTEENTH CENTURY PRESENTED TO DAVID NICHOL SMITH IN HONOUR OF HIS SEVENTIETH BIRTHDAY. Ed. James Sutherland and F.P. Wilson. Oxford: Clarendon Press, 1945, pp. 49-64.

Speculates on Pope's poetic working habits in 1730, and by reference to parts of the ESSAY ON MAN and the

EPISTLES TO SEVERAL PERSONS describes "four stages of mental and manual labor" involved in the creative process: notes, often in prose; composition of verse paragraphs; structuring of fragments; and perfecting and polishing the couplet rhetoric. See no. 124.

1782    Sigworth, Oliver F. "Alexander Pope: Renaissance and Modern Poet." ARIZONA QUARTERLY, 31 (1975), 249-64.

Intended for a general audience, this graceful essay points out that the kind of poetry Pope wrote and his approach to literature and art in general resemble the poets and poetry of the Renaissance and that he is very modern in his alienation from and disgust with contemporary society.

1783    Spacks, Patricia Meyer. AN ARGUMENT OF IMAGES: THE POETRY OF ALEXANDER POPE. Cambridge, Mass.: Harvard Univ. Press, 1971.

Reading of Pope viewing imagery as the force holding in balance the basic opposition in his poems between creative energy and rational control; wit is essentially a controlling force in the early AN ESSAY ON CRITICISM, whereas images of madness discipline the passions themselves in the later DUNCIAD.

1784    _____. "Pope's Satiric Use of Nature." SLitL, 5, ii (1972), 39-52.

Interesting discussion of Pope's satiric use of natural imagery, in both its attractive and ugly aspects, as a form of natural process by which to judge human "modes of action."

1785    Tillotson, Geoffrey. ON THE POETRY OF POPE. 2nd ed. Oxford: Clarendon Press, 1950.

Lucid discussion of Pope's indebtedness to classical literary theory and neoclassical formulations of "correctness." Important early revaluation of Pope.

1786    _____. POPE AND HUMAN NATURE. Oxford: Clarendon Press, 1958.

A comprehensive account of the theme of nature (mankind or human nature) as a philosophical and moral basis for Pope's art.

1787    Van Rennes, Jacob J. BOWLES, BYRON AND THE POPE CONTROVERSY. Amsterdam: H.J. Paris, 1927.

Explores ramifications of this pamphlet war and controversy
carried on in a number of periodicals and sparked by
William Bowles's attack on Pope's moral and poetical
character and Byron's subsequent defense in ENGLISH
BARDS AND SCOTCH REVIEWERS (1809).

1788    Warren, Austin.  ALEXANDER POPE AS CRITIC AND HUMANIST.
Princeton, N.J.:  Princeton Univ. Press, 1929.

Revaluation of Pope and the eighteenth century, treating
major works and criticism in terms of their stated aims
and standards.

1789    _____.  "The Mask of Pope."  SR, 54 (1946), 19-33.

Pope's genius for the burlesque, a kind of mockery that
is in fact "affectionate homage," depends for its effect
on the irrelevancy of the heroic or sublime for the age
and in the process successfully reconciles classicism and
rationalism, the past and present.  See no. 1533.

1790    Warton, Joseph.  ESSAY ON THE GENIUS AND WRITINGS OF
POPE.  1782; Facs. rpt.  4th ed.  2 vols.  New York:  Garland,
1970.

Important (but often misused) critique of Pope's verse,
which allegedly anticipated the romantic disparagement
of Pope's neoclassicism, but actually employs the norms
of neoclassical criticism as a basis of judgment, faulting
Pope for not attempting the most sublime genre in poetry--
the epic.

1791    Williams, Aubrey.  "Submerged Metaphor in Pope."  EIC, 9 (1959),
197-201.

Rejoinder to the argument that Pope's images are "suppressed"
and also a fine discussion of the nature and function of
metaphor in Pope's poetry, demonstrating the care, sensitivity, and artistic control he exhibits in the service of
satire.  See no. 1715.

1792    Williams, Kathleen.  "The Moralized Song:  Some Renaissance Themes
in Pope."  ELH, 41 (1974), 578-601.

Emphasizes Pope's indebtedness in language, line, theme,
and mythic traditions to Renaissance poets, especially
Spenser.

1793    Wimsatt, William K.  "One Relation of Rhyme to Reason."  In THE
VERBAL ICON:  STUDIES IN THE MEANING OF POETRY.  Knoxville:  Univ. of Kentucky Press, 1954, pp. 153-66.

Demonstrates from Pope (among others) how rhyme contributes to poetic structure by imposing "upon the logical
pattern of expressed argument a kind of fixative counter-
pattern of alogical implication." See no. 131.

1794    _____. "Rhetoric and Poems: Alexander Pope." In his THE VERBAL
ICON: STUDIES IN THE MEANING OF POETRY. Knoxville: Univ.
of Kentucky Press, 1954, pp. 169-85.

Discussion of Pope's couplet rhetoric in relation to the
neoclassical theory of "correctness," demonstrating the
infinite suggestiveness and richness of meaning generated
by his practice. See no. 131.

1795    Woodman, Tom. "Pope and the Polite." EIC, 28 (1978), 19-37.

Political and social compromises struck between the old
aristocratic and the new emerging middle class influenced
changing literary tastes and practices of the Restoration
and early eighteenth century and affected Pope's early
polite attitude toward his readers and his later attacks on
society's corruption.

# MATTHEW PRIOR (1664-1721)

## A. MAJOR EDITIONS

1796    POEMS ON SEVERAL OCCASIONS, 1709.    1709; Facs. rpt. Ilkley,
        Yorkshire, Engl.: Scolar Press, 1973.

>       This edition was issued in response to a number of piracies.

1797    POEMS ON SEVERAL OCCASIONS. Ed. Alfred R. Waller. Cam-
        bridge: Cambridge Univ. Press, 1905.

>       Prints the 1718 folio, a subscription edition, and attempts
>       some collation with earlier editions.

1798    DIALOGUES OF THE DEAD AND OTHER WORKS IN PROSE AND
        VERSE. Ed. Alfred R. Waller. Cambridge: Cambridge Univ. Press,
        1907.

>       Prints new poems from the Longleat manuscripts.

1799    THE LITERARY WORKS OF MATTHEW PRIOR.    Ed. H. Bunker Wright
        and Monroe K. Spears. 2 vols. Oxford: Clarendon Press, 1959.

>       Based on collation of all extant manuscripts and early
>       publications.   Includes new materials, excludes previous
>       titles wrongly attributed to Prior, and classifies some as
>       doubtful.   Full commentary carried separately in volume
>       2.   Standard modern edition.   Contains useful list of
>       collected editions.

## B. CORRESPONDENCE

1800    Wright, H. Bunker.    "Matthew Prior and Elizabeth Singer."   PQ,
        24 (1945), 71-82.

>       Examines the nine Prior letters extant and suggests that

the wit and teasing quality displayed could be either "a
disguise for genuine feeling or a mere substitute for it."

## C. BIBLIOGRAPHY AND TEXTUAL STUDIES

1801    Aitken, George A. "Notes on the Bibliography of Matthew Prior."
TRANSACTIONS OF THE BIBLIOGRAPHICAL SOCIETY [London], 14
(1915-17), 39-68.

From contemporary newspaper accounts, discusses the order
of appearance of individual poems as well as monographic
publication and notes Prior's successful career in the
limited arena of light verse.

1802    Ellis, Frank H., and David Foxon. "Prior's SIMILE." PBSA, 57
(1963), 337-39.

The variant "Pindar's," for the "Pindus" of the 1718
edition, in an early printing of the poem shows that
Johnson was correct in observing that Prior, like others
in the early period, was "infatuated" by Pindarism and
that Prior explicitly ridiculed fashionable but inferior
Pindarics.

1803    Godshalk, William Leigh. "Prior's Copy of Spenser's 'Works' (1679)."
PBSA, 61 (1967), 52-55.

Marginalia and underlinings in Prior's copy of Spenser's
WORKS in the Widener Collection at Harvard reveal his
poetic debt to the Elizabethan poet.

1804    Wright, H. Bunker. "Ideal Copy and Authoritative Text: The Problem of Prior's POEMS ON SEVERAL OCCASIONS, 1718." MP, 49
(1952), 234-41.

Prior's careful supervision of the 1718 volume, published
by Tonson and Barber, makes it not only the "perfect
state" of the book from the publisher's viewpoint, but
also the authoritative version textually and the one
representative of his intentions.

## D. BIOGRAPHY

1805    Bickley, Francis. THE LIFE OF MATTHEW PRIOR. London: Sir
Isaac Pitman, 1914.

Popular life in response to the Marquess of Bath correspondence.

1806     Eves, Charles K. MATTHEW PRIOR: POET AND DIPLOMATIST.
         New York: Columbia Univ. Press, 1939. Index.

>    Standard biography, viewing Prior as an accomplished
>    diplomat and talented author of both light and serious
>    verse and prose. Well researched.

## E. CRITICISM

1807     Bronson, Bertrand H. "On Choosing Fit Subjects for Verse; or, Who
         Now Reads Prior?" In his FACETS OF THE ENLIGHTENMENT:
         STUDIES IN ENGLISH LITERATURE AND ITS CONTEXTS. Berkeley:
         Univ. of California Press, 1968, pp. 26-44.

>    Critique of Prior's verse as well as an assessment of his
>    achievement as a minor poet delightfully produced in the
>    form of a witty dialog between Prior the poet and Samuel
>    Johnson the critic. See no. 100.

1808     Ewing, Majl. "Musical Settings of Prior's Lyrics in the Eighteenth
         Century." ELH, 10 (1943), 159-71.

>    In contrast to unaccompanied Elizabethan song sung in
>    parts, Prior's "smoothly and elegantly turned" lyrics
>    had instrumental accompaniment and were intended for
>    professional entertainment; the many settings indicate
>    their popularity in the eighteenth century.

1809     Fellows, Otis. "Prior's 'Pritty Spanish Conceit.'" MLN, 87 (1972),
         3-11.

>    Discussion of this expression, coined by Prior in an un-
>    finished essay, describing the notion that one's mood and
>    intelligence enters through the feet and hence upward
>    through the body, and its application to Prior's satiric
>    vision and skeptical view of all rational systems and
>    metaphysical speculations.

1810     Jack, Ian. "The 'Choice of Life' in Johnson and Matthew Prior."
         JEGP, 49 (1950), 523-30.

>    Both RASSELAS and THE VANITY OF HUMAN WISHES
>    contain evidence that Johnson was deeply impressed by
>    Prior's SOLOMON, despite its faults, and that it
>    flattered his own vision of the human condition and
>    stood squarely in the tradition of Christian pessimism.

1811     Ketton-Cremer, Robert Wyndham. MATTHEW PRIOR (The Rede Lecture,
         1957). Cambridge: Cambridge Univ. Press, 1957.

Appreciation of Prior's diplomatic talents and the curious combination in his poetry of humor, wit, and touch of the wistful and elegiac.

1812   Kline, Richard B. "Tory Prior and Whig Steele: A Measure of Respect." SEL, 9 (1969), 527-37.

Argues that, despite differences in political persuasion, Prior and Steele respected one another's literary talents and professionalism.

1813   Mack, Maynard. "Matthew Prior: Et Multa Prior Arte." SR, 68 (1960), 165-76.

Beneath Prior's playfully comic treatment of human folly and absurdity lies warmth, honesty, and self-knowledge. A brief but superb critique of Prior's strengths and weaknesses as an Augustan.

1814   Spears, Monroe K. "Matthew Prior's Attitude Toward Natural Science." PMLA, 63 (1948), 485-507.

Comprehensive account of Prior's attitudes toward natural science in the context of his skeptical philosophy, his questioning of attempts to reconcile science and religious faith, and his rejection of the materialistic basis of modern science.

1815   _____. "Matthew Prior's Religion." PQ, 27 (1948), 159-80.

Studies the religious problems perplexing Prior throughout his life--the interplay between religious demands and political expediency--and sums up his philosophical position as Anglican Fideism. Concentrates on SOLOMON and PREDESTINATION.

1816   _____. "The Meaning of Matthew Prior's ALMA." ELH, 13 (1946), 266-90.

Answers charges that ALMA has no discernible design by showing that it continually burlesques metaphysical systems at the same time that it represents a coherent expression of the central Pyrrhonist arguments.

1817   _____. "Some Ethical Aspects of Matthew Prior's Poetry." SP, 45 (1948), 606-29.

Lengthy consideration of Prior's verse in light of Pyrrhonistic ethics, concluding that his characteristic pessimism and melancholy are directly related to his temperament and overall intellectual position.

1818    Wright, H. Bunker. "Biographical Allusions in Prior's 'The Mice, a Tale.'" MLN, 53 (1938), 498-501.

> The signature on the epistle is not Prior's, but Matthew Drift's. This fact does not clear up the question of authorship, but it does explain discrepancies between details in the poem and Prior's life.

1819    _____. "Matthew Prior's Cloe and Lisetta." MP, 36 (1938), 9-23.

> New manuscript materials, along with other resources, make more exact the identification and characterization of Anne Durham and Elizabeth Cox, explain their relationship with Prior, and reclarify allusions in his poems.

# ROCHESTER, JOHN WILMOT, 2ND EARL OF (1648-80)

## A. MAJOR EDITIONS

1820    POEMS BY JOHN WILMOT, EARL OF ROCHESTER.  Ed. Vivian
        de Sola Pinto.  London:  Routledge and Kegan Paul, 1953, rev. 1964.

> This edition represents renewed modern interest in Rochester's
> poetic art.

1821    THE COMPLETE POEMS OF JOHN WILMOT, EARL OF ROCHESTER.
        Ed. David M. Vieth.  New Haven, Conn.:  Yale Univ. Press, 1968.
        Bibliog.

> Modern scholarly edition of poems arranged in chronologi-
> cal order and intended for both scholar as well as general
> reader.  Includes a short biography, criticism of the poems,
> helpful critical apparatus, and useful basic bibliography
> of Rochester studies from 1925 to 1967.

1822    ROCHESTER'S "POEMS ON SEVERAL OCCASIONS."  Ed. James
        Thorpe.  Princeton, N.J.:  Princeton Univ. Press, 1950.

> Facsimile of the "Antwerp," the earliest edition (1680)
> of Rochester's poems and a discussion of authorship, early
> texts, and the textual interrelations of the sixty-one
> poems.  Contains some poems not written by Rochester,
> but is nonetheless an essential text in establishing the
> canon.

1823    THE "GYLDENSTOLPE MANUSCRIPT" MISCELLANY OF POEMS BY
        JOHN WILMOT, EARL OF ROCHESTER, AND OTHER RESTORATION
        AUTHORS.  Ed. Bror Danielsson and David M. Vieth.  Stockholm:
        Almquist and Wiksell, 1967.

> Facsimile of manuscript with an excellent introduction,
> notes on authorship, and textual history of this "loose-
> sheet" miscellany.

## B. CORRESPONDENCE

1824    THE ROCHESTER-SAVILE LETTERS, 1671-1680. Ed. John Harold
        Wilson. Columbus: Ohio State Univ. Press, 1941.

> Letters between Rochester and one of his best-known
> and important correspondents.

1825    THE LETTERS OF JOHN WILMOT, EARL OF ROCHESTER. Ed. Jeremy
        Treglown. Oxford: Blackwell, 1980.

> Standard modern edition of the correspondence with some
> undated fragments. Fully annotated and glossed; includes
> letters to Rochester.

## C. BIBLIOGRAPHY, TEXTUAL STUDIES, AND CONCORDANCES

1826    Moehlmann, John F. A CONCORDANCE TO THE COMPLETE POEMS
        OF JOHN WILMOT, EARL OF ROCHESTER. Troy, N.Y.: Whitson,
        1979.

> Keyed to the 1968 Vieth edition, but omits 173 words,
> including "neither," "no," "nor," "not," and some con-
> junctive adverbs. An introduction discusses style in
> general terms.

1827    Todd, William B. "The 1680 Editions of Rochester's POEMS with
        Notes on Earlier Texts." PBSA, 47 (1953), 43-58.

> Argues that more extensive collation, including texts of
> poems antedating a book form of publication, would es-
> tablish the printing of the Pforzheimer copy over that in
> the Huntington. See no. 1833.

1828    Treglown, Jeremy. "The Dating of Rochester's 'Scaen.'" RES, NS
        30 (1979), 434-36.

> Sir Robert Howard's letter to Rochester about the play-
> scene establishes 1676, not 1672 or 1678, as the date
> of the fragment.

1829    Vieth, David M. ATTRIBUTION IN RESTORATION POETRY: A
        STUDY OF ROCHESTER'S "POEMS" OF 1680. New Haven, Conn.:
        Yale Univ. Press, 1963.

> Analysis of Rochester's poems, demonstrating principles
> essential for the establishing of authorship and an authentic
> canon, especially with respect to Restoration poets. An
> important study. See no. 1830.

1830 _____. "Order of Contents as Evidence of Authorship: Rochester's POEMS of 1680." PBSA, 53 (1959), 293-308.

> Important essay in attribution theory, arguing, on the basis of the sixty-one poems of the 1680 edition, that the arrangement of poems in a printed book or in a manuscript may indirectly provide significant evidence of authenticity and of authorship.

1831 _____. "Rochester and the Restoration: An Introductory Note and Bibliography." PLL, 12 (1976), 260-77. Bibliog.

> Excellent survey of trends in Rochester criticism and scholarship, with praise for recent work, a few quarrels with recent studies of the period, and some mild warnings about future directions. A bibliography supplements Vieth's "Rochester Studies 1925-67" and Griffin's list. See nos. 1821 and 1851.

1832 _____. "Rochester's 'Scepter' Lampoon on Charles II." PQ, 37 (1958), 424-32.

> Most editors of Rochester's poems have considered this satire as part of the canon, despite hitherto unreliable evidence; however, numerous early manuscript copies of the poem, fixing its date and circumstances, reliably substantiate Rochester's authorship of "this memorable satiric picture of the complex personality who ruled England during the Restoration."

1833 _____. "The Text of Rochester and the Editions of 1680." PBSA, 50 (1956), 243-63.

> Studies the Yale manuscript and its complex relation to the copy-text of the first edition as a method for determining the disputed question of priority among the ten 1680 editions of Rochester's poems. See no. 1827.

## D. BIOGRAPHY

1834 Greene, Graham. LORD ROCHESTER'S MONKEY: BEING THE LIFE OF JOHN WILMOT, SECOND EARL OF ROCHESTER. New York: Viking, 1974. Illus.

> Written around 1931 in a Victorian atmosphere of suppression, but still relevant as a shrewd appreciation and understanding of Rochester's poetry and character, which are seen as sharing with Donne "something of the same dark concentration, the confusion of love and lust and death and hate."

1835 Pinto, Vivian de Sola. ENTHUSIAST IN WIT: A PORTRAIT OF JOHN WILMOT: EARL OF ROCHESTER, 1647-1680. Lincoln: *Univ. of Nebraska Press, 1962.

    Comprehensive but sometimes untrustworthy biography of Rochester.

1836 Wilson, John Harold. "Rochester, Dryden, and the Rose-Street Affair." RES, 15 (1939), 294-301.

    Examines the value of three items of evidence (a statement by A. Wood and two letters from Rochester to Savile) offered to prove Rochester responsible for the "cudgelling" of Dryden by hired assistants on December 18, 1679, and exonerates Rochester.

## E. CRITICISM

1837 Beal, Peter. "Ben Jonson and Rochester's 'Rodomontade on His Cruel Mistress.'" RES, NS 29 (1978), 320-24.

    An unnoticed version of this poem was published seven years before Rochester was born in the 1640 folio of Jonson's WORKS; moreover, changes and modifications, even though characteristic of Restoration satire against women, seem more the work of a compiler of a miscellany than that of a skillful artist.

1838 Berman, Ronald. "Rochester and the Defeat of the Senses." KR, 26 (1964), 354-68.

    Failure of the senses is Rochester's "great obsession," and if pleasure is the highest good and ultimately that fails too, then philosophy ends and "man is estranged from the only experience he finds meaningful; to be aware of this possibility, in a milieu in which nothing really matters, is to commit an act of morality."

1839 Bruser, Fredelle. "Disproportion: A Study in the Work of John Wilmot, Earl of Rochester." UTQ, 15 (1945-46), 483-96.

    Views Rochester the poet and man as troubled and tormented by doubts, at once the prophet and jester in need of the present, sensuous apprehension of things, yet thoroughly cynical about the enduring nature of worldly pleasure.

1840 Clark, John R. "Satiric Singing: An Example from Rochester." ENGLISH RECORD, 24 (1973), 16-20.

    In the tradition of I.A. Richard's PRACTICAL CRITICISM (1929), discusses uninstructed student responses to "A Song of a Young Lady to Her Ancient Lover," concluding that "con-

tradiction" characterizes the "continuous strategy" of the
poem, which is a "tissue of paradoxes."

1841    Crocker, S.F.  "Rochester's 'Satire Against Mankind': A Study of Certain Aspects of the Background."  WEST VIRGINIA UNIV. STUDIES:
3 PHILOLOGICAL PAPERS  2 (1937), 57-73.

Contends that Boileau's "Satire VIII" is not necessarily the
model for Rochester's poem by thorough examination of the
common stock of antirationalistic pieces and of some verbal
parallels among especially La Rochefoucauld, Montaigne's
APOLOGIE DE RAIMOND SEBOND, and A SATIRE AGAINST
MANKIND.

1842    Davies, Paul C.  "Restoration Liberalism."  EIC, 22 (1972), 226-39;
24 (1974), 213-16.

Argues that the themes of "political stability and reverence
for authority" are missing from most Restoration literature and
that in effect it is actually "subversive," the obvious exception being Dryden.

1843    _____.  "Rochester: Augustan and Explorer."  DUJ, 30 (1969), 59-64.

Rochester anticipates the great Augustans, not in his allegi-
ance to stability and order but in his "skeptical, ironical,
subversive" vision of the world and in his concern with the
exposure of vice and folly rather than with any recommenda-
tion of good sense or virtue.

1844    _____.  "Rochester and Boileau:  A Reconsideration."  CL, 21 (1969),
348-55.

Opposes the view that Montaigne is a major influence on "A
Satyr Against Mankind" and that the content is dissimilar from
Boileau's "Satire VIII" by demonstrating the similarities between
Boileau's and Rochester's handling of their themes and arguing
for the French poet's "discernible influence" and inspiration.

1845    Erskine-Hill, Howard.  "Rochester: Augustan or Explorer?" In RENAIS-
SANCE AND MODERN ESSAYS PRESENTED TO VIVIAN DE S. PINTO
IN CELEBRATION OF HIS SEVENTIETH BIRTHDAY.  Ed. G.R. Hibbard.
London: Routledge and Kegan Paul, 1966, pp. 51-64.

If the choice is between characterizing Rochester as, like
Dryden and Pope, an Augustan, assured of Christian-classical
values, or as an explorer in the realms of skepticism and un-
belief, the second of the two would appear the most accurate
in light of "A Satyr against Mankind."

1846    Fabricant, Carol.  "Rochester's World of Imperfect Enjoyment."  JEGP,
73 (1974), 338-50.

Despite Rochester's fascination with "genitalia of various
sizes and capacities" and his exaltation of the body's
functions, his writings portray the "failure" of sexuality
and picture sensual pleasures in "bleak terms," undermining
his portrayal of the physical ideal and erotic fantasies
with a vision of "impotence and decay."

1847 _____. "The Writer as Hero and Whore: Rochester's LETTER FROM
ARTEMISIA TO CHLOE." ESSAYS IN LITERATURE, 3 (1976), 152–66.

Conveying her observation in ambiguous language reflecting both complicity and detachment makes Artemisia an
attractive, sympathetic figure of imperfect humanity and
"invites comic, aesthetically satisfying awareness rather
than rigid moral censure."

1848 Farley-Hills, David. ROCHESTER'S POETRY. Totowa, N.J.: Row-
man and Littlefield, 1978.

Rochester's "central preoccupation" is to achieve order
in the world through imposition of conventional poetic
forms on essentially disorderly experience. A study
making little use of previous criticism and textual
scholarship.

1849 _____, ed. ROCHESTER: THE CRITICAL HERITAGE. London:
Routledge and Kegan Paul, 1972.

Various comments from 1672 to 1903, many deflected
by noncritical considerations, prejudices, and inadequate
theoretical assumptions, but still valuable as an index to
literary tastes and as a testimony to Rochester's presence
as a man.

1850 Fujimura, Thomas. "Rochester's 'Satyr Against Mankind': An Analysis." SP, 55 (1958), 576–90.

Divides the poem into three parts: the first addressing
questions of epistemology; the second consisting of moral
satire, both sections often paralleling as well as differing
from Hobbes's philosophy; and the epilogue, which reinforces his already-established contempt for human nature.

1851 Griffin, Dustin H. SATIRES AGAINST MAN: THE POEMS OF
ROCHESTER. Berkeley: Univ. of California Press, 1973. Bibliog.

Examination of Rochester's complex and multivoiced poetic
art within the social, intellectual, and literary contexts
of the Restoration period. Excellent critical study.

1852     Johnson, J.W. "Lord Rochester and the Tradition of Cyrenaic Hedonism, 1670-1790." SVEC, 153 (1976), 1151-67.

> Places Rochester's works in the long history of the hedonistic philosophy, indicates that he became disillusioned with sensuality, passing to Epicureanism and deathbed Christianity, and sees these ideas of happiness as holding a fascination for eighteenth-century writers.

1853     Johnson, Joseph A. "'An Allusion to Horace': The Poetics of John Wilmot, Earl of Rochester." DUJ, 35 (1973), 52-59.

> Rochester is an unfairly neglected but serious satirist whose attacks on others were justified and whose moral goal is to "improve by constructive instruction."

1854     Johnson, Ronald W. "Rhetoric and Drama in Rochester's 'Satyr against Reason and Mankind.'" SEL, 15 (1975), 365-73.

> The structure of "Satyr" combines rhetorical and dramatic principles of poetic discourse in a narrator "who elicits our support but figures forth Rochester's satiric aims."

1855     Knight, Charles A. "The Paradox of Reason: Argument in Rochester's SATYR AGAINST MANKIND." MLR, 65 (1970), 254-60.

> Focuses on the tone and rhetorical structure of the poem, remarking on the essential "playfulness" inhering in Rochester's facile manipulation of argumentative method and his paradoxical treatment of reason that produces a shifting satiric perspective and artistic richness.

1856     Love, Harold. "Rochester and the Traditions of Satire." In RESTORATION LITERATURE: CRITICAL APPROACHES. Ed. H. Love. London: Methuen, 1972, pp. 145-75.

> Traces Rochester's development as satirist from early use of the informal lampoon tradition, which is subsequently modified and enriched by interest in character, scene, generalized moralizing, to a final stage in which expression as man and artist of public and collective values replaces the narrow lampoon ethos. See no. 118.

1857     Main, C.F. "The Right Vein of Rochester's SATYR." In ESSAYS IN LITERARY HISTORY PRESENTED TO J.M. FRENCH. Ed. R. Kirk and C.F. Main. New Brunswick, N.J.: Rutgers Univ. Press, 1960.

> Analyzes the poem as a formal verse satire utilizing fictional identities and assumed moral positions for rhetorical effects.

1858    Moore, John. "The Originality of Rochester's SATYR AGAINST MANKIND." PMLA, 58 (1943), 393-401.

> Discusses possible sources and models for Rochester's poem and concludes that he should be accorded "the same degree of eclectic originality" as other writers who absorb ideas from reading and develop them into an original synthesis.

1859    O'Neill, John H. "Rochester's 'Imperfect Enjoyment': 'The True Veine of Satyr' in Sexual Poetry." TSL, 15 (1980), 57-71.

> Contra Swift's contention that "obscene wit" constitutes a disgression "from the central traditions of ancient learning," argues that obscene poetry in the Restoration belongs "to a central literary tradition, that of general satire," and closely reads "The Imperfect Enjoyment" to show its affinity with "The True Veine of Satyre."

1860    Paulson, Kristoffer F. "The Reverend Edward Stillingfleet and the Epilogue to Rochester's A SATYR AGAINST REASON AND MANKIND." PQ, 50 (1971), 657-63.

> A sermon by Stillingfleet preached before Charles II on February 24, 1675, helps to date Rochester's poem; but the much-disputed epilogue is in fact a poetical retort to the sermon, presenting a satirical vignette on the figure of a churchman and, therefore, written at a later date.

1861    See no. 1663.

1862    Paulson, Ronald. "Rochester: The Body Politic and the Body Private." In THE AUTHOR IN HIS WORK: ESSAYS ON A PROBLEM IN CRITICISM. Ed. Louis L. Martz and Aubrey Williams. New Haven, Conn.: Yale Univ. Press, 1978, pp. 103-21.

> Opposes the view of Rochester as a "proto-Augustan" and asserts that sex and obscenity are not only symbols of personal debauchery, but also one half of an analogy Rochester draws between public and private worlds. See no. 119.

1863    Pinto, Vivian de Sola. "John Wilmot, Earl of Rochester, and the Right Veine of Satire." ESSAYS AND STUDIES, NS 6 (1953), 56-70.

> Famous appreciation of Rochester as a poet of realistic satire, whose themes involve the contradictions and ironies of a professedly "rational," "elegant," and "polite" society.

1864 _____. "Rochester and Dryden." RMS, 5 (1961), 29-48.

Contends that the relationship between Dryden and
Rochester is not that of a major to a minor Restoration
poet but that they represent one of an interesting number
of paired writers in literary history, the former an "industrious professional," the latter a "brilliant, dynamic,
aristocratic amateur."

1865 Righter, Anne. "John Wilmot, Earl of Rochester." PBA, 53 (1967),
46-69.

An appreciation of Rochester's poetic art in general terms,
touching on the biographical problems, acknowledging his
paradoxical attitudes, and locating the ironies informing
his best lyrics.

1866 Robinson, K.E. "Rochester and Hobbes and the Irony of A SATYR
AGAINST REASON AND MANKIND." YES, 3 (1973), 108-19.

Argues that critical controversies and interpretations embracing "A Satyr" suggest a complexity that makes the
poem rewarding as art and that Rochester indeed did
accept Hobbes's theory of knowledge, but was disaffected
from certain aspects of the political theory.

1867 Sheehan, David. "The Ironist in Rochester's 'A Letter from Artemisia
in the Town to Chloe in the Country.'" TSL, 15 (1980), 72-83.

Previous readings of the poem fail to recognize the function of Artemisia's "most distinctive characteristic, her
ironic way of viewing the world," a procedure which,
while exposing unsatisfactory views of love, helps to
clarify the satiric intention.

1868 Silverman, Stuart. "Rochester's 'The Maim'd Debauchee': A Poem to
Rival Marvell." EnlE, 3, iii/iv (1972), 208-16.

Closely analyzes the poem as a complexly organized
structure involving such sexual matters as voyeurism and
impotence and finds it superior to poems of Marvell.

1869 _____. "Upon Rochester's 'Upon Nothing.'" EnlE, 2, iii/iv (1971),
190-200.

Curiously rearranges the poem for "textual and expressive"
antiphilosophical consistency in order to reveal Rochester's
wit and power.

1870 Sitter, John E. "Rochester's Reader and the Problem of Satiric
Audience." PLL, 12 (1976), 285-98.

Rochester employs four strategies to resist establishing the satirist's "solidarity with the reader": (1) undermining of familiar normative terms; (2) redefinition of honorific terms; (3) use of obscenity as moral standard; and (4) employing of the "qualified persona" that undermines and subverts all assumed perspectives.

1871    Smith, Harold Wendall.   "'Reason' and Restoration Ethos." SCRUTINY, 18 (1951), 118-36.

General and far-reaching discussion of various attitudes toward and definitions of reason in the Restoration, ranging from abstract intellectualism based on Aristotle, the representation of empiricism of a pristine golden age, to Rochester's conception of right reason.  Also treats Dryden, Butler, Sprat, and Bunyan.

1872    Treglown, Jeremy.   "The Satirical Inversion of Some English Sources in Rochester's Poetry."  RES, NS 24 (1973), 42-48.

An important element in Rochester's poetry is imitation, not just of classical satires but of native English practices, the result of which is "travesty by inversion."

1873    Vieth, David M.   "'Pleased with the Contradiction and the Sin': The Perverse Artistry of Rochester's Lyrics."  TSL, 15 (1980), 35-56.

Analyzes four lyrics of Rochester in the context of his penchant for "open-ended" poetic structures which produce "many-sided awarenesses" of the human situation, a poetic practice as thoroughly modern as it is characteristic of the seventeenth-century approach to the experience of love.

1874    _____.   "Toward an Anti-Aristotelian Poetic:  Rochester's SATYR AGAINST MANKIND and ARTEMISIA TO CHLOE, with Notes on Swift's TALE OF A TUB and GULLIVER'S TRAVELS."  LANGUAGE AND STYLE, 5 (1972), 123-45.

Interesting discussion of Rochester's two poems (with brief glances at Swift) under the rubric of anti-Aristotelian stylistics that deny the artistic unity characterized by beginnings, middles, and endings and also deny poetic autonomy to works that consciously generate amusement, discontinuities, ironies, conflicting norms, depressions, multiple voices, and dramatic speakers.

1875    Weinbrot, Howard D.   "The 'Allusion to Horace': Rochester's Imitative Mode."  SP, 69 (1972), 348-68.

A thoughtful study of Rochester's allusive mode that finds "Allusion to Horace" falling short of the more complex use of allusion in Pope's "To Augustus" because Rochester's stance vis à vis the original is simpler and his use of the resources of the classical mode less fully utilized.

1876 _____. "The Swelling Volume: The Apocalyptic Satire of Rochester's LETTER FROM ARTEMISIA IN THE TOWN TO CHLOE IN THE COUNTRY." SLitI, 5, ii (1972), 19-37.

Views the poem as Rochester's masterpiece, demonstrating his most successful satiric talents and mastery of the most pessimistic, apocalyptic brand of serious contemporary satire.

1877 Wilcoxon, Reba. "Pornography, Obscenity, and Rochester's 'The Imperfect Enjoyment.'" SEL, 15 (1975), 375-90.

Combines studies of the pornography with reference to the classical heritage and contemporary precedent to argue for a complex moral, psychological, and aesthetic context behind the poem.

1878 _____. "The Rhetoric of Sex in Rochester's Burlesque." PLL, 12 (1976), 273-84.

Constantly alternating between two systems of value in his burlesques of popular seventeenth-century forms, Rochester's ambivalent attitudes toward the romantic ideal and sexuality comprise a "reciprocating process" of affirmation and qualification of attitudes.

1879 _____. "Rochester's Philosophical Premises: A Case for Consistency." ECS, 8 (1974-75), 183-201.

The Epicureanism, skepticism, and empiricism characterizing Rochester's thinking reveal "some general premises" underlying his poetry: rejection of Christian orthodoxy; distrust of a priori rationalism; and an ethic based on "pleasure as the summum bonum."

1880 _____. "Rochester's Sexual Politics." STUDIES IN EIGHTEENTH-CENTURY CULTURE, 8 (1979), 137-49.

Incorporating the term sexual politics from recent feminist polemics, argues that Rochester's poetry asserts the ideal of rational and sexual politics by satirizing male or female dominance in love and sex as a means of social or political power.

1881    Wilson, John Harold. "Satiric Elements in Rochester's VALENTINIAN."
        PQ, 16 (1937), 41-48.

> This discussion of the play throws light on Rochester's satiric
> temperament and attitudes toward Charles II and his court,
> both relevant for understanding the poems.

# WILLIAM SHENSTONE (1714-63)

## A. MAJOR EDITIONS

1883    POEMS ON VARIOUS OCCASIONS. Oxford: n.p., 1737.

Contains the early twelve-stanza version of "The School-Mistress."

1884    THE WORKS IN VERSE AND PROSE. Ed. Robert Dodsley. 3 vols. London: J. Dodsley, 1769.

One of a number of collections edited by Shenstone's friend and correspondent. Volume 3 contains some letters.

1885    THE POETICAL WORKS OF WILLIAM SHENSTONE, WITH LIFE, CRITICAL DISSERTATION, AND EXPLANATORY NOTES. Ed. Reverend George Gilfillan. New York: D. Appleton, 1854.

Well-known edition.

1886    THE SCHOOL-MISTRESS, A POEM. 1742; Facs. Oxford: Clarendon Press, 1924.

Runs twenty-eight stanzas and includes an advertisement, index, and the Latin mottoes.

1887    SHENSTONE'S MISCELLANY, 1759-1763. Ed. Ian A. Gordon. Oxford: Clarendon Press, 1952.

Valuable collection (edited from the manuscript for the first time) representing an important but neglected aspect of Shenstone's literary career: his strong desire to be an "arbiter of taste" by gathering together and editing verses by a group of literary friends for the purpose of "illustrating his conception of poetry, with its praise of simplicity, pastoral elegance, and the innocent pleasures of the country life."

# William Shenstone

## B. CORRESPONDENCE

1888     THE LETTERS OF WILLIAM SHENSTONE. Ed. Duncan Mallam. Minneapolis: Univ. of Minnesota Press, 1939.

> Annotated edition of the correspondence with marginal illustrations in pen by Shenstone redrawn for clarity's sake. Complements the Williams edition, both of which were compiled from the same manuscripts and printed sources. See no. 1889.

1889     THE LETTERS OF WILLIAM SHENSTONE. Ed. Marjorie Williams. Oxford: Basil Blackwell, 1939. Appendix.

> Annotated edition with marginal illustrations reproduced from original source. Contains notes and Shenstone's "billets." Complements Mallam edition and derives from the same manuscripts and printed materials. See no. 1888.

1890     Fullington, J.F. "Some Early Versions of William Shenstone's Letters." MP, 29 (1932), 323-34.

> The letters in the volume published by Thomas Hull (1778) are earlier versions of the texts of letters in volume 3 of the WORKS (1769) and in several manuscript collections, and the alterations and revisions reveal the poet's careful attention to the art of letter writing.

1891     See no. 1899.

1892     Lewis, Roy. "William Shenstone and Edward Knight, Some New Letters." MLR, 42 (1947), 422-33.

> Discusses the friendship between Shenstone and the Knight family and their mutual interest in landscape gardening. Prints the nine letters Shenstone wrote to Edward Knight, Jr., between 1755 and 1762.

1893     See no. 1902.

1894     Tierney, James E. "Four New Shenstone Letters." PLL, 11 (1975), 264-78.

> Four new letters, three never before printed and one a manuscript of a much-altered version, provide literary historians with new information and insights as well as corroborating some previously known information about the Shenstone circle.

353

1895 _____. "Two More Shenstone Letters." PLL, 14 (1978), 470-72.

> Prints for the first time letters addressed to John Livie and John Scott Hylton, verifying some facts surrounding Shenstone's relationship with his publisher, Robert Dodsley.

1896 Williams, Marjorie. "William Shenstone, Letter-Writer." RES, 9 (1933), 291-305.

> Finds his correspondence "charming," stylistically elegant, and affectionate, and also a useful vehicle for interpreting the changing aesthetics of gardening reflected by discussions involving his small circle of friends.

## C. BIBLIOGRAPHY AND TEXTUAL STUDIES

1897 Burns, F.D.A. "The First Published Version of Shenstone's 'Pastoral Ballad.'" RES, NS 24 (1973), 182-85.

> This LONDON MAGAZINE printing in 1751 was not submitted or authorized by Shenstone, and his note in POEMS UPON VARIOUS OCCASIONS (1737) makes it clear that he had no role in its publication and also provides evidence for the relationship of this text to other known versions of the poem.

1898 Churchill, Irving L. "Shenstone's Billets." PMLA, 52 (1937), 114-21.

> Lists songs and ballads on which Shenstone comments and which he forwarded to Percy during the preparation of the RELIQUES.

1899 Fullington, J.F. "The Dating of Shenstone's Letters." PMLA, 46 (1931), 1128-36.

> Corrects the dating of twenty-two letters in the Dodsley collection (1769) by examining allusions to topical matters and situations mentioned in letters correctly dated, and thus completes the redating begun by Wells (no. 1905).

1900 Gordon, I.A. "Shenstone's Miscellany." RES, 23 (1947), 43-59.

> Detailed description of the genesis of this unpublished miscellany that helps clear up a number of biobibliographical puzzles in the correspondence and firmly establishes the collection as evidence of the judgments and tastes of this arbiter elegantiarum.

1901     See no. 1906.

1902     Mallam, Duncan. "The Dating of Lady Luxborough's Letters to William Shenstone." PQ, 19 (1940), 139-45.

> Detailed essay devoted to problems of accurately dating the correspondence of Henrietta Knight to Shenstone—a series of letters that provides an illuminating memoir of a relationship throwing light on the "Warwickshire Coterie" and Shenstone's circle of friends at The Leasowes.

1903     Sambrook, A.J. "Another Early Version of Shenstone's PASTORAL BALLAD." RES, NS 18 (1967), 169-73.

> The version published in the LONDON MAGAZINE of December 1751 is the earliest extant printing and possibly the first written.

1904     Smith, David Nichol. "The Early Version of Shenstone's PASTORAL BALLAD." RES, 17 (1941), 47-54.

> Prints the form of the poem surviving in a transcript by Bishop Percy that occupies the two final fly-leaves of the first volume in Percy's copy of the collected edition of Shenstone published in 1764 and notes Percy's claim that his version reflects Shenstone's original "easy un-affected simplicity" which is lost in the "elaborate" revision of 1755.

1905     Wells, J.E. "The Dating of Shenstone's Letters." ANGLIA, 35 (1912), 429-52.

> Points out that Dodsley's dating of Shenstone's correspondence (in volume 3 of WORKS) is often in error and that the ordering and chronology are also suspect; offers some corrections and discussion relating to the task of accurate dating through reference to public events. See no. 1899.

## D. BIOGRAPHY

1906     Hazeltine, Alice Isabel. A STUDY OF WILLIAM SHENSTONE AND OF HIS CRITICS, WITH FIFTEEN OF HIS UNPUBLISHED POEMS AND FIVE OF HIS UNPUBLISHED LATIN INSCRIPTIONS. Menasha: Wis.: George Banta, 1918.

> General treatment of Shenstone the man and his career, inspired by a manuscript containing fifteen unpublished poems and others altered when included in his WORKS.

1907    Hughes, Helen Sard. "Shenstone and the Countess of Hertford."
        PMLA, 46 (1931), 1113-27.

> Traces the connections between Lady Hertford, a lady-
> in-waiting to Queen Caroline, and the nature of her
> friendship with Shenstone that led to the dedication to
> her of his ode on RURAL ELEGANCE to express his
> admiration for her gardens at Percy Lodge.

1908    McKillop, Alan D. "Thomson's Visit to Shenstone." PQ, 23 (1944),
        283-86.

> Shenstone set great store in Thomson's visit, recording
> the fact in numerous places, and he memorialized
> Thomson in a short elegy inscribed on an urn set up in
> Virgil's grove at The Leasowes.

1909    Purkis, E. Monro. WILLIAM SHENSTONE: POET AND LANDSCAPE
        GARDENER. Wolverhampton, Engl.: Whitehead Brothers, 1931.

> Rather maudlin biography at times, but appreciative of
> Shenstone's curious mixture of conventionality, "querulous"
> nature, and "unsatisfying" character representing in the
> Augustan age one of the "almost forgotten springs of the
> romantic revival."

1910    Williams, Marjorie. WILLIAM SHENSTONE: A CHAPTER IN
        EIGHTEENTH-CENTURY TASTE. Birmingham, Engl.: Cornish
        Brothers, 1935.

> Affectionate biography noting Shenstone's personality
> as realized in seemingly inconsequential private amuse-
> ments and activities and viewing his responses to these
> as an index to the tastes and aesthetic principles of
> the period.

1911    _____. WILLIAM SHENSTONE AND HIS FRIENDS. Oxford:
        Oxford Univ. Press, 1933.

> An appreciation of Shenstone's successful achievement
> of the "art of living," and an assessment of the "purity
> of taste" he hoped would become a standard to be
> emulated by the "most refined of his generation."

## E. CRITICISM

1912    Bond, Richmond P. "Shenstone's Heroi-Comical Poem." SP, 28
        (1931), 742-49.

> Although lacking in overall organization, Shenstone's

THE SNUFF-BOX often catches the mild burlesque tone proper for the heroi-comical genre, as well as exhibiting some lines and passages approaching Pope's performance in the genre.

1913    Churchill, Irving L.  "William Shenstone's Share in the Preparation of Percy's RELIQUES."  PMLA, 51 (1936), 960-74.

Gives a comprehensive account of the collaboration of these two writers in order to correct certain misconceptions about the question of indebtedness and extent of the influence, concluding that Shenstone's death before publication of the RELIQUES (1765) brought to an untimely conclusion a long literary friendship and significant editorial collaboration.

1914    Fisher, J.  "Shenstone, Gray, and the 'Moral Elegy.'"  MP, 34 (1937), 273-94.

Well-documented argument for Shenstone's pioneer use of the alternatively rhyming elegiac stanza in the eighteenth century, pointing to the circulation of his ELEGIES in manuscript before the composition of Gray's famous poem.  See no. 1307.

1915    Grammans, Harold W.  "Shenstone's Appreciation of Vergil."  CLASSICAL WEEKLY, 22 (1929), 90-91.

Brings together Shenstone's scattered references to and remarks on Virgil, summarizing that he held the Latin poet in higher repute than Pope.

1916    Hill, Charles J.  "Shenstone and Richard Graves' COLUMELLA."  PMLA, 49 (1934), 566-76.

The character of Columella, portrayed by Graves as a promising but indolent man who fails to realize his potential to benefit society, was created in the image of Shenstone.

1917    Humphreys, Arthur R.  WILLIAM SHENSTONE: AN EIGHTEENTH CENTURY PORTRAIT.  Cambridge: Cambridge Univ. Press, 1937.

Views Shenstone's life and interests as an important index to the literary and social values of English country society with its lovely landscapes, elegant estates, conscious pose of unsophistication, "completeness of spirit," and "unconscious decorum."

1918    Mallam, Duncan.  "Some Inter-Relationships of Shenstone's Essays, Letters, and Poems."  PQ, 28 (1949), 458-64.

The repetition of aesthetic motifs and themes among his
essays, letters, and poems shows Shenstone to be a
conscious artist in his attempts to control his thoughts
and to polish, rephrase, and experiment with language.

1919    Prettyman, Virginia F. "Shenstone's Reading of Spenser." In THE
AGE OF JOHNSON: ESSAYS PRESENTED TO CHAUNCEY BREW-
STER TINKER. Ed. Frederick W. Hilles. New Haven, Conn.:
Yale Univ. Press, 1949, pp. 227-37.

The three surviving versions of "The Schoolmistress" attest
to Shenstone's developing knowledge of and appreciation
for Spenser's "mood and music," while demonstrating his
own particular balance between sentiment and humor.
See no. 109.

1920    Sirén, Osvald. CHINA AND THE GARDENS OF EUROPE IN THE
EIGHTEENTH CENTURY. New York: Ronald Press, 1950. Illus.

Interesting discussion of the Chinese influence on the art
of gardening in England (and elsewhere) during the latter
part of the period with chapters devoted to Pope and the
Burlington circle and to "amateur landscape gardeners
and litteratti," such as Shenstone, showing the connections
between the design of The Leasowes and its gardens and
the pastoral poet of simple elegance.

1921    Street, John. "The Poets and the English Garden." LISTENER, 70
(1963), 503-04.

Although no longer read as a poet, Shenstone is still
famous for his garden at The Leasowes; and his short
essay on the subject not only represented his greatest
achievement, but also influenced late eighteenth- and
nineteenth-century garden designs.

1922    Tillotson, Geoffrey. "William Shenstone." In ESSAYS IN CRITI-
CISM AND RESEARCH. Cambridge: Cambridge Univ. Press, 1942,
pp. 105-10.

Discussion of the combination of artistic gifts that made
Shenstone a product of the mid-eighteenth century and
an important force in guiding that age into the one
which followed.

# CHRISTOPHER SMART (1722-71)

## A. MAJOR EDITIONS

1923    POEMS OF THE LATE CHRISTOPHER SMART. Ed. Christopher Hunter.
        2 vols. Reading, Engl.: Smart and Cowslade, 1791.

        Omits A SONG TO DAVID, but contains a brief un-
        documented life written by Smart's nephew, a sometimes
        perverse and unsympathetic commentator.

1924    THE POETICAL WORKS OF CHRISTOPHER SMART. Ed. Karina
        Williamson. Vol. 1: JUBILATE AGNO. Oxford English Texts
        Series. Oxford: Clarendon Press, 1980.

        First of projected five-volume work to provide a complete
        edition of the poems and verse translations. Texts es-
        tablished by examination of relevant manuscripts and
        printed editions. Introduction and commentary.

1925    THE COLLECTED POEMS OF CHRISTOPHER SMART. Ed. Norman
        Callan. 2 vols. London: Routledge and Kegan Paul, 1949.

        Muses' Library edition omitting translations and operatic
        libretti. Poems grouped under five headings within which
        the order of publication is followed. Some annotation.

1926    POEMS BY CHRISTOPHER SMART. Ed. Robert Brittain. Princeton,
        N.J.: Princeton Univ. Press, 1950.

        Designed to give a fairer representation of Smart's poetic
        achievement by reproducing poems of permanent value.
        Based on editions published in Smart's lifetime with
        variants based on previously reprinted poems. Helpful
        critical commentary included in the notes.

1927    CHRISTOPHER SMART'S VERSE TRANSLATION OF HORACE'S "ODES":
        TEXT AND INTRODUCTION. Ed. Arthur Sherbo. Victoria: English
        Literary Studies, 1979.

>    Convenient printing of these delightful translations accom-
>    panied by a comprehensive introduction explaining Horace's
>    influence on the period in general and on Smart in par-
>    ticular.

1928    HYMNS FOR THE AMUSEMENT OF CHILDREN. Ed. Thomas L.
        Minnick. 1772; Facs. rpt. Menston, Yorkshire, Engl.: Scolar
        Press, 1973.

1929    HYMNS FOR THE AMUSEMENT OF CHILDREN. Oxford: Blackwell
        for the Luttrell Society, 1948.

>    Reproduction of the Bodleian Library copy of the third
>    edition, London, 1775.

1930    "JUBILATE AGNO," RE-EDITED FROM THE ORIGINAL MANUSCRIPT.
        By William H. Bond. Cambridge, Mass.: Harvard Univ. Press, 1954.

>    Rearranges the parts of the poem on the basis of "the
>    secret of its original structure": an adaptation of the
>    antiphonal or responsive character of Hebrew poetry into
>    English, as Smart in all probability intended.

1931    "REJOICE IN THE LAMB": A SONG FROM BEDLAM. Ed. William
        Force Stead. London: Oxford Univ. Press, 1939.

>    First publication of the autograph manuscript, fragments
>    of which are arranged chronologically and accompanied
>    by exhaustive explanatory notes. See no. 1934.

1932    A SONG TO DAVID. Ed. John B. Broadbent. London: Bodley
        Head, Rampant Lions Press, 1960.

>    Convenient printing of poem.

## B. CORRESPONDENCE

1933    Price, Cecil. "Six Letters by Christopher Smart." RES, NS (1957),
        144-48.

>    An account of letters written to Paul Panton, a Flintshire
>    landowner, offering a pathetic picture of Smart's depen-
>    dence on others at the end of his difficult life.

## C. BIBLIOGRAPHY AND TEXTUAL STUDIES

1934    Bond, William H.  "Christopher Smart's JUBILATE AGNO."  HLB,
4 (1950), 39-52.

Description of the Stead manuscript and a tribute to
Stead's rearrangement of materials, as well as a re-
construction from the surviving parts of Smart's holograph
manuscript in order to establish the underlying design of
the poem.  See no. 1931.

1935    Brittain, Robert E.  "Christopher Smart's 'Hymns for the Amusement
of Children.'"  PBSA, 35 (1941), 61-65.

Considers these poems, like much of Smart's later work,
as uneven and often mediocre in quality, but finds flashes
of "graceful simplicity" and an uncanny ability to re-
create a child's experience from the child's point of view.

1936    _____.  "An Early Model for Smart's A SONG TO DAVID."  PMLA,
56 (1941), 165-74.

Argues that BENEDICTE PARAPHRASED (1746) is part of
the Smart canon and establishes that DAVID is not a
product of insanity, but rather a logical development
of Smart's natural talent for the composition of religious
verse.

1937    Gray, George J.  A BIBLIOGRAPHY OF THE WRITINGS OF
CHRISTOPHER SMART WITH BIOGRAPHICAL REFERENCES. TRANS-
ACTIONS OF THE BIBLIOGRAPHICAL SOCIETY [London], 6 (1903),
269-303.

Valuable but incomplete listing.

1938    Macgregor, C.P.  "The Origin and Significance of the 'Let: For'
Couplet in Smart's JUBILATE AGNO."  HLB, 24 (1976), 180-93.

Smart owes his "Let: For" couplet verse form to Hobbes's
description of the kinds of knowledge available to many;
this unique pattern is, thus, more than a technical experiment.

1939    _____.  "A Reconsideration of the Dating of Fragments B1 and B2
of Smart's JUBILATE AGNO."  HLB, 25 (1977), 322-31.

Reopens the question of the dating of these fragments
advanced by Sherbo and suggests that references to the
liturgical calendar in the text provide a strong basis
for dating.  See no. 1942.

1940    Rizzo, Betty W.  "Christopher Smart's 'Chaucerian' Poems."  LIBRARY, 28 (1973), 124-30.

Publishes three "Chaucerian" songs written by Smart in the mid-1740s, which show his already developed technical skill.

1941    Ryskamp, Charles.  "Problems in the Text of Smart."  LIBRARY, 5th ser., 14 (1959), 293-98.

Discusses the "extraordinarily complicated" matter of identifying Smart's poems in magazines and miscellanies, singling out several difficult cases of attribution.

1942    Sherbo, Arthur.  "The Probable Time of Composition of Christopher Smart's SONG TO DAVID, PSALMS, and HYMNS AND SPIRITUAL SONGS."  JEGP, 55 (1956), 41-57.

Argues that the evidence in JUBILATE AGNO and the parallels and verbal echoes within it and with verses of DAVID, the PSALMS, and the HYMNS AND SPIRITUAL SONGS suggest composition during "a somewhat rigidly dated period," not in the sequence traditionally thought. See no. 1939.

1943    Williamson, Karina.  "Another Edition of Smart's HYMNS FOR THE AMUSEMENT OF CHILDREN."  LIBRARY, 5th ser., 10 (1955), 280-82.

An anonymous edition, published in Dublin and standing separate from the London editions by virtue of an extra plate and new appendix, was probably anticipated by only one London edition.

1944    _____.  "Christopher Smart in the Songbooks."  RES, NS 25 (1974), 410-21.

Finds the songbooks, music magazines, and broadsheets of immense importance as evidence of Smart's popularity as an author of light verse, as documentation of textual history, and as an aid to problems of attribution.  Contains a checklist of the earliest publication of Smart's songs and of their publication in books, music magazines, and songsheets.

1945    _____.  "Christopher Smart's Problems of Attribution Reconsidered."  LIBRARY, 28 (1973), 116-23.

Discusses the three main sources of the accepted canon and warns that attribution is an industry "as subject as any to the law of diminishing returns" and that in the case of Smart a skeptical, not sanguine, spirit is now appropriate.

## D. BIOGRAPHY

1946    Ainsworth, Edward G., and Charles E. Noyes. CHRISTOPHER SMART: A BIOGRAPHICAL AND CRITICAL STUDY. Univ. of Missouri Studies, vol. 18, no. 4. Columbia: Univ. of Missouri Press, 1943.

Thorough study, incorporating information based on the records kept during Smart's lifetime, on newspapers, magazines, periodicals, and data from Pembroke College, and on Smart's own writings; intended to set the stage for a serious study of Smart's verse, especially the neglected religious poetry.

1947    Ryskamp, Charles. "Christopher Smart and the Earl of Northumberland." In THE AUGUSTAN MILIEU: ESSAYS PRESENTED TO LOUIS LANDA. Ed. Henry Knight Miller, Eric Rothstein, and G.S. Rousseau. Oxford: Clarendon Press, 1970, pp. 320-32.

Smart was pathetically and ironically caught up in the dilemma faced by writers of the mid-century when the rewards of patronage were few and payments and royalties uncertain, and his relationship with Northumberland illustrates the situation. See no. 120.

## E. CRITICISM

1948    Abbot, Charles David. "Christopher Smart's Madness." PMLA, 45 (1930), 1014-22.

General discussion of the facts as well as legends concerning the period of Smart's madness and confinement, arguing that he remained at home until sometime in 1760, and then was committed soon after until 1762, the funds for his commitment probably having been raised through the charitable acts of such writers as Garrick and Goldsmith during the years 1759-60.

1949    Adams, Francis D. CHRISTOPHER SMART. New York: Twayne, 1974.

Establishes the context in which Smart wrote, considering the influence of his experiences, ideas, and attitudes toward his art; critically evaluates the poetry with special emphasis on the SONG TO DAVID; and concludes that while Smart shares with Blake idealism, imagination, and intellectual integrity, he seems nearer to Cowper, not only in his bouts with madness, but also in his paradoxical freeing of poetic expression from literary artificialities of the period at the same time preserving many neoclassical features.

1950       . "JUBILATE AGNO and the 'Theme of Gratitude.'" PLL, 3 (1967), 195-209.

The poem is really two poems: one a personal and chronologically arranged account of Smart's imprisonment; the other an attempt to "confess" the Lord's presence and "report" his praise, a plan deduced from the "theme of gratitude."

1951       . "The Seven Pillars of Christopher Smart." PLL, 1 (1965), 125-32.

Rather than representing numbers, these Greek symbols are the utterances of David, the speaker in the pillar stanzas; and each is representative of an individual psalm.

1952       . "Wordplay in the D Fragment of JUBILATE AGNO." PQ, 48 (1969), 82-91.

This earlier section of the poem is rich in word play, usually in the form of bilingual Latin-English, Greek-English puns; and this verbal complexity, though erratic, often accounts for the linkage Smart makes between natural objects and proper names.

1953 Binyon, Lawrence. THE CASE OF CHRISTOPHER SMART. London: Oxford Univ. Press, 1934.

Interesting biocritical commentary on the SONG TO DAVID, which judges it, except for an occasional line or stanza, as the only poem of "enduring power" he wrote, ironically enough, during the period he was confined in a madhouse.

1954 Blaydes, Sophia B. CHRISTOPHER SMART AS A POET OF HIS TIME: A RE-APPRAISAL. The Hague: Mouton, 1966.

Gives a biographical and historical survey of Smart's critical reputation, discusses the extent of Smart's conformity with neoclassical poetics, assesses the hostilities created by his religious enthusiasm, and carefully analyzes the major and minor poems, asserting that Smart was not a romantic "precursor," but a product of his own age and "one of literature's few great religious lyricists."

1955   See no. 1389.

1956   Browning, Robert. "Parleyings with Certain People of Importance in their Day." In THE COMPLETE POETICAL WORKS OF BROWNING. Ed. Horace E. Scudder. Boston: Houghton Mifflin, 1895, pp. 959-61.

>    Browning's penchant for the grotesque and bizarre and his obsession with the "mad" creative mind drew him to Smart's life and art. Fascinating study.

1957   Christenson, Allan C. "Liturgical Order in Smart's JUBILATE AGNO: A Study of Fragment C." PLL, 6 (1970), 366-73.

>    Uses musical terminology--counterpoint, melody, and accompaniment--to explain the relationship between the "Let" and "For" sections, concluding that the chronology of the "Let" verses parallels the thematic development of the "For" verses, despite the fact that the fragment is "a completely successful unit" on its own merits.

1958   Davie, Donald. "Christopher Smart: Some Neglected Poems." ECS, 3 (1969), 242-64.

>    General consideration of Smart's lesser-known poems, concluding that whether he writes poems conveying ecstasy and wonder or more mundane verse, he is not preromantic but wholly of the eighteenth century, as HYMNS FOR THE AMUSEMENT OF CHILDREN (1775) can surely attest.

1959   Dearnley, Moira. THE POETRY OF CHRISTOPHER SMART. London: Routledge and Kegan Paul, 1969.

>    Attempts to treat Smart's work as a "coherent whole," focusing on four main poetic categories--the secular poems, the early religious works, the mad poetry, and the religious verse written after madness in the larger context of the literary conventions of the age--in order to determine the relationship between his idiosyncratic features and the conventional bases of the hymn, psalms, and oratorio.

1960   Dennis, Christopher M. "A Structural Conceit in Smart's SONG TO DAVID." RES, NS 29 (1978), 257-66.

>    Clear evidence indicates that Smart's mind worked typologically and that he understood the concept in the widest sense: God is the Creator of all nature, and the world is unified in its obligation to praise God. Thus, the devotional lyricism of his religious poetry reflects

structural regularity, symmetry, harmony, and balance, combining a creative passion and rational order which reenact the action of divine wisdom in the world.

1961    Devlin, Christopher. POOR KIT SMART. Carbondale: Southern Illinois Univ. Press, 1961.

There are three Christopher Smarts: the coffee house habituate who knew and befriended many important literary persons of the day; the creator of a single religious lyric "of surpassing grandeur"; and the compli- cated genius the twentieth century is "trying to discover and reconstruct."

1962    Fitzgerald, Robert P. "The Form of Christopher Smart's JUBILATE AGNO." SEL, 8 (1968), 487-99.

Attention to Smart's literary activity during his confine- ment when he composed JUBILATE AGNO suggests that his rendering of each biblical verse into a metrical stanza in his translation of the Psalms may have dictated the bipartite structure of the "For" and "Let" sections, and suggests two sets of sheets recording both a public and private poem he may later have found unwieldy.

1963    Friedman, John Block. "The Cosmology of Praise: Smart's JUBILATE AGNO." PMLA, 82 (1967), 250-56.

The poem can be seen as a prayer, offering thanksgiving as the Psalmist had done, and as a choral work written to praise God's creation, but it also is a personal glorifi- cation of God and man's part in a new world in which God will be eternally praised.

1964    Greene, Donald. "Smart, Berkeley, the Scientists and the Poets: A Note on Eighteenth-Century Anti-Newtonianism." JHI, 14 (1953), 327-52.

Interesting contribution to the ongoing discussions of the relationships between science and poetry in the eighteenth century, demonstrating that Smart shared, with Berkeley, an appreciation of the physical world as well as of its fancied version and that both men emphasized the con- crete, substantial quality of language.

1965    Hartman, Geoffrey H. "Christopher Smart's MAGNIFICAT: Toward a Theory of Representation." ELH, 41 (1974), 429-54.

Dense and learned analysis of mimesis or artistic represen- tation in Smart as questioning the very validity of the

"visionary language" he employs and the authenticity of
his religious vision.

1966     Havens, Raymond D.  "The Structure of Smart's SONG TO DAVID ."
         RES, 14 (1938), 178–82.

> In addition to other kinds of patterning, the poem is
> constructed throughout in one or another formal patterns,
> and the general divisions are made up of stanzas grouped
> in threes or sevens or their multiples--interestingly enough,
> the mystic numbers.

1967     Hope, Alec D.  "The Apocalypse of Christopher Smart: A Preliminary
         Sketch."  In STUDIES IN THE EIGHTEENTH CENTURY I:  PAPERS
         PRESENTED AT THE DAVID NICHOL SMITH MEMORIAL SEMINAR,
         CANBERRA, 1966.  Ed. R.F. Brissenden.  Toronto:  Univ. of Toronto
         Press, 1968, pp. 269–84.

> Understanding of Smart's conception of the universe
> created by a "musical-artist-Creator" leads to a better
> understanding of his great A SONG TO DAVID, whose
> theme concerns poetry "as a celebration . . . of the
> world by the creation of something that adds to and
> completes the order of nature."  See no. 97.

1968     Kuhn, Albert J.  "Christopher Smart:  The Poet as Patriot of the
         Land."  ELH, 30 (1963), 121–36.

> Smart was obsessed, during the last fifteen years of his
> life, with his self-imposed sense of a "messianic mission,"
> creating the persona of the "patriot par excellence, the
> hero of art and arms who suffers martyrdom in the cause
> of the Lord."

1969     See no. 1328.

1970     Merchant, W. Moelwyn.  "Patterns of Reference in Smart's JUBILATE
         AGNO."  HLB, 14 (1960), 20–26.

> Sees a rich allusiveness and play of wit in the poem as
> indicating Smart's ability to bring together a "remarkable
> body of heterogeneous learning" into a coherent whole,
> despite the fragmentary nature of the poem.

1971     See no. 847.

1972     Parkin, Rebecca Price.  "Christopher Smart's Sacramental Cat."  TSLL,
         11 (1969), 1191–96.

> Argues that in a sense Jeoffry is a "sacramental cat,"

"an outward and visible sign of an inward and spiritual
grace" (BOOK OF COMMON PRAYER), and that Smart
uses small or large, noble or ridiculous, animals as symbols of correspondence between the animal world, the
human world, and the divine.

1973    Parish, Charles. "Christopher Smart's Knowledge of Hebrew." SP,
58 (1961), 516-32.

A preliminary investigation which concludes that some
passages in JUBILATE AGNO would indicate a surprising
familiarity with the language, grammar, and syntax of
Hebrew.

1974    _____. "Christopher Smart's 'Pillars of the Lord.'" MLQ, 24
(1963), 158-63.

The poem is a Heiligedanksgesang (holy song of thanksgiving) and the pillar section a miniature of this "paean
of devotion, sanctification, and consecration," both David
and the singer-poet being truly sanctified by Smart's
creative act.

1975    Rogers, K.M. "The Pillars of the Lord: Some Sources of 'A Song
to David.'" PQ, 40 (1961), 525-34.

Smart's religious views were mostly conventional, and he
utilized the religious, ethical, and mystical wisdom contained in the Old and New Testaments, Talmud, Cabala,
Masonic lore, and classical ethics, giving these influences
"brilliant individual expression."

1976    Saltz, Robert D. "Reason in Madness: Christopher Smart's Poetic
Development." SHR, 4 (1970), 57-68.

General overview of Smart's poetic achievement, finding
"a coherent pattern of growth developing from a conception of the sublime poet as the conveyer of the apocalyptic
vision and manifest in the evolution of a style that was at
once both traditional in its reliance on the trappings of
'sublime' rhetoric and highly personal as a formalized
statement of his emotional experience of the model."

1977    Sherbo, Arthur. "Christopher Smart, Free and Accepted Mason."
JEGP, 54 (1955), 664-69.

Smart's JUBILATE AGNO, rather than his masterpiece
A SONG, affords greater opportunities for discovering
Masonic symbolism, ritual, and history and affirms his
interest in occult literature generally.

1978 _____. "Christopher Smart, Reader of Obituaries." MLN, 71 (1956), 177-82.

Evidence strongly suggests that names in the last section of JUBILATE AGNO are drawn from obituary notices in contemporary newspapers and periodicals, especially the GENTLEMAN'S MAGAZINE.

1979 _____. CHRISTOPHER SMART: SCHOLAR OF THE UNIVERSITY. East Lansing: Michigan State Univ. Press, 1967.

Scholarly biography and sensitive critical evaluation of the poetry, covering all aspects of Smart's life, education, and literary career and noting that the anti-David prejudices contained in contemporary sermons and periodicals influenced the conception and organization of Smart's SONG, a brilliant but "palpably uneven" work.

1980 _____. "Christopher Smart's Knowledge of Occult Literature." JHI, 18 (1957), 233-41.

Challenges those who view Smart as fully conversant with the literature of the occult and suggests that many of his allusions and echoes are not to specific mystical treatises or religio-scientific literature but to contemporary commonplaces of religious imagery.

1981 Side, Karina. "Christopher Smart's Heresy." MLN, 69 (1954), 316-19.

A "curious feature" of Smart's theology--the concept of the tripartite nature of man (mercy, soul, and sense)--helps to interpret A SONG TO DAVID; but this human trichotomy was neither heretical nor a theological aberration peculiar to Smart, as critics have thought.

1982 Sutton, Max Keith. "Smart's 'Compleat Cat.'" CE, 24 (1963), 302-04.

Unlike other eighteenth-century cats, Smart's Jeoffry exists in his own right as an animal at the same time that he carries symbolic significance in the human world, in the cosmic order, and as an aesthetic object.

1983 Walker, Jeanne Murray. "'Jubilate Agno' as Psalm." SEL, 20 (1980), 449-59.

Compares the poem with the structure of the psalms and treats the motif of poet-musician in the figures of David and Smart as representing the artist's "will to order" through an act of the imagination that denies human alienation and redeems time.

1984    Williamson, Karina. "Christopher Smart's HYMNS AND SPIRITUAL SONGS." PQ, 38 (1959), 413-24.

>   The originality of these poems emerges only when considered in relation to the conventions of hymn writing involving arrangements of the texts according to the cycle of the ecclesiastical year.

1985    Wood, Frederick T. "Christopher Smart." ENGLISCHE STUDIEN, 71 (1936), 191-213.

>   General remarks on Smart's achievement, including biographical information and some critical commentary on his religious instincts and imaginative theories.

# JONATHAN SWIFT (1667-1745)

## A. MAJOR EDITIONS

1986    THE POEMS OF JONATHAN SWIFT. Ed. Sir Harold Williams. 2nd
        ed. 3 vols. Oxford: Clarendon Press, 1958.

> First published in 1937; second edition adds new material
> based on discoveries of two autograph manuscripts, con-
> temporary transcripts, and additional biographical and
> bibliographical information that has come to light. Groups
> poems, not by date, but to reflect the major events in
> Swift's life. The standard edition.

1987    SWIFT: POETICAL WORKS. Ed. Herbert Davis. London: Oxford
        Univ. Press, 1967.

> Based on Williams' text, but poems arranged in chronologi-
> cal order according to date of composition with textual
> apparatus excluded. Incorporates into Williams text "the
> variants he records [from] the later corrections of the
> author."

1988    COLLECTED POEMS OF JONATHAN SWIFT. Ed. Joseph Horrell.
        2 vols. Cambridge, Mass.: Harvard Univ. Press, 1958.

> Accepts Williams' determination of the canon, but adds
> "A Description of Mother Ludwell's Cave," rejected in
> the standard edition. Some modernization of accidentals
> and few textual variants and bibliographical matters noted.
> Provides a general introduction to the poems.

## B. CORRESPONDENCE AND JOURNALS

1989    THE CORRESPONDENCE OF JONATHAN SWIFT, D.D. Ed. F.
        Elrington Ball. 6 vols. London: Bell, 1910-14.

Important edition of the letters, although incomplete; remains a source of pertinent comment and the basis for the Williams edition.

1990    THE CORRESPONDENCE OF JONATHAN SWIFT. Ed. Harold Williams. 5 vols. Oxford: Clarendon Press, 1963-65. Index.

Standard edition, superseding all previous collections. Carefully edited and annotated.

1991    Freeman, A. Martin. VANESSA AND HER CORRESPONDENCE WITH JONATHAN SWIFT. Boston: Houghton Mifflin, 1921.

Prints known letters together as a basis for further study of the relationship between Swift and Esther Vanhomrigh.

1992    Smith, David Nichol. LETTERS OF JONATHAN SWIFT TO CHARLES FORD. Oxford: Clarendon Press, 1935.

Fifty-one letters involving Swift and one of his most trusted friends and confidantes not known to earlier editors of the correspondence. Introduction discusses the nature of the relationship.

1993    JONATHAN SWIFT: JOURNAL TO STELLA. Ed. Harold Williams. 2 vols. Oxford: Clarendon Press, 1948.

Intimate glimpse into Swift's life during the Harley ministry in 1710 to 1713, indicating the extent of his involvement in the Tory cause and also revealing his charming, self-effacing, witty, affectionate, and personable side.

## C. BIBLIOGRAPHY, TEXTUAL STUDIES, AND CONCORDANCES

1994    Lamont, Claire. "A Checklist of Critical and Biographical Writings on Jonathan Swift, 1945-65." In FAIR LIBERTY WAS ALL HIS CRY: A TERCENTENARY TRIBUTE TO JONATHAN SWIFT, 1667-1745. Ed. A. Norman Jeffares. London: Macmillan, 1967, pp. 356-91.

Covers publications of this twenty-year period, many of which form the basis of Quintana's accompanying bibliographical essay (no. 2001).

1995    Landa, Louis A., and James E. Tobin, eds. JONATHAN SWIFT: A LIST OF CRITICAL STUDIES PUBLISHED FROM 1895 TO 1945, TO WHICH IS ADDED REMARKS ON SOME SWIFT MANUSCRIPTS IN THE UNITED STATES BY HERBERT DAVIS. New York: Cosmopolitan Science and Art Service Co., 1945.

Unannotated.

1996     Mayhew, George P. "Jonathan Swift's 'On the burning of Whitehall in 1697' Re-examined." HLB, 19 (1971), 399-411.

Argues for the readmission of "On the burning" to the canon, excluded since Scott's edition of 1814, on the evidence that Scott printed the poem from a copy of Swift's manuscript made by Henry Weber before he returned to Ireland where it was destroyed by fire.

1997     _____. RAGE OR RAILLERY: THE SWIFT MANUSCRIPTS AT THE HUNTINGTON LIBRARY. Forward by Herbert Davis. San Marino, Calif.: Huntington Library, 1968.

Valuable account (chapter 5) of Huntington manuscript 81494 containing variant handwritten versions of AN EPISTLE TO A LADY (1733) and satirical passages omitted from ON POETRY: A RAPSODY (1733), two politically oriented poems considered libelous in their time.

1998     _____. "Recent Swift Scholarship." In JONATHAN SWIFT, 1667-1967: A DUBLIN TERCENTENARY TRIBUTE. Ed. Roger McHugh and Philip Edwards. Dublin: Dolmen Press, 1967, pp. 187-97.

Bibliographical essay dealing with the range of critical topics on Swift as well as with the specific controversies (dating from around 1926 to the middle 1960s) surrounding problematical works. See no. 2008.

1999     _____. "Swift's 'On the Day of Judgement' and Theophilus Swift." PQ, 54 (1975), 213-21.

Bibliographical evidence would suggest that the version of the poem published in ST. JAMES'S CHRONICLE, 12 April 1774, and signed "Mercutio" was the work of Theophilus Swift, Deane Swift's son.

2000     Murtuza, Arthur. "Twentieth-Century Critical Response to Swift's 'Scatological' Verse: A Checklist." BB, 30 (1973), 18-19.

Cites many already familiar titles, but includes doctoral dissertations.

2001     Quintana, Ricardo. "A Modest Appraisal: Swift Scholarship and Criticism, 1945-65." In FAIR LIBERTY WAS ALL HIS CRY: A TERCENTENARY TRIBUTE TO JONATHAN SWIFT, 1667-1745. Ed. A. Norman Jeffares. London: Macmillan, 1967, pp. 342-55.

Part 1 consists of a survey of new editions, bibliographically related items, and important scholarly books and criticism; part 2 consists of selective representation of specialized essays on Swift topics. See no. 2007.

2002    Shinagel, Michael, ed. A CONCORDANCE TO THE POEMS OF JONA-
THAN SWIFT. Ithaca, N.Y.: Cornell Univ. Press, 1972.

Based on the 1958 edition of Williams and recording 13,600
word-forms, among them Swift's colloquialisms and archaic
spellings. The index to word frequency indicates not only
the language Swift favored, but more important the appeal of
his poetry to both the intellect and the senses.

2003    Stathis, James J. A BIBLIOGRAPHY OF SWIFT STUDIES, 1945-1965.
Nashville: Vanderbilt Univ. Press, 1967.

Covers the two decades of Swift scholarship after the Landa-
Tobin checklist, recording the acceleration of interest in Swift's
writings and indicating the variety of approaches to his works.
Briefly annotated. See no. 1995.

2004    Teerink, Herman. A BIBLIOGRAPHY OF THE WRITINGS OF JONATHAN
SWIFT. 2nd ed. Rev. by Arthur H. Scouten. Philadelphia: Univ. of
Pennsylvania Press, 1965.

First appeared in 1937. Lists primary and secondary resources
through 1895. An invaluable research source.

2004A   Vieth, David M. SWIFT'S POETRY 1900-1980: AN ANNOTATED BIB-
LIOGRAPHY OF STUDIES. New York: Garland, 1982.

Lists 582 items, with generous annotations.

## D. COLLECTIONS AND FESTSCHRIFTEN

2005    Davis, Herbert. JONATHAN SWIFT: ESSAYS ON HIS SATIRE AND
OTHER STUDIES. New York: Oxford Univ. Press, 1964.

Reprints previously published essays from 1931 to 1962 on
various aspects of Swift's life and works.

2006    Fischer, John Irwin, and Donald C. Mell, Jr., eds. CONTEMPORARY
STUDIES OF SWIFT'S POETRY. Newark: Univ. of Delaware Press,
1981.

The first collection of essays devoted exclusively to Swift's
verse, utilizing biographical, bibliographical, and rhetorical
methods of criticism to show Swift's versatility and seriousness
as a poet.

2007    Jeffares, A. Norman, ed. FAIR LIBERTY WAS ALL HIS CRY: A TERCEN-
TENARY TRIBUTE TO JONATHAN SWIFT, 1667-1745. London: Macmillan, 1967.

Reprints a number of important articles appearing during the
century and also presents several new additions to Swift criticism.

2008    McHugh, Roger, and Philip Edwards, eds.  JONATHAN SWIFT,
        1667-1967:  A DUBLIN TERCENTENARY TRIBUTE.  Dublin: Dolmen
        Press, 1967.

        Eleven essays.

2009    Probyn, Clive T., ed.  THE ART OF JONATHAN SWIFT.  New
        York: Barnes and Noble, 1978.

        Essays devoted to the rhetorical complexity of Swift's
        satires on such topics as the persistent misuses and mis-
        understandings of language.

2010    Rawson, Claude J., ed.  FOCUS:  SWIFT.  London:  Sphere Books,
        1971.

        Essays (some previously published) on Swift the satirist,
        pamphleteer, and poet; Rawson's and Traugott's contribu-
        tions represent important new trends in Swift criticism,
        focusing as they do on Swift's self-involvement in the
        very irrationalities and disorders he satirizes.

2011    Tuveson, Ernest, ed.  SWIFT:  A COLLECTION OF CRITICAL
        ESSAYS.  Englewood Cliffs, N.J.:  Prentice-Hall, 1964.

        Well-known essays, some often reprinted, on all aspects
        of Swift's career and art.  Stresses the prose.

2012    Vickers, Brian, ed.  THE WORLD OF JONATHAN SWIFT: ESSAYS
        FOR THE TERCENTENARY.  Cambridge, Mass.:  Harvard Univ.
        Press, 1968.

        Essays (two previously published) written for the tercente-
        nary year by distinguished Swiftians from both England
        and America.

## E. BIOGRAPHY

2013    Brain, Walter Russell.  "The Illness of Dean Swift."  IRISH JOURNAL
        OF MEDICAL SCIENCE, 6th ser., 320-1 (1952), 337-45.

        The most comprehensive study of Swift's health during
        his last years, laying to rest the charge of insanity in
        the following words:  "It is rather surprising that there
        should have been so much discussion about Swift's sanity,
        since he showed no symptoms suggesting mental deterioration
        until he was over seventy years of age."

2014    Craik, Henry.  THE LIFE OF JONATHAN SWIFT.  2nd ed.  2 vols.
        1894; rpt.  New York: Burt Franklin, 1969.

Among the first critics of the Victorian age to make careful distinctions between Swift and his various personae and to separate his writing from myths about the man.

2015    Ehrenpreis, Irvin. THE PERSONALITY OF JONATHAN SWIFT. Cambridge, Mass.: Harvard Univ. Press, 1958.

A model use of biographical data to illuminate Swift's works, avoiding the earlier tendencies toward sensationalist and bizarre connections between the man and his art.

2016    _____. SWIFT: THE MAN, HIS WORKS, AND THE AGE. 2 vols. to date. Vol. 3, projected. Cambridge, Mass.: Harvard Univ. Press, 1962-- .

Definitive biography of Swift in progress, correcting speculations of the past and furnishing an accurate assessment of England's greatest prose satirist.

2017    Ferguson, Oliver W. JONATHAN SWIFT AND IRELAND. Urbana: Univ. of Illinois Press, 1962.

Basic study of Swift's activities as pamphleteer and propagandist for the cause of Ireland and his emergence as a bona fide Hibernian patriot.

2018    Landa, Louis A. SWIFT AND THE CHURCH OF IRELAND. Oxford: Clarendon Press, 1954.

Thorough study of Swift's many-sided career as priest in the Anglican Church of Ireland, emphasizing the factual details of his ecclesiastical associations and his career as churchman.

2019    Murry, John Middleton. JONATHAN SWIFT: A CRITICAL BIOGRAPHY. London: J. Cape, 1954.

General introduction to Swift's life and works, but marred at times by the failure to recognize Swift's irony and playfulness and by drawing conclusions about the works from overly solemn readings.

2020    Orrery, Lord (John Boyle). REMARKS ON THE LIFE AND WRITINGS OF DR. JONATHAN SWIFT. Dublin: G. Faulkner, 1752.

Swift's first biographer described him as marked by a "moroseness of temper" and made other such unflattering judgments--all of which have subsequently influenced uninformed opinion about Swift.

2021    Rowse, Alfred Leslie. JONATHAN SWIFT. London: Thames and Hudson, 1975.

   Popular biography, marred by many inaccuracies and a number of flip judgments.

2022    Stephen, Leslie. SWIFT. London: Macmillan, 1902.

   An early life by a sensitive critic who recognizes previous interpretive shortcomings, but who is often given to an unexamined acceptance of Swift's misanthropy.

2023    Wilson, T.G. "Swift's Deafness and His Last Illness." IRISH JOURNAL OF MEDICAL SCIENCE, ser. 6, 162 (1939), 241-56.

   A detailed discussion of Swift's bouts with shingles, gout, and thyroid cartilege difficulties during his last years.

## F. CRITICISM

2024    Aden, John M. "Those Gaudy Tulips: Swift's 'Unprintables.'" In QUICK SPRINGS OF SENSE: STUDIES IN THE EIGHTEENTH CENTURY. Ed. Larry S. Champion. Athens: Univ. of Georgia Press, 1974, pp. 15-32.

   Enthusiastic defense of five "scatological" poems as works of art that utilize "disgusting" imagery, juxtapose comic and grotesque scenes, descredit myths or familiar analogies-- all in the service of correcting human perversity, conduct, and morality. See no. 104.

2025    Ball, F. Elrington. SWIFT'S VERSE: AN ESSAY. London: John Murray, 1929.

   An early attempt to establish the canon, discussing the poetry in chronological order and supplying dates of composition and interpretations.

2026    Barnett, Louise K. "Fictive Self-Portraiture in Swift's Poetry." In CONTEMPORARY STUDIES OF SWIFT'S POETRY. Ed. John Irwin Fischer and Donald C. Mell, Jr. Newark: Univ. of Delaware Press, 1981, pp. 101-11.

   Refines the persona approach to Swift by arguing that in the poems "self tends to be its own end rather than a strategy for presenting something else" and that Swift was to become "the monument he himself constructed for posterity--the poetic memorial to self." Sensitive analysis of Swift's self-creation. See no. 2006.

2027 ____. "'Saying the thing that is not': Swift's Metalinguistic Satire." CP, 12, i (1979), 21-27.

Analyzes the satire on the abuse of language in selected poems, concluding that Swift "remains convinced of a primal language integrity" as the vehicle for the realities words stand for.

2027A ____. SWIFT'S POETIC WORLDS. Newark: Univ. of Delaware Press, 1981.

An approach to the verse as structurally and thematically co-herent, involving an ongoing struggle between the shaping power of language and art and chaotic forces, both within Swift and outside in the public world of politics, that threaten to overwhelm poetic design and order.

2028 Bateson, Frederick Wilse. ENGLISH POETRY: A CRITICAL INTRODUC-TION. London: Longmans, Green, 1950.

Provides shrewd insights into Swift's satiric strategies, describ-ing his method as one in which he insinuates himself "into the enemy ranks disguised as a friend, and once he is there to spread all the alarm and despondency he can."

2029 Berwick, Donald M. THE REPUTATION OF JONATHAN SWIFT: 1781-1882. Philadelphia: n.p., 1941. Bibliog.

Analyzes Swift studies during the years his reputation was controversial and the object of much hostility.

2030 Brown, Norman O. "The Excremental Vision." In LIFE AGAINST DEATH: THE PSYCHOANALYTICAL MEANING OF HISTORY. Middle-town, Conn.: Wesleyan Univ. Press, 1959, pp. 179-201.

Despite occasional special pleading, a sound psychoanalytic approach to the scatological poems, distinguished between Swift and his romantics whose sterile fear and denial of the body represents "the universal neurosis of mankind." Best-known Freudian interpretation. See no. 2011.

2031 Bullit, John M. JONATHAN SWIFT AND THE ANATOMY OF SATIRE: A STUDY OF SATIRIC TECHNIQUE. Cambridge: Harvard Univ. Press, 1953.

Touches on the poetry as exemplifying techniques of the kind of satire Swift directs against mechanistic thinking, false appearances, and artifice.

2032 ____. "Swift's 'Rules of Raillery.'" In VEINS OF HUMOR. Ed. Harry Levin. Harvard English Studies, no. 3. Cambridge: Harvard Univ. Press, 1972.

Excellent explanation of Swift's employment of raillery, a

playful form of bantering and ridicule, fashioned out of negative materials but operating as a positive and affectionate
type of humor easily identified and understood by his eighteenth-
century audience.

2033    Carnochan, W.B. "The Consolation of Satire." In THE ART OF JONA-
THAN SWIFT. Ed. Clive T. Probyn. New York: Barnes and Noble,
1978, pp. 19–42.

A brilliantly argued proposition that the very satiric art through
which Swift acknowledges his own folly, ineffectiveness, and
moral impotence provides, through its form, technique and
ironic awareness, the only possible "consolations" against
pain, loss, and the facts of time and morality. Treats a number of poems. See no. 2009.

2034    _____. "The Occasion of Swift's 'Day of Judgement.'" PMLA, 87
(1972), 518–20.

Argues that although there is no evidence Swift was acquainted
with the chiliastic group called the Philadelphia Society, it is
unlikely he missed such "an enthusiastic lot" and that their
mystical and eccentric views about the God of the apocalypse
could well have inspired Swift's denunciation.

2035    Clarke, Austin. "The Poetry of Swift." In JONATHAN SWIFT, 1667–
1967: A DUBLIN TERCENTENARY TRIBUTE. Ed. Roger McHugh and
Philip Edwards. Dublin: Dolmen Press, 1967, pp. 94–115.

An appreciation of the range of feeling and poetic inventiveness of Swift's verse, pointing out that in temperament and
style he seems close to the seventeenth-century tradition of
English poetry. See no. 2008.

2036    Davis, Herbert. "Alecto's Whip." REL, 3 (1962), 7–17.

Views Swift, in his poetry and prose, as a moralist whose lash
is meant to heal not hurt. Treats passages from early and late
poems.

2037    _____. "A Modest Defence of THE LADY'S DRESSING ROOM." In
RESTORATION AND EIGHTEENTH-CENTURY LITERATURE: ESSAYS IN
HONOR OF ALAN DUGALD McKILLOP. Ed. Carroll Camden. Chicago:
Univ. of Chicago Press, 1963, pp. 39–48.

Fascinating account of Pope's witty and ingenious reply to
criticisms of Swift's scatological poem, arguing that both poets
viewed such verse as satire of human pride in the humanistic
moral tradition. See no. 103.

2038    _____. "Swift's View of Poetry." In his JONATHAN SWIFT: ESSAYS
ON HIS SATIRE AND OTHER STUDIES. New York: Oxford Univ. Press,

1964, pp. 163-98.

> An early appraisal of the verse (1931) as an "extreme example"
> of the reaction against the heroic or romantic view of the nature
> and function of poetry. Sets the stage for later antipoetic crit-
> icism. See no. 2005.

2039    Donoghue, Denis. JONATHAN SWIFT: A CRITICAL INTRODUCTION.
Cambridge: Cambridge Univ. Press, 1969.

> Balanced account of Swift's work, noting that irony is not al-
> ways the key to understanding his meaning and that for all his
> modernism he was a man of his age. Chapter on the poem ack-
> nowledges their range of feeling and technique, but insists
> on their essentially light and comic quality.

2039A   Elliott, Robert C. "Jonathan Swift: The Presentation of Self in Doggerel
Rhyme." In THE POETRY OF JONATHAN SWIFT. Los Angeles, Calif.:
William Andrews Clark Memorial Library, 1981, pp. 3-23.

> Discusses the various levels of involvement in Swift's use of
> himself in the poetry, concluding that all of Swift's selves are
> imaginatively "true," but that "some are truer than others."

2040    England, A.B. ENERGY AND ORDER IN THE POETRY OF SWIFT. Lewisburg, Pa.: Bucknell Univ. Press, 1980.

> Studies the various ways in which Swift's verse departs from the
> orderly forms of poetic discourse traditionally called Augustan
> and analyzes subversive tendencies and disconcerting stresses
> manifest in Swift's verbal configurations and alignments.

2041    _____. "Rhetorical Order and Emotional Turbulence in 'Cadenus and
Vanessa.'" PLL, 14 (1978), 116-23.

> Argues that the fruitless and protracted debate between the
> characters reveals the inadequacies of pure rationality as a
> means for ordering and containing the experiential world of
> passion and impulse. See no. 2006.

2042    _____. "The Subversion of Logic in Some Poems by Swift." SEL, 15
(1975), 409-18.

> "The Description of a Salamander," "The Fable of Midas," and
> "The Virtues of Sid Hamet the Magician's Rod" exemplify
> Swift's characteristic "disrespect for rigid argumentative pro-
> cedures" and ridicule of traditional methods of formal logic.

2043    _____. "World Without Order: Some Thoughts on the Poetry of Swift."
EIC, 16 (1966), 32-43.

> Treating a number of familiar poems, shows that Swift's or-

ganization of poetic materials would suggest that his "hold on
the Popean ideal of a simplifying 'Order' was less than confi-
dent" and that his poems dramatize this satiric apprehension
of disunity, which extends from metrics to use of allusion.

2044    Fabricant, Carole. "The Garden as City: Swift's Landscape of Alienation." ELH, 42 (1975), 531-55.

Like Pope's villa and grotto at Twickenham, the "physical details" of Swift's environment--namely, the landscape, houses,
and estates of friends--provide thematic focus and carry symbolic meaning; but unlike Pope's vision of an "edenic and
civilized" community of friends, Swift's countryside is "an
extended wasteland" destroyed by corrupt materialists.

2045    Fischer, John Irwin. "Apparent Contraries: A Reading of Swift's
'A Description of a City Shower.'" TSL, 19 (1974), 21-34.

Excellent reconciliation of the cheerful (Ehrenpreis) and
dark (O Hehir) interpretations of "A City Shower" showing
that both views are valid and focused by Swift's "vibrant
consciousness" of both the pain and joy constituting life's
paradoxes and contradictions.

2046    _____. "The Dean CONTRA Heathens: Swift's THE DAY OF
JUDGEMENT." RLV, 43 (1977), 592-97.

Considers the particular occasion and specific targets of
the satire together with the poem's universal meaning,
concluding that Jove's condemnation does not represent
Swift's real sentiments but rather reflects his belief that
such hatred was a reflection of pride potentially redeem-
able through the kinds of poetic strategies employed in
the poem.

2047    _____. "Faith, Hope, and Charity in Swift's Poems to Stella."
PLL, 14 (1978), 123-29.

Examines these poems as Christian verse inculcating in Stella
these three theological virtues, the most important and poig-
nant being charity, involving the final offer to her of his life
and the request for her forgiveness in return. See no. 2006.

2048    _____. "How to Die: VERSES ON THE DEATH OF DR. SWIFT."
RES, NS 21 (1970), 422-41.

Drawing on biblical sources and the BOOK OF COMMON
PRAYER, argues that Swift structures his poem in the form
of a seventeenth-century meditation on death and, unlike
his "friends," is thus able to discover self-understanding,
leading to a final transformation of his self-interest into
a positive good through faith, hope, and charity.

Jonathan Swift

2049    _____. ON SWIFT'S POETRY. Gainesville: Univ. Presses of
Florida, 1978.

> Penetrating study of selected poems from the early and
> middle periods and of the Stella poems, VERSES, and
> ON POETRY as occasions for Swift "to judge and laugh,
> judge and hope, judge and trust, and in brief to judge
> himself."

2050    _____. "The Uses of Virtue: Swift's Last Poem to Stella." In
ESSAYS IN HONOR OF ESMOND LINWORTH MARILLA. Ed.
Thomas Austin Kirby and William John Olive. Baton Rouge:
Louisiana State Univ. Press, 1970, pp. 201-09.

> "Stella's Birth-Day, 1726/27" reflects Swift's belief that
> virtue is both its own reward and a means to salvation
> and that by offering himself as an object of pity he
> provides Stella with an occasion for and a model of the
> "earthly efficacy of human virtue."

2051    Fricke, Donna G. "Jonathan Swift's Early Odes and the Conversion
to Satire." EnlE, 5, ii (1974), 3-17.

> Steers between the two critical extremes that write off
> Swift's early poems as artistic failures or view them as
> skillfully controlled mock-panegyrics and views them
> instead as qualified successes.

2052    _____. "Swift and the Tradition of Informal Satiric Poetry." In
CONTEMPORARY STUDIES OF SWIFT'S POETRY. Ed. John Irwin
Fischer and Donald C. Mell, Jr. Newark: Univ. of Delaware
Press, 1981, pp. 36-45.

> Treats Swift's verse against the background and tradition
> of English colloquial satire and sees it as reviving some
> medieval satiric practices. See no. 2006.

2053    Gilbert, Jack G. JONATHAN SWIFT: ROMANTIC AND CYNIC
MORALIST. Austin: Univ. of Texas Press, 1966.

> Discussion of the complex body of Swift's ethical opinions
> as the basis for his satire. Touches on the poems.

2054    Gilmore, Thomas B., Jr. "The Comedy of Swift's Scatological
Poems." PMLA, 91 (1976).

> Argues that in these five poems Swift may be satirizing
> those who would ignore or deny the need to evacuate,
> but at the same time his willingness to treat such denials
> with playful self-mockery, tolerance, and ultimately the
> good sense that is the hallmark of the comic vision.

2055 _____. "Freud, Swift, and Narcissism: A Psychological Reading of 'Strephon and Chloe.'" In CONTEMPORARY STUDIES OF SWIFT'S POETRY. Ed. John Irwin Fischer and Donald C. Mell, Jr. Newark: Univ. of Delaware Press, 1981, pp. 159-68.

> Thoughtful addition to the growing number of psychological readings of this difficult poem, contending that, like Freud, Swift understood the need to make moral choices and "civilizing renunciations" in regard to sociosexual relationships. A longer, more comprehensive version of an earlier essay entitled "Freud and Swift: A Psychological Reading of STREPHON AND CHLOE." (PLL, 14 [1978], 147-51). See no. 2006.

2056 Goldgar, Bertrand A. THE CURSE OF PARTY: SWIFT'S RELATIONS WITH ADDISON AND STEELE. Lincoln: Univ. of Nebraska Press, 1961.

> Thorough examination of the personal, political, and literary relations of these three writers, setting forth the facts about their friendships and disagreements against the background of party controversy, political journalism, and propaganda during the last six years of Queen Anne's reign.

2057 Greenacre, Phyllis. SWIFT AND CARROLL: A PSYCHOANALYTIC STUDY OF TWO LIVES. New York: International Universities Press, 1955.

> A distorted Freudian approach to Swift, identifying numerous signs of coprophilia, masturbation fantasies, a homosexuality associated with childhood and his substitute father (Sir William Temple), and hidden transvestite tendencies in his role as Anglican priest.

2058 Greene, Donald. "On Swift's 'Scatological Poems.'" SR, 75 (1967), 672-89.

> Psychoanalytic and/or Freudian readings of the scatological poems ignore Swift's "perfectly orthodox" Christian message exposing an idealized and romanticized vision of the world and condemning the arrogance or pride that fails to acknowledge the imperfect nature of things.

2059 Halsband, Robert. "'The Lady's Dressing-Room' Explicated by a Contemporary." In THE AUGUSTAN MILIEU: ESSAYS PRESENTED TO LOUIS LANDA. Ed. Henry Knight Miller, Eric Rothstein, and G.S. Rousseau. Oxford: Clarendon Press, 1970, pp. 225-31.

> Discusses three replies to Swift's famous scatological poem as indication of its contemporary reception, quoting verses

by Lady Mary Wortley Montagu that employ coarse diction and crude figures to attack the same in Swift. See no. 120.

2060    Harris, Kathryn Montgomery. "'Occasions So Few': Satire as a Strategy of Praise in Swift's Early Odes." MLQ, 31 (1970), 22-37.

Swift's employment of praise and blame in these six early odes signals rhetorical strategies and moral positions characteristic of his mature writing; but their failure as poems suggests Swift's awareness of the need for a new kind of poetic form to keep alive "the Christian humanist heritage."

2061    Hill, Geoffrey. "Jonathan Swift: The Poetry of 'Reaction.'" In THE WORLD OF JONATHAN SWIFT: ESSAYS FOR THE TERCEN-TENARY. Ed. Brian Vickers. Cambridge, Mass.: Harvard Univ. Press, 1968, pp. 195-212.

Surveys themes and attitudes expressed in a wide range of poems, explaining the ways Swift's language and art "transfigure" by sheer creative energy the moral orderings of acceptance and rejection, compassion and anger. See no. 2012.

2062    Horne, Colin J. "'From a Fable form a Truth': A Consideration of the Fable in Swift's Poetry." In STUDIES IN THE EIGHTEENTH CENTURY I: PAPERS PRESENTED AT THE DAVID NICHOL SMITH MEMORIAL SEMINAR, CANBERRA, 1966. Ed. R.F. Brissenden. Toronto: Univ. of Toronto Press, 1968, pp. 193-204.

Rather than consistently mocking the entertaining and instructive features of fable, Swift employs the figure of Aesop in both positive and negative ways, depending on whether the story confirms his view of human pride or falsely compliments human nature. See no. 97.

2063    _____. "Swift's Comic Poetry." In AUGUSTAN WORLDS: ESSAYS IN HONOUR OF A.R. HUMPHREYS. Ed. J.C. Hilson, M.M.B. Jones, and J.R. Watson. Leicester, Engl.: Leicester Univ. Press, 1978, pp. 51-67.

Deplores the tendencies to over-solemnize Swift's temperament and emphasizes his jocular nature, affection for others, and sense of humor, especially manifest in the social verse where "exploitation of comic effects lurking in analogies is akin to the metaphysical conceit, here converted to a comic role." See no. 111.

2064    Hunting, Robert. JONATHAN SWIFT. New York: Twayne, 1967.

Chapter on the poetry refers to the variety of tones,
stances, and satiric methods present in Swift's verse,
but concentrates its analysis on well-known, anthologized
selections.

2065    Irwin, W.R.  "Swift the Verse Man."  PQ, 54 (1975), 222-38.

Describes the art of Swift's light verse as characterized
by word games, obtrusive rhymes, odd diction, and
idiosyncratic prosody, but at the same time achieving
unity of purpose and method through the "pretended detachment of the performer from the performance" and
satiric force through adaptation of the "willful posture
of an observer, refusing to be involved."

2066    Jaffe, Nora Crow.  THE POET SWIFT.  Hanover: Univ. Press of
New England, 1977.

Claims that traditional approaches to Augustan poetry
often do not adequately explain the charm, craft, and
power of Swift's verse and instead attempts to establish
a more reliable critical framework and critical vocabulary to describe his considerable poetic achievement.

2067    _____.  "Swift and the 'agreeable young Lady, but extremely lean.'"
PLL, 14 (1978), 129-37.

Points out that "Death and Daphne" (1730) was an occasional poem written to entertain the Achesons, but also
demonstrates Swift's expert incorporation into the poem's
texture of several mythologies to shape the autobiographi-
cal content and define his relationships with Lady Acheson.
See no. 2006.

2068    Jefferson, D.W.  "The Poetry of Age."  In FOCUS: SWIFT.  Ed.
Claude J. Rawson.  London: Sphere Books, 1971, pp. 121-37.

Generalized account of Swift's poetic career, noting
his adaptation of classical models and myths, his social
realism and brutal frankness about man's physical nature,
and the personal element and overt didacticism in poems
of the 1730s; but also emphasizing his "agility" and "inventiveness" and the playfulness and generosity of
spirit of the verse addressed to his Irish friends.  See
no. 2010.

2069    Johnson, Maurice.  THE SIN OF WIT: JONATHAN SWIFT AS A
POET.  Syracuse, N.Y.: Syracuse Univ. Press, 1950.  Appendix.

An important pioneering study of Swift's verse, demonstrating the satirical art characterizing his mocking, humorous, burlesquing, and ironic antipoetry. An appendix suggestively links Swiftian poetic procedures to such moderns as Eliot, Hardy, Joyce, and Yeats.

2070        . "Swift's Poetry Reconsidered." In ENGLISH WRITERS OF THE EIGHTEENTH CENTURY. Ed. John H. Middendorf. New York: Columbia Univ. Press, 1971, pp. 233-48.

Emphasis on the "biographical presence" and impact of events informing the verse represents an interesting shift away from the familiar rhetorical approach to the Augustans in general and Swift in particular, especially by the critic who originally championed it, especially in the case of Swift. Signals a new biographical emphasis.

2071        . "Text and Possible Occasion for Swift's 'Day of Judgement.'" PMLA, 86 (1971), 210-16.

Skillfully uses bibliographical data to argue that the poem was written in 1732 or 1733 as a response to a new attempt by nonconformists to repeal the Sacramental Test Act and that it also resembles many serious eighteenth-century millenialist poems. Shows the crucial nature of bibliographical data in determining Swift's intentions.

2072    Johnston, Oswald. "Swift and the Common Reader." In IN DEFENSE OF READING. Ed. Reuben A. Brower and Richard Poirier. New York: E.P. Dutton, 1963, pp. 174-90.

Approaches Swift's verse (in contrast to Pope's) as antipoetic, playing "some kind of practical joke on poetic language" and thus distrusting the grander and solemn pretensions of poetry and ultimately of language itself as a vehicle for expressing moral value.

2073    Jones, Gareth. "Swift's CADENUS AND VANESSA: A Question of 'Positives.'" EIC, 20 (October 1970), 424-40.

Argues that this poem (and much of Swift's best verse) is "a masterpiece of satiric counterpointing" in which "positives" are wholly relative, "requiring us to be critically aware of our certainties, our habits of response."

2074    Kulisheck, Clarence L. "Swift's Octosyllabics and the Hudibrastic Tradition." JEGP, 53 (1954), 361-68.

Explores what Swift owes to the tradition of popular verse satire in England and demonstrates the flexibility and adaptability of the octosyllabic couplet to Swift's comic as well as serious tones.

2075    Landa, Louis A. "Jonathan Swift: The Critical Significance of Biographical Evidence." In ENGLISH INSTITUTE ESSAYS, 1946. Ed. James L. Clifford, Rudolf Kirk, and David Allan Robertson, Jr. New York: Columbia Univ. Press, 1947, pp. 20-40.

    Important attempt to responsibly consider Swift's biography as a crucial factor in the understanding of his artistic intentions, concluding that traditional Christian apologetics influenced much of his writing.

2076    Lawrence, D.H. "The Private Printed Edition of PANSIES." In PHOENIX: THE POSTHUMOUS PAPERS OF D.H. LAWRENCE. Ed. Edward D. McDonald. Harmondsworth, Middlesex, Engl.: Penguin Books, 1936, pp. 279-82.

    Includes a number of trenchant remarks about scatology in Swift's "Celia" poems, asserting that the fact of defecation did not trouble Swift but rather the thought.

2077    Leavis, F.R. "The Irony of Swift." In DETERMINATIONS. Ed. F.R. Leavis. London: Chatto and Windus, 1934, pp. 79-108.

    Widely reprinted essay on the satire (especially the prose), arguing for the essentially "negative" and "destructive" force of Swift's "ironic intensities." One of the two or three most influential viewpoints of this century, providing the underpinning for many recent critical studies. See nos. 2007 and 2011.

2078    Lee, Jae Num. SWIFT AND SCATOLOGICAL SATIRE. Albuquerque: Univ. of New Mexico Press, 1971.

    Focuses on Swift's use of scatology as a literary device in the context of its traditions and antecedents, ranging from Aristophanes and Martial to Catullus and Rabelais, and in terms of its success or failure as an instrument of satire and humor.

2079    Mell, Donald C., Jr. "Elegiac Design and Satiric Intention in VERSES ON THE DEATH OF DR. SWIFT." CP, 6, ii (1973), 15-24.

    The "elegiac sentiments" expressed in the poem are treated ironically and the fashionable pieties satirized, but only to affirm indirectly the ideal of art as a defense against time and the value of poetry as a vehicle of truth.

2080    _____. "Imagination and Satiric Mimesis in Swift's Poetry: An Exploratory Discussion." In CONTEMPORARY STUDIES OF SWIFT'S

POETRY. Ed. John Irwin Fischer and Donald C. Mell, Jr. Newark: Univ. of Delaware Press, 1981, pp. 123-35.

> Places Swift's verse alongside the tradition of mimetic literature and demonstrates by analysis of the ironies and deliberate artifice of "On Poetry: A Rapsody" Swift's "awareness of the capacities and limitations of the satiric imagination to render moral truths and aesthetic ideals." See no. 2006.

2081    Nussbaum, Felicity. "Juvenal, Swift and THE FOLLY OF LOVE." ECS, 9 (1976), 540-52.

> Explores the traditions of satires directed against women (beginning with Ovid and Juvenal) and generalizes about the resulting "context of commonplaces and set scenes" that help in understanding Swift's "boudoir" poems.

2082    O Hehir, Brendan. "Meaning in Swift's 'Description of a City Shower.'" ELH, 27 (1960), 194-207.

> Points out the classical allusions and models behind Swift's mock-georgic exercise and concludes that references to destructive storms and floods amount to "an oblique denunciation of cathartic doom upon the corruption of the city."

2083    Ohlin, Peter. "'Cadenus and Vanessa': Reason and Passion." SEL, 4 (1964), 485-96.

> Swift utilizes the form of a dialog between the principles of reason and passion as a controlling poetic device to mock romantic love.

2084    Parkin, Rebecca Price. "Swift's BAUCIS AND PHILEMON: A Sermon in the Burlesque Mode." SNL, 7 (1970), 109-14.

> Using as a frame the burlesque form of a saint's legend, Swift inveighs against imprudent hospitality, superstition, naive acceptance of external signs as proof of God's grace, and the low estimate of priests, saints, and "parson's-wife-hood."

2085    Paulson, Ronald. "Swift, Stella, and Permanence." ELH, 27 (1960), 298-314.

> In his early poems, Swift's persona was conventionally Augustan, but in the later poems it moves toward the autonomy of symbol with the satirist as Everyman; and this progression reveals Swift's tendency toward the self-dramatization of the romantics, a direct result of his

perception of the incompatibility of flesh and spirit, a
theme running through all his work.

2086    Peake, Charles. "Swift's 'Satirical Elegy on a Late Famous General.'"
REL, 3, iii (1962), 80-89.

Views the poem as exhibiting the wit, emotional impact,
unified imagery, controlled dictum, and tight logical
structure worthy of a great poet.

2087    Price, Martin. SWIFT'S RHETORICAL ART: A STUDY IN STRUCTURE
AND MEANING. New Haven, Conn.: Yale Univ. Press, 1953.

Some helpful comments on Swift's use of "witty extravagance" and comic incongruities in his poems.

2088    Probyn, Clive T. "Realism and Raillery: Augustan Conversation and
the Poetry of Swift." DUJ, NS 39 (1977), 1-14.

Conversation, the dialog of human voices representing
sociability and communication, is an important moral
ideal in Swift's verse (as for all the Augustans), and
throughout his career he directs comic satire at violations
of this ideal in both the social and literary realms, but
never at the expense of his own carefully contrived
rhetorical effects of structural discourse.

2089    Quintana, Ricardo. THE MIND AND ART OF JONATHAN SWIFT.
London: Oxford Univ. Press, 1936.

One of the best general treatments of Swift as a conscious
literary artist employing a variety of rhetorical strategies;
the verse is occasionally treated less as successful poetry
and more as an index to Swift's thinking and biography.

2090    _____. SWIFT: AN INTRODUCTION. London: Oxford Univ.
Press, 1955.

Best short introduction to Swift with especially helpful
(if generalized) remarks on the early "Description" poems
and the poetic masterpieces of the 1730s.

2091    _____. TWO AUGUSTANS: JOHN LOCKE, JONATHAN SWIFT.
Madison: Univ. of Wisconsin Press, 1978.

Excellent discussion, directed toward the general reader,
of these two important figures of the Augustan age who,
whatever their differences, share a belief in man's capacity
to reason and the need for an empirical approach to experience. Especially strong on the seventeenth-century
intellectual backgrounds and changing approaches to Swift's
satire.

2092     Rawson, Claude J. GULLIVER AND THE GENTLE READER: STUDIES
         IN SWIFT AND OUR TIME. London: Routledge and Kegan Paul,
         1973.

> Chapter 2 brilliantly analyzes the varying appearances
> in Swift, Pope, and Johnson of conflicts between official
> ideologies and a certain "inner subversiveness" and creative
> anarchy that challenge ethical norms and violate systems
> of morality.

2093     _____. "The Nightmares of Strephon: Nymphs of the City in the
         Poems of Swift, Baudelaire, Eliot." In ENGLISH LITERATURE IN
         THE AGE OF DISGUISE. Ed. Maximillian E. Novak. Berkeley
         and Los Angeles: Univ. of California Press, 1977, pp. 57-99.

> With brief illuminating comparisons to Baudelaire and
> Eliot, argues that repudiation of all forms of poetic con-
> vention and rhetorical exaggeration resulting from his
> employment of the unadorned octosyllabic couplet charac-
> terizes Swift's realistic but moving appraisal of city life
> and his vision of human love.

2094     _____. "Order and Cruelty: A Reading of Swift (with some
         Comments on Pope and Johnson)." EIC, 20 (1970), 24-56.

> Mostly devoted to Swift's prose, but incisive remarks
> concerning the clash in Swift between the ordering
> potentialities of style and a psychological restlessness
> threatening moral order.

2095     Rodino, Richard H. "Blasphemy or Blessing? Swift's 'Scatological'
         Poems." PLL, 14 (1978), 152-70.

> Shows how Swift compels the reader by means of a
> complicated set of rhetorical strategies toward a "fraudu-
> lent" and unsatisfactory moral dilemma only to force him
> finally to recognize the "hard fact" of physical and
> moral realities, "the first step to real human engagement"
> and self-understanding.

2096     _____. "Notes on the Developing Motives and Structures of Swift's
         Poetry." In CONTEMPORARY STUDIES OF SWIFT'S POETRY. Ed.
         John Irwin Fischer and Donald C. Mell, Jr. Newark: Univ. of
         Delaware Press, 1981, pp. 87-99.

> Argues that Swift's entire output falls into four distinct
> phases: the first, demonstrating the incompatibility of
> the demands of idealism and honesty; two and three,
> exhibiting as operative but often unsatisfactory, reconcili-
> ation of the ideal and real; and the fourth, utilizing
> language and conversation to deceive the reader into

accepting moral norms that are essentially unacceptable in human terms. See no. 2006.

2097 _____. "The Private Sense of CADENUS AND VANESSA." CP, 11, ii (1978), 41-47.

Swift imitates and parodies the "normative" Augustan properties of balance and poise while positively depicting his love relationship with Vanessa through a series of ironic paradoxes which provide twists and flows in the poem's movement and sequences suggesting the extra-logical, private character of this relationship.

2098 Rosenheim, Edward W., Jr. SWIFT AND THE SATIRIST'S ART. Chicago: Univ. of Chicago Press, 1963.

Focuses mainly on the prose; but the distinctions between "persuasive" and "punitive" effects of satire and the assertion that it attacks "discernible, historically authentic particulars" have important implications for the verse. Thoughtful study.

2099 _____. "Swift's ODE TO SANCROFT: Another Look." MP, 73 (1976), 24-39.

Not an uncongenial and awkward Pindaric exercise, the ode combines "authentic sentiment" with the rhetorical pose of a speaker "forced from his professed panegyric task into hapless rage at the enormities which surround him."

2100 Rothstein, Eric. "Jonathan Swift as Jupiter: 'Baucis and Philemon.'" In THE AUGUSTAN MILIEU: ESSAYS PRESENTED TO LOUIS LANDA. Ed. Henry Knight Miller, Eric Rothstein, and G.S. Rousseau. Oxford: Clarendon Press, 1970, pp. 205-24.

Interesting analysis of Swift's changes and revisions in the second version of "Baucis and Philemon" suggesting that consideration of the poem's intentions, structure, and historical context reveals several things: Swift's poetic tact, the mute presence of Dryden's "genial" and "sentimental" adaptation, and Swift's characteristic multiple perspectives and stances resulting from moral skepticism and human inadequacy. See no. 120.

2101 Rowse, Alfred Leslie. "Swift as Poet." In FAIR LIBERTY WAS ALL HIS CRY: A TERCENTENARY TRIBUTE TO JONATHAN SWIFT, 1667-1745. Ed. A. Norman Jeffares. London: Macmillan, 1967, pp. 98-106.

Defends Swift's poetry from the charge that it lacks

variety of tone, arguing that it was "dominantly intellectual" and, given his frame of mind, mainly satirical. See
no. 2007.

2102    Said, Edward W.   "Swift's Tory Anarchy."   ECS, 3 (1969), 48-66.

A learned and suggestive discussion investigating "the
highly dramatic encounter in Swift between the anarchy
of resistance (agraphia) to the written page, and the
abiding Tory order of the page."

2103    San Juan, Epifanio, Jr.   "The Anti-Poetry of Jonathan Swift."   PQ,
44 (1965), 387-96.

The antipoetic element in Swift's verse is a manifestation
of an "intense awareness" and "unified sensibility" that
results from the process of "deidealizing" and demythologizing the meaning of facts.

2104    Savage, Roger.   "Swift's Fallen City, 'A Description of the Morning.'"
In THE WORLD OF JONATHAN SWIFT:  ESSAYS FOR THE TERCEN-
TENARY.   Ed. Brian Vickers.   Cambridge, Mass.:  Harvard Univ.
Press, 1968, pp. 171-94.

Scholarly and sensitive discussion of Augustan description-
of-the-morning motifs in the context of their Virgilian
models, focusing on the complex irony of Swift's parodic
version in which the classical ideal seems irrelevant to
the realities of the London setting at the same time that
reality is chided for not equalling the standards implied
by the classical ideal.   See no. 2012.

2105    Schakel, Peter J.   THE POETRY OF JONATHAN SWIFT:  ALLUSION
AND THE DEVELOPMENT OF A POETIC STYLE.   Madison:  Univ.
of Wisconsin Press, 1978.

Study of Swift's poetic art, noting its allusiveness and use
of literary convention and recognizable forms "to clarify
or reinforce themes and to establish or strengthen his
tones."   Represents an important response to arguments
stressing Swift's use of popular English modes and his
uniquely individualized antipoetic practices.

2106    _____.   "The Politics of Opposition in VERSES ON THE DEATH
OF DR. SWIFT."   MLQ, 35 (1974), 246-56.

Characterizing the eulogist at the Rose Tavern as a power-
less patriot in a disreputable setting employing the rhetoric
of opposition propaganda, suggests that Swift is both
promoting his political cause and at the same time
seriously praising himself through irony, a clear proof
of La Rochefoucauld's maxim.

2107     _____. "Swift's 'dapper Clerk' and the Matrix of Allusions in 'Cadenus and Vanessa.'" CRITICISM, 17 (1975), 246-61.

> More than an autobiographical projection of the Swift-Esther Vanhomrigh relationship, the allusions to Virgil's and Ovid's lovers provide ironic contrast to Cadenus and Vanessa's relationship and contribute structurally to Swift's examination of the need for self-acceptance and self-sacrifice in love.

2108     _____. "Swift's Remedy for Love: The 'Scatological' Poems." PLL, 14 (1978).

> Reads the scatological poems against the background of Ovid's REMEDIA AMORES and concludes that though Swift could not tolerate Ovid's dispassionate and comic treatment of the physical, he discloses his own fallibility and uncertain feelings about the body. See no. 2006.

2109     _____. "Virgil and the Dean: Christian and Classical Allusion in THE LEGION CLUB." SP, 70 (1973), 427-38.

> Swift's selective use of Virgil and the Bible provides literary authority and a universal moral standard for his strong condemnation of corrupt politicians, making the poem "his finest political satire in verse."

2109A   Scouten, Arthur H. "Jonathan Swift's Progress from Prose to Poetry." In THE POETRY OF JONATHAN SWIFT. Los Angeles, Calif.: William Andrews Clark Memorial Library, 1981, pp. 27-52.

> Argues interestingly that Swift's attempts to write in pentameter couplets, especially between 1729-31, reveal a seriousness of literary purpose and concern with public image and fame that brought him into conflict with Pope, who did not understand his desires and fears.

2110     _____. "Swift's Poetry and the Gentle Reader." In CONTEMPORARY STUDIES OF SWIFT'S POETRY. Ed. John Irwin Fischer and Donald C. Mell, Jr. Newark: Univ. of Delaware Press, 1981, pp. 46-55.

> Points out the importance of Swift's particular audience and readership and the need to distinguish between public and private contexts when analyzing his poems. See no. 2006.

2111   Scouten, Arthur H., and Robert Hume. "Pope and Swift: Text and Interpretation of Swift's Verses on His Death." PQ, 52 (1973), 205-31.

> Studies the textual difficulties of the poem from bibliographical evidence and ventures a theory of structural coherence and meaning dependent on a series of contrasting dramatic speakers espousing "artificial" points of view, none of which is entirely Swift's own, resulting finally in ironic qualifications of the

panegyric at the Rose Tavern that makes Swift's self-portrait
more attractive and convincing.

2112    Sena, John F.  "Swift as Moral Physician: Scatology and the Tradition of Love Melancholy."  JEGP, 76 (1977), 346-62.

Swift's knowledge of Burton and Lucretius would indicate
he understood that love melancholia was a disease to be
cured by shock therapy, in the case of the scatological
poems his motives being less medical than spiritual and
moral.

2113    Sheehan, David.  "Swift, Voiture, and the Spectrum of Raillery."
PLL, 14 (1978), 171-88.

Using Voiture's urbane letters as a model, discusses
raillery in Swift's Stella poems, ranging from the simpler
form of praise-by-blame to the more complex balancing
of praise and/or blame, notably in "To Stella, Who Collected and Transcribed his Poems" (1720), in which blame
is wittily transformed into praise.

2114    _____.  "Swift on High Pindaric Stilts."  In CONTEMPORARY
STUDIES OF SWIFT'S POETRY.  Ed. John Irwin Fischer and Donald
C. Mell, Jr.  Newark: Univ. of Delaware Press, 1980, pp. 25-35.

Interprets Swift's early odes in the tradition of seventeenth-
century satiric Pindarics, demonstrating his expert merging
of the panegyrical and satiric modes.  See no. 2006.

2115    Slepian, Barry.  "The Ironic Intention of Swift's Verses on his own
Death."  RES, NS 14 (1963), 249-56.

Treats the famous eulogy as ironic and fully supportive
of Swift's thesis about self-love, pride, and vanity con-
suming all men and, thus, the logical conclusion of an
implied syllogism: all men are vain; Swift is like other
men; therefore, Swift is vain.  This article has been the
impetus for numerous other approaches to irony in Swift's
poetry generally and in VERSES in particular.

2116    Solomon, Harry M.  "'Difficult Beauty': Tom D'Urfey and the Context of Swift's 'The Lady's Dressing Room.'"  SEL, 19 (1979), 431-44.

Swift's "mock variation" of D'Urfey's scatological experiments also borrows situations, diction, and imagery from
early Augustan pastoral and Restoration scatology.

2117    Timpe, Eugene F.  "Swift as Railleur."  JEGP, 69 (1970), 41-49.

Swift achieved the "delicate irony" characterizing Voiture's

form of the ancient practice of raillery, learning the art
of successfully converting "seeming criticism" into "graceful praise."

2118    Tyne, James. "Gulliver's Maker and Gullibility." CRITICISM, 7
(1965), 151-67.

As a satirist, Swift "preferred to set man as he is against
man as he thinks he is" on the notion that self-understanding preceded moral reform; thus, his poems are filled with
"naive and gullible souls" who accept artistic illusion and
fancy for fact and reality and unsuccessfully try to govern
their lives according to poetic fictions.

2119    _____. "'Only A Man of Rhimes': Swift's Bridled Pegasus." PLL,
14 (1978), 189-204.

Quoting from the correspondence, revisions of the poems,
and his critiques of Pope's and Tickell's verse, argues
that sense and mastery of rhyme are of paramount importance in Swift's theory and practice of poetry and take
precedence over "such aesthetic refinements as imagery
or emotion."

2120    _____. "Swift and Stella: The Love Poems." TSL, 19 (1974),
35-47.

In an age not usually noted for its genuine love poetry,
Swift's eleven poems to Esther Johnson are "love poems
of considerable power," celebrating not _amor concupi-
scientiae_ but _amor benevolentiae_, the most superior kind
of love that can be attained by imperfect human beings.

2121    _____. "Swift's Mock Panegyrics in 'On Poetry: A Rapsody.'"
PLL, 10 (1974), 279-86.

Briefly examines the encomiums of such laureates as Eusden
and Cibber and show how Swift skillfully parodies their
crude stylistic practices in his mocking of the royal family
and Walpole while invoking "classical precedent and perfection" against which to measure Hanoverian England, a
satiric strategy not often utilized by Swift.

2122    _____. "Vanessa and the Houyhnhnms: A Reading of 'Cadenus and
Vanesa.'" SEL, 11 (1971), 517-34.

The poem's action, fluctuating between mythological and
real worlds and verbal exchanges of the fictionalized Swift
and Esther Vanhomrigh, dramatizes a perennial theme of
Swift's concerning the price paid for denying one's humanity.

2123     Uphaus, Robert W. "From Panegyric to Satire: Swift's Early Odes and A TALE OF A TUB." TSLL, 13 (1971), 55-70.

> Swift's failure to accommodate Pindaric inventiveness and praise to his satiric vision "becomes one of the models for the persona's eccentric inventiveness in A TALE" and, thus, the relative artistic failure of the odes becomes the artistic virtue of A TALE.

2124     _____. "Swift's Irony Reconsidered." In CONTEMPORARY STUDIES OF SWIFT'S POETRY. Ed. John Irwin Fischer and Donald C. Mell, Jr. Newark: Univ. of Delaware Press, 1981, pp. 169-77.

> Using both Pope's reference to Swift's satires as libels and Leavis' characterization of the satire as essentially negative and destructive to establish a critical rationale, considers the later poems (after 1726) as overt revelations of Swift's personality and feeling through art, consisting often of outright attack and self-defense. See no. 2006.

2125     _____. "Swift's Poetry: The Making of Meaning." ECS, 5 (1972), 569-86.

> Effectively attacks the antipoetry school of Swift criticism by demonstrating that poetry is his "vehicle for truth" in opposition to the visionary and romantic, and, in a way of committing himself to the world of experience.

2126     _____. "Swift's Stella Poems and Fidelity to Experience." Éire, 5, iii (1970), 40-52.

> Discusses the poems as units and views them as Swift's attempt to separate out, in his relationship with Stella, what is permanent and valuable from what is superficial and transitory, and to affirm the achievement of self-knowledge based on virtue.

2127     _____. "Swift's 'whole character': The Delany Poems and 'Verses on the Death of Dr. Swift.'" MLQ, 34 (1973), 406-16.

> Distinct departures from his usual ironic strategies, these poems mark a change in Swift's literary direction by making the autobiographical Swift, rather than poetic convention and artifice, the poems' governing form.

2128     Vieth, David M. "Fiat Lux: Logos versus Chaos in Swift's 'A Description of the Morning.'" PLL, 8 (1972), 302-07.

> In addition to being a mock-pastoral and realistic description of urban London, the poem parodies the "divine fiat of Creation" and thus depicts a fallen world of dis-

order and imperfection, an effect created by Swift's
imagery and couplet rhetoric.

2129 _____. "Metaphors and Metamorphoses: Basic Techniques in the
Middle Period of Swift's Poetry, 1698-1719." In CONTEMPORARY
STUDIES OF SWIFT'S POETRY. Ed. John Irwin Fischer and Donald
C. Mell, Jr. Newark: Univ. of Delaware Press, 1981, pp. 56-68.

Describes the distinctive metaphoric features of poems
during this period as involving comic metamorphosis and
other forms of ironic transformations within Ovidian and
Christian contexts. See no. 2006.

2130 _____. "The Mystery of Personal Identity: Swift's Verses on His
Own Death." In THE AUTHOR IN HIS WORK: ESSAYS ON A
PROBLEM IN CRITICISM. Ed. Louis L. Martz and Aubrey Williams.
New Haven, Conn.: Yale Univ. Press, 1978, pp. 245-62.

Account of the range and variety of modern interpretations of VERSES, emphasizing the multiplicity of identities Swift assumes or creates and concluding that the
poem is "yet another instance of Swift's uncanny skill
in perpetrating hoaxes," in this case a serious one involving the creation of a Swift for historical posterity.
The notes provide a comprehensive bibliography of the
variety of interpretations. See no. 119.

2131 Voight, Milton. SWIFT AND THE TWENTIETH CENTURY. Detroit:
Wayne State Univ. Press, 1964.

Valuable accounting of the major developments in the
critical, biographical, and textual study of Swift in
this century. Deals with nineteenth-century opinions,
textual editing of the major works and poems, the
diverse responses to A TALE OF A TUB and GULLIVER'S
TRAVELS, and impressions of Swift the man.

2132 Waingrow, Marshall. "'Verses on the Death of Dr. Swift.'" SEL,
5 (1965), 513-18.

Defends the famous eulogy, which concludes the poems, as
a serious and thoughtful exercise showing Swift as "a
model of moral perception and behavior" precisely because
he has achieved the self-knowledge on which virtue is
built.

2133 Williams, Aubrey L. "Swift and the Poetry of Allusion: 'The
Journal.'" In LITERARY THEORY AND STRUCTURE: ESSAYS IN
HONOR OF WILLIAM K. WIMSATT. Ed. Frank Brady, John
Palmer, and Martin Price. New Haven, Conn.: Yale Univ. Press,
1973, pp. 227-43.

Far from a "graceless lampoon" directed against Swift's hosts, the Rochforts of Gaulstown, "The Journal" is a seriocomic account of a day in a country manor which ridicules "the patterns of life in rural retreat" and the poetic tradition praising such life while acknowledging the "inherent dissatisfactions of mortal life."

2134       _____. "'A Vile Encomium': That 'Panegyric on the Reverend D--n S---t." In CONTEMPORARY STUDIES OF SWIFT'S POETRY. Ed. John Irwin Fischer and Donald C. Mell, Jr.  Newark:  Univ. of Delaware Press, 1981, pp. 178-90.

Calls Swift's authorship into question on the basis of internal evidence of voice and tone, concluding that the attack on Swift is so virulent and unrelieved as to be uncharacteristic of his ironic and parodic technique and that George Faulkner was correct in attributing the poem to Swift's enemy, James Arbuckle.  See no. 2006.

2135       Williams, Kathleen.  JONATHAN SWIFT AND THE AGE OF COM-PROMISE.  Lawrence:  Univ. of Kansas Press, 1958.

Studies Swift's writings in relation to "the conditions of his time," concluding that they reflect traditional humanistic ideas of "a Christian classical heritage" and demonstrate the "compromise" required in an age beset with ambivalent attitudes about the nature of man and society.  Brief remarks on the poetry.

2136       _____.  SWIFT:  THE CRITICAL HERITAGE.  New York:  Barnes and Noble, 1970.

Acknowledges the difficulties faced in collecting dis-passionate eighteenth-century commentary on Swift's writing, noting the often predictably personal and partisan nature of much so-called "literary criticism" in the age; nevertheless, provides a fair representation, both favorable and hostile, of critical comments on Swift, from William King's witty critique of A TALE OF A TUB to Coleridge's insightful fragments.

2137       Wimsatt, William K.  "Rhetoric and Poems:  The Example of Swift." In THE AUTHOR IN HIS WORK:  ESSAYS ON A PROBLEM IN CRITICISM.  Ed. Louis L. Martz and Aubrey Williams.  New Haven, Conn.:  Yale Univ. Press, 1978, pp. 229-44.

Brilliant treatment of Swift's verse, noting the "inventive extravagance" of his poetic techniques and analyzing his octosyllabic couplet rhythm, suggestive manipulation of rhyme scheme, ironic juxtaposition of the serious with everyday speech, and his anticlassical (not antipoetic) burlesque. See no. 119.

2138   Woolley, James. "Arbuckle's 'Panegyric' and Swift's Scrub Libel: The Documentary Evidence." In CONTEMPORARY STUDIES OF SWIFT'S POETRY. Ed. John Irwin Fischer and Donald C. Mell, Jr. Newark: Univ. of Delaware Press, 1980, pp. 191-209.

Painstaking examination of the bibliographical evidence relating to both Swift's and Arbuckle's poems, offering an analysis of handwriting samples and library materials to argue that Arbuckle wrote the "Panegyric" (as Faulkner asserted) and that the famous "scrub libel" in question is actually Swift's "An Answer to Dr. Delany's Fable of the Pheasant and the Lark." See no. 2006.

2139   _____. "Autobiography in Swift's Verses on His Death." In CONTEMPORARY STUDIES OF SWIFT'S POETRY. Ed. John Irwin Fischer and Donald C. Mell, Jr. Newark: Univ. of Delaware Press, 1981, pp. 112-22.

Adds significantly to the body of commentary surrounding the famous "panegyric" at the Rose, citing facts, opinions, and sentiments expressed elsewhere in the prose and corre-spondence to demonstrate that "Verses" is truly representa-tive of Swift's real understanding of himself. See no. 2006.

2140   _____. "Friends and Enemies in VERSES ON THE DEATH OF DR. SWIFT." STUDIES IN EIGHTEENTH-CENTURY CULTURE, 8 (1979), 205-32.

Excellent account of the Augustan concepts of friendship (as well as enmity) informing Swift's depiction of personal relations and poetic stances in the poem and a suggestive rationalization of the self-portrait of Swift in the con-cluding eulogy as actually affirming his integrity and humanity as satirist.

# JAMES THOMSON (1700-1748)

## A. MAJOR EDITIONS

2141    POETICAL WORKS OF JAMES THOMSON. Ed. J. Logie Robertson.
London: Oxford Univ. Press, 1908.

> Only complete edition available of the poetry, with
> variorum text for THE SEASONS. Standard edition.

2142    THOMSON'S SEASONS: CRITICAL EDITION, BEING A REPRODUC-
TION OF THE ORIGINAL TEXTS, WITH ALL THE VARIOUS READ-
INGS OF THE LATER EDITIONS, HISTORICALLY ARRANGED. Ed.
Otto Zippel. Berlin: Mayer and Müller, 1908.

> Collation provided as well as a discussion of the compli-
> cated history of Thomson's revisions and a record of
> sources and models for many passages. Important scholarly
> edition.

2143    THE CASTLE OF INDOLENCE AND OTHER POEMS. Ed. Alan D.
McKillop. Lawrence: Univ. of Kansas Press, 1961.

> Presents the definitive texts and full scholarly apparatus
> for many important poems except THE SEASONS and in-
> cludes a long critical discussion of the poetry. Excellent
> edition, though incomplete. See no. 2150.

2144    THE SEASONS AND THE CASTLE OF INDOLENCE. Ed. James
Sambrook. Oxford: Clarendon Press, 1972. Index.

> Substantially annotated text, based on the 1746 version
> (corrected by the author) with helpful notes. Some
> normalization and modernization of accidentals. Con-
> venient edition.

2145    JAMES THOMSON: THE SEASONS. Oxford English Texts Series.
Ed. James Sambrook. Oxford: Clarendon Press, 1981. Appendix.

A critical edition based on full collation of all editions
published in Thomson's lifetime. Variants introduced into
later editions are listed. A commentary explains Thomson's
relationship to the intellectual context of his time, and
an introduction accounts for the poem's complicated publication history.

## B. CORRESPONDENCE

2146    JAMES THOMSON (1700-1748): LETTERS AND DOCUMENTS. Ed.
Alan D. McKillop. Lawrence: Univ. of Kansas Press, 1958.

Scholarly presentation of the extant letters, fully annotated
with relevant biographical information supplied. Supplements earlier biographical studies.

## C. BIBLIOGRAPHY AND TEXTUAL STUDIES

2147    Campbell, Hilbert H. JAMES THOMSON (1700-1748): AN ANNO-
TATED BIBLIOGRAPHY OF SELECTED EDITIONS AND IMPORTANT
CRITICISM. New York: Garland, 1976. Index.

An attempt to reflect the extensive interest in and popularity of Thomson (especially THE SEASONS) in England,
Scotland, and America since the eighteenth century.
Notes editions published during his lifetime and also
during the nineteenth and twentieth centuries. Fully
annotates secondary materials; in the index cross-references
names appearing in annotations for purposes of comparison
and for highlighting critical disagreements.

2148    See no. 2157.

2149    Corney, Bolton. "Memorandum on the Text of THE SEASONS."
GENTLEMAN'S MAGAZINE, 169 (1841), 145-49.

Corney is the first to follow the 1746 text, the last in
Thomson's lifetime, for his edition of 1842. See no. 2151.

2150    Todd, William B. "The Text of THE CASTLE OF INDOLENCE."
ES, 34 (1953), 117-21.

Early bibliographical study establishing a basis for the
definitive text of the poem, the one accepted by later
scholars. See no. 2143.

2151    Wells, J.E. "Thomson's SEASONS 'Corrected and Amended.'"
JEGP, 42 (1943), 104-14.

Study of George Lyttelton's edition of Thomson's works, pointing out the emendations and extensive modifications that affected all texts until Comey's 1842 edition based on the 1746 text. See no. 2149.

## D. BIOGRAPHY

2152    Grant, Douglas. JAMES THOMSON: POET OF THE SEASONS. London: Cresset, 1951.

The standard biography, incorporating new materials about Thomson's love affair with Elizabeth Young ("Amanda"), assessing its destructive effects on Thomson's professional and personal life, and placing the poet in his intellectual setting.

## E. CRITICISM

2153    Aden, John M. "Scriptural Parody in Canto I of THE CASTLE OF INDOLENCE." MLN, 71 (1956), 574-77.

Since the general theme of this canto is the temptation and fall of man, Thomson appropriately alludes to Scripture and a variety of examples of ensnarement of the innocent and virtuous through disguise.

2154    Campbell, Hilbert H. JAMES THOMSON. Boston: Twayne, 1979.

Provides a critical account of Thomson's poetic and dramatic career, placing him in the context of his historical background, poetic ideals, and intentions in order to correct numerous nineteenth-century attempts to make him an anomaly in his age and a forerunner of Wordsworth. Incorporates recent materials and interpretations.

2155    Chalker, John. "Thomson's SEASONS and Virgil's GEORGICS: The Problem of Primitivism and Progress." STUDIA NEOPHILOLOGICA, 35 (1963), 41-56.

Thomson was not violating the decorum of descriptive poetry, but employing the same contrasting views, eclectic subject matter, and poetic methods as did Virgil in his GEORGICS.

2156    Clifford, James L., ed. "James Thomson: 1748-1948." JOHN-SONIAN NEWS LETTER, 8 (September 1948), 1-5.

Reviews the work of McKillop and includes a bibliographical notation by Geoffrey Tillotson.

2157    Cohen, Ralph. THE ART OF DISCRIMINATION: THOMSON'S
        THE SEASONS AND THE LANGUAGE OF CRITICISM. Berkeley:
        Univ. of California Press, 1964. Bibliog.

        Using Thomson's poem as a particular case, discusses the
        various readings of the poem during the eighteenth and
        nineteenth centuries as a reflection of differing critical
        assumptions, premises, use of evidence, and aesthetic
        theories. Also provides forty-six illustrations that reflect
        sentimentalizing and idealizing attitudes toward the poem.
        Contains a checklist of separate editions from 1726 to 1929.

2158    _____. "Thomson's Poetry of Space and Time." In STUDIES IN
        CRITICISM AND AESTHETICS, 1660-1800: ESSAYS IN HONOR OF
        SAMUEL HOLT MONK. Ed. Howard Anderson and John S. Shea.
        Minneapolis: Univ. of Minnesota Press, 1967, pp. 176-92.

        Thomson's intentional mixing of personification with
        natural description is integral to his unified conception
        of man and nature contained within a comprehensive and
        holistic spatial framework that admits complex variation.
        See no. 93.

2159    _____. THE UNFOLDING OF THE SEASONS. Baltimore: Johns
        Hopkins Press, 1970.

        Shows that Thomson's poem is part of mainstream Augustan
        poetry, successfully combining an awareness of man's
        imperfection, his need for religious faith, and the im-
        portance of the natural world in a "unified vision" that
        encompasses the historical and literary past in its asser-
        tion of man's humanity in the midst of spatial vastness
        and the continuum of time.

2160    Drennon, Herbert. "James Thomson's Contact with Newtonianism
        and His Interest in Natural Philosophy." PMLA, 49 (1934), 71-80.

        Explores the nature and extent of Thomson's interest in
        science and in Newton while a student at Edinburgh, from
        1715 to 1725, and argues that by the time Thomson
        wrote the lament for Newton and "Summer" (1727) he
        was directly responding to the implications of the
        Newtonian scientific outlook.

2161    _____. "James Thomson's Ethical Theory and Scientific Rationalism."
        PQ, 14 (1935), 70-82.

        Thomson's acceptance of the principles of scientific
        rationalism meant that analogies between the natural
        and moral worlds were discovered through man's rational
        faculty and that moral law and order could be under-

403

stood by philosophic observation of the harmonies of
the natural world.

2162        . "Newtonianism in James Thomson's Poetry." ES, 70 (1936),
358-72.

Thomson believed that an empirical and rational approach
to nature can not only discover the laws of the universe,
but also lead to a belief in God as the creative force
as well as the sustainer of creation itself.

2163        . "Scientific Rationalism and James Thomson's Poetic Art."
SP, 31 (1934), 453-71.

Argues that Thomson's artistic consciousness is strongly
influenced by his belief in scientific rationalism and
that his aesthetic response to nature was mainly rationalistic and largely devoid of emotional content.

2164    Durliny, Dwight L. GEORGIC TRADITION IN ENGLISH POETRY.
New York: Columbia Univ. Press, 1935.

Describes the impact of Virgil's GEORGICS on the theme,
method, and style of Thomson's THE SEASONS (as well
as on a number of other minor poets) and traces both
poets' influence in establishing the "European descriptive-
didactic tendency" in the eighteenth and nineteenth
centuries.

2165    Greene, Donald. "From Accidie to Neuroses: THE CASTLE OF
INDOLENCE Revisited." In ENGLISH LITERATURE IN THE AGE
OF DISGUISE. Ed. Maximillian E. Novak. Berkeley: Univ. of
California Press, 1977, pp. 131-56.

Both the biographical and intentional "fallacies" have
long inhibited critical interpretation of this "mature"
poem of Thomson's which explores different forms of
neuroses associated with the psychological, psychiatric,
and finally theological ramifications of pride, a familiar
theme in literature ranging from the RAPE OF THE LOCK
to RASSELAS.

2166    Hamilton, Horace E. "James Thomson's SEASONS: Shifts in the
Treatment of Popular Subject Matter." ELH, 15 (1948), 110-21.

Thomson incorporated into early versions of the poem
descriptions of storms, earthquakes, icebergs, sandstorms,
and other natural phenomena drawn from superstition and
popular literature; but by 1744 he omitted many of these
spectacular scenes and replaced them with scientific explanation.

2167    Havens, Raymond D. "Primitivism and the Idea of Progress in Thomson." SP, 29 (1932), 41-52.

Thomson's poetic attitudes were marked by oppositions: he naturally loved the rural life and simple existence but at the same time was proud of Britain's trade, progress, and role as a world power; this ambivalence characterized his life, work, values, and artistic taste.

2168    McKillop, Alan D. THE BACKGROUND OF THOMSON'S LIBERTY. RICE INSTITUTE PAMPHLET, 38, no. 2 (1951): entire work.

Explains the various influences--historical, political, moral, and geographical--on the poem, accounting for Thomson's attempted synthesis of these in the art of the poem.

2169    _____. THE BACKGROUND OF THOMSON'S SEASONS. Minneapolis: Univ. of Minnesota Press, 1942.

Studies the poem in the philosophical and literary contexts of the age, showing its indebtedness to many works on science, philosophy, geography, and travel and also argues for the importance of recognizing these influential interests in order to interpret the text accurately.

2170    _____. "Ethics and Political History in Thomson's LIBERTY." In POPE AND HIS CONTEMPORARIES: ESSAYS PRESENTED TO GEORGE SHERBURN. Ed. James L. Clifford and Louis A. Landa. New York: Oxford Univ. Press, 1949, pp. 215-29.

Analyzes the political background of the poem, concluding that its professed "Whiggism" is anti-Walpole and often activated by premises espoused in Bolingbroke's CRAFTSMAN. See no. 107.

2171    _____. "Thomson Studies." JOHNSONIAN NEWS LETTER, 8 (December 1948), 1-3.

Review-essay discussing and evaluating recent studies and indicating new areas for possible exploration in biography, bibliography, criticism, and intellectual backgrounds.

2172    Moore, Cecil A. "A Predecessor of Thomson's SEASONS." MLN, 34 (1919), 278-81.

Suggests that William Hinchliffe's THE SEASONS: A POEM, along with such common sources as Virgil and Milton, influenced the general plan and structure of Thomson's poem.

2173　Peck, Richard E.  "Two Lost Bryant Poems:  Evidence of Thomson's Influence."  AL, 39 (1967), 88-94.

> Two unpublished juvenile nature poems by Bryant, THE SEASONS and "A Thunderstorm," owe much to Thomson's "vitalized" storm sections in "Summer" and suggest a link between Bryant's "mature" verse and that of Thomson.

2173A　Potter, G.R.  "James Thomson and the Evolution of Spirits." ENGLISCHE STUDIEN, 61 (1926), 57-65.

> Thomson applies the Pythagorean doctrine of the trans- migration of souls from man to animals and back again to the level of superior being, theorizing that spirit translates itself successfully to higher forms of existence until achieving perfection and immortality.

2174　Reisner, Thomas A.  "The Vast Eternal Springs: Ancient and Modern Hydrodynamics in Thomson's 'Autumn.'"  MOSAIC, 10 (1977), 97- 110.

> Between 1719, the date of composition of his PARAPHRASE OF PSALM CIV, and 1744, the date of the vernal SEA- SONS, Thomson's scientific position on the percolation hypothesis changed radically.  This fact raises questions about the "intellectual provenance" of his early view of the water cycle and the reasons that he so vehemently repudiated his original theory in the later version of THE SEASONS.

2175　Smith, David Nichol.  "Thomson and Burns."  In his SOME OBSERVA- TIONS ON EIGHTEENTH CENTURY POETRY.  London:  Oxford Univ. Press, 1937, pp. 56-80.

> Emphasizes Pope's positive influence on and personal encouragement of such poets as Thomson and asserts that the literary diction of THE SEASONS did not preclude Pope's appreciation of Thomson's pictorially rendered nature as a backdrop for human activity.

2176　Spacks, Patricia Meyer.  THE VARIED GOD:  A CRITICAL STUDY OF THOMSON'S THE SEASONS.  Berkeley:  Univ. of California Press, 1959.

> An important study of the strengths and weaknesses in Thomson's poem, arguing that the increased concern for human affairs and moral issues indicated by the various revisions of the texts alters the original conception and weakens the more successful depictions of the natural world.

2177    See no. 856.

2178    Weathersby, Harrell.  "An Analysis of Pope's AN ESSAY ON CRITI-
        CISM and Thomson's 'Winter' As Examples of Edmund Burke's Con-
        cepts of the Beautiful and the Sublime."  SOUTHERN QUARTERLY,
        10 (1972), 375-83.

            Views Thomson's images of the terrifying aspects of nature,
            his prosody, and his insistent alliteration as moving toward
            ideas of the beautiful and sublime espoused by Burke and
            away from the more conventional norms of nature and
            beauty depicted in Pope's ESSAY.

2179    Williams, Ralph M.  "Thomson and Dyer:  Poet and Painter."  In
        THE AGE OF JOHNSON:  ESSAYS PRESENTED TO CHAUNCEY
        BREWSTER TINKER.  Ed. Frederick W. Hilles.  New Haven, Conn.:
        Yale Univ. Press, 1949, pp. 209-16.

            Stylistic changes from descriptions of nature as an activity
            ("Winter," 1726) to a static verbal painting ("Spring,"
            1727) were probably influenced by Thomson's friendship
            with John Dyer, the painter-poet.  See no. 109.

# THOMAS WARTON THE ELDER (1688?-1745)
# JOSEPH WARTON (1722-1800)
# THOMAS WARTON THE YOUNGER (1728-90)

## A. MAJOR EDITIONS

2180    Warton, Thomas the Elder.  POEMS ON SEVERAL OCCASIONS
        (1748).  New York: Facsimile Text Society, 1930.

> Reproduced from a copy in New York Public Library
> collated with a copy at Harvard University.  Although
> not a distinguished collection, these poems influenced
> his two sons and reveal the search for new subject
> matter in older English poets.

2181    Warton, Joseph.  ODES ON VARIOUS SUBJECTS (1746).  Intro.
        Richard Wendorf.  1746; Facs. rpt.  Los Angeles:  Augustan Re-
        print Society, no. 197, 1979.

> Introduction provides a helpful discussion of contributions
> made by both Collins and Joseph Warton to the intro-
> duction of a new poetic sensibility into English poetry,
> viewing Warton as the "most extravagant" and Collins
> the "most successful" proponent of this new sensibility.

2182    _____.  ODES ON VARIOUS SUBJECTS (1746).  1746; Facs. rpt.
        Intro. Joan Pittock.  Delmar, N.Y.:  Scholars Facsimiles and Re-
        prints, 1977.

> Confirms his status as rising poet and leader in reaction
> against Pope.

2183    COLLECTION OF POEMS BY SEVERAL HANDS.  Ed. Robert Dodsley.
        London:  R. and J. Dodsley, 1748-58.

> Good source for Joseph Warton's verse, although some
> poems are revised and differ from those in earlier printings.

2184    Warton, Thomas the Younger. HISTORY OF ENGLISH POETRY.
        Ed. W. Carew Hazlitt. 4 vols. London: Reeves and Turner, 1871;
        rpt. Hildeshelm, W. Ger.: George Olms Verlagsbuchhandlung,
        1968.

        Standard edition available in modern reprint of the 3
        volumes, 1774-81. Contains invaluable comment relating
        to the Wartons and to the developing historical sense in
        the poetry and criticism of the age.

2185    _____. POEMS BY THOMAS WARTON. London: T. Becket, 1779.

        An edition of the collected poems of 1777 with some
        additions of pieces previously printed separately and of
        new poems.

2186    _____. THE POETICAL WORKS OF THE LATE THOMAS WARTON,
        D.D. TOGETHER WITH MEMOIRS OF HIS LIFE AND WRITINGS.
        Ed. Richard Mant. 5th ed. 2 vols. Oxford: Oxford Univ. Press,
        1802.

        Some annotation and biographical materials. Best known
        nineteenth-century edition. Still valuable.

2187    _____. VERSES ON SIR JOSHUA REYNOLDS' PAINTED WINDOW
        AT NEW COLLEGE, OXFORD, 1782. Facs. rpt. 1782; Oxford:
        Oxford Univ. Press, 1930.

2188    THE THREE WARTONS: A CHOICE OF THEIR POETRY. Ed. Eric
        Partridge. London: Scholartis Press, 1927.

        Good selection from all three Wartons. Also contains
        a critical essay on bibliography.


## B. CORRESPONDENCE

2189    Churchill, Irving L. "The Percy-Warton Letters--Additions and
        Corrections." PMLA, 48 (1933), 301-03.

        Corrects some dates and bibliographical misinformation
        resulting from the Dennis edition of the correspondence
        between Bishop Percy and Thomas Warton the Younger.
        See no. 2190.

2190    Dennis, Leah. "The Text of the Percy-Warton Letters." PMLA, 46
        (1931), 1166-1201.

        Presents a rationale for the publication of the correspon-
        dence, noting that the letters form "if not a chapter in

the development of romanticism, footnote material for
such a chapter." See no. 2189.

2191    Watkin-Jones, A. "Bishop Percy, Thomas Warton, and Chatterton's
        Rowley Poems, 1773-1790." PMLA, 50 (1935), 769-84.

        Unpublished letters relating to the Rowley Poems show
        the high esteem in which Percy and Warton held the
        poet, despite the controversy surrounding the matter of
        fake authorship.

## C. BIBLIOGRAPHY AND TEXTUAL STUDIES

2192    Baxter, Ralph C. "A Sonnet Wrongly Ascribed to Thomas Warton,
        Jr." BSUF, 11, iv (1970), 51-53.

        Studies the publication history of a sonnet lamenting the
        death of Thomas Gray, often attributed to Warton, con-
        cluding that there is little justification for the attribution.

2193    Martin, Burns. "Some Unpublished WARTONIANA." SP, 29 (1932),
        53-67.

        Discusses the Joseph Warton the Younger manuscripts in
        the collection owned by John B. Swann, a great-great
        grandson of the poet. Includes some poems.

2194    Miller, Frances S. "Did Thomas Warton Borrow from Himself?"
        MLN, 51 (1936), 151-54.

        Parallel conceptions, word choice, and metrics in "Verses
        written in a blank leaf of Mr. Warton's OBSERVATIONS
        on Spenser" and his later sonnet "Written in a Blank
        Leaf of Dugdale's MONASTICON" indicate bibliographical
        connections between the anonymous publication of "Verses"
        and Warton's acknowledged sonnet and help date the pub-
        lication of the Spenser essay in 1754.

2195    Sambrook, A.J. "Thomas Warton's GERMAN ECLOGUES." RES,
        NS 20 (1969), 61-62.

        A letter from Robert Dodsley to Warton while at Oxford,
        written in March 1745, verifies the attribution often
        doubted over the years by editors of Warton the Younger's
        verse.

2196    Smith, David Nichol. "Thomas Warton's Miscellany: THE UNION."
        RES, 19 (1943), 263-75.

        A description of the bibliographical history of this minor

but highly successful miscellany edited by the younger Warton, a collection that included poems by a number of well-known eighteenth-century poets.

2197    Willoughby, Edwin E.  "The Chronology of the Poems of Thomas Warton the Elder."  JEGP, 30 (1931), 87-89.

Examines POEMS ON SEVERAL OCCASIONS (1748) to determine the correct dating and chronology and to refute the notion that Warton wrote all of his poetry after retiring from his professorship at Oxford, concluding that he began writing poems in 1705 and continued to write throughout his life, in effect providing his sons with an example of a practicing poet.

## D. BIOGRAPHY

2198    Wooll, John.  BIOGRAPHICAL MEMOIRS OF THE LATE REVD. JOSEPH WARTON, D.D., TO WHICH ARE ADDED A SELECTION FROM HIS WORKS AND LITERARY CORRESPONDENCE. London: Luke Hansard, 1806.

Brings to light a number of interesting facts about Joseph Warton's career; for example, that his insistence on translations of verse as a pedagogical exercise at Winchester encouraged promising poetic talents among his students.

## E. CRITICISM

2199    Bishop, David H.  "The Father of the Wartons."  SAQ, 16 (1917), 357-68.

Points out that in the heyday of Pope, the elder Thomas Warton gave early signs of supporting the romantic revolt so assiduously carried on by his two sons.

2200    Fairbanks, A. Harris.  "'Dear Native Brook': Coleridge, Bowles, and Thomas Warton, the Younger."  WORDSWORTH CIRCLE, 6 (1975), 313-15.

Coleridge's "Sonnet: To the River Otter" was influenced by Bowles's "To the River Itchin" but also by Warton's "To the River Lodon," which furnished Coleridge with several ideas and phrases and also acted as a model for Bowles's own sonnet.

2201    Fairer, David.  "The Poems of Thomas Warton the Elder?"  RES, NS 26 (1975), 287-300; 395-406.

A fascinating study that calls into question the almost universally held assumption that the elder Thomas Warton pioneered the romantic movement by arguing that (1) POEMS ON SEVERAL OCCASIONS (1748) contains much verse in the Pope-Prior school of Augustan satire; (2) poems attributed to him reached print only in a volume edited by Thomas the Younger; and (3) the Warton papers show that Joseph not only heavily edited and improved his father's poems, but that he also wrote at least ten himself. See no. 2192.

2202 _____. "The Poems of Thomas Warton the Elder? A Postscript." RES, NS 29 (1978), 61-65.

A sequel to the earlier, important article (above), repeating the argument that the elder Warton was hardly the romantic innovator often alleged and that "Retirement: An Ode" demonstrates the kinds of editorial changes made by his two sons. See no. 2201.

2203 Fenner, Arthur, Jr. "The Wartons 'Romanticize' Their Verse." SP, 93 (1956), 501-08.

Though not denying the importance of THE ENTHUSIAST, ODE TO FANCY, and THE PLEASURES OF MELANCHOLY to the emerging romantic mode in the mid-century, calls attention to the textual revisions of these poems as "constituting a partial history-in-miniature of eighteenth-century poetry" and illustrating a growing emphasis on the Gothic and utilization of the senses.

2204 Gosse, Edmund. TWO PIONEERS OF ROMANTICISM: JOSEPH AND THOMAS WARTON. London: Humphrey Milford, 1915.

Unabashedly romantic view of the poetry and criticism of Joseph and Thomas Warton the Younger, identifying what in poetry up to this age stimulated them and what they disapproved of in the fashionable and popular verse of the day.

2205 Havens, Raymond D. "Thomas Warton and the Eighteenth-Century Dilemma." SP, 25 (1928), 36-50.

Counters the "misconception" that in both critical theory and poetic practice, the younger Warton was a conscious rebel against the school of Pope and recommends instead a dispassionate examination of the successes as well as failures of such typical figures of the period to determine the mixture of "conventionality and conservatism" in their search for "originality and liberalism."

2206    Hysham, Julia. "Joseph Warton's Reputation as a Poet." SIR, 1
(1962), 220-29.

An interesting discussion of changing critical opinion
regarding Joseph Warton's poetry and of the problems
raised by attempts to place his verse in English literary
history, concluding that in our modern reappraisals of
poetic technique, literary forms, and overall poetic
achievements, his verse has acted "as a kind of barom-
eter of shifting sensibilities in his decade" and has by
its nature and the critical commentary devoted to it under-
scored the difficulties of assessing the worth of the
poetry of this transitional period.

2207    Kirschbaum, Leo. "A Postscript to the Imitations of Thomas Warton
the Elder." PQ, 24 (1945), 89-90.

On the basis of his borrowings from Shakespeare, sur-
mises that Warton kept a commonplace book in which
he recorded passages he wanted to remember under
specific topic headings.

2208    Leisy, Ernest E. "John Trumbull's Indebtedness to Thomas Warton."
MLN, 36 (1921), 313-14.

An examination of interesting parallels between the prosody,
spirit, and content of two satires on college life, namely
Trumbull's "The Progress of Dulness Part I" (1772) and
Thomas Warton the Younger's "The Progress of Discontent"
(1746).

2209    McKillop, Alan D. "Shaftesbury in Joseph Warton's ENTHUSIAST."
MLN, 70 (1955), 337-39.

Shaftesbury's distinction between material possession and
higher aesthetic experience in CHARACTERISTICKS (1737-38)
was seized on by Warton in his "facile" contrast between nature and art in the opening lines of THE ENTHUSIAST (1744),
where he employs imagery and themes emphasizing the
beauties of primitivism.

2210    Martin, Leonard C. THOMAS WARTON AND THE EARLY POEMS
OF MILTON. London: Humphrey Milford, 1934.

Essentially a discussion of the aesthetic and historical
importance of the younger Warton's highly praised edition
of Milton's early poems (1785; 1791), but a valuable
index to the tastes and cultural inclinations of the age
reflected in mid-century poetry.

2211    Miller, Frances S.  "The Historic Sense of Thomas Warton, Jr."
        ELH, 5 (1938), 71-92.

> Argues that Warton's "historic-sense" insists on the reality
> of the past in poetry and that his views on literary history
> are closely connected with his creative work: the enthu-
> siasm for the past and fascination with such matters as
> courtly legend, the Crusades, the picturesque, the high
> life, "ancient manners," and architectural remains.

2212    Morris, David B.  "Joseph Warton's Figure of Virtue:  Poetic In-
        direction in THE ENTHUSIAST."  PQ, 50 (1971), 678-83.

> States that readers knowledgeable in the classics would
> have noticed in 11.220-32 an allusion not only to
> Astraea's departure from earth, but also to Virgil's
> description of Venus' departure from Aeneas in THE
> AENEID, book 1; judges further that the equation be-
> tween the figures of virtue and innocence and those of
> Venus and Cupid seems to reflect the enthusiast's newly
> found comfort in "the active love of nature and in the
> creative powers of the imagination" once virtue has
> flown the corrupted modern world.

2213    Pittock, Joan.  THE ASCENDANCY OF TASTE:  THE ACHIEVEMENT
        OF JOSEPH AND THOMAS WARTON.  London:  Routledge and
        Kegan Paul, 1973.

> Though basically a study of changing literary tastes in
> the period and the central importance of Joseph and
> Thomas Warton the Younger's criticism, the issues ad-
> dressed relate to the poetic themes and style reflected
> in the poetry of these two dominant figures.

2214    _____.  "Lives and Letters:  New Wartoniana."  DUJ, 70 (1978),
        193-203.

> The distinctive poetical feature of the School of Warton
> was a "conscious individualism," but materials from the
> Swann Collection and other substantial collections reveal
> the Warton's ability to employ the devices and practices
> of their English and classical predecessors.  See no. 2193.

2215    Rinaker, Clarissa.  THOMAS WARTON:  A BIOGRAPHICAL AND
        CRITICAL STUDY.  Univ. of Illinois Studies in Language and
        Literature, vol. 2, no. 1.  Urbana:  Univ. of Illinois, 1916.
        Bibliog.

> A full-fledged critical biography, assessing the younger
> Warton's contributions to poetry, criticism, the study of
> literary history, and antiquarianism in light of the literary

movements of the day, noting his themes, use of picturesque imagery, interest in nature, and revival of the
sonnet form. Includes a bibliography of printed sources
for the HISTORY OF ENGLISH POETRY (1774-81) and
a list of editors and critical works on Warton.

2216 _____. "Thomas Warton's Poetry and its Relation to the Romantic
Movement." SR, 23 (1915), 140-63.

Although overshadowed by his more famous literary criticism and scholarship, the younger Warton's poetry nonetheless is an important contribution in the development
of the new romantic sensibility, the promotion of the
sonnet form, and the revival of the spirit of the medieval
Gothic and English antiquity that culminated in Wordsworth and Scott.

2217 Schick, George Baldwin. "Joseph Warton's Conceptions of the
Qualities of a True Poet." BUSE, 3 (1957), 77-87.

Devoted to a reappraisal of Warton's critical conceptions
of the essential qualities of the truly great poet, this
article also throws light on his poetic practices, describing the ideal poet as enthusiastically committed to the
past, inventively reworking inherited traditions, capable
of creating sublime and pathetic effects, and being able
to make use of real people and events without distortion
or banality.

2218 Sena, John F. "A Miltonic Echo in THE ENTHUSIAST." RESEARCH
STUDIES, 46 (1978), 202-03.

Lines in which Warton compares the poetic styles of
Addison and Shakespeare allude to Milton's differentiation
between Jonson and Shakespeare in "L'Allegro" and permit
Warton to remark on distinctions between learned and
"natural" literary works by making the eighteenth-century
reader an active participant in the creative act.

2219 Smith, Audley L. "The Primitivism of Joseph Warton." MLN, 42
(1927), 501-04.

Although references to "the bard" in 11. 108-09 of THE
ENTHUSIAST would indicate the possibility of Lucretius'
supplying certain details to the idealized picture of primitive life, the Lucretian concept of early man differs radically from that of Warton which emphasizes primitive
violence.

2220    Trowbridge, Hoyt. "Joseph Warton on the Imagination." MP, 25
        (1937), 73-87.

> Warton's theory of the imagination insisted on the delight
> produced by the visual image as opposed to an imagina-
> tive love of "the castles and palaces of Fancy"; such
> emphasis would indicate a demand for concrete particu-
> larity over generalization--all concepts that fall within
> the broad general framework of "imitation of nature."

2221    _____. "Joseph Warton's Classification of English Poets." MLN,
        51 (1936), 515-18.

> Ostensibly a discussion of the poetic categories to which
> Warton assigned English poets in his "Essay on Pope"
> throughout its five editions, but in fact chiefly a dis-
> cussion of Warton's changing tastes and perhaps too
> easy acquiescence to reviewers' objections.

2222    Wellek, René. THE RISE OF ENGLISH LITERARY HISTORY. Chapel
        Hill: Univ. of North Carolina Press, 1941.

> "In [Thomas] Warton [the younger] a recognition of
> classical standards and a (tempered appreciation of
> Gothic picturesqueness or sublimity went hand in hand . . . .
> This idea of a contrast between early imaginative and
> modern refined poetry was accepted by Warton." Classic
> account of the "historical sense," in the developing
> literary consciousness of the eighteenth century coupled
> with a recognition of individual talent within tradition.

# WINCHILSEA, ANNE FINCH, COUNTESS OF (1661-1720)

## A. MAJOR EDITIONS

2223    THE POEMS OF ANNE, COUNTESS OF WINCHILSEA. Ed. Myra
        Reynolds. Chicago: Univ. of Chicago Press, 1903.

> Based on the MISCELLANY POEMS OF 1713 (reissued as
> POEMS ON SEVERAL OCCASIONS [1714]) and manuscripts
> at Reynolds' disposal. Standard edition with some commentary
> and introduction bearing on Winchilsea's life and literary career.

2224    POEMS BY ANNE, COUNTESS OF WINCHILSEA. Ed. J. Middleton
        Murry. London: J. Cape, 1928.

> Selections of the poems. Superseded by Rogers' edition below.

2225    SELECTED POEMS OF ANNE FINCH, COUNTESS OF WINCHILSEA.
        Ed. Katharine M. Rogers. New York: Frederick Unger, 1979.

> Good selection with brief notes. The helpful introduction
> highlights the essential features of Winchilsea's poetry: its
> concern with difficulties encountered by female authors; the
> themes of female liberation and domestic freedom; a romantic's
> painful awareness of the discrepancy between human aspirations
> and achievement; the Augustan acceptance of human limita-
> tions; and her own distinctively personal touches.

## B. BIBLIOGRAPHY AND TEXTUAL STUDIES

2226    Anderson, Paul B. "Mrs. Manley's Texts of Three of Lady Winchilsea's
        Poems." MLN, 45 (1930), 95-99.

> Although not challenging the notion of Winchilsea's popularity,
> argues that Manley's NEW ATALANTIS (1709-10) prints a num-
> ber of poems in versions earlier than the 1713 MISCELLANY,
> a fact that suggests Winchilsea substituted "honest Hebraisms"
> for earlier "poetical paganism" instead of the reverse, as
> Reynolds, her modern editor, believes.

2227    See no. 2231.

2228    Hughes, Helen Sard. "Lady Winchilsea and Her Friends." LONDON MERCURY, 19 (1929), 624-35.

> Discussion based on a manuscript volume of her poems and documents in the possession of the Countess of Hertford at Alnwick Castle.

## C. CRITICISM

2229    Brower, Reuben A. "Lady Winchilsea and the Poetic Tradition of the Seventeenth Century." SP, 42 (1945), 61-80.

> Argues that the Lady Winchilsea is not a romantic poet born too early, but more accurately an Augustan in the company of Prior or Gay still capable of incorporating the witty metaphysical idiom of Donne, Herbert, and Marvell.

2230    Buxton, John. "The Countess of Winchilsea." In his A TRADITION OF POETRY. London: Macmillan, 1967, pp. 157-83.

> Combines biography with literary criticism to assess "the first English woman to write poetry that no man could have written who found her best inspiration in the domestic happiness of her marriage and in the refined life which she shared with her husband . . . and the social round of visits to friends."

2231    Dowden, Edward. "A Noble Authoress." In his ESSAYS, MODERN AND ELIZABETHAN. London: J.M. Dent, 1910, pp. 234-49.

> Adds a fragment on Mary Magdalen at the Tomb (not included in the Reynolds edition) to the canon and generally assesses Lady Winchilsea's achievement, pointing out that her warmth of feeling and ardor often seemed at odds with the didactic and moralizing tendencies of the age.

2232    Drew, Elsie. "Lady Winchilsea." In her EIGHTEENTH CENTURY LITERATURE: AN OXFORD MISCELLANY. Oxford: Clarendon Press, 1909, pp. 42-55.

> An appreciation of a writer who is judged to be neither important historically nor a great enough writer to influence tastes or style, but one whose unpolished and often commonplace poems sometimes "reveal a character whose charm and delicate originality make her dear as a friend to the hearts of her readers."

2233    Gosse, Sir Edmund. "Lady Winchilsea's Poems." In his GOSSIP IN
        A LIBRARY. London: William Heinemann, 1891, pp. 121-32.

        Rather effusive appreciation of "divine Ardelia," describ-
        ing her as "a little oasis of delicate and pensive refine-
        ment" at the "hot close" of the seventeenth century.

2234    Messenger, Ann P. "'Adam Pos'd': Metaphysical and Augustan
        Satire." WEST COAST REVIEW, 8, no. 4 (1974), 10-11.

        Notes the connections between Lady Winchilsea's "Adam
        Pos'd" and Donne's "Satyre IV" and analyzes the subtle-
        ties of tone and complex use of the persona device
        that reveal the skill of a "civilized satirist."

2234A    _____. "Publishing Without Perishing: Lady Winchilsea's MIS-
        CELLANY POEMS of 1713." RESTORATION, 5 (1981), 27-37.

        "A comparison of her published with her unpublished
        poems sheds light not only on some of the conventions
        of Augustan poetry but also on the nature and extent
        of the self-censorship a woman writer had to exercise
        in order to escape calumny, and the strategies she could
        sometimes use to circumvent her own censorship."

2235    Peacock, Markham L., Jr., ed. THE CRITICAL OPINIONS OF
        WILLIAM WORDSWORTH. Baltimore: Johns Hopkins Press, 1950.

        Reprints excerpts from the correspondence to Alexander
        Dyce that convey Wordsworth's admiration for the Countess
        of Winchilsea's poetry, while expressing some reservations
        about THE SPLEEN (1701) and her use of classical models.

2236    Reynolds, Myra. THE TREATMENT OF NATURE IN ENGLISH
        POETRY BETWEEN POPE AND WORDSWORTH. Chicago: Univ.
        of Chicago Press, 1909.

        Distinguishes between the concern for externals charac-
        terizing the classical concept of nature and the impulse
        of the modern poet to approach nature with a passionate
        longing, and considers Lady Winchilsea's "Nightingale,"
        "Tree," and "A Nocturnal Revery" as exemplifying a
        celebration of nature based not on the artifices of the
        pastoral but on the personal experience of the natural
        world.

2237    Rogers, Katharine M. "Anne Finch, Countess of Winchilsea: An
        Augustan Woman Poet." In SHAKESPEARE'S SISTERS: FEMINIST
        ESSAYS ON WOMEN POETS. Ed. Sandra M. Gilbert and Susan
        Gubar. Bloomington: Indiana Univ. Press, 1979, pp. 32-46.

Though working within the Augustan tradition and forms, Winchilsea "adapted them as necessary to fit her distinctive talent and point of view, and in doing so she added a much-needed feminine voice to a masculine tradition" and made "a woman's consciousness the center of awareness." An important interpretation from the feminist perspective.

2238    Sena, John F.  "Melancholy in Anne Finch and Elizabeth Carter: The Ambivalence of an Idea."  YES, 1 (1971), 108-19.

Argues that although the "softer sex" presumably suffered more from delusions and neuroses than men and that Winchilsea's poems often treat this "English Malady" from a romantic viewpoint, THE SPLEEN (1701) is a rationalistic treatment of melancholy.

2239    Wordsworth, William.  "Essay, Supplementary to the Preface of 1815."  In THE PROSE WORKS OF WILLIAM WORDSWORTH. Ed. W.J.B. Owen and Jane Worthington Smyser.  Vol. 3.  Oxford: Clarendon Press, 1974, p. 73.

In his supplementary essay to the "Preface of 1815," on the theme and purpose of Thomson's THE SEASONS and on nature poetry in general, Wordsworth treats Lady Winchilsea's "Nocturnal Reverie" (and several passages in Pope's WINDSOR FOREST) as an exception to his blanket condemnation of poetry between PARADISE LOST and Thomson's THE SEASONS as devoid of "a single new image of external nature."

# EDWARD YOUNG (1683-1765)

## A. MAJOR EDITIONS

2240    THE COMPLETE WORKS OF THE REV. EDWARD YOUNG, REVISED, AND COLLATED WITH THE EARLIEST EDITIONS. Ed. J. Doran. Preface and annotations, J. Nichols. 2 vols. London: William Tegg, 1854.

        Standard edition.

2241    POETICAL WORKS AND A LIFE BY REV. J. MITFORD. 2 vols. London: W. Pickering, 1844.

        The Aldine edition of British poets. A standard nineteenth-century source of the poems.

2242    SELECTED POEMS. Ed. Brian Hepworth. Cheshire, Engl.: Carcanet Press, 1975.

        Valuable edition with helpful notes and commentary; stresses the romantic features of Young.

2243    NIGHT THOUGHTS, OR THE COMPLAINT AND THE CONSOLA-TION. Ed. Robert Essick and Jenijoy La Belle. 1797; Facs. rpt. New York: Dover, 1975.

        Provides commentary along with reprinting, in mono-chrome, Blake's forty-three engravings for the first four nights of Young's poem reduced from the original size by 35 percent.

2244    CONJECTURES ON ORIGINAL COMPOSITION. Ed. Edith J. Morley. London: Longmans, Green, 1918.

        Introduction and bibliographical information. Standard edition.

2245      CONJECTURES ON ORIGINAL COMPOSITION, 1759. Facs. Leeds, Engl.: Scolar Press, 1966.

> Important statement about originality and the poetic imagination.

## B. CORRESPONDENCE

2246      THE CORRESPONDENCE OF EDWARD YOUNG, 1683-1765. Ed. Henry Pettit. Oxford: Clarendon Press, 1971.

> Brings together previously published correspondence and unpublished letters notable for their low-keyed depiction of English familiar life.

## B. BIBLIOGRAPHY AND TEXTUAL STUDIES

2247      Pettit, Henry. A BIBLIOGRAPHY OF YOUNG'S NIGHT-THOUGHTS. Boulder: Univ. of Colorado Press, 1954.

> Compares existing copies of the poem in order to list authorized and unauthorized printings of the text through Young's lifetime, indicating the peculiar fascination of the poem for readers in the first part of the eighteenth century.

2248      _____. "The Dating of Young's NIGHT-THOUGHTS." MLN, 55 (1940), 194-95.

> Evidence from periodical advertisements and from the Stationers' Register points to publication of "Consolation," the ninth and final NIGHT-THOUGHTS, in January 1746, not in 1745 as commonly thought.

2249      _____. "Preface to a Bibliography of Young's NIGHT-THOUGHTS." In his ELIZABETHAN STUDIES AND OTHER ESSAYS IN HONOR OF GEORGE F. REYNOLDS. Univ. of Colorado Studies, Series B, vol. 2, no. 4. Boulder: Univ. of Colorado, 1945, pp. 215-22.

> Discusses the difficulties in approaching a bibliography of the poem, stressing problems of the changing title, anonymity of the poem's early editions, its serialization, and number of printers and booksellers involved.

## D. BIOGRAPHY

2250      Johnson, Samuel. "The Life of Young." In THE LIVES OF THE

ENGLISH POETS. Ed. G. Birkbeck Hill. Vol. 3. Oxford: Oxford
Univ. Press, 1905, pp. 361-99.

Noteworthy even though the biographical and character
sections of this life were written by Herbert Croft, a
friend of Young's son and a source of much biographical
misinformation and uncritical thinking regarding Young's
poetic career and public life.

2251    Shelley, Henry C. THE LIFE AND LETTERS OF EDWARD YOUNG.
London: Sir Isaac Putnam, 1914.

Contains letters to the Duchess of Portland reflecting
Young's efforts to secure preferment in the Church and
treating other personal matters.

## E. CRITICISM

2252    Bailey, Margery. "Edward Young." In THE AGE OF JOHNSON:
ESSAYS PRESENTED TO CHAUNCEY BREWSTER TINKER. Ed.
Frederick W. Hilles. New Haven, Conn.: Yale Univ. Press, 1949,
pp. 197-207.

Good account of Young--the friend of Addison, Swift,
and Pope--not only as a graveyard poet but also as a
moralist and satirist "straining at the bonds of correctness
and regularity" and as an "exponent of originality and
the imagination as the key to creative genius." See no.
109.

2253    Bliss, Isabel St. John. EDWARD YOUNG. New York: Twayne,
1969.

Study of Young as artist, viewing his work against the
background of his age and assessing what he wrote in
relation to the poetic traditions and conventions of the
Augustan age. Chapters on the satires and on NIGHT
THOUGHTS. Corrects the often biased image of him as
a man by citing correspondence.

2254    _____. "Young's NIGHT THOUGHTS in Relation to Contemporary
Christian Apologetics." PMLA, 49 (1934), 37-70.

Rather than idiosyncratic or strictly confessional religious
poetry or conventional meditations on death as such,
NIGHT THOUGHTS draws on many issues found in contemporary defenses of religion, and recognition of these
arguments adds to the understanding and appreciation of
the originality of Young's achievement.

2255    Clark, Harry H. "A Study of Melancholy in Edward Young." MLN, 39 (1924), 125-36.

>    NIGHT THOUGHTS marks a transition in the character and literary depiction of melancholy and, thus, shares tendencies with two kinds: that provoked by solitude and "hypersensibility" in the Elizabethan age and that of a more sentimental, subjective, and self-indulgent later Romanticism.

2256    Crawford, Charlotte E. "What was Pope's Debt to Edward Young." ELH, 13 (1946), 157-67.

>    Examines Pope's indebtedness after 1728 to Young's UNIVERSAL PASSION, not only in relation to verbal similarities, direct borrowings, topical allusions, and satirical norms but to a shared social, intellectual, and literary context.

2257    Eliot, George. "Worldliness and Other-Worldliness: The Poet Young." In ESSAYS OF GEORGE ELIOT. Ed. Thomas Pinney. New York: Columbia Univ. Press, 1963, pp. 335-85.

>    Famous reversal of a youthful enthusiasm, and a scathing attack on Young as immoral and lacking in artistic integrity.

2258    Goldstein, Laurence. "Immortal Longings and 'The Ruines of Time.'" JEGP, 75 (1976), 337-51.

>    Using as a springboard the passage on immortality in Book 7 of NIGHT THOUGHTS, examines the progenitors in the Renaissance (especially in Spenser) of this desire for permanence within change and self-perpetuation within flux through the creative act.

2259    Hall, Mary S. "On Light in Young's NIGHT THOUGHTS." PQ, 48 (1969), 452-63.

>    Argues that Young intended his poem to be a rebuttal of Pope's ESSAY ON MAN and that the progression from images of darkness to those of light in the overall argument emphasize Young's philosophical optimism, not the gloom and pessimism associated with darkness and melancholy.

2260    Mutschmann, Heinrich. THE ORIGIN AND MEANING OF NIGHT THOUGHTS. 1939; rpt. Folcroft, Pa.: Folcroft Press, 1969.

>    Psychological study of Young's metaphysical problem: the fear of death that nearly drove him mad and his desire for survival and everlasting fame.

2261    Odell, Daniel W. "Locke, Cudworth and Young's NIGHT THOUGHTS."
        ELN, 4 (1967), 188-93.

> Passages in Young's sixth NIGHT THOUGHTS embrace
> both Locke's sensationalism and the Platonism of Ralph
> Cudworth, and his imaginative expression of these views
> converts the more passive idea of the mind in relation
> to the senses "into an active partnership of 'giving,'
> 'making' and 'creation.'"

2262    _____. "Young's NIGHT THOUGHTS and the Tradition of Divine
        Poetry." BSUF, 12, ii (1971), 3-13.

> Argues that Young allies himself with the exponents of
> the Christian sublime and that NIGHT THOUGHTS is in
> conformity with the conception of religious poetry as
> represented in the Augustan tradition of Dennis, Watts,
> and Blackmore.

2263    _____. "Young's NIGHT THOUGHTS as an Answer to Pope's
        ESSAY ON MAN." SEL, 12 (1972), 481-501.

> Young's view of man's place in nature differs from Pope's
> more rationalistic and static conception of man's fixed
> position in the chain of being, and Young's belief in
> Christ's Resurrection and human immortality supports a
> more progressivist view of man's material, intellectual,
> and spiritual situation.

2264    Wicker, Cecil V. "Edward Young and the Fear of Death: A Study
        in Romantic Melancholy." UNIV. OF MEXICO PUBLICATIONS IN
        LANGUAGE AND LITERATURE, no. 10. Albuquerque: Univ. of
        New Mexico, 1952.

> Argues that Young's treatment of melancholy is neither
> conventional nor traditional, but is shaped by his inner
> fears and broodings.

INDEX

# INDEX

This index includes the names of all authors, editors, compilers and translators, as well as references to the thirty-one poets contained in this guide. Primary titles are listed under the poet (e.g., THE DUNCIAD is under Pope). Secondary titles are listed alphabetically (e.g., POETRY OF POPE'S "DUNCIAD," THE). Underlined item numbers indicate main entries for an author. Page numbers ("p.") are given in cases where a name or title occurs in the introduction or in the Blake headnote. Alphabetization is letter by letter.

# Index

# Index

# Index

"Blake's Seasons" 662
"Blake's 'The Lamb': The Punctuation
    of Innocence" 635
"Blake's Tree of Knowledge Grows
    Out of the Enlightenment" 723
BLAKE STUDIES 593, 620
BLAKE STUDIES: ESSAYS ON HIS
    LIFE AND WORKS 607
"Blake's 'Tyger': The Nature of the
    Beast" 625
BLAKE'S VISIONARY FORMS DRAMA-
    TIC 603
BLAKE'S VISIONARY UNIVERSE 626
"Blasphemy or Blessing? Swift's
    'Scatological' Poems" 2095
Blaydes, Sophia B. 1954
Bliss, Isabel St. John 2253-54
Bliss, Philip 221
Blom, T.E. 332
Bloom, Edward A. 453, 1384-88
Bloom, Harold 110, 386, 629-32,
    677, 681, 862, 1296-97, 1319,
    1412, 1650. See also "Harold
    Bloom's Revisionary Ratios"
Bloom, Lillian D. 453, 1386-88,
    1521
Bluestone, Max 1715
Bluhm, Heinz 673
Blunden, Edmund 937, 1158
Blunt, Anthony 633
Bogel, Fredric V. 333, 1389, 1646A
Bogen, Nancy W. 634
Bogue, Ronald L. 1562
BOLINGBROKE 151
BOLINGBROKE AND HARLEY 139
BOLINGBROKE AND HIS CIRCLE
    177
"Bolingbroke's Deism and Gray's
    ELEGY" 1325
Bond, Donald F. 15, 56-57, 290
Bond, Richmond P. 454, 1912. See
    also THE DRESS OF WORDS
Bond, William H. 94, 1270, 1388,
    1934
"BOOK OF GENESIS and the Genesis
    of Books: The Creation of
    Pope's DUNCIAD, The" 1670
Borck, Jim S. 635
BOROUGH OF GEORGE CRABBE,
    THE 914

Boswell, James 140, 1375
BOSWELL'S CLAP AND OTHER
    ESSAYS: MEDICAL ANALYSES
    OF LITERARY MEN'S AFFLIC-
    TIONS 250
BOSWELL'S LIFE OF JOHNSON
    1375
Boulton, James T. 224, 1390
Bowers, Clementian Francis, F.S.C.
    942
BOWLES, BYRON AND THE POPE
    CONTROVERSY 1787
Boyce, Benjamin 509, 1185, 1539,
    1613, 1716
Boyd, David V. 890, 1391
Boyle, John. See Orrery
Boys, Richard C. 95, 334, 1168
Bracher, Frederick 1717
Brady, Frank 96, 1296, 1632, 2133
Brain, Walter Russell 2013
Bredvold, Louis I. 291, 455-56,
    1100. See also CONTEXTS OF
    DRYDEN'S THOUGHT
Brennecke, Ernest, Jr. 1068
Brett, R.L. 292
Brewer, John 141
Brewer, Stella M. 142
Brewster, Elizabeth 930, 943
BRIEF LIVES 136
Brisman, Leslie 636
Brissenden, R.F. 97-99, 1178, 1410,
    1624, 1738, 1967, 2062
BRISTOL BIBLIOGRAPHY 758
BRITISH BROADSIDE BALLAD AND
    ITS MUSIC, THE 278
BRITISH LIBRARY RESOURCES: A
    BIBLIOGRAPHICAL GUIDE 9
BRITISH MUSEUM GENERAL CATA-
    LOGUE OF PRINTED BOOKS
    5
"British Philippic, A" 576
BRITISH POLITICS IN THE AGE OF
    ANNE 170
Brittain, Robert E. 1926, 1935-36
Broadley, A.M. 931
Brockbank, J. Philip 1670
Brogan, Terry V.F. 529A
"Broken Dream of THE DESERTED VIL-
    LAGE, The" 1258
Broman, Walter E. 944

# Index

# Index

# Index

# Index

'Sense' in Eighteenth-Century
Poetry" 390
"From Satire to Description" 1437
FROM SENSIBILITY TO ROMANTI-
CISM: ESSAYS PRESENTED
TO FREDERICK A. POTTLE
110, 386, 677, 681, 862,
1296-97, 1319, 1412, 1650
Frosch, Thomas R. 653
Frost, William 1113-15, 1578
Fry, Paul H. 516
Frye, Northrop 333, 361, 597,
605, 647, 654-56, 685, 697.
See also "Structure and Sub-
stantiality"
Fujimura, Thomas 1056-57, 1116-
18, 1850
Fullington, J.F. 1890, 1899
FUNERAL ELEGY AND THE RISE OF
ENGLISH ROMANTICISM, THE
464
Furnival, R.G. 1161
Fussell, Paul 362, 536-37, 1399

# G

Gabriner, Paul 1649
GAELIC SOURCES OF MACPHER-
SON'S OSSIAN, THE 1480
Gallant, Christine 657
Gallon, D.N. 950
"Game of Ombre in THE RAPE OF
THE LOCK, The" 1598
Gantz, Kenneth F. 1467
"Garden, and a Grave': The Poetry
of Oliver Goldsmith, 'A" 1265
GARDEN AND THE CITY: RETIRE-
MENT AND POLITICS IN THE
LATER POETRY OF POPE, THE
1757
"Garden as City: Swift's Landscape
of Alienation, The" 2044
Gardner, Stanley 658
Gardner, William B. 986
Garrison, James D. 1119
Garrod, Heathcote William 839,
1284
Garth, Sir Samuel 1181-93
Works:
DISPENSARY, THE 1181,
1183, 1185, 1187-93

"Garth's DISPENSARY and Pope's
RAPE OF THE LOCK" 1190
"Gateway to Innocence: Ossian and
the Nordic Bard as Myth, The"
1468
Gatrell, S. 921
Gay, John 23, 137, 177, 301,
342, 442, 478, 480, 530,
1194-1225, 1503
Works:
"Contemplation on Night, A"
1210
FABLES 1213
RURAL SPORTS 1199, 1207
SHEPHERD'S WEEK, THE 1208-
09, 1214, 1224
"Saturday" 1214, 1217
"Thought on Eternity, A" 1210
TRIVIA 478, 1203, 1220
"Welcome to Mr. Pope" 1219
Gay, Peter 235
"Gay, Swift, and the Nymphs of
Drury-Lane" 1218
"Gay among the Defenders of the
Faith" 1210
"Gay Augustan" 1216
Gaye, Phoebe Fenwick 1201
"Gay's Bowzybeus and Thomas
D'Urfey" 1214
"Gay's Burlesque of Sir Richard
Blackmore's Poetry" 1217
"Gay's Mastery of the Heroic
Couplet" 1206
"Gay's TRIVIA and the Art of
Allusion" 1203
"Generality in Augustan Satire" 550
"Genesis of Cowper's 'Yardley Oak,'
The" 875
"Genesis of John Oldham's SATYRS
UPON THE JESUITS, The" 1493
GENIUS OF THE PLACE: THE ENG-
LISH LANDSCAPE GARDEN
1620-1820, THE 263
George, M. Dorothy 157-61
GEORGE CRABBE (Bareham) 941
GEORGE CRABBE (Chamberlain) 945
GEORGE CRABBE: AN ANTHOLOGY
913
"George Crabbe: Not Quite the
Sternest" 976
"George Crabbe, Poet of Penury" 951

453

# Index

GRACES OF HARMONY 526
Graham, Edwin 1213
Graham, W.H. 951
Grammans, Harold W. 1915
Granger, Bruce Ingham 739
Gransden, K.W. 1058
Grant, Douglas 791, 1401, 2152
Grant, John E. 584, 591, 603,
    606, 668-72
Gray, George J. 1937
"Gray, Jaques, and the Man of
    Feeling" 1323
Gray, Thomas 19, 117, 323, 333,
    351, 386-87, 403, 410-11,
    415, 451, 454, 458-59, 490,
    509, 512, 516, 520, 522,
    546-47, 568, 675, 684, 716,
    823-25, 858, 1277-1350, 1477,
    1499
    Works:
        "Bard, The" 1303, 1320, 1337
        ELEGY WRITTEN IN A
        COUNTRY CHURCHYARD 330,
        403, 825, 1284, 1286, 1289,
        1291, 1295-99, 1302, 1304,
        1306, 1309, 1311, 1314, 1317,
        1319, 1323-25, 1332-34, 1337-
        40, 1343, 1345-49
        "Ode on a Distant Prospect of
        Eton College" 1310, 1314,
        1329A
        "Ode on the Death of a
        Favourite Cat" 1318, 1331,
        1341
        "Ode on the Spring" 1320,
        1342
        PROGRESS OF POETRY, THE
        1337
        "Sonnet on the Death of Richard
        West" 1309, 1314, 1330
        "Triumphs of Owen, The" 1285
"Gray and Chatterton" 782
"Gray Parody in BRAVE NEW WORLD,
    The" 1334
"Gray's Audiences" 1314
"Gray's Cat and Pope's Belinda" 1318
"Gray's Craftsmanship" 1337
"Gray's ELEGY: A Poem of Moral
    Choice and Resolution" 1347
"Gray's ELEGY: The Biographical

Problem in Literary Criticism"
    1304
"Gray's ELEGY: 'The Skull Beneath
    the Skin'" 1311
"Gray's ELEGY Revisited" 1319
"Gray's 'Epitaph' Reconsidered" 1332
"Gray's Eton College Ode: The
    Problem of Tone" 1305
"Gray's 'Frail Memorial' to West"
    1309
"Gray's 'Ode on the Death of a
    Favourite Cat': A Rationalist's
    Aesthetic" 1331
"Gray's 'Ode on the Death of a
    Favourite Cat, Drowned in a
    Tub of Gold Fishes'" 1341
"Gray's Ode on the Spring" 1342
"Gray's Opinion of Parnell" 1507
"Gray's Personal Elegy" 1299
"Gray's Sensibility" 1316
"Gray's Storied Urn" 1298
"Gray's 'The Triumphs of Owen'"
    1285
"Gray's Use of the Gorchesty Beirdd
    in THE BARD" 1320
GREAT CHAIN OF BEING: A STUDY
    OF THE HISTORY OF AN IDEA,
    THE 242
Green, Stanley 236
Greenacre, Phyllis 774, 2057
Greene, Donald J. 299-300, 368-
    69, 517, 1313, 1360-61, 1371,
    1402-06, 1650, 1964, 2058,
    2165
Greene, Graham 1834
Greenway, John L. 1468
Greever, Garland 1169
Gregor, Ian 952
Gregory, Housag K. 880
Griffin, Dustin H. 1020, 1071,
    1314, 1407, 1702, 1741, 1851
Griffith, Reginald H. 1516, 1525,
    1675
"Grimeses, The" 948
GRONGAR HILL (Boys) 1168
"GRONGAR HILL: An Introduction
    and Texts" 1171
"Grongar Hill: Its Origin and De-
    velopment" 1177
Groom, Bernard 538

# Index

Grove, Robin 1579
"Groves of Eden: Design in a Satire by Pope, The" 1633
GROWTH OF POLITICAL STABILITY IN ENGLAND, 1675-1725, THE 197
GRUB STREET: STUDIES IN A SUB-CULTURE 203
GRUB STREET STRIPPED BARE 193
Gubar, Susan 2237
Guerinot, Joseph V. 1526, 1532
Guibbory, Achsah 1120
GUIDE TO ENGLISH AND AMERI-CAN LITERATURE, A 4
Guilhamet, Leon 370, 1021, 1315
GULLIVER AND THE GENTLE READER 2092
"Gulliver's Maker and Gullibility" 2118
Guthke, Karl S. 775
Gwynn, Stephen 1242
"GYLDENSTOLPE MANUSCRIPT" MISCELLANY OF POEMS BY JOHN WILMOT, EARL OF ROCHESTER, THE 1823

# H

Haddakin, Lilian 953
Hagstrum, Jean H. 301, 471, 673-77, 1316, 1408
Haley, Kenneth H.D. 162
Halgerson, Richard 1261
Hall, Mary S. 2259
Halsband, Robert 163-64, 1580, 2059
Hamilton, Horace E. 2166
Hamilton, Kenneth G. 539, 1121
Hamm, Victor M. 1059-60
Hammond, Barbara 165
Hammond, John Lawrence 165
HANDEL, DRYDEN, AND MILTON 272
Hanson, Laurence W. 166, 167
HAPPY MAN: STUDIES IN THE METAMORPHOSES OF A CLASSICAL IDEAL, THE 320
Hardin, Richard F. 371, 838A
Hardy, John P. 1409-11, 1581, 1651
Hare, Maurice F. 752

"Harlequin Intrudes: William Cowper's Venture into the Satiric Mode" 896
"Harold Bloom's Revisionary Ratios and the Augustan Satirists" 427
Harp, Richard L. 1243
Harris, Kathryn Montgomery 2060
Harris, Ronald W. 237
Hart, Jeffrey 168, 556
Harth, Phillip 108A, 311, 369, 471A, 515, 1122
Hartley, Lodwick C. 872, 881-83, 896-99
Hartman, Geoffrey H. 568, 840, 1965
Hartog, Curt 1317
Harvey, Paul 10
Hatch, Ronald B. 932, 954-56
Hauser, David R. 1553
Havens, Raymond D. 372-74, 1505, 1966, 2167, 2205
Hayley, William 884
Hazeltine, Alice Isabel 1906
Hazen, Allen T. 1351, 1358
Hazlitt, William 933
HEAVENLY CITY OF THE EIGH-TEENTH-CENTURY PHILOSO-PHERS, THE 222
HEAV'N'S FIRST LAW: RHETORIC AND ORDER IN POPE'S ESSAY ON MAN 1621
"Heirs to Vitruvius: Pope and the Idea of Architecture" 1635
Helmstadter, Thomas H. 678
Hemphill, George 1123
Hendrickson, John R. 1279
Hennig, John 1470
"Henry St. John: A Reappraisal of the Young Bolingbroke" 233
Hepworth, Brian 2242
"Heroic and Anti-Heroic Elements in THE HIND AND THE PANTHER" 1064
HEROIC COUPLET, THE 543
HEROIC MOCKERY: VARIATIONS ON EPIC THEMES FROM HOMER TO JOYCE 487
HEROIC NATURE: IDEAL LANDSCAPE IN ENGLISH POETRY FROM MARVELL TO THOMSON 416

Heuston, Edward F.   1214
Hibbard, George R.   472, 957
Hill, Charles J.   1916
Hill, Christopher   169
Hill, Geoffrey   2061
Hill, George Birkbeck   1354-55, 1375, 2250
Hilles, Frederick W.   109-10, 386, 510, 525, 677, 681, 770, 862, 885, 1296-97, 1308, 1319, 1372, 1392, 1412, 1436, 1650, 1919, 2179, 2252
Hilson, J.C.   111, 1601, 1616, 1737, 2063
Hilton, Nelson   679
Hipple, Walter J.   302
Hirsch, E.D., Jr.   680
HIS MAJESTY'S OPPOSITION, 1714-1830   156
"Historical Allusions in ABSALOM AND ACHITOPHEL"   1026
"Historic Sense of Thomas Chatterton, The"   781
"Historic Sense of Thomas Warton, Jr., The"   2211
"History and Rhetoric of the Triplet, The"   529
HISTORY AND SOURCES OF PERCY'S MEMOIR OF GOLDSMITH, THE   1239
"History and Structure of Pope's TO A LADY, The"   1632
HISTORY OF EIGHTEENTH CENTURY LITERATURE, 1660-1780, A   31
HISTORY OF ENGLAND IN THE EIGHTEENTH CENTURY, A   178
HISTORY OF ENGLISH POETRY   2184
HISTORY OF ENGLISH THOUGHT IN THE EIGHTEENTH CENTURY   257
HISTORY OF LITERATURE IN THE ENGLISH LANGUAGE, THE   32A, 378, 399, 1109, 1755
HISTORY OF MODERN CRITICISM 1750-1950, A   52
"History of the Future, A"   311
HISTORY OF THE REBELLION AND CIVIL WARS IN ENGLAND   147
HISTORY OF THE ROYAL SOCIETY, THE   256

Hodgart, Matthew T.C.   1413
Hodgart, Patricia   934
Hoffman, Arthur W.   1072, 1124
HOGARTH: HIS LIFE, ART, AND TIMES   274
HOGARTH'S GRAPHIC WORKS   275
Hollander, John   375, 681
Holloway, John   32
Holmes, Geoffrey   170-71
"HOMER IN ENGLISH CRITICISM: THE HISTORICAL APPROACH IN THE EIGHTEENTH CENTURY   297
"Homer of the North Translates Homer, The"   1452
Hone, P.P.   933
HONEST MUSE: A STUDY IN AUGUSTAN VERSE, THE   432
Hook, Judith   172
Hooker, Edward Niles   24, 979, 1061, 1073, 1567
Hooven, Evelyn   1600
Hope, Alec D.   1074, 1967
"Hope and Fear in Johnson"   1409
Hopkins, Kenneth   376, 473, 812
Hopkins, Robert H.   1262
HORACE IN THE ENGLISH LITERATURE OF THE EIGHTEENTH CENTURY   363
Horne, Colin J.   1364, 1414, 2062-63
Horne, William C.   740
Horrell, Joseph   1988
Horsely, Lee   474
Hotch, Ripley   1566, 1652
Houpt, Charles T.   562
Houtchens, C.W.   597
Houtchens, L.H.   597
Howard, William J.   1676
Howell, Wilbur J.   238
"How Really to Play the Game of Ombre in Pope's RAPE OF THE LOCK"   1582
"How to Die: VERSES ON THE DEATH OF DR. SWIFT"   2048
Hsia, Chih-tsing   958
Huang, Ts'ui-en (Roderick)   900
Hubbard, Lester A.   996
Hubble, Douglas   935
Huchon, René L.   936

# Index

# Index

# Index

# Index

NEW PERSPECTIVES ON COLERIDGE
AND WORDSWORTH 568
NEW POEMS BY GEORGE CRABBE
912
"New Satire of Augustan England,
The" 497
Newton, A. Edward 1234
NEWTON DEMANDS THE MUSE:
NEWTON'S "OPTICKS" AND
THE EIGHTEENTH CENTURY
POETS 247
"Newtonianism in James Thomson's
Poetry" 2162
"'New World' of Pope's DUNCIAD,
The" 1672
Nichols, John 38, 2240
Nicholson, Norman 886
Nicolson, Marjorie Hope 247-49,
396, 1540. See REASON AND
THE IMAGINATION
Nierenberg, Edwin 1569
NIGHT BATTLE, THE 1614
NIGHTMARES AND HOBBYHORSES:
SWIFT, STERNE, AND
AUGUSTAN IDEAS OF MAD-
NESS 347
"Nightmares of Strephon: Nymphs of
the City in the Poems of Swift,
Baudelaire, Eliot, The" 2093
NIGHT THOUGHTS, OR THE
COMPLAINT AND THE CON-
SOLATION 2243
Nobbe, George 799
"Noble Authoress, A" 2231
"Nonstructure of Augustan Verse,
The" 522
"NORTH BRITON": A STUDY IN
POLITICAL PROPAGANDA,
THE 799
Northup, Clark S. 782, 1287
Norton, John 573
"No Single Scholiast: Pope's THE
DUNCIAD" 1694
NOTABLE MAN: THE LIFE AND
TIMES OF OLIVER GOLDSMITH,
THE 1241
NOTEBOOK OF WILLIAM BLAKE:
A PHOTOGRAPHIC AND TYPO-
GRAPHIC FACSIMILE, THE
587-88

"Note in Defence of Satire, A" 456
"Note on the Composition of Gray's
ELEGY" 1284
"Note on the First Edition of THE
PLEASURES OF IMAGINATION,
A" 555
"Notes for a Bibliography of Cowper's
Letters" 874
"Notes on Some Lesser Poets of the
Eighteenth Century" 404
"Notes on the Bibliography of
Matthew Prior" 1801
"Notes on the Developing Motives and
Structures of Swift's Poetry"
2096
"Notes on the Prosody of THE
VANITY OF HUMAN WISHES"
1380
"Notes on Three Editions of George
Crabbe's TALES" 923
Novak, Maximillian E. 1105, 1728,
2093, 2165
Noyes, Charles E. 1946
Noyes, George R. 980
Nurmi, Martin T. 593-94, 597,
693-97
Nussbaum, Felicity A. 1640, 2081

# O

Oates, Mary I. 520
Ober, William B. 250, 847
OBSERVATIONS, ANECDOTES, AND
CHARACTERS OF BOOKS AND
MEN 1547
"Occasion of Swift's 'Day of Judge-
ment,' The" 2034
"'Occasions So Few': Satire as a
Strategy of Praise in Swift's
Early Odes" 2060
OCLC 13-14
"Octosyllabic Couplet, The" 544
Odell, Daniel W. 2261-63
Oden, Richard L. 1046
"Ode on Anne Killigrew" 1092
ODES ON VARIOUS SUBJECTS
(1746) 2181-82
OF BOOKS AND HUMANKIND 1722
"OF DRAMATIC POESY" AND OTHER
CRITICAL ESSAYS 985

# Index

# Index

Poirier, Richard 550, 2072
POLITICAL BALLADS ILLUSTRATING
THE ADMINISTRATION OF SIR
ROBERT WALPOLE 40
POLITICAL DIARY OF GEORGE BUBB
DODINGTON, THE 154
POLITICAL PRINTS IN THE AGE OF
HOGARTH: A STUDY OF
IDEOGRAPHIC REPRESENTA-
TIONS OF POLITICS 135
"Political Satire in Dryden's ALEX-
ANDER'S FEAST" 1086
"Political Satires of Charles Churchill"
804
POLITICS AND POETRY IN RESTORA-
TION ENGLAND: THE CASE
OF DRYDEN'S ANNUS MIRA-
BILIS 1078
"Politics in THE HIND AND THE
PANTHER" 1063
"Politics of Opposition in 'Verses
on the Death of Dr. Swift,'
The" 2106
POLITICS OF SAMUEL JOHNSON,
THE 1405
Pollard, Arthur 912, 919, 966
Pollard, Graham 927
Poole, Austin Lane 823
POOR COLLINS: HIS LIFE, HIS
ART, AND HIS INFLUENCE
831
"'Poor Collins' Reconsidered" 834
POOR KIT SMART 1961
"Pope" (Strachey) 1549
"Pope" (Tillotson) 1528
POPE: A COLLECTION OF CRITICAL
ESSAYS 1532
Pope, Alexander (pp. xi, xiii), 63,
117, 137-38, 149, 163-64, 177,
226, 287, 301, 314, 328,
335, 338-39, 341-42, 348,
351, 353, 356, 362, 364,
369, 380, 385, 387-88, 390,
392, 394, 405, 412, 419,
423, 425, 430, 432, 438,
441-42, 454, 472, 482-84,
486, 489-90, 501, 505, 517-
18, 522, 526-27, 529, 535,
538, 546-47, 549, 550, 807,
813, 821, 860A, 904, 958,

970, 1018, 1096, 1126, 1128,
1162, 1190-91, 1197, 1223,
1398, 1503, 1508-1795, 2092,
2094
Works:
DUNCIAD, THE 388, 475,
478, 487, 535, 1018, 1510,
1561, 1585, 1670-1700, 1729,
1749, 1753, 1783
"Elegy to the Memory of an Unfortunate Lady" 1601, 1605,
1610
"Eloisa to Abelard" 383, 1599-
1600, 1602-04, 1606-09, 1611
EPILOGUE TO THE SATIRES
1643, 1649, 1715
EPISTLE TO A LADY 1303,
1524, 1632, 1640, 1642
"Epistle to Augustus" 441,
1658, 1665-66
"Epistle to Bathurst" 1512,
1631
EPISTLE TO. BURLINGTON 479,
1522, 1633, 1638, 1641
"Epistle to Cobham" 1637
"Epistle to Dr. Arbuthnot, An"
164, 423, 535, 1646A, 1647,
1651-52, 1655, 1660, 1663
"Epistle to Harley" 1705
"Epistle to Lord Bolingbroke"
1657, 1667
EPISTLE TO MR. ADDISON
1701
EPISTLES TO SEVERAL PERSONS
475, 1510, 1632, 1635-36,
1731
ESSAY ON CRITICISM, AN
1510, 1561-71, 1715, 1783,
2178
ESSAY ON MAN, AN 412,
1510, 1545, 1585, 1612-29,
1753, 2259, 2263
HOMER 1726, 1750
HORATIAN IMITATIONS 1636,
1653-54, 1661, 1668, 1731,
1747
"Messiah" 394
MORAL ESSAYS 535, 1753.
See also EPISTLES TO SEVERAL
PERSONS

476

# Index

# Index

# Index

# Index

# Index